A Glossary of Literary Terms

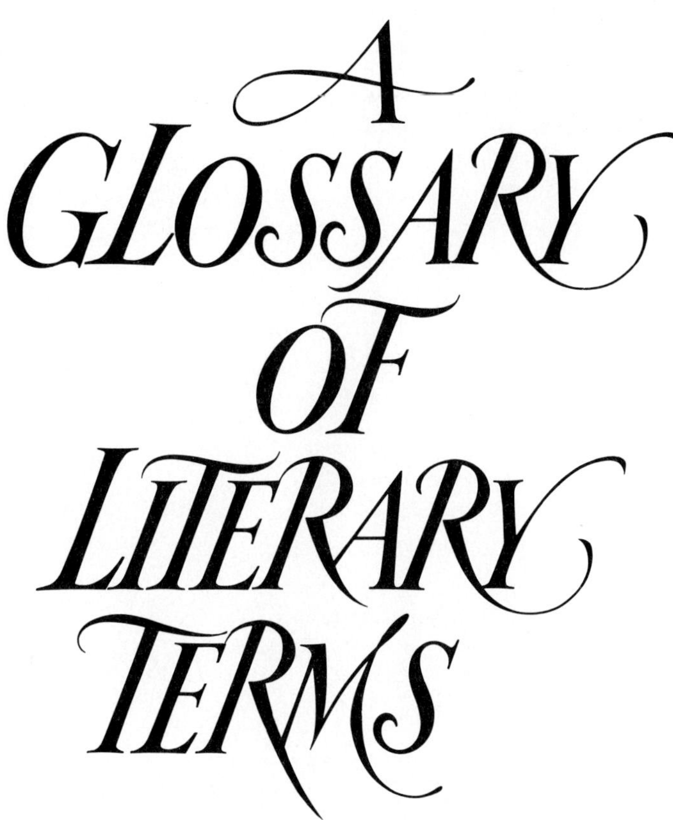

FIFTH EDITION

M. H. ABRAMS
Cornell University

Harcourt Brace Jovanovich College Publishers
Fort Worth Philadelphia San Diego
New York Orlando Austin San Antonio
Toronto Montreal London Sydney Tokyo

Library of Congress Cataloging in Publication Data

Abrams, M. H. (Meyer Howard), 1912-
A glossary of literary terms.

Includes index.
1. Literature—Dictionaries. I. Title.
PN41.A184 1988 803'.21 87-291

ISBN 0-03-011953-7

Printed in the United States of America

1 2 3 090 9 8

Harcourt Brace Jovanovich, Inc.
The Dryden Press
Saunders College Publishing

Contents

Preface to the Fifth Edition

This book defines and discusses terms, concepts, and points of view that are commonly and profitably used in the history, analysis, interpretation, and criticism of works of literature. The level of discussion and the guides to further reading are oriented especially toward undergraduate students of English, American, and other literatures; over the decades, however, the book has proved its usefulness as a reference work for advanced literary students as well.

The *Glossary* is organized as a series of succinct essays in the alphabetic order of the title word or phrase. Terms that are subsidiary, or that denote subclasses of a topic, are discussed under the title heading of the major or generic term, and words that are commonly used in conjunction or as contraries *(distance and involvement, empathy and sympathy, objective and subjective, primitivism and progress)* are discussed in the same essay. The alternative organization—a dictionary of single terms defined in isolation—is not only forbidding to the reader and repetitive in content, but may be misleading as well, because the application of many terms becomes clear only in the context of other concepts to which they are related, subordinated, or opposed. The essay presentation also makes it possible to supplement the standard, or the most useful, definition of a technical word with enough indications of its changes of meaning over time, and of its diversity in current usage, to help students steer their way through the shifting references and submerged ambiguities in historical and critical treatments of literature. In addition, this discursive way of treating literary terms provides the author with the opportunity to write discussions that are readable as well as useful. Each essay prints in **boldface** the terms for which it supplies the principal discussion; it prints in *italics* other terms that occur in the course of this discussion but are treated more fully elsewhere in the *Glossary*.

This new edition has been prepared in response to recent changes in the literary scene, to important new books on literature and literary criticism, and to a constant stream of suggestions for improvements or additions, some of them solicited and others contributed by generous users of the *Glossary*. The revision has provided the opportunity to rewrite all the articles, some of them drastically, in order to clarify the exposition, to take account of recent innovations, and to add further references and illustrations, especially from American literature and from women and Black authors; to such references and illustrations, a date or temporal indication has now in most instances been affixed, in order to give the student some sense of their place in literary history. The suggested readings in each essay have also been expanded and made current; books written in French and German are listed in their English translations.

Following the suggestions of many users, a number of terms have been added, either as entries themselves or within other entries, including *American Renaissance, aubade, automatic writing, baroque, Black writers, caricature, décor, echoism, fabulation, golden age, Harlem Renaissance, ideology, ivory tower, jeremiad, kenning, lampoon, magic realism, malapropism, positivism,* the Shakespearean *problem play, proscenium,* and *solecism.* There are also extensive new essays, with illustrative references and suggested readings, on the *canon of literature, negative capability, periods of American literature,* and *Transcendentalism in America.*

I follow the advice of several consultants by introducing an important change in format. Ours is an age of many and varied new "theories" of literature, literary language, and literary criticism. In the attempt to record these innovations, recent editions of the *Glossary* have tended to submerge treatments of the traditional and enduring literary terms and concepts amid fairly lengthy discussions of recent critical modes. These latter essays are now printed in a separate section of the *Glossary,* pp. 201–247, under the heading "Modern Theories of Literature and Criticism," together with new essays on *feminist criticism, Marxist criticism,* and *psychological and psychoanalytic criticism.* The general introduction to the topic of *criticism* remains in the body of the text. The new section includes seventeen essays on the innovative critical views and procedures of the last half-century, ranging from *New Criticism* and *archetypal criticism* through *phenomenology* and *reader-response criticism* to *deconstruction* and *semiotics;* the section is preceded by a list of the approximate dates at which each of these critical modes was developed. There is a double advantage in this rearrangement. Students can now read the treatment of the more traditional literary and critical terms—whether sequentially or by selected assignments adapted to the subject matter of a course—without impediment by what are, inescapably, fairly abstruse discussions of modern theory. On the other hand, reading through the section on "Modern Theories" can provide a terse yet inclusive overview of all the major developments in this lively era of competing points of view and modes of literary analysis and evaluation. And despite this division, the place of the discussion of any literary term or critical mode, whether traditional or new, can readily be located by reference to the inclusive Index.

How to Use the *Glossary*

Always look up the word or phrase you are investigating in the alphabetic Index at the end of the volume. Although the essays in the *Glossary* are in the alphabetic order of their title terms, by far the larger number of terms are discussed within the body of these essays. In the Index readers will find, in **boldface,** the page number of the principal discussion of the term; this is sometimes followed, in *italics,* by the page numbers of its occurrences in other essays which serve further to clarify and exemplify the ways in which the word or expression is in fact used. Note that the word referred to by an italicized entry may be a modified form of the index-term; thus the forms "parodies" and "parodied" are listed under the entry "parody." Note also that those terms in the Index (mainly foreign in origin) which are most likely to be mispronounced by a student are followed by simplified guides to pronunciation; the key to these guides is on the first page of the Index.

Some of the more general entries in the Index are also supplemented by a list of references to closely related specific or analytic terms. These secondary references not only expedite the fuller exploration of a topic but make it easy to locate items that serve the needs of a particular course in literature. They identify, for example, the separate essays in the *Glossary* that deal with particular types and movements of literary *criticism,* the terms most relevant to the analysis of *style,* the separate entries defining classes of *figurative language* or literary *genres,* and the many essays which treat the form, component features, history, and criticism of the *drama, lyric,* and *novel.*

This edition owes a great deal to the counsel of teachers at many colleges and universities who suggested changes and additions that would make the book more useful to students in a wide variety of courses in American, English, and foreign literatures. I am especially grateful for advice by A. R. Ammons, Walter Cohen, Jonathan Culler, Nelly Furman, Mary Jacobus, and Cushing Strout at Cornell University; and for many and detailed suggestions by Nina Baym, University of Illinois; Martha Woodmansee, Case Western Reserve University; Ray Craig, University of Illinois at Urbana–Champaign; Christopher Herbert, Northwestern University; Owen Jenkins, Carleton College; James M. Kee, College of the Holy Cross; Steven Strang, Wheaton College; Nathaniel Strout, Hamilton College; Linda Venis, University of California, Los Angeles. Dianne Ferriss has been an unfailingly cheerful and helpful research assistant and secretary; Kate Morgan, Associate Editor at Holt, Rinehart and Winston, has instigated this revision; and Jean Ford, Senior Project Editor at Holt, has excellently supervised its accomplishment. All these friends and advisers have helped me come closer to the goal I announced in the original edition: to write the kind of handbook that I would most have valued when I was myself a college student of literature.

M. H. Abrams
Ithaca, New York

A Glossary of Literary Terms

Literary Terms

Absurd, Literature of the. The name is applied to a number of works in drama and prose fiction which have in common the sense that the human condition is essentially and ineradicably absurd, and that this condition can be adequately represented only in works of literature that are themselves absurd. This literature has its roots in the movements of *expressionism* and *surrealism,* as well as in the fiction, in the 1920s, of James Joyce (*Ulysses*) and of Franz Kafka (*The Trial, Metamorphosis*). The current movement, however, emerged after World War II as a rebellion against the essential beliefs and values both of traditional culture and traditional literature. Central to this earlier tradition had been the assumptions that human beings are mainly rational creatures who live in an at least partially intelligible universe, that they are part of an orderly social structure, and that they may be capable of heroism and dignity even in defeat. Since the 1940s, however, there has been a widespread tendency, especially prominent in the *existential philosophy* of men of letters such as Jean-Paul Sartre and Albert Camus, to view a human being as an isolated existent who is cast into an alien universe, to conceive the universe as possessing no inherent human truth, value, or meaning, and to represent human life, as it moves from the nothingness whence it came toward the nothingness where it must end, as an existence which is both anguished and absurd. As Camus said in *The Myth of Sisyphus* (1942),

> In a universe that is suddenly deprived of illusions and of light, man feels a stranger. His is an irremediable exile. . . . This divorce between man and his life, the actor and his setting, truly constitutes the feeling of Absurdity.

Or as Eugène Ionesco, a leading writer of the drama of the absurd, has put it in an essay on Kafka: "Cut off from his religious, metaphysical, and transcendental roots, man is lost; all his actions become senseless, absurd, useless."

Samuel Beckett, the most eminent and influential of writers in this mode, is an Irishman living in Paris who writes in French and then translates many of his own works into English. His plays project the irrationalism, helplessness, and absurdity of life, in dramatic forms that reject realistic settings, logical reasoning, or a consistently evolving plot. *Waiting for Godot* (1955) presents two tramps in a waste place, fruitlessly and all but hopelessly waiting for an unidentified person, Godot, who may or may not exist and with whom they sometimes think they remember that they may have an appointment; as one of them remarks, "Nothing happens, nobody comes, nobody goes, it's awful." Like most works in this mode, the play is "absurd" in the double sense that it is grotesquely comic as well as irrational and nonconsequential; it is a deliberate parody not only of the traditional assumptions of Western culture, but of traditional drama, and even of its own inescapable participation in the dramatic medium. The lucid but eddying and pointless dialogue is often funny, and pratfalls and other modes of slapstick are used to project metaphysical alienation and anguish. Beckett's prose fiction, such as *Malone Dies* (1958) and *The Unnamable* (1960), present an *antihero* who plays out the absurd moves of the end game of civilization in a nonwork which tends to undermine the coherence of its own medium, language itself. See *unstable irony.*

Another French playwright of the absurd is Jean Genet (who combines absurdism and diabolism); some of the dramatic work of the Englishman Harold Pinter and the American Edward Albee are recognizably in a similar mode. The plays of Tom Stoppard, such as *Rosencrantz and Guildenstern Are Dead* (1966) and *Travesties* (1974), exploit the devices of absurdist drama more for comic than philosophical ends. There are also affinities with this movement in the numerous recent works which exploit **black comedy:** baleful, naive, or inept characters in a fantastic or nightmarish modern world play out their roles in what Ionesco called a "tragic farce," in which the events are often simultaneously comic, horrifying, and absurd. Examples are Joseph Heller's *Catch-22* (1961), Thomas Pynchon's *V* (1963), John Irving's *The World According to Garp* (1978), and some of the novels by the German Günter Grass and the Americans Kurt Vonnegut, Jr., and John Barth.

See *wit, humor, and the comic,* and refer to: Martin Esslin, *The Theatre of the Absurd* (rev., 1969); David Grossvogel, *The Blasphemers: The Theatre of Brecht, Ionesco, Beckett, Genet* (1965); Arnold P. Hinchliffe, *The Absurd* (1969); Charles B. Harris, *Contemporary American Novelists of the Absurd* (1972); and Max F. Schultz, *Black Humor Fiction of the Sixties* (1980).

Act. A major division in the action of a play. Such a division was introduced into England by Elizabethan dramatists, who imitated the Roman playwright Seneca by structuring the action so that it fell into five acts. Late in the nineteenth century, a number of writers followed the example of Chekhov and Ibsen by constructing plays in four acts. In the present century the most common form for nonmusical dramas has been three acts.

Acts are often subdivided into **scenes,** which in modern plays usually consist of units of action in which there is no change of place or break in the continuity of time. (Some recent plays dispense with the division into acts, and are structured as a sequence of scenes, or episodes.) In the conventional theater with a **proscenium arch** that frames the front of the stage, the end of a scene is usually indicated by a dropped curtain, and the end of an act by a dropped curtain and an intermission.

Aestheticism and Decadence. Aestheticism, or "the Aesthetic Movement," was a European phenomenon during the latter nineteenth century that had its chief philosophical headquarters in France. Its roots lie in the German theory, proposed by Kant in his *Critique of Aesthetic Judgment* (1790), that the pure aesthetic experience consists of a "disinterested" contemplation of an object without reference to reality or to the "external" ends of its utility or morality; it was also influenced by the view of Edgar Allan Poe (in "The Poetic Principle," 1850) that the supreme work is a "poem *per se,*" a "poem written solely for the poem's sake." In defiance of the indifference or hostility of the society of their time to any art that did not inculcate utilitarian and social values, French writers developed the doctrine that a work of art is the supreme value among human products precisely because it is self-sufficient and has no aim beyond itself: the end of a work of art is simply to exist in its formal perfection, and to be beautiful.

French Aestheticism, as a self-conscious movement, is often said to date from Théophile Gautier's witty defense of his claim that art lacks all utility (Preface to *Mademoiselle de Maupin,* 1835), and it was developed by Baudelaire, Flaubert, Mallarmé, and many other writers. A rallying cry of Aestheticism became the phrase "l'art pour l'art"—**art for art's sake.** This claim often involved also the view of life for art's sake, with the artist envisioned as a priest who renounces the practical and self-seeking concerns of ordinary existence in the service of what Flaubert and others called "the religion of beauty."

Some proponents of Aestheticism, especially Baudelaire, also espoused views and values which developed into a movement called the **Decadence.** The term was based on qualities attributed to the literature and art of the later Roman Empire, and of Greece in the Byzantine era, which were said to possess the refinements and subtle beauties of a culture and art which have passed their vigorous prime and fallen into the sweet savor of decay. Such was also held to be the state of European civilization in the later nineteenth century. The precepts of the Decadence were summarized by Gautier in the "Notice" he prefixed to an edition of Baudelaire's poems, *Les Fleurs du mal* ("Flowers of Evil"), in 1868. Central to this movement was the view that art is totally opposed to "nature," both in the sense of biological nature and of the standard, or "natural," norms of morality and sexual behavior. The thoroughgoing Decadent writer cultivates high artifice in his style and, often, the bizarre in his subject matter, recoils from the fecundity and exuberance of instinctual and organic life, prefers elaborate dress over the living form and cosmetics over the natural hue, and sometimes sets out to violate what is "natural" in human experience by resorting to drugs, depravity, or sexual deviation in the attempt to achieve (in a phrase echoed from the French poet Rimbaud) "the systematic derangement of all the senses." The movement reached its height in the last two decades of the century; extreme products were the novel *À rebours* ("Against the Grain"), written by J. K. Huysmans in 1884, and some of the paintings of Gustave Moreau. This period is also known as the **fin de siècle** (end of the century); the phrase connotes the lassitude, satiety, and ennui expressed by many writers of the Decadence.

The doctrines of French Aestheticism were introduced into England by Walter Pater, with his emphasis on painstaking artifice and stylistic subtlety, his recommendation to crowd one's life with the maximum of exquisite sensations, and his concept of the supreme value of beauty and of "the love of art for its own sake." (See his Conclusion to *The Renaissance*, 1873.) Both the Aesthetic and Decadent modes are manifested in some of Swinburne's early poems of the 1860s, and in the 1890s by writers such as Oscar Wilde, Arthur Symons, Ernest Dowson, and Lionel Johnson and by the artist Aubrey Beardsley. In the search for strange sensations, a number of English Decadents in this period experimented with drugs and with illicit or deviant amours; several of them died young. Representative literary products are Wilde's novel *The Picture of Dorian Gray* (1891), his play *Salomé* (1893), and the poems of Ernest Dowson.

The influence of certain ideas of Aestheticism—such as the view of the "autonomy" (self-sufficiency) of art, the concept of the poem or novel as an isolated object with inherent value, the derogation of spontaneous "nature" as against art and artifice—has been important in the writings of such prominent recent authors as W. B. Yeats, T. E. Hulme, and T. S. Eliot, as well as in the theory of the *New Critics.* And the emphasis in the Decadence on drugged perception, extreme or deviant sexuality, and the deliberate inversion of conventional moral and social values has recently reappeared, with modern variations, in the *Beat* poets and novelists and in various writers of *black humor* and other modes of experimental prose fiction (see *novel*).

See *ivory tower,* and refer to Holbrook Jackson, *The Eighteen Nineties* (1913); Mario Praz, *The Romantic Agony* (1933); William Gaunt, *The Aesthetic Adventure* (1945); A. E. Carter, *The Idea of Decadence in French Literature, 1830–1900* (1958); Frank Kermode, *Romantic Image* (1957); Enid Starkie, *From Gautier to Eliot* (1960); Richard Gilman, *Decadence: The Strange Life of an Epithet* (1979).

Affective Fallacy. In an essay published in 1946, W. K. Wimsatt and Monroe C. Beardsley defined the affective fallacy as the error of evaluating a poem by its effects—especially its emotional effects—upon the reader. As a result of this fallacy "the poem itself, as an object of specifically critical judgment, tends to disappear," so that criticism "ends in impressionism and relativism." Beardsley has since modified the earlier claim by the admission that "it does not appear that critical evaluation can be done at all except in relation to certain types of effect that aesthetic objects have upon their perceivers." So modified, the doctrine becomes a claim for *objective criticism,* in which the critic does not describe the effects of a work upon himself, but concentrates upon the analysis of the attributes, devices, and form of the work by which such effects are achieved. For an extreme reaction against this view, see *reader-response criticism;* compare also *intentional fallacy.*

Wimsatt and Beardsley, "The Affective Fallacy," reprinted in W. K. Wimsatt, *The Verbal Icon* (1954); Monroe C. Beardsley, *Aesthetics: Problems in the Philosophy of Criticism* (1958), p. 491 and Chap. 11.

Allegory. An allegory is a narrative in which the agents and action, and sometimes the setting as well, are contrived so as to make coherent sense on the "literal," or primary, level of signification, and also to signify a second, correlated order of agents, concepts, and events. We can distinguish two main types:

(1) Historical and political allegory, in which the characters and actions that are signified literally in turn signify, or "allegorize," historical personages and events. So in Dryden's *Absalom and Achitophel* (1681), King David represents Charles II, Absalom represents his natural son the Duke of Monmouth, and the biblical plot allegorizes a political crisis in contemporary England. (2) The allegory of ideas, in which the literal characters represent abstract concepts and the plot incorporates and exemplifies a doctrine or thesis. Both types of allegory may either be sustained throughout a work, as in *Absalom and Achitophel* and Bunyan's *The Pilgrim's Progress* (1678), or else serve merely as an episode in a nonallegorical work. A famed example of episodic allegory is the encounter of Satan with his daughter Sin, as well as with Death—who is represented allegorically as the son born of their incestuous relationship—in Milton's *Paradise Lost*, Book II (1667).

The central device in the second type, the sustained allegory of ideas, is the personification of abstract entities such as virtues, vices, states of mind, modes of life, and types of character; in the more explicit allegories, such reference is specified by the names given to characters and places. Thus Bunyan's *The Pilgrim's Progress* allegorizes the doctrines of Christian salvation by telling how Christian, warned by Evangelist, flees the City of Destruction and makes his way laboriously to the Celestial City; en route he encounters characters with names like Faithful, Hopeful, and the Giant Despair, and passes through places like the Slough of Despond, the Valley of the Shadow of Death, and Vanity Fair. A passage from this work will indicate the nature of a clear-cut allegorical process:

> Now as Christian was walking solitary by himself, he espied one afar off come crossing over the field to meet him; and their hap was to meet just as they were crossing the way of each other. The Gentleman's name was Mr. Worldly-Wiseman; he dwelt in the Town of Carnal-Policy, a very great Town, and also hard by from whence Christian came.

Works which are primarily nonallegorical may introduce **allegorical imagery** (the personification of abstract entities who perform a brief allegorical action) in short passages. Familiar instances are the opening lines of Milton's *L'Allegro* and *Il Penseroso* (1645). This device was exploited especially in the *poetic diction* of authors in the mid-eighteenth century. An example—so brief that it presents an allegoric tableau rather than a narrative—is the passage in Gray's "Elegy Written in a Country Churchyard" (1751):

> Can Honour's voice provoke the silent dust,
> Or Flatt'ry sooth the dull cold ear of Death?

Allegory is a strategy which may be employed in any literary form or genre. *The Pilgrim's Progress* is a moral and religious allegory in a prose narrative; Spenser's *The Faerie Queene* (1590–96) fuses moral, religious, historical, and political allegory in a verse romance; the third book of Swift's *Gulliver's*

Travels, the voyage to Laputa and Lagado (1726), is an allegorical satire directed primarily against philosophical and scientific pedantry; and William Collins' "Ode on the Poetical Character" (1747) is a lyric poem which allegorizes a topic in literary criticism—the nature, sources, and power of the poet's creative imagination. John Keats makes a subtle use of allegory throughout his ode "To Autumn" (1820), most explicitly in the magnificent second stanza, which represents autumn personified as a female figure amid the scenes and activities of that season.

Sustained allegory was a favorite form in the Middle Ages, when it produced masterpieces—especially in the mode of the *dream vision,* in which the narrator falls asleep and experiences an allegoric dream—including, in the fourteenth century, Dante's *Divine Comedy,* the French *Roman de la Rose,* Chaucer's *House of Fame,* and Langland's *Piers Plowman,* as well as, early in the sixteenth century, the drama *Everyman.* (See *morality play.*) But sustained allegory has been written in all literary periods, and is the form of such major nineteenth-century poetic works as Goethe's *Faust, Part II,* Shelley's *Prometheus Unbound,* Hardy's *The Dynasts,* and in the present century the stories and novels of Franz Kafka.

Various literary *genres* may be classified as special types of allegory, in that they all narrate, though in varied forms, one coherent set of circumstances which signify a second order of correlated meanings. A **fable** is a short story that exemplifies an abstract moral thesis or principle of human behavior; usually in its conclusion either the narrator or one of the characters states the moral in the form of an *epigram.* Most common is the **beast fable,** in which animals talk and act like the human types they represent. In the familiar fable of the fox and the grapes, the fox—after vainly exerting all his wiles to get the grapes hanging beyond his reach—concludes that they are probably sour anyway: the express moral is that human beings belittle what they cannot get. An early set of beast fables was attributed to Aesop, a Greek slave of the sixth century B.C.; in the seventeenth century a Frenchman, Jean de La Fontaine, wrote a set of witty fables in verse which are the classics of this literary kind. Chaucer's "The Nun's Priest's Tale," the story of the cock and the fox, is a beast fable; the American Joel Chandler Harris (1848–1908) wrote many Uncle Remus stories which are beast fables, told in Black southern dialect and based on Black *folktales;* James Thurber's *Fables for Our Time* (1940) is a recent set of short fables; and in *Animal Farm* (1945) George Orwell expanded the beast fable into a sustained satire on the political and social conditions of our era.

A **parable** is a short narrative presented so as to stress the tacit analogy between its component parts and a thesis or lesson that the narrator is trying to bring home to his listeners or readers. The parable was one of Christ's favorite devices as a teacher; examples are His parables of the good Samaritan and of the prodigal son. Here is Christ's parable of the fig tree, Luke 13:6–9:

> He spake also this parable: A certain man had a fig tree planted in his vineyard; and he came and sought fruit thereon, and found none. Then said he unto the dresser of his vineyard, "Behold, these three years I come seeking fruit on this fig tree, and

find none: cut it down; why cumbereth it the ground?" And he answering said unto him, "Lord, let it alone this year also, till I shall dig about it, and dung it. And if it bears fruit, well: and if not, then after that thou shalt cut it down."

An **exemplum** is a story told as a particular narrative instance of the general theme of a sermon. The device was popular in the Middle Ages, when extensive collections of exempla were prepared for use by preachers. In Chaucer's "The Pardoner's Tale" the Pardoner, preaching on the thesis "Greed is the root of all evil," incorporates as exemplum the tale of the three drunken revelers who set out to find Death, find a heap of gold instead, only after all to find Death by killing one another in the attempt to gain sole possession of the treasure. By extension the term "exemplum" is also applied to tales used in a formal, though nonreligious, exhortation. Thus Chaucer's Chanticleer, in "The Nun's Priest's Tale," borrows the preacher's technique in the ten exempla he tells in a vain effort to persuade his skeptical wife, Dame Pertelote the hen, that bad dreams forebode disaster.

See *didactic, symbol* (for the distinction between allegory and symbol), and (on the fourfold allegorical interpretation of the Bible) *interpretation: typological and allegorical.* On allegory in general, consult C. S. Lewis, *The Allegory of Love* (1936), Chap. 2; Edwin Honig, *Dark Conceit: The Making of Allegory* (1959); Angus Fletcher, *Allegory: The Theory of a Symbolic Mode* (1964); Rosemund Tuve, *Allegorical Imagery* (1966); Michael Murrin, *The Veil of Allegory* (1969); Maureen Quilligan, *The Language of Allegory* (1979). On the exemplum, see G. R. Owst, *Literature and Pulpit in Medieval England* (2d ed., 1961), Chap. 4.

Alliteration is the repetition of speech sounds in a sequence of nearby words; the term is usually applied only to consonants, and especially when the recurrent sound occurs in a conspicuous position at the beginning either of a word or of a stressed syllable within a word. In Old English **alliterative meter,** alliteration is the principal organizing device of the verse line; each line is divided into two half-lines of two strong stresses by a decisive pause, or *caesura,* and at least one, and usually both, of the two stressed syllables in the first half-line alliterate with the first stressed syllable of the second half-line. (In this versification a vowel was considered to alliterate with any other vowel.) A number of Middle English poems, such as *Piers Plowman* and *Gawain and the Green Knight* in the fourteenth century, continued to use and play variations upon the old alliterative meter. (See *strong-stress meters.*) In the opening line of *Piers Plowman,* for example, all four of the stressed syllables alliterate:

In a *s*ómer *s*éson, whan *s*óft was the *s*ónne . . .

In later English versification, however, alliteration is used only for special stylistic effects, such as to reinforce the meaning, to link related words, or to provide tone color. An example is the repetition of the *s, th,* and *w* consonants in Shakespeare's Sonnet 30:

When to the *s*essions of *s*weet *s*ilent *th*ought
I *s*ummon up remembrance of *th*ings past,
I *s*igh the lack of many a *th*ing I *s*ought
And *w*ith old *w*oes new *w*ail my dear time's *w*aste. . . .

Various other repetitions of speech sounds are identified by special terms. **Consonance** is the repetition of a sequence of two or more consonants, but with a change in the intervening vowel: live-love, lean-alone, pitter-patter. W. H. Auden's poem of the 1930s " 'O where are you going?' said reader to rider" makes prominent use of this device; the last stanza reads:

"Out of this house"—said *rider* to *reader*,
"Yours never will"—said *farer* to *fearer*,
"They're looking for you"—said *hearer* to *horror*,
As he left them there, as he left them there.*

Assonance is the repetition of identical or similar vowel sounds—especially in stressed syllables—in a sequence of nearby words. Note the recurrent long *i* in the opening lines of Keats's "Ode on a Grecian Urn" (1820):

Thou still unravished br*i*de of qu*i*etness,
Thou foster ch*i*ld of s*i*lence and slow t*i*me.

The richly assonantal effect at the beginning of William Collins' "Ode to Evening" (1747) depends on a patterned sequence both of identical and of similar vowels:

If aught of oaten stop or pastoral song,
May hope, chaste Eve, to soothe thy pensive ear . . .

For a special case of the repetition of vowels and consonants in combination, see *rhyme*.

Allusion in a literary text is a reference, explicit or indirect, to a well-known person, place, or event, or to another literary work or passage. In the Elizabethan Thomas Nashe's "Litany in Time of Plague,"

Brightness falls from the air,
Queens have died young and fair,
Dust hath closed Helen's eye,

there is an explicit allusion to Helen of Troy. Most allusions serve to illustrate or enhance a subject, but some are used in order to undercut it ironically by the

*From "O where are you going?" Copyright 1934 and renewed 1962 by W. H. Auden. Reprinted from *Collected Shorter Poems, 1927–1957*, by W. H. Auden, by permission of Random House, Inc., and Faber and Faber Ltd.

discrepancy between the subject and the allusion. In the lines from T. S. Eliot's *The Waste Land* (1922) describing a woman at her modern dressing table,

> The Chair she sat in, like a burnished throne,
> Glowed on the marble,*

the ironic allusion, by the indirect mode of echoing some of Shakespeare's phrasing, is to Cleopatra's magnificent barge in *Antony and Cleopatra* (II. ii. 196 ff.):

> The barge she sat in, like a burnish'd throne,
> Burn'd on the water.

For discussion of a poet who makes persistent and complex use of this device, see Reuben A. Brower, *Alexander Pope: The Poetry of Allusion* (1959).

In older literature the author assumed that his allusions were well enough known to be recognized by the educated readers of the day. But a number of modern authors (including Joyce, Pound, and Eliot) often employ allusions that are highly specialized, or else are drawn from the author's private reading and experience, in the knowledge that very few readers will recognize them without the help of scholarly annotation. The current term *intertextuality* includes allusion among the many ways in which one text is interlinked with other texts.

Ambiguity. In ordinary usage "ambiguity" is commonly applied to a fault in style; that is, the use of a vague or equivocal expression when what is wanted is precision and particularity of reference. Since William Empson published *Seven Types of Ambiguity* (1930), however, the term has been widely used in criticism to identify a poetic device: the deliberate use of a word or expression to signify two or more distinct references, or to express two or more diverse attitudes or feelings. **Multiple meaning** and **plurisignation** are alternative terms for this use of language; they have the advantage of avoiding the pejorative association with the word "ambiguity."

When Shakespeare's Cleopatra, exciting the asp to a frenzy, says (*Antony and Cleopatra;* V. ii. 306 ff.),

> Come, thou mortal wretch,
> With thy sharp teeth this knot intrinsicate
> Of life at once untie. Poor venomous fool,
> Be angry, and dispatch,

her speech is richly multiple in significance. For example, "mortal" means "fatal" or "death-dealing," and at the same time signifies that the asp is itself mortal, or subject to death. "Wretch" in this context serves to express both contempt and pity (Cleopatra goes on to refer to the asp as "my baby at my

*From *The Waste Land* by T. S. Eliot (1922). Reprinted by permission of Harcourt, Brace & World, Inc., and Faber and Faber Ltd.

breast,/That sucks the nurse asleep"). And the two meanings of "dispatch"—"make haste" and "kill"—are equally relevant.

A special type of multiple meaning is the **portmanteau word.** The term was introduced into literary criticism by Humpty Dumpty, the expert on semantics in Lewis Carroll's *Through the Looking Glass* (1871). He is explicating to Alice the meaning of the opening lines of "Jabberwocky":

> 'Twas brillig, and the slithy toves
> Did gyre and gimble in the wabe.

"Slithy," Humpty Dumpty explained, "means 'lithe and slimy' . . . You see it's like a portmanteau—there are two meanings packed up into one word." A portmanteau word thus consists of a fusion of two or more existing words. James Joyce exploited this device to the full in order to sustain the multiple levels of meaning in his dream narrative *Finnegans Wake* (1939); an example is his comment on girls who are "yung and easily freudened"; "freudened" fuses "frightened" and "Freud," while "yung" fuses "young" and Sigmund Freud's rival in depth psychology, C. J. Jung. (Compare *pun.*) "Différance," a key analytic term of the philosopher of language Jacques Derrida, is a portmanteau noun which he describes as a fusion of two diverse meanings of the French verb "différer": "to differ" and "to defer." (See *deconstruction.*)

William Empson (who named and enlarged upon a literary phenomenon that had been noted by earlier writers) helped make current a mode of explication which has greatly expanded our sense of the complexity and richness of poetic language. The risk, exemplified both by Empson and other recent critics, is that the intensive search for ambiguities easily leads to **over-reading:** ingenious, overdrawn, and sometimes contradictory explications of multiple significations.

For related terms see *connotation and denotation* and *pun.* Refer to Empson, above, and to Philip Wheelwright, *The Burning Fountain* (1954), especially Chap. 4. For critiques of Empson's theory and practice, see John Crowe Ransom, "Mr. Empson's Muddles," *The Southern Review*, 4 (1938), and Elder Olson, "William Empson, Contemporary Criticism and Poetic Diction," in *Critics and Criticism*, ed. R. S. Crane (1952).

Antithesis is a contrast or opposition in the meanings of contiguous phrases or clauses, emphasized by **parallelism**—that is, a similar order and structure—in the *syntax*. An example is Alexander Pope's description of Atticus in his *Epistle to Dr. Arbuthnot* (1735), "Willing to wound, and yet afraid to strike." In the second line of Pope's description of the Baron's designs against Belinda, in *The Rape of the Lock* (1714), syntactic parallelism is stressed by *alliteration* in the correspondent nouns:

> Resolved to win, he meditates the way,
> By *f*orce to ravish, or by *f*raud betray.

In a sentence from Samuel Johnson's prose fiction *Rasselas* (1759), Chap. 26, the antithesis is heightened by the alliteration of a pair of contrasted nouns: "Marriage has many *p*ains, but celibacy has no *p*leasures."

Archaism. The use in literature of words and expressions that have become obsolete in the common speech of an era. Spenser in *The Faerie Queene* (1590–96) deliberately employed archaisms (many of them derived from Chaucer's medieval English) in the attempt to achieve a specialized poetic style appropriate to his revival of the medieval *chivalric romance.* The translators of the King James Version of the Bible (1611) gave weight, dignity, and sonority to their prose by archaic revivals. Both Spenser and the King James Bible have in their turn been major sources of archaisms in Milton and many later poets. When Keats, for example, in his ode (1820) described the Grecian urn as "with *brede*/Of marble men and maidens *overwrought,*" he used archaic words for "braid" and "worked [that is, ornamented] all over." Until fairly recent times many poets continued to use "I ween," "methought," "steed," "taper" (for candle), and "morn," but only in their verses, not their speech.

Atmosphere (alternative terms are **mood** and **ambience**) is the tonality pervading a literary work, which fosters in the reader expectations as to the course of events, whether happy or (more commonly) terrifying or disastrous. Shakespeare establishes the tense and fearful atmosphere of *Hamlet* at the beginning, by the terse and nervous dialogue of the sentinels as they anticipate a reappearance of the ghost; Coleridge engenders a compound of religious and superstitious terror by his manner of describing the initial scene of the narrative poem *Christabel* (1816); and Hardy in his novel *The Return of the Native* (1878) makes Egdon Heath an immense and brooding presence which reduces to pettiness and futility the human struggle for happiness for which it is the setting.

Augustan Age. The original Augustan Age was the brilliant literary period of Vergil, Horace, and Ovid under the Roman emperor Augustus (27 B.C.–A.D. 14). In the eighteenth century and later, however, the term was frequently applied also to the literary period in England from approximately 1700 to 1745, on the ground that the leading writers of the time (such as Pope, Swift, and Addison) greatly admired the Roman Augustans, themselves drew the parallel between the two ages, and deliberately imitated their literary forms and subjects, their emphasis on social concerns, and their ideals of moderation, decorum, and urbanity. See *neoclassicism.*

Ballad. A short definition of the **popular ballad** (known also as the "folk ballad" or "traditional ballad") is that it is a song, transmitted orally, which tells a story. Ballads are thus the narrative variety of *folk songs*, which originate among illiterate, or only partly literate, people. In all probability the initial version of a ballad was composed by a single author, but he or she is unknown; and since each singer who learns a ballad by word of mouth is apt to introduce changes in both the text and the tune, it exists in many variant forms. Typically, the popular ballad is dramatic, condensed, and impersonal: the narrator begins with the climactic episode, tells the story tersely by means of action and dialogue (sometimes by means of the dialogue alone), and tells it without self-reference or the expression of personal attitudes or feelings.

The most common stanza form—called the **ballad stanza**—is a *quatrain* in alternate four- and three-stress *iambic* lines; usually only the second and fourth lines rhyme. This is the form of "Sir Patrick Spens"; the first stanza of this ballad also exemplifies the conventionally abrupt opening and the manner of proceeding by third-person narration, curtly sketched setting and action, sharp transition, and spare dialogue:

> The king sits in Dumferling towne,
>   Drinking the blude-red wine:
> "O Whar will I get a guid sailor,
>   To sail this schip of mine?"

Many ballads employ set formulas (which helped the singer remember the song) including (1) stock descriptive phrases like "blood-red wine" and "milk-white steed," (2) a *refrain* in each stanza ("Edward," "Lord Randal"), and (3) **incremental repetition,** in which a line or stanza is repeated, but with an addition that advances the story ("Lord Randal," "Child Waters").

The collecting and printing of popular ballads began in England, then in Germany, during the eighteenth century. In 1765 Thomas Percy published his *Reliques of Ancient English Poetry,* which, although most of the contents had been rewritten in the style of that time, did much to inaugurate widespread interest in folk literature. The basic collection is Francis J. Child's *English and Scottish Popular Ballads* (1882–98), which includes 305 ballads, together with many variant versions. Bertrand H. Bronson has edited *The Traditional Tunes of the Child Ballads* (4 vols.; 1959–72). Popular ballads are still being sung—and collected, now with a tape recorder—in the British Isles and remote rural areas of America. To the songs it inherited from Great Britain, America has added native forms of the ballad, such as those sung by lumberjacks, cowboys, laborers, and social protesters. A number of recent folk singers, from Woody Guthrie to Bob Dylan and Joan Baez, themselves compose ballads; most of these, however, such as "Bonnie and Clyde" (about a notorious gangster and his moll), are closer to the journalistic "broadside ballad" than to the primitive and heroic mode of the popular ballads in the Child collection.

A **broadside ballad** is a ballad that was printed on one side of a single sheet (called a "broadside"), dealing with a current event or person or issue, and sung to a well-known tune. Beginning with the sixteenth century, these broadsides were hawked in the streets or at country fairs in Great Britain.

The ballad has had an enormous influence on the form and style of poetry, especially, in England, since Wordsworth and Coleridge's *Lyrical Ballads* (1798). A **literary ballad** is a narrative poem written by a learned poet in deliberate imitation of the form and spirit of the popular ballad. Some of the greatest of these were composed in the *Romantic Period:* Coleridge's "Rime of the Ancient Mariner" (which, however, is much longer and more elaborately developed than the folk ballad), Scott's "Proud Maisie," and Keats's "La Belle Dame sans Merci." Wordsworth begins the narration in "We Are Seven" by introducing the narrator as an agent—"I met a little cottage girl"—which is probably one reason that he called it "a *lyrical* ballad." Coleridge's "Ancient Mariner," on the other hand, opens with the abrupt impersonal narration of the traditional ballad:

> It is an ancient Mariner
> And he stoppeth one of three.

Gordon H. Gerould, *The Ballad of Tradition* (1932); M. J. C. Hodgart, *The Ballads* (2d ed., 1962); John A. and Alan Lomax, *American Ballads and Folk Songs* (1934). For the broadside ballad see *The Common Muse,* eds. V. de Sola Pinto and Allan E. Rodway (1957).

Baroque is a term derived from the Spanish and Portuguese words for a pearl that is roughly shaped. It was applied (at first derogatorily, but now merely descriptively) to a style of architecture, sculpture, and painting that developed in Italy in the late-sixteenth and seventeenth centuries and then spread to Germany and other countries in Europe. The style employs the classical forms of the *Renaissance,* but breaks them up and intermingles them to achieve elaborate, grandiose, energetic, and highly dramatic effects.

In literature, the term has varied uses. It may be applied to any elaborately formal and magniloquent style in verse or prose—for example, some verse passages in Milton's *Paradise Lost* (1667) and De Quincey's prose descriptions of his dreams in *Confessions of an English Opium Eater* (1822) have both been called baroque. Occasionally—though oftener on the Continent than in England—it serves as a period term for post-Renaissance literature. More frequently it is applied to the elaborate verses and extravagant conceits of the late-sixteenth- and early-seventeenth-century poets Giambattista Marino in Italy and Luis de Góngora in Spain. In English literature the metaphysical poems of John Donne are sometimes described as baroque; but the term is more often, and more precisely, applied to the elaborate style, fantastic conceits, and extreme religious emotionalism of the poet Richard Crashaw, 1612–49. (See under *metaphysical conceit.*)

Bathos and Anticlimax. Bathos is Greek for "depth," and it has been an indispensable term to critics since Alexander Pope, parodying the Greek Longinus' famous essay *On the Sublime* (that is, "loftiness"), wrote in 1727 an essay *On Bathos: Of the Art of Sinking in Poetry.* With mock solemnity Pope assures his readers that he undertakes "to lead them as it were by the hand . . . the gentle down-hill way to Bathos; the bottom, the end, the central point, the *non plus ultra,* of true Modern Poesy!" The word ever since has been used for an unintentional descent in literature when, straining to be pathetic or passionate or elevated, the writer overshoots the mark and drops into the trivial or the ridiculous. Among his examples Pope records "the modest request of two absent lovers" in a contemporary poem:

> Ye Gods! annihilate but Space and Time,
> And make two lovers happy.

The slogan "For God, for Country, and for Yale!" is bathetic because it moves to intended **climax** (that is, an ascending sequence of importance) in rhetorical order and to unintended descent in reference—at least for someone who is not a Yale student. The greatest of poets sometimes fall unwittingly into the same rhetorical figure. In the early version of *The Prelude* (1805; Book IX), Wordsworth, after recounting at length the tale of the star-crossed lovers Vaudracour and Julia, tells how Julia died, leaving Vaudracour to raise their infant son:

> It consoled him here
> To attend upon the Orphan and perform
> The office of a Nurse to his young Child
> Which after a short time by some mistake
> Or indiscretion of the Father, died.

The Stuffed Owl: An Anthology of Bad Verse, eds. D. B. Wyndham Lewis and Charles Lee (rev., 1948), is a rich mine of bathos.

Anticlimax is sometimes used as an equivalent of bathos—the writer aims at rhetorical climax and achieves semantic descent. In a second usage, however, "anticlimax" is nonpejorative, and denotes a writer's intentional drop from the serious and elevated to the trivial and lowly, in order to achieve a comic or satiric effect. Thus Thomas Gray in his *mock-heroic* "Ode on the Death of a Favorite Cat" (1748)—the cat drowned when she tried to catch a goldfish—gravely inserts the moral observation:

> What female heart can gold despise?
> What cat's averse to fish?

And in *Don Juan* (1819–24; I. ix) Byron thus exemplifies the would-be gallantry of Juan's father:

> A better cavalier ne'er mounted horse,
> Or, being mounted, e'er got down again.

Beat Writers identifies a loose-knit group of poets and novelists, writing in the second half of the 1950s, who shared a set of social attitudes—antiestablishment, antipolitical, anti-intellectual, opposed to reigning cultural and moral values, and in favor of unfettered self-realization and self-expression. "Beat" signified both "beaten down" (that is, by the oppressive culture of the time) and "beatific" (many of the Beat writers cultivated ecstatic states of mind by way of Buddhism, Jewish and Christian mysticism, and/or drugs that induced visionary experiences). The group included such diverse figures as the poets Allen Ginsberg, Gregory Corso, and Lawrence Ferlinghetti and the novelists William Burroughs and Jack Kerouac. Ginsberg's *Howl* (1956) is a central Beat achievement in its breathless, chanted celebration of the down-and-out and the subculture of drug addicts, social misfits, and compulsive wanderers, as well as in its exhibition of the derangement of the intellect and the senses effected by a combination of sexual abandon, drugged hallucinations, and religious ecstasies. (Compare *decadence.*) A representative novel of the movement is Jack Kerouac's *On the Road* (1958). While the Beat movement was short-lived, it left its imprint on the subjects and forms of many writers of the 1960s and 1970s; see *counterculture.*

Lawrence Lipton, *The Holy Barbarians* (1959); Seymour Krim, ed., *The Beats* (1960).

Biography. Late in the seventeenth century, Dryden defined biography neatly as "the history of particular men's lives." The name now connotes a relatively full account of a person's life, involving the attempt to set forth character, temperament, and milieu, as well as the facts of the subject's experiences and activities. English biography proper—as distinguished from the generalized chronicles of the deeds of a king, or the stylized and pious lives of the Christian saints—appeared in the seventeenth century; an example is Izaak Walton's *Lives* (of John Donne, George Herbert, Richard Hooker, and others), written between 1640 and 1678. In the eighteenth century both the theory and the practice of biography as a special literary *genre* were greatly advanced; it was the age of Dr. Johnson's monumental *Lives of the English Poets* (1779–81) and of James Boswell's *Life of Samuel Johnson* (1791), which many readers hold to be the greatest of all biographies. In our own time it has become one of the most popular of literary forms, and usually there is at least one biographical title high on the best-seller list. The recent increase of interest in notable women has led to a number of biographies of such pioneers of *feminism* as Mary Wollstonecraft in England and Margaret Fuller in America. (See also *psychobiography.*)

Autobiography is a biography written by the subject about himself or herself. It is to be distinguished from the **memoir**—in which the emphasis is not on the author's developing self, but on the people and events that the author has known or witnessed—and from the private **diary** or **journal,** which is a day-to-day record of the events in a person's life, written for personal use and pleasure, with little or no thought of publication. Examples of the latter type are the seventeenth-century diaries of Samuel Pepys and John Evelyn, and the eighteenth-century journals of James Boswell. The first fully developed autobiography is also one of the greatest: the *Confessions* of St. Augustine, written in the fourth century. The design of this profound and subtle **spiritual autobiography** centers on the author's mental crisis and a recovery in which he discovers his Christian identity and religious vocation. This design of the spiritual history of the self has been repeated in many later autobiographies. Some of these, like Augustine's, are religious confessions of crisis and conversion such as John Bunyan's *Grace Abounding to the Chief of Sinners* (1666). Others are secular works in which the crisis is resolved by the author's discovery of his identity and vocation as a poet or artist, as in Wordsworth's great autobiography in verse, *The Prelude* (completed 1805, published in revised form 1850), or in the partly autobiographical works of prose fiction such as Marcel Proust's *À la recherche du temps perdu* (1913–27) and James Joyce's *Portrait of the Artist as a Young Man* (1915).

Notable American and British autobiographies are those by Benjamin Franklin, John Stuart Mill, Anthony Trollope, Henry Adams, and Sean O'Casey. Among the masterpieces of this genre in other languages are Rousseau's *Confessions,* written 1764–70, and Goethe's *Dichtung und Wahrheit* ("Poetry and Truth"), written 1810–31.

On biography: Donald A. Stauffer, *English Biography before 1700* (1930), and *The Art of Biography in Eighteenth-Century England* (1941); Leon Edel, *Literary Biography* (1957); Richard D. Altick, *Lives and Letters: A History of Literary Biography in England and America* (1965); David Novarr, *The Lines of Life: Theories of Biography, 1880–1970* (1986). On autobiography: Wayne Shumaker, *English Autobiography* (1954); Roy Pascal, *Design and Truth in Autobiography* (1960); Estelle C. Jellinek, ed., *Women's Autobiography: Essays in Criticism* (1980); James Olney, *Metaphors of Self: The Meaning of Autobiography* (1981). John N. Morris, in *Versions of the Self: Studies in English Autobiography from John Bunyan to John Stuart Mill* (1966), deals both with religious and secular spiritual autobiographies.

Blank Verse consists of lines of *iambic pentameter* which are unrhymed—hence the term "blank." Of all English verse forms it is closest to the natural rhythms of English speech, yet the most flexible and adaptive to diverse levels of discourse; as a result it has been more frequently and variously used than any other type of verse. Soon after blank verse was introduced by the Earl of Surrey in his translations from Vergil's *The Aeneid* (about 1540), it became the standard meter for Elizabethan and later poetic drama; a free form of blank verse is still the medium in such recent verse plays as those by Maxwell Anderson and T. S. Eliot. Milton used blank verse for his epic *Paradise Lost* (1667), James Thomson for his descriptive and philosophical *Seasons* (1726–30), Wordsworth for his autobiographical *Prelude* (1805), Tennyson for the narrative *Idylls of the King* (1891), Browning for *The Ring and the Book* (1868–69) and many dramatic monologues, and T. S. Eliot for much of *The Waste Land* (1922). Many meditative lyrics, from the *Romantic Period* to the present, have also been written in blank verse, including Coleridge's "Frost at Midnight," Wordsworth's "Tintern Abbey," Tennyson's "Tears, Idle Tears" (in which the blank verse is divided into five-line stanzas), and Wallace Stevens' "Sunday Morning."

The usual divisions in blank verse poems, setting off a sustained passage, are called **verse paragraphs.** See, for example, the great verse paragraph of twenty-six lines which initiates Milton's *Paradise Lost,* beginning with "Of man's first disobedience" and ending with "And justify the ways of God to men," or the opening verse paragraph of twenty-two lines in Wordsworth's "Tintern Abbey" (1798).

See *meter,* and refer to Moody Prior's critical study of blank verse in *The Language of Tragedy* (1964).

Bombast originally meant "cotton stuffing"; the word was adopted to signify verbose and inflated diction that is disproportionate to the matter it expresses. The high style of even so fine a poet as Christopher Marlowe is at times inappropriate to its occasion, as when Faustus declares (*Dr. Faustus,* 1604; III. i. 47 ff.):

Now by the kingdoms of infernal rule,
Of Styx, Acheron, and the fiery lake
Of ever-burning Phlegethon I swear
That I do long to see the monuments
And situation of bright-splendent Rome;

which is to say: "By Hades, I'd like to see Rome!" Bombast is a frequent component in the *heroic drama* of the late seventeenth and early eighteenth centuries. The pompous language of that drama is parodied in Henry Fielding's *Tom Thumb the Great* (1731), as in the famous opening of Act II. v, in which the lover cries:

Oh! Huncamunca, Huncamunca, oh!
Thy pouting breasts, like kettle-drums of brass,
Beat everlasting loud alarms of joy;
As bright as brass they are, and oh! as hard;
Oh! Huncamunca, Huncamunca, oh!

Fielding points out in a note the inspiration for this parody in James Thomson's lines in *The Tragedy of Sophonisba* (1730):

Oh! Sophonisba, Sophonisba, oh!
Oh! Narva, Narva, oh!

Bowdlerize. To expurgate from an edition of a literary work passages considered indecent or indelicate. The word derives from the Reverend Thomas Bowdler, who tidied up his *Family Shakespeare* in 1815 by omitting, as he put it, "whatever is unfit to be read by a gentleman in a company of ladies." Swift's *Gulliver's Travels* (1726) and Shakespeare's plays are often bowdlerized in editions intended for the young, and until fairly recently, even some compilers of anthologies for college students availed themselves of Bowdler's prerogative in editing Chaucer.

Burlesque has been succinctly defined as "an incongruous imitation"; that is, it imitates the matter or manner of a serious literary work, or of a literary genre, but makes the imitation amusing by a ridiculous disparity between its form and style and its subject matter. The burlesque may be written for the sheer fun of it; usually, however, it is a form of *satire.* The butt of the satiric ridicule may be the particular literary work or general type that is being imitated, or the subject matter to which the imitation is incongruously applied, or (often) both of these together.

"Burlesque," "parody," and "travesty" are sometimes applied interchangeably; simply to equate these terms, however, is to surrender useful critical distinctions. It is better to follow the critics who use "burlesque" as the generic name and use the other terms to discriminate various species of burlesque. The application of these terms will be clearer if we make two preliminary distinctions: (1) In a burlesque imitation, the form and style may be either lower or higher in level and dignity than the subject to which it is incongruously applied. (See the discussion of levels under *style.*) If the form and style are elevated but the subject is low or trivial, we have "high burlesque"; if the subject is high in status and dignified but the style and manner of treatment are low and undignified, we have "low burlesque." (2) A burlesque may also be distinguished according to whether it imitates a general type or *genre,* or a particular work or author. Applying these two distinctions, we get the following species of burlesque.

(I) Varieties of high burlesque:

(1) A **mock epic** or **mock-heroic** poem imitates the elaborate form and ceremonious style of the *epic* genre, but applies it to a commonplace or trivial subject matter. In a masterpiece of this type, *The Rape of the Lock* (1714), Pope views through the grandiose epic perspective a quarrel between the belles and elegants of his day over the theft of a lady's curl. The story includes such elements of traditional epic protocol as supernatural *machinery,* a voyage on board ship, a visit to the underworld, and a heroically scaled battle between the sexes—although with metaphors, hatpins, and snuff for weapons. The term "mock-heroic" is often applied to other dignified poetic forms which are purposely mismatched to a lowly subject; for example, to Thomas Gray's comic "Ode on the Death of a Favorite Cat" (1748).

(2) A **parody** imitates the serious materials and manner of a particular literary work, or the characteristic style of a particular author, or the stylistic and other features of a serious literary form, and applies them to a lowly or comically inappropriate subject. John Phillips' "The Splendid Shilling" (1705) parodied the epic style of Milton's *Paradise Lost* (1667) by exaggerating its high formality and applying it to the description of a tattered poet composing in a drafty attic. Henry Fielding in *Joseph Andrews* (1742) parodied Richardson's novel *Pamela* (1740–41) by putting a hearty male hero in place of Richardson's sexually beleaguered heroine. Here is Hartley Coleridge's parody of the first stanza of Wordsworth's "She Dwelt among the Untrodden Ways":

> He lived amidst th' untrodden ways
> To Rydal Lake that lead,
> A bard whom there were none to praise,
> And very few to read.

From the early nineteenth century to the present, parody has been the favorite form of burlesque. Among the gifted parodists of the present century have been Max Beerbohm in England (see his *A Christmas Garland,* 1912) and such American writers for *The New Yorker* as James Thurber, Robert Benchley, and E. B. White.

(II) Varieties of low burlesque:

(1) The **Hudibrastic poem** is named from Samuel Butler's *Hudibras* (1663), which satirizes rigid Puritanism by describing the adventures of a Puritan knight, Sir Hudibras; instead of the doughty deeds and dignified style of the traditional genre of the *chivalric romance,* however, we find the knightly hero experiencing mundane and humiliating misadventures which are described in *doggerel* verses and a ludicrously colloquial idiom.

(2) The **travesty,** like the parody, mocks a particular work; but it does so by treating its lofty subject in a jocular and undignified manner and style. As Boileau put it, describing a travesty of Vergil's *Aeneid,* "Dido and Aeneas are made to speak like fishwives and ruffians."

The term **lampoon** is applied to a short satirical work, or a passage in a longer work, which burlesques, not a literary work or general subject, but the appearance and character of a particular person; it typically employs **caricature,** which in a verbal description (as in graphic art) designates the exaggeration or distortion, for comic effect, of a person's distinctive physical features or other characteristics. John Dryden's *Absalom and Achitophel* (1681) includes a famed twenty-five-line lampoon of Zimri (Dryden's contemporary the Duke of Buckingham), which begins:

In the first rank of these did Zimri stand;
A man so various, that he seemed to be
Not one, but all mankind's epitome:
Stiff in opinions, always in the wrong;
Was everything by starts, and nothing long. . . .

The modern sense of "burlesque" as a theater form derives, historically, from plays which mocked serious types of drama by an incongruous imitation. John Gay's *Beggar's Opera* (1728)—which in turn became the model for the German *Threepenny Opera,* by Bertolt Brecht and Kurt Weill (1928)—was a high burlesque of Italian opera, applying its dignified formulas to a company of beggars and thieves; a number of the musical plays by Gilbert and Sullivan in the Victorian era also burlesqued grand opera.

George Kitchin, *A Survey of Burlesque and Parody in English* (1931); Richmond P. Bond, *English Burlesque Poetry, 1700–1750* (1932). Anthologies: Walter Jerrold and R. M. Leonard, eds., *A Century of Parody and Imitation* (1913); Robert P. Falk, ed., *The Antic Muse: American Writers in Parody* (1955); Dwight MacDonald, ed., *Parodies: An Anthology* (1960).

Canon of Literature. In the original Greek, "canon" signified a measuring rod; the term came to be applied to the list of books in the Hebrew Bible and the New Testament which were officially recognized by the Christian Church as Holy Scripture. A number of writings closely related to those in the Bible, but not accepted as canonical, are called **apocrypha;** eleven books which have been included in the Roman Catholic biblical canon are considered apocryphal by Protestants.

The term "canon" was later used in a literary application, to signify the list of works accepted by experts as genuinely written by a particular author. We speak thus of "the Chaucer canon" and "the Shakespeare canon," and refer to other works that have sometimes been attributed to an author, but on evidence judged to be inadequate or invalid, as "apocryphal." In recent decades the phrase **literary canon** has come to denote—either in all of European literature, or else in a national literature—those authors whose works, by a cumulative consensus of authoritative critics and scholars, as well as by their conspicuous and continued influence on later authors, have come to be widely recognized as "major." These canonical writers are the ones most frequently and fully treated by literary critics and historians, and most likely to be included in anthologies and courses with titles such as "World Masterpieces," "Major English Authors," or "The Great American Writers."

The collective cultural process by which an author comes to be firmly and durably recognized as canonical is often called "canon formation." Such a process involves, along with other factors, the wide concurrence of critics with diverse critical viewpoints and sensibilities, as well as the passage of a considerable period of time. In his "Preface to Shakespeare" (1765), for example, Samuel Johnson said that a century is "the term commonly fixed as the test of literary merit." It seems clear, however, that some writers of the present century such as Proust, Kafka, Thomas Mann, and Joyce—and perhaps even a writer so recent as Vladimir Nabokov—have already entered the general European canon, and others, including Yeats, T. S. Eliot, Hemingway, Virginia Woolf, and Wallace Stevens, seem at this early stage to be very likely candidates for their national canons, at least.

Even after a long period, the overall consensus about authors of the highest literary merit remains loose-boundaried, while within the bounds of any literary canon, some writers are clearly central and others marginal. Occasionally an earlier author who was for long on the fringe of the canon, or even outside it gets to be reevaluated and admitted to a high position. A conspicuous recent example was John Donne, who from the eighteenth century on was regarded mainly as an interestingly eccentric poet. T. S. Eliot, followed by Cleanth Brooks and other *New Critics* in the 1930s and later, made Donne the very paradigm of the self-ironic and paradoxical poetry they most admired, and helped elevate him to a prominent status in the English canon. (See *metaphysical poets.*) Once firmly established as a central figure, however, an author shows remarkable resistance to being disestablished by adverse criticism and changing literary preferences and criteria. For example, many New Critics, while lauding Donne, vigorously attacked the romantic poet Shelley as embodying the poetic qualities they most condemned; but although a number of critics over a few decades joined in this derogation of Shelley, the long-term effect was merely to swell the flood of critical attention, whether in the mode of praise or dispraise, which serves to sustain the position of an author in the canon.

Discussions of the literary canon and of the "canonicity" of individual authors has become a central issue in recent decades, in diverse attempts to enlarge and reorder the standard canon so as to include "popular" cultural products such as fiction written for a mass audience, the writings of ethnic minorities and especially *Black writers,* and literature written by women. The general charge is that the standard literary canon has been deeply biased toward writers who are white, male, and Anglo-Saxon, and who aim their works toward an elite audience dominated by a white, male, and middle-class *ideology* and literary sensibility. For attempts to expose and correct the "patriarchal" bias in canon formation, see *feminist criticism;* on claims for the canonicity of Black writers and other ethnic literature, see Houston A. Baker, Jr., ed., *Reading Black: Essays in the Criticism of African, Caribbean, and Black American Literature* (1976); Dexter Fisher and Robert B. Stepto, eds., *Afro-American Literature: The Reconstruction of Instruction* (1979); Leslie A. Fiedler and Houston A. Baker, Jr., eds., *English Literature: Opening Up the Canon* (1981). In current critical usage, the term "canon" is sometimes used to signify the major authors within a literary subgroup, in such phrases as "the canon of Black writers," or "the canon of women novelists."

Caroline Age. The reign of Charles I, 1625–49; the name is derived from "Carolus," the Latin version of "Charles." This was the time of the English Civil War, fought between the supporters of the king (known as "Cavaliers") and the supporters of Parliament (known as "Roundheads," from their custom of wearing their hair cut short). Milton began his writing during this period; and it was the age of the religious poet George Herbert and of the prose writers Robert Burton and Sir Thomas Browne.

Associated with the court were the **Cavalier poets,** writers of witty and polished lyrics of courtship and gallantry. The group included Richard Lovelace, Sir John Suckling, and Thomas Carew. Robert Herrick, although a country parson, is often classified with the Cavalier poets because, like them, he was a **Son of Ben**—that is, an admirer and follower of Ben Jonson—in many of his lyrics of love and gallant compliment.

See Robin Skelton, *Cavalier Poets* (1960).

Carpe Diem, meaning "seize the day," is a Latin phrase from one of Horace's *Odes* (I. xi) which has become the name for a very common literary *motif,* especially in lyric poetry. The speaker in a carpe diem poem emphasizes that life is short and time is fleeting in order to enjoin his auditor—who is often a virgin reluctant to change her state—to make the most of present pleasures. A frequent emblem of the brevity of physical beauty and the finality of death is the rose, as in Spenser's *The Faerie Queene,* 1590–96 (II. xii. 74–75: "Gather therefore the Rose, whilst yet is prime"), and in the seventeenth century, Herrick's "To the Virgins, to Make Much of Time" ("Gather ye rosebuds, while ye may") and Waller's "Go, Lovely Rose." The greatest poems of this kind communicate the poignant sadness—or else desperation—of the pursuit of pleasures under the sentence of inevitable death; see Andrew Marvell's "To His Coy Mistress"

(1681) and the set of variations on the carpe diem motif *The Rubáiyát of Omar Khayyám* by the Victorian poet Edward Fitzgerald. In 1747 the early *feminist* Lady Mary Wortley Montagu wrote "The Lover: A Ballad," a brilliant antitype to the carpe diem poems written by male poets, in which the woman explains why she finds her importunate lover utterly resistible.

Celtic Revival, also known as the **Irish Literary Renaissance,** identifies the creative period in Irish literature from about 1885 to the death of William Butler Yeats in 1939. The aim of Yeats and other early leaders of the movement was to create a distinctively national literature by going back to Irish history, legend, and folklore, as well as to native literary models. The major writers, however, wrote not in the native Irish (one of the Celtic languages) but in English, and under the influence of various non-Irish literary forms; a number of them also turned increasingly for their subject matter to modern Irish life rather than to the ancient past.

Notable poets in addition to Yeats were AE (George Russell) and Oliver St. John Gogarty. The dramatists included Yeats himself, as well as Lady Gregory (who was also an important patron and publicist for the movement), John Millington Synge, and later Sean O'Casey. Among the novelists were George Moore and James Stephens, as well as James Joyce, who, although he abandoned Ireland for Europe and ridiculed some of the excesses of the nationalist writers, adverted to Irish subject matter and characters in all his writings. As these names indicate, the Celtic Revival produced some of the greatest poetry, drama, and prose fiction written in English during the first four decades of the twentieth century.

E. A. Boyd, *Ireland's Literary Renaissance* (1916, rev. 1922); Herbert Howarth, *The Irish Writers* (1958); Phillip L. Marcus, *Yeats and the Beginning of the Irish Renaissance* (1970), and "The Celtic Revival: Literature and the Theater," in *The Irish World: The History and Cultural Achievements of the Irish People* (1977).

Character and Characterization. (1) **The character** is the name of a literary *genre;* it is a short, and usually witty, sketch in prose of a distinctive type of person. The genre was inaugurated by Theophrastus, a Greek author of the second century B.C., who wrote a lively book called *Characters.* The form had a great vogue in the earlier seventeenth century; the books of characters then written by Joseph Hall, Sir Thomas Overbury, and John Earle influenced later writers in the essay, history, and fiction. The titles of some of Overbury's sketches will indicate the nature of the form: "A Courtier," "A Wise Man," "A Fair and Happy Milkmaid." See Richard Aldington's anthology *A Book of "Characters"* (1924).

(2) **Characters** are the persons presented in a dramatic or narrative work, who are interpreted by the reader as being endowed with moral, dispositional, and emotional qualities that are expressed in what they say—the **dialogue**—and by what they do—the **action.** The grounds in the characters' temperament, desires, and moral nature for their speech and actions constitute their **motivation.** A character may remain essentially "stable," or unchanged in outlook and

dispositions, from beginning to end of a work (Prospero in *The Tempest,* Micawber in Dickens' *David Copperfield,* 1849–50), or may undergo a radical change, either through a gradual development (the title character in Jane Austen's *Emma,* 1816) or as the result of a crisis (Shakespeare's *King Lear,* Pip in Dickens' *Great Expectations*). Whether a character remains stable or changes, the reader of a traditional, realistic work expects "consistency"—the character should not suddenly break off and act in a way not plausibly grounded in his or her temperament as we have already come to know it.

E. M. Forster, in *Aspects of the Novel* (1927), introduced popular new terms for an old distinction by discriminating between flat and round characters. A **flat character** (also called a **type,** or "two-dimensional"), Forster says, is built around "a single idea or quality" and is presented without much individualizing detail, and therefore can be fairly adequately described in a single phrase or sentence. A **round character** is complex in temperament and motivation and is represented with subtle particularity; such a character therefore is as difficult to describe with any adequacy as a person in real life, and like most persons is capable of surprising us. Almost all dramas and narratives, properly enough, have some characters who serve merely as functionaries and are not characterized at all, as well as other characters who are relatively flat: there is no need, in Shakespeare's *Henry IV, Part 1,* for Mistress Quickly to be as globular as Falstaff. The degree to which characters need to be three-dimensional depends on their function in the plot; in many types of narrative, such as in the detective story or adventure novel or farce comedy, even the protagonist usually is two-dimensional. Sherlock Holmes and Long John Silver do not require, for their own excellent literary roles, the roundness of a Hamlet, a Becky Sharp, or a Jay Gatsby. In his *Anatomy of Criticism* (1957), Northrop Frye has proposed that even lifelike characters are identifiable variants, more or less individualized, of stock types which are inherited from prior literary genres; examples in the comic genre are the self-deprecating "eiron," the boastful "alazon," and the "senex iratus," or choleric old father. (See *stock characters.*)

A broad distinction is frequently made between alternative methods for **characterizing** (i.e., establishing the distinctive characters of) the persons in a narrative: showing and telling. In **showing** (also called "the dramatic method"), the author merely presents the characters talking and acting and leaves the reader to infer what motives and dispositions lie behind what they say and do. In **telling,** the author intervenes authoritatively in order to describe, and often to evaluate, the motives and dispositional qualities of the characters. For example, in the fine opening chapter of *Pride and Prejudice* (1813), Jane Austen first shows us Mr. and Mrs. Bennet as they talk to one another about the young man who has just rented Netherfield Park, then tells us about them, and so confirms and expands the inferences that the reader has already begun to make from what has been shown:

> Mr. Bennet was so odd a mixture of quick parts, sarcastic humour, reserve, and caprice, that the experience of three-and-twenty years had been insufficient to make his wife understand his character. *Her* mind was less difficult to develop. She was a woman of mean understanding, little information, and uncertain temper.

Especially since the novelistic theory and practice of Flaubert and Henry James, a critical tendency has been to consider "telling" a violation of artistry and to recommend only the technique of "showing" characters; authors, it is often said, should efface themselves in order to write "objectively," "impersonally," or "dramatically." Such judgments, however, glorify a modern kind of artistic limitation which is suited to particular novelistic effects, and decry an alternative method of characterization which all the greatest novelists, until recently, have employed to produce masterpieces. (See *point of view.*)

Innovative writers in the present century—including novelists from James Joyce to French writers of the *new novel,* and authors of the dramas and novels of the *absurd* and other experimental forms—often present the persons in their works in ways which run counter to the earlier way of analyzing them as lifelike characters who manifest in what they say and do a consistent substructure of individuality. Recent structuralist critics have undertaken to dissolve even the lifelike characters of traditional novels into a system of literary conventions and codes which are *naturalized* by the readers; that is, readers project lifelikeness upon them by assimilating them to their conceptions of individuals in real life. Such conceptions about individuality, however, are in turn analyzed by a thoroughgoing structuralist as consisting of nothing more than intersections, or "nodes," of cultural stereotypes and conventions. See *structuralist criticism* and *text and writing* (*écriture*), and refer to Jonathan Culler, *Structuralist Poetics* (1975), Chap. 9, "Poetics of the Novel."

On the traditional problems and methods of characterization, including discussions of showing and telling, see in addition to E. M. Forster (above), Percy Lubbock, *The Craft of Fiction* (1926); Wayne C. Booth, *The Rhetoric of Fiction* (1961), especially Chaps. 1–4; W. J. Harvey, *Character and the Novel* (1966); Robert Scholes and Robert Kellogg, *The Nature of Narrative* (1966).

Chivalric Romance (or **medieval romance**) is a narrative *genre* which developed in twelfth-century France, spread to the vernacular literatures of other countries, and displaced in popularity the various *epic* and heroic forms of narrative. ("Romance" originally signified a work written in the French language, which evolved from a dialect of the Roman language, Latin.) Romances were at first written in verse, but later in prose as well. The **romance** is distinguished from the epic in that it represents, not a heroic age of tribal wars, but a courtly and chivalric age, often one of highly developed manners and civility. Its standard plot is that of a quest undertaken by a single knight in order to gain a lady's favor; frequently its central interest is *courtly love,* together with tournaments fought and dragons and monsters slain for the damsel's sake; it stresses the chivalric ideals of courage, honor, mercifulness to an opponent, and exquisite and elaborate manners; and it delights in wonders and marvels. Supernatural events in the epic had their causes in the will and actions of the gods; romance shifts the supernatural to fairyland, and makes much of the mysterious effect of magic, spells, and enchantments.

The recurrent materials of medieval romances are divided by scholars into four classes of subjects: (1) "The Matter of Britain" (that is, Celtic subject matter, especially stories centering on the court of King Arthur); (2) "The Matter of Rome" (stories based on classical antiquity, including the exploits of Alexander and of the heroes of the Trojan War); (3) "The Matter of France" (Charlemagne and his knights); and (4) "The Matter of England" (concerned with heroes such as King Horn and Guy of Warwick). The cycle of tales which developed around the pseudohistorical British King Arthur produced many of the finest romances, some of them (stories of Sir Perceval and the quest for the Holy Grail) with a religious instead of a purely secular interest. Chrétien de Troyes, the great twelfth-century French poet, wrote Arthurian romances; *Gawain and the Green Knight* is a superb "metrical" (that is, versified) romance about an Arthurian knight, written in fourteenth-century England; and Malory's *Morte d'Arthur* (fifteenth century) is an English version in prose of the cycle of earlier versified romances about Arthur and his Knights of the Round Table.

See *prose romance,* and refer to W. P. Ker, *Epic and Romance* (1897); L. A. Hibbard, *Medieval Romance in England* (rev., 1961); R. S. Loomis, *The Development of Arthurian Romance* (1963), and *The Grail* (1963); and the anthology *Medieval Romances,* eds. R. S. and L. H. Loomis (1957). For modern adaptations and extensions of the concept of the romance genre, see *myth critics,* and Eleanor T. Lincoln, *Pastoral and Romance: Modern Essays in Criticism* (1969).

Chorus. Among the ancient Greeks the chorus was a group, wearing masks, who sang or chanted verse while performing dancelike maneuvers at religious festivals. A similar chorus played a part in Greek tragedies, where (in the plays of Aeschylus and Sophocles) they served mainly as commentators on the characters and events who expressed traditional moral, religious, and social attitudes; beginning with Euripides, however, the chorus assumed primarily a lyrical function. The Greek ode, as developed by Pindar, was also chanted by a chorus; see *ode.*

Roman playwrights such as Seneca took over the chorus from the Greeks, and in the mid-sixteenth century some English dramatists (for example, Norton and Sackville in *Gorbuduc*) imitated the Senecan chorus. The classical type of chorus was never widely adopted by English dramatic writers. John Milton, however, included a chorus in *Samson Agonistes* (1671), Shelley employed a chorus in *Prometheus Unbound* (1820) and Hardy in *The Dynasts* (1904–08), and more recently, T. S. Eliot made effective use of the classical chorus in his religious tragedy *Murder in the Cathedral* (1935).

During the Elizabethan Age the term "chorus" was applied also to a single character who spoke the prologue and epilogue to a play, and sometimes introduced each act as well. This character served as the author's vehicle for commenting on the play and for exposition to the audience concerning its subject, offstage events, and setting; see Marlowe's *Dr. Faustus* and Shakespeare's *Henry V.* In Shakespeare's *Winter's Tale,* the fifth act begins with "Time, the Chorus," who asks the audience that they "impute it not a crime/To me or my swift passage that I slide/O'er sixteen years," then summarizes what has happened during those years and announces that the setting for this act is Bohemia.

A recent and extended use of a chorus in this sense is the Stage Manager in Thornton Wilder's *Our Town* (1938).

Modern scholars use the term **choral character** to identify a person within the play itself who stands largely apart from the action and by his comments provides the audience with a special perspective (often an ironic perspective) through which to view characters and events. Examples in Shakespeare are the Fool in *King Lear,* Enobarbus in *Antony and Cleopatra,* and Thersites in *Troilus and Cressida;* a modern instance is Seth Beckwith in O'Neill's *Mourning Becomes Electra* (1931). "Choral character" is sometimes applied also to one or more persons in a novel who represent a communal point of view or the perspective of a cultural group, and so provide norms by which to judge other characters and what they do; instances are Thomas Hardy's peasants and the old Black women in William Faulkner's novels.

For the alternative use of the term "chorus" to signify a recurrent stanza in a song, see *refrain.* Refer to A. W. Pickard-Cambridge, *Dithyramb, Tragedy and Comedy* (1927), and *The Dramatic Festivals of Athens* (1953); T. B. L. Webster, *Greek Theater Production* (1956).

Chronicle. Chronicles, the predecessors of modern "histories," were accounts, in prose or verse, of national or worldwide events over a considerable period of time. If the chronicles deal with events year by year, they are often called **annals.** Unlike the modern historian, most chroniclers tended to take their information as they found it, and made little attempt to separate fact from legend. The most important English chronicles are the *Anglo-Saxon Chronicle,* started by King Alfred in the ninth century and continued until the twelfth century, and the *Chronicles of England, Scotland, and Ireland* (1577–87) by Raphael Holinshed and other writers; the latter documents were important sources of materials for Elizabethan drama.

Chronicle Plays were dramatic renderings of the historical materials in the English *Chronicles* by Raphael Holinshed and others. They achieved high popularity late in the sixteenth century, when the patriotic fervor following the defeat of the Spanish Armada in 1588 fostered a demand for plays dealing with English history. The early chronicle plays presented a loosely knit series of events during the reign of an English king and depended for effect mainly on a bustle of stage battles, pageantry, and spectacle. Marlowe, however, in his *Edward II* (1592) selected and rearranged materials from Holinshed's *Chronicles* to compose a unified drama of character, and Shakespeare's series of chronicle plays, encompassing the succession of English kings from Richard II to Henry VIII, includes such major artistic achievements as *Richard II, Henry IV, Parts 1 and 2,* and *Henry V.*

The Elizabethan chronicle plays are often called **history plays.** This latter term is also applied more broadly to any drama based mainly on historical materials, such as Shakespeare's *Julius Caesar* and *Antony and Cleopatra,* and including such recent examples as Arthur Miller's *The Crucible* (1953), which treats the Salem witch trials of 1692, and Robert Bolt's *A Man for All Seasons* (1962), about the sixteenth-century judge, author, and martyr Sir Thomas More.

E. M. Tillyard, *Shakespeare's History Plays* (1946); Lily B. Campbell, *Shakespeare's "Histories"* (1947); Irving Ribner, *The English History Play in the Age of Shakespeare* (rev., 1965); Max M. Reese, *The Cease of Majesty: A Study of Shakespeare's History Plays* (1962).

Cliché, which is French for the stereotype used in printing, signifies an expression which deviates enough from ordinary usage to call attention to itself and has been used so often that it is felt to be hackneyed or cloying. "I beg your pardon" or "sincerely yours" are standard usages which do not call attention to themselves; but "point with pride," "my better half," "the eternal verities," and "lock, stock, and barrel" are considered clichés, as are indiscriminate uses of terms taken from specialized vocabularies such as "alienation," "identity crisis," and "interface." Some clichés are foreign phrases which are used as an arch or elegant equivalent for a common English term ("aqua pura," "terra firma"). Others are hackneyed literary echoes. "The cup that cheers" is an inaccurate quotation from Cowper's *The Task* (1785), referring to tea—"the cups/That cheer but not inebriate."

> Come, and trip it as you go
> On the light fantastic toe

was charming in Milton's "L'Allegro," but "to trip the light fantastic" has become an annoying substitute for "to dance." In his *Essay on Criticism* (II, ll. 350 ff.) Alexander Pope comments satirically on some clichés which early eighteenth-century **poetasters** (untalented pretenders to the poetic art) used in order to eke out their rhymes:

> Where'er you find "the cooling western breeze,"
> In the next line it "whispers through the trees";
> If crystal streams "with pleasing murmurs creep,"
> The reader's threatened (not in vain) with "sleep."

See Eric Partridge, *A Dictionary of Clichés* (4th ed., 1950).

Comedy. A comedy is a work in which the materials are selected and managed primarily in order to interest, involve, and amuse us: the characters and their discomfitures engage our delighted attention rather than our profound concern, we feel confident that no great disaster will occur, and usually the action turns out happily for the chief characters. The term "comedy" is customarily applied only to dramas; it should be noted, however, that the comic form, so defined, also occurs in prose fiction and narrative poetry.

Within the broad spectrum of dramatic comedy, the following types are frequently distinguished:

(1) **Romantic comedy,** as developed by Shakespeare and some of his Elizabethan contemporaries, is concerned with a love affair that involves a beautiful and idealized heroine (sometimes disguised as a man); the course of this love does not run smooth, but overcomes all difficulties to end in a happy union. Many of the boy-meets-girl plots of later writers are instances of romantic comedy. In *The Anatomy of Criticism* (1957), Northrop Frye points out that some of Shakespeare's romantic comedies manifest a movement from the normal world of conflict and trouble into "the green world"—the Forest of Arden in *As You Like It,* or the fairy-haunted wood of *A Midsummer Night's Dream*—in which the problems and injustices of the ordinary world are dissolved, enemies reconciled, and true lovers united. Frye regards that phenomenon (together with other aspects of these comedies, such as their festive conclusion in the social ritual of a wedding, a feast, a dance) as evidence that comic plots reflect primitive myths and rituals celebrating the victory of spring over winter.

(2) **Satiric comedy** ridicules political policies or philosophical doctrines, or else attacks the disorders of society by making ridiculous the violators of its standards of morals or manners. (See *satire.*) The early master of satiric comedy was the Greek Aristophanes, c. 450–c. 385 B.C., whose plays mocked political, philosophical, and literary matters of his age. In *Volpone* and *The Alchemist* by Shakespeare's contemporary Ben Jonson, the greed and ingenuity of one or more intelligent but rascally swindlers, and the equal greed but stupid gullibility of their victims, are made grotesquely ludicrous rather than lightly amusing.

(3) The **comedy of manners** originated in the **New Comedy** of the Greek Menander, c. 342–292 B.C. (as distinguished from the **Old Comedy** represented by Aristophanes), and was developed by the Roman dramatists Plautus and Terence in the third and second centuries B.C. Their plays dealt with the vicissitudes of young lovers and included what became the *stock characters* of much later comedy, such as the clever servant, old and stodgy parents, and the wealthy rival. The English comedy of manners was early exemplified by Shakespeare's *Love's Labour's Lost* and *Much Ado about Nothing,* and was brought to a high polish in **Restoration comedy** (1660–1700). This form owes much to the brilliant dramas of the French writer Molière, 1622–73. It deals with the relations and intrigues of men and women living in a sophisticated upper-class society, relying for comic effect in large part on the wit and sparkle of the dialogue—often in the form of *repartee,* a witty conversational give-and-take which constitutes a kind of verbal fencing match—and to a lesser degree, on the violations of social conventions and decorum by stupid characters such as would-be wits, jealous husbands, and foppish dandies. Excellent examples are Congreve's *The Way of the World* and Wycherley's *The Country Wife.* A middle-class reaction against the immorality of situation and the frequent indecency of dialogue in the courtly Restoration comedy resulted in the *sentimental comedy* of the eighteenth century. In the latter part of the century, however, Oliver Goldsmith (*She Stoops to Conquer*) and his contemporary Richard Brinsley Sheridan (*The Rivals* and *A School for Scandal*) revived the wit and gaiety, but deleted the indecency, of Restoration comedy. The comedy of manners lapsed in the early nineteenth century, but was revived by many skillful practi-

tioners, from A. W. Pinero and Oscar Wilde (*The Importance of Being Earnest,* 1895), through George Bernard Shaw and Noel Coward, to Neil Simon, Alan Ayckbourn, and other writers of our own era.

(4) **Farce** is a type of comedy designed to provoke the audience to simple, hearty laughter—"belly laughs," in the parlance of the theater. To do so it commonly employs highly exaggerated or *caricatured* types of characters, puts them into improbable and ludicrous situations, and makes free use of broad verbal humor and physical horseplay. Farce was a component in the comic episodes in medieval *miracle plays,* such as the Wakefield plays "Noah" and the "Second Shepherd's Play," and constituted the matter of the Italian *commedia dell'arte* in the Renaissance. In the enduring English drama, farce is usually an episode in a more complex form of comedy—for example, the knockabout scenes in Shakespeare's *The Taming of the Shrew* and *The Merry Wives of Windsor.* Brandon Thomas' *Charley's Aunt,* however, an American play of 1892 which has often been revived, is a true farce throughout, as are some of the current plays of Tom Stoppard. Many of the movies by such comedians as Charlie Chaplin, Buster Keaton, W. C. Fields, and Woody Allen are excellent farce. Farce is often employed in single scenes of musical revues, and is standard fare in television "situation comedies."

(5) A distinction is frequently made between high and low comedy. **High comedy,** as described by George Meredith in the classic essay *The Idea of Comedy* (1877), evokes "intellectual laughter"—thoughtful laughter from spectators who remain emotionally detached from the action—at the spectacle of folly, pretentiousness, and incongruity in human behavior. Meredith finds its highest form within the comedy of manners, in the combats of wit (sometimes identified now as the "love duels") between such intelligent, highly verbal, and well-matched lovers as Benedick and Beatrice in Shakespeare's *Much Ado about Nothing* (1598–99) and Mirabell and Millamant in Congreve's *The Way of the World* (1700). **Low comedy,** at the other extreme, makes little or no intellectual appeal, but undertakes to arouse laughter by jokes, or "gags," and by slapstick humor or boisterous or clownish physical activity; it is, therefore, one of the common components of farce.

See also *comedy of humours, tragicomedy,* literature of the *absurd,* and *wit, humor, and the comic.* On comedy and its varieties: H. T. E. Perry, *Masters of Dramatic Comedy* (1939); G. E. Duckworth, *The Nature of Roman Comedy* (1952); Louis Kronenberger, *The Thread of Laughter* (1952); W. K. Wimsatt, ed., *English Stage Comedy* (1954); Leo Hughes, *A Century of English Farce* (1956); Elder Olson, *The Theory of Comedy* (1968). On the relation of comedy to myth and ritual: Northrop Frye, *Anatomy of Criticism* (1957), pp. 163–86; C. L. Barber, *Shakespeare's Festive Comedy* (1959). On the history of low comedy and farce from the Greeks to the present: Anthony Caputi, *Buffo: The Genius of Vulgar Comedy* (1978). On television comedy: Horace Newcomb, *Television: The Most Popular Art* (1974), Chap. 2.

Comedy of Humours. A type of comedy developed by Ben Jonson, the Elizabethan playwright, based on the ancient and still current physiological theory of the **four humours.** The "humours" were held to be the four primary fluids—blood, phlegm, choler (or yellow bile), and melancholy (or black bile)—whose "temperament," or mixture, determined both a man's physical condition and his character type. An imbalance of one or another humour in a temperament was said to produce four kinds of disposition, whose names have survived the underlying theory: sanguine (from the Latin "sanguis," blood), phlegmatic, choleric, and melancholic. In Jonson's comedy of humours each of the major characters, instead of being a well-balanced individual, has a preponderant humour that gives him a characteristic distortion or eccentricity of disposition. Jonson expounds his theory in the "Induction" to his play *Every Man in His Humour* (1598) and exemplifies the mode in his later comedies as well. The Jonsonian type of humours character remained influential in the *comedies of manners* by Wycherley, Etheredge, Congreve, and other dramatists of the English *Restoration,* 1660–1700.

Comic Relief is the introduction of comic characters, speeches, or scenes in a serious or tragic work, especially a dramatic work. Such elements were almost universal in *Elizabethan* tragedy. Sometimes they occur merely as episodes of dialogue or horseplay for purposes of alleviating tension and adding variety; in more carefully wrought plays, however, they are also made integral to the plot, in a way that counterpoints and enhances the serious or tragic significance. Examples of such complex uses of comic elements are the gravediggers in *Hamlet* (V. i), the scene of the drunken porter after the murder of the king in *Macbeth* (II. iii), the Falstaff scenes in *Henry IV, Part 1,* and the roles of Mercutio and the old nurse in *Romeo and Juliet.*

See Thomas De Quincey's classic essay "On the Knocking at the Gate in *Macbeth*" (1823).

Commedia dell'Arte was a form of comic drama developed about the mid-sixteenth century by guilds of professional Italian actors. The actors, playing *stock characters,* largely improvised the dialogue around a given **scenario**—a brief outline of a drama, indicating merely the entrances of the main characters and the development of the action. In a typical play, a pair of young lovers outwit a rich old father ("Pantaloon"), aided by a clever and intriguing servant ("Harlequin"), in a plot enlivened by the buffoonery of "Punch" and other clowns. Wandering Italian troupes played in all the large cities of Renaissance Europe and influenced various writers of comedies in Elizabethan England and, later, Molière in France. The modern Punch and Judy show is a descendant of this old Italian comedy.

See Kathleen M. Lea, *Italian Popular Comedy, 1560–1620* (2 vols.; 1934).

Commonwealth Period, also known as the **Puritan Interregnum,** extends from the end of the Civil War and the execution of Charles I in 1649 to the restoration of the Stuart monarchy under Charles II in 1660. In this period England was ruled by Parliament under the Puritan leader Oliver Cromwell; his death in

1658 marked the dissolution of the Commonwealth. Drama almost disappeared for eighteen years after the Puritans, on moral and religious grounds, closed the public theaters in September 1642. It was the age of Milton's political pamphlets, of Hobbes's political treatise *Leviathan* (1651), of the prose writers Sir Thomas Browne, Thomas Fuller, Jeremy Taylor, and Izaak Walton, and of the poets Vaughan, Waller, Cowley, Davenant, and Marvell.

Conceit. Originally meaning a concept or image, "conceit" came to be the term for figures of speech which establish a striking parallel—usually an elaborate parallel—between two very dissimilar things or situations. The term, once derogatory, is now best employed as a neutral identification of a poetic device. Two types of conceit are often distinguished:

(1) The **Petrarchan conceit** is a type of figure used in love poems which had been novel and effective in the Italian poet Petrarch, but became hackneyed in some of his imitators, the *Elizabethan* sonneteers. The figure consists of detailed, ingenious, and often exaggerated comparisons applied to the disdainful mistress, as cold and cruel as she is beautiful, and to the distresses and despair of the worshipful lover. (See *courtly love.*) Sir Thomas Wyatt (1503–42), for example, in his sonnet "My Galley Chargèd with Forgetfulness," circumstantially compares the lover's state to a ship laboring in a storm; and in another sonnet, "Like to These Unmeasurable Mountains," he details its parallels to an Alpine landscape. A third sonnet by Wyatt begins with a familiar Petrarchan conceit, an *oxymoron* describing the simultaneous fever and chills experienced by a sufferer from the disease of love:

> I find no peace; and all my war is done;
> I fear and hope; I burn and freeze in ice.

Shakespeare (who at times employed this type of conceit himself) *parodied* some standard objects pressed into service for *similes* by Petrarchan sonneteers, in his Sonnet 130 beginning

> My mistress' eyes are nothing like the sun;
> Coral is far more red than her lips' red:
> If snow be white, why then her breasts are dun;
> If hairs be wires, black wires grow on her head.

(2) The **metaphysical conceit** is a characteristic figure in John Donne (1572–1631) and other *metaphysical poets* of the seventeenth century. It was described by Samuel Johnson, in a famed passage in his "Life of Cowley" (1779–81), as "wit" which is

> a kind of *discordia concors;* a combination of dissimilar images, or discovery of occult resemblances in things apparently unlike. . . . The most heterogeneous ideas are yoked by violence together.

The metaphysical poets exploited all knowledge—commonplace or esoteric, practical, theological, or philosophical, true or fabulous—for the vehicles of these figures; and their comparisons, whether succinct or expanded, were novel, witty, and at their best startlingly effective. In sharp contrast to both the concepts and figures of conventional Petrarchism is Donne's "The Flea," a poem that uses a flea who has bitten both lovers as the basic reference for its argument against the lady's coyness. In Donne's "The Canonization," as the poetic argument develops, the comparisons for the relationship between lovers move from the area of commerce and business, through various actual and mythical birds and diverse forms of historical memorials, to a climax which equates the sexual acts and the moral status of worldly lovers with the ascetic life and heavenly destination of unworldly saints. The most famous sustained conceit is Donne's parallel (in "A Valediction: Forbidding Mourning") between the continuing relationship of his and his lady's soul, despite their physical parting, and the coordinated movements of the two feet of a draftsman's compass. A well-known instance of the chilly and *hyperbolic* ingenuity of the metaphysical conceit when it is overdriven is Richard Crashaw's description, in his mid-seventeenth-century poem "Saint Mary Magdalene," of the tearful eyes of the repentant Magdalene as

> two faithful fountains
> Two walking baths, two weeping motions,
> Portable and compendious oceans.

Following the great revival of the metaphysical poets in the early decades of the twentieth century, a number of modern poets exploited this type of conceit. Examples are T. S. Eliot's comparison of the evening to "a patient etherized upon a table" in "The Love Song of J. Alfred Prufrock," and the series of startling figurative vehicles in Dylan Thomas' "In Memory of Ann Jones." The vogue for such conceits extended even to popular love songs, in the 1920s and later, by well-educated composers such as Cole Porter: "You're the Cream in My Coffee" and "You're the Top."

See *figurative language*, and refer to Rosemond Tuve, *Elizabethan and Metaphysical Imagery* (1947); K. K. Ruthven, *The Conceit* (1969).

Concrete and Abstract. In traditional philosophy a "concrete term" is defined as a word which denotes a particular person or thing, and an "abstract term" is defined as a noun (such as "brightness," "beauty," "evil," "despair") which denotes qualities that exist only as attributes of particular persons or things. A sentence, accordingly, is said to be concrete if it makes an assertion about a particular subject (T. S. Eliot's "Grishkin is nice . . ."), and abstract if it makes an assertion about an abstract subject (Pope's "Hope springs eternal in the human breast"). With reference to literature, however, these terms are often used in an extended way: a passage is called abstract if it represents its subject matter in general or nonsensuous words or with only a thin realization of its experienced qualities; it is called concrete if it represents its subject matter with striking particularity and sensuous detail. In his "Ode to Psyche" (1820) Keats's

'Mid hush'd, cool-rooted flowers, fragrant-eyed,
Blue, silver-white, and budded Tyrian

is a concrete description of a locale which involves qualities that are perceived by four senses: hearing, touch, sight, and smell. And in the opening of his "Ode to a Nightingale," Keats communicates concretely, by a combination of literal and figurative language, how it felt to experience the full-throated song of the nightingale:

My heart aches, and a drowsy numbness pains
My sense, as though of hemlock I had drunk,
Or emptied some dull opiate to the drains . . .

It is frequently asserted that "poetry is concrete," or, as John Crowe Ransom put it in *The World's Body* (1938), that its proper subject is "the rich, contingent materiality of things." Most poetry is certainly more concrete than other modes of language, especially in its use of *imagery.* It should be kept in mind, however, that poets do not hesitate to use abstract language when the situation or purpose calls for it. Keats, though he was one of the most concrete of poets, began *Endymion* with a sentence composed of abstract terms:

A thing of beauty is a joy forever:
Its loveliness increases; it will never
Pass into nothingness; . . .

And some of the most moving and memorable passages in poetry are not concrete; for example, the statement about God in Dante's *Paradiso,* "In His will is our peace," or the bleak comment by Edgar in the last act of *King Lear,*

Men must endure
Their going hence, even as their coming hither;
Ripeness is all.

See John Crowe Ransom, *The World's Body* (1938); Richard H. Fogle, *The Imagery of Keats and Shelley* (1949), Chap. 5.

Concrete Poetry is a recent term for an ancient type, **pattern poems,** which are experiments with the visual shape in which a text is presented on the page. Some Greek poets, beginning in the third century B.C., shaped a text in the form of the object which the poem describes or suggests. In the Renaissance and seventeenth century there was a considerable vogue of such patterned forms, called **emblem poems,** in which the lines vary in length in such a way that their printed shape is in the outline of the subject of the poem; familiar examples in English are George Herbert's "Easter Wings" and "The Altar." Prominent later experiments with pictorial or suggestive typography include Mallarmé's *Un Coup de dés* ("A Throw of Dice," 1897), and Guillaume Apollinaire's *Calli-*

grammes (1918); in the latter publication, for example, Apollinaire printed the poem "Il pleut" ("It rains") so that the component letters trickle down the page.

The writing of **concrete poetry** is a worldwide movement that was largely inaugurated in 1953 by the Swiss poet Eugen Gomringer. The practice of such poetry varies widely, but the common feature is the use of a radically reduced language, typed or printed in such a way as to force the text on the reader's attention as an object which is itself to be perceived as a visual whole. Many concrete poems, in fact, cannot be read at all in the conventional way, since they consist of a single word or phrase which is subjected to systematic alterations in the order and position of the component letters, or else are composed of fragments of words, or of nonsense syllables, or even of single letters, numbers, and marks of punctuation. In their shaped patterns, concrete poets often use a variety of type fonts and sizes and different colors of type, and sometimes supplement the text with drawings or photographs; some of their shapes are called "kinetic," in that they evolve as we turn page after page.

America had its native tradition of pattern poetry in the typographical experiments of Ezra Pound, and especially of E. E. Cummings; see, for example, Cummings' "r-p-o-p-h-e-s-s-a-g-r," in which—by way of representing textually the way we at first vaguely perceive, then identify, the leaping insect—scrambled sequences of letters gradually shape themselves into the word "grasshopper." Americans who have been influenced by the international vogue for concrete poetry include Emmett Williams, Jonathan Williams, and Mary Ellen Solt.

Collections of concrete poems in a variety of languages are Emmett Williams, ed., *An Anthology of Concrete Poetry* (1967); Mary Ellen Solt, ed. (with a useful historical introduction), *Concrete Poetry: A World View* (1968). For a noted early-eighteenth-century attack on pattern poems, see Addison's comments on "false wit" in the *Spectator*, Nos. 58 and 63.

Confessional Poetry designates a type of narrative and lyric verse, given impetus by Robert Lowell's *Life Studies* (1959), which deals with the facts and intimate experiences of the poet's own life. It differs in subject matter from poems of the *Romantic Period* about the poet's own circumstances, experiences, and feelings, such as Wordsworth's "Tintern Abbey" and Coleridge's "Dejection: An Ode," in the candor and detail—and sometimes the *psychoanalytic* insight—with which the poet reveals intimate or clinical matters about himself or herself. Confessional poems have been written by Allen Ginsberg, Theodore Roethke, Sylvia Plath, Anne Sexton, John Berryman, and other recent American poets.

Confidant (the feminine form is "confidante") is a character in a drama or novel who plays only a minor role in the action, but serves the protagonist as a trusted friend to whom he or she confesses intimate thoughts and feelings. The confidant thus provides the playwright with a plausible device for communicating to the audience the knowledge, state of mind, and intentions of a principal character without the use of stage devices such as the *soliloquy* or the *aside;* an example is Hamlet's friend Horatio in Shakespeare's *Hamlet,* and Cleopatra's maid Charmion in his *Antony and Cleopatra.*

A famous confidant in prose fiction is Dr. Watson in A. Conan Doyle's stories about Sherlock Holmes (1887 and following). The device is particularly useful to modern writers who, like Henry James, have largely renounced the novelist's earlier privilege of intruding in order to address information directly to the reader. To the confidant James also applied the term **ficelle,** French for the string by which the puppeteer manages his puppets. Discussing Maria Gostrey, Strether's confidante in *The Ambassadors,* James remarks that she is a "ficelle" who is not, "in essence, Strether's friend. She is the reader's friend much rather" (James, *The Art of the Novel,* ed. R. P. Blackmur, 1934, pp. 321–22).

See *stock characters,* and on the nonintrusive author, *point of view.* On the confidant, refer to W. J. Harvey, *Character and the Novel* (1966).

Connotation and Denotation. In literary usage, the **denotation** of a word is its primary significance or reference, such as the dictionary primarily specifies; its **connotation** is the range of secondary or associated significances and feelings which it commonly suggests or implies. Thus "home" denotes the place where one lives, but connotes privacy, intimacy, and coziness; that is the reason real estate agents like to use "home" instead of "house" in their advertisements. "Horse" and "steed" denote the same quadruped, but "steed" has a different connotation, deriving from the chivalric or romantic narratives in which this word was often used.

The connotation of a word is only a potential range of shared secondary significance; which of these connotations are evoked depends on the overall context in which the word is used. Poems typically establish contexts which bring into play some part of the connotative as well as the denotative meaning of words. In his poem "Virtue" George Herbert wrote,

> Sweet day, so cool, so calm, so bright,
> The bridal of the earth and sky . . .

The denotation of "bridal"—a union between human beings—serves as part of the *ground* for applying the word as a *metaphor* to the union of earth and sky; but the specific poetic context in which the word occurs also evokes such connotations of "bridal" as sacred, joyous, and ceremonial. (Note that "marriage," although metrically and denotatively equivalent to "bridal," would have been less richly effective in this context, because more commonplace and modern in its connotation.) Even the way a word is spelled may alter its connotation. Keats, in a passage of his "Ode to a Nightingale" (1819),

> Charmed magic casements, opening on the foam
> Of perilous seas, in *faery* lands forlorn,

altered his original spelling of "fairy" to the older form "faery" in order to evoke the connotations of antiquity and of the magic world of Spenser's *The Faerie Queene*.

On connotation and denotation see Isabel C. Hungerland, *Poetic Discourse* (1958), Chap. 1, and Monroe C. Beardsley, *Aesthetics: Problems in the Philosophy of Criticism* (1958), Chap. 3.

Conventions. (1) In one sense of the term, conventions (derived from the Latin term for "coming together") are necessary, or at least convenient, devices, accepted by a kind of implicit agreement between author and audience, for solving the problems imposed by a particular artistic medium in representing reality. In watching a production of a Shakespearean play, for example, the audience accepts without question the convention by which a *proscenium* stage with three walls (or if it is a **theater in the round,** with no walls) represents a room with four walls. It also accepts the convention of characters speaking in *blank verse* instead of prose, and uttering *soliloquies* and *asides,* as well as the convention by which actions presented on a single stage in less than three hours may represent events which take place in a great variety of places, and over a span of many years.

(2) In a second sense of the term, conventions are conspicuous features of subject matter, form, or technique which recur repeatedly in works of literature. Conventions in this sense may be recurrent types of character, turns of plot, forms of versification, or kinds of diction and style. *Stock characters* such as the Elizabethan braggart soldier, or the languishing and fainting heroine of Victorian fiction, or the sad young men of the lost-generation novels of the 1920s, were among the conventions of their age. The abrupt reform of the villain at the end of the last act was a common convention of *melodrama. Euphuism* in prose, and the *Petrarchan* and *metaphysical conceits* in verse, were conventional devices of style. It is now just as much a literary convention to be outspoken on sexual matters as it was to be reticent in the age of Dickens.

(3) In the most inclusive sense, common in structuralist criticism, all literary works, no matter how seemingly realistic, are held to be totally constituted by purely literary conventions, or "codes"—of genre, plot, character, language, and so on—which a reader *naturalizes,* by assimilating these conventions to the world of discourse and experience which his culture regards as real, or "natural." (See *structuralist criticism* and *character and characterization.*)

Invention was originally a term used in theories of *rhetoric,* and later in literary criticism, to signify the "finding" of the subject matter by the orator or the poet; it then came to be used to signify novelty in a work, in contrast to the deliberate "imitation" of the forms and subjects of prior literary models. (See *imitation.*) Now "invention" is often opposed to "convention" (in sense 2, above) to signify the inauguration by a writer of a new subject or theme or form or style, and the resulting work is said to possess **originality.** The history of literature shows a repeated process in which innovative writers, such as Donne or Wordsworth or Joyce or Beckett, rebel against reigning conventions of their time to produce highly original works, only to have their inventions imitated by other writers, who thereby convert literary novelties into a new set of literary conventions.

There is nothing either good or bad in the degree or obviousness of conformity to preexisting conventions; all depends on how effective a use the individual writer makes of them. The *pastoral elegy,* for example, is one of the most conspicuously convention-bound of literary forms, yet in "Lycidas" (1638) Milton achieved one of the greatest lyrics in the language. He did this by employing the ancient pastoral rituals with freshness and power, so as to absorb an individual's death into the experience of the race and to add to his own voice a resonance achieved by echoing the many earlier pastoral laments for the untimely death of a poet.

See E. E. Stoll, *Poets and Playwrights* (1930); M. C. Bradbrook, *Themes and Conventions of Elizabethan Tragedy* (1935); Harry Levin, "Notes on Convention," in *Perspectives of Criticism* (1950); and the issue *On Convention* of *New Literary History,* 14 (1983). On convention and originality see John L. Lowes, *Convention and Revolt in Poetry* (1919); Graham Hough, *Reflections on a Literary Revolution* (1960).

Courtly Love. A philosophy of love, including an elaborate code governing the relations of aristocratic lovers, which was widely represented in the lyric poems and *chivalric romances* of western Europe during the Middle Ages. The development of the conventions of courtly love is usually attributed to the **troubadours** (poets of Provence, in Southern France), in the period from the latter eleventh century through the twelfth century. Love, with its erotic aspect spiritualized, is regarded as the noblest passion this side of heaven. The courtly lover idealizes and idolizes his beloved, and subjects himself entirely to her every whim. (This love is often that of a bachelor knight for another man's wife, as in the stories of Tristan and Isolde or of Lancelot and Guinevere; it must be remembered that marriage among the medieval upper classes was usually a kind of business contract, for utilitarian and political purposes.) The lover suffers agonies and sickness of body and spirit at the caprices of his imperious sweetheart, but remains devoted to her, manifesting his honor by his unswerving fidelity and his adherence to a rigorous code of behavior, both in knightly battles and in the complex ceremonies of courtly speech and conduct.

The development of courtly love has been traced in part to a serious reading of the Roman poet Ovid's mock-serious book *The Remedies of Love;* to an imitation in lovers' relations of the politics of feudalism (the lover is a vassal, and both his lady and the god of love are his lords); and to an importation into amatory situations of Christian concepts and ritual, especially from the cult of the Virgin Mary. Thus, the lady is exalted and worshiped; the lover sins and repents; and if his faith stays steadfast, he may be admitted at last into the lover's heaven through his lady's "gift of grace."

From southern France the literature of courtly love spread to Chrétien de Troyes (flourished 1170–90) and other poets and romance writers in northern France, to Dante (*La Vita Nuova,* 1290–94), Petrarch, and other writers in fourteenth-century Italy, and to the love poetry of Germany and northern Europe. To the reader of English literature the *conventions* of courtly love are best known in the medieval romance *Gawain and the Green Knight,* in Chaucer's *Troilus and Criseyde,* and in their later manifestation in the Petrarchan subject matter and the *Petrarchan conceits* of the Elizabethan sonneteers. There has long been a debate as to whether medieval courtly love was merely a literary convention and a topic for elegant conversation at courts, or whether to some degree it reflected the actual conditions of aristocratic life of the time. What is clear is that its views of the intensity and the ennobling power of love as "the grand passion," of the special sensibility and spiritual status of women, and of the complex decorum governing relations between the sexes have profoundly affected not only the literature of love but also the lived experience of "being in love" in the Western world, through the nineteenth century and (though to a diminished extent) even into our own day of sexual candor, freedom, and the movement for total equality between the sexes.

C. S. Lewis, *The Allegory of Love* (1936); A. J. Denomy, *The Heresy of Courtly Love* (1947); M. J. Valency, *In Praise of Love* (1958); F. X. Newman, ed., *The Meaning of Courtly Love* (1968); Denis de Rougemont, *Love in the Western World* (rev., 1974); Roger Boase, *The Origin and Meaning of Courtly Love: A Critical Study of European Scholarship* (1977). For skeptical views of some commonly held opinions, see Peter Dronke, *Medieval Latin and the Rise of European Love-Lyric* (1965–66); E. Talbot Donaldson, "The Myth of Courtly Love," in *Speaking of Chaucer* (1970). For a *feminist* reappraisal of the role of women in the tradition, see Andrée Kahn Blumstein, *Misogyny and Idealization in the Courtly Romance* (1977).

Criticism is the overall term for studies concerned with defining, classifying, analyzing, interpreting, and evaluating works of literature. **Theoretical criticism** undertakes to establish, on the basis of general principles, a set of terms, distinctions, and categories to be applied to the identification and analysis of literature, as well as the **criteria** (the standards, or norms) by which these works and their writers are to be evaluated. The earliest great work of theoretical criticism was Aristotle's *Poetics* (fourth century B.C.). Especially influential works of theoretical criticism in the first half of the present century are I. A. Richards, *Principles of Literary Criticism* (1924); Kenneth Burke, *The Philosophy of Literary Form* (1941, rev. 1957); Eric Auerbach, *Mimesis* (1946); R. S. Crane, ed., *Critics and Criticism* (1952); and Northrop Frye, *Anatomy of Criticism* (1957). Since the 1970s there has been a flood of writings, Continental, American, and English, proposing diverse new and radical forms of "critical theory"—see under *criticism* in the Index, and the section of the *Glossary* titled "Modern Theories of Literature and Criticism," beginning p. 201. **Practical criticism,** or **applied criticism,** concerns itself with the discussion of particular works and writers; in an applied critique, the theoretical principles controlling the analysis, interpretation, and evaluation are often left implicit, or brought in only as the occasion demands. Among the major works of applied criticism in England are the literary essays of Dryden in the *Restoration,* Dr. Johnson's *Lives of the En-*

glish Poets (1779–81), Coleridge's chapters on the poetry of Wordsworth in *Biographia Literaria* (1817) and his lectures on Shakespeare, Matthew Arnold's *Essays in Criticism* (1865 and following), T. S. Eliot's *Selected Essays* (1932), and the many critical essays by Virginia Woolf, F. R. Leavis, and Lionel Trilling. Cleanth Brooks's *The Well Wrought Urn* (1947) is an instance of the "close reading" of single texts which was characteristic of the *New Criticism* in America.

Practical criticism is sometimes distinguished into impressionistic and judicial criticism:

Impressionistic criticism attempts to represent in words the felt qualities of a particular passage or work, and to express the responses (the "impression") that the work directly evokes from the critic. As Hazlitt put it in his essay "On Genius and Common Sense" (1824): "You decide from feeling, and not from reason; that is, from the impression of a number of things on the mind . . . though you may not be able to analyze or account for it in the several particulars." And Walter Pater later said that in criticism "the first step toward seeing one's object as it really is, is to know one's own impression as it really is, to discriminate it, to realise it distinctly," and posed as the basic question, "What is this song or picture . . . to *me*?" (Preface to *Studies in the History of the Renaissance*, 1873). At its extreme this mode of criticism becomes, in Anatole France's phrase, "the adventures of a sensitive soul among masterpieces."

Judicial criticism, on the other hand, attempts not merely to communicate, but to analyze and explain the effects of a work by reference to its subject, organization, techniques, and style, and to base the critic's individual judgments on general standards of literary excellence. Rarely are the two modes of criticism sharply distinct in practice, but good examples of primarily impressionistic commentary can be found in the Greek Longinus (see the characterization of the *Odyssey* in his essay *On the Sublime*), Hazlitt, Pater (the locus classicus of impressionism is his description of Leonardo's *Mona Lisa* in *The Renaissance*, 1873), and some of the twentieth-century critical essays of E. M. Forster and Virginia Woolf.

Types of traditional critical theories and applied criticism can be discriminated according to whether, in explaining and judging a work of literature, they refer the work primarily to the outer world, or to the reader, or to the author, or else look upon the work as an entity in itself:

(1) **Mimetic criticism** views the literary work as an imitation, or reflection, or representation of the world and human life, and the primary criterion applied to a work is that of the "truth" of its representation to the objects it represents, or should represent. This mode of criticism, which first appeared in Plato and (in a qualified way) in Aristotle, is characteristic of modern theories of literary realism. (See *imitation.*)

(2) **Pragmatic criticism** views the work as something which is constructed in order to achieve certain effects on the audience (effects such as aesthetic pleasure, instruction, or kinds of emotion), and it tends to judge the value of the work according to its success in achieving that aim. This approach, which dom-

inated literary discussion from the versified *Art of Poetry* by the Roman Horace (first century B.C.) through the eighteenth century, has been revived in recent *rhetorical criticism,* which emphasizes the artistic strategies by which an author engages and influences the responses of readers to the matters represented in a literary work, as well as by *structuralists* such as Roland Barthes, who analyze a literary work as a systematic play of *codes* which effect the interpretative responses of the reader.

(3) **Expressive criticism** treats a literary work primarily in relation to its author. It defines poetry as an expression, or overflow, or utterance of feelings, or as the product of the poet's imagination operating on his or her perceptions, thoughts, and feelings; it tends to judge the work by its sincerity, or genuineness, or adequacy to the poet's individual vision or state of mind; and it often looks in the work for evidences of the particular temperament and experiences of the author who, consciously or unconsciously, has revealed himself in it. Such views were developed mainly by romantic critics and remain current in our own time, especially in the writings of *psychological and psychoanalytic critics* and in *critics of consciousness* such as George Poulet and the Geneva School.

(4) **Objective criticism** approaches the work as something which stands free from reference to the poet, the audience, and the environing world. It describes the literary product as a self-sufficient and autonomous object, or else as a world-in-itself, which is to be analyzed and judged by "intrinsic" criteria such as complexity, coherence, equilibrium, integrity, and the interrelations of its component elements. This is the approach of a number of important critics since the 1920s, including the *New Critics,* the *Chicago School,* and proponents of European *formalism.*

An essential literary enterprise that the ordinary reader takes for granted is **textual criticism,** whose aim is to establish as accurately as possible what an author actually wrote, or intended to be the final version. The textual critic **collates** (that is, puts side by side for comparison) the printed texts of a work, together with any surviving manuscripts, in order to detect variants and to identify and correct sources of error. For problems and current methods, see Fredson Bowers, *Textual and Literary Criticism* (1959), and G. T. Tanselle, "Textual Scholarship," in Joseph Gibaldi, ed., *Introduction to Scholarship in Modern Language and Literature* (1981).

It is also common to distinguish types of criticism which bring to bear upon literature various special areas of knowledge and theory, in the attempt to account for the influences or causes which determined the particular characteristics of a literary work. Accordingly, we have "historical criticism," "biographical criticism," "sociological criticism" (see *sociology of literature* and *Marxist criticism*), *psychological criticism* (a subspecies is *psychoanalytic criticism*), and *archetypal* or *myth criticism* (which undertakes to explain types of literature by reference to the theories of myth and ritual in modern cultural anthropology).

On types of criticism and of critical approaches to literature, refer to René Wellek and Austin Warren, *Theory of Literature* (3rd ed., 1956), and M. H. Abrams, *The Mirror and the Lamp* (1953), Chap. 1. Histories of criticism: J. W.

Atkins, *Literary Criticism in Antiquity* (2 vols.; 1934), and *English Literary Criticism: The Renascence* (1947); W. K. Wimsatt and Cleanth Brooks, *Literary Criticism: A Short History* (1957); René Wellek, *A History of Modern Criticism, 1750–1950* (6 vols.; 1955 ff.). On criticism in the earlier nineteenth century see Abrams, *The Mirror and the Lamp,* and on twentieth-century criticism, S. E. Hyman, *The Armed Vision* (1948); Murray Krieger, *The New Apologists for Poetry* (1956); Jonathan Culler, *Structuralist Poetics* (1975); Grant Webster, *The Republic of Letters: A History of Postwar American Literary Opinion* (1979); Frank Lentricchia, *After the New Criticism* (1980). Convenient anthologies of literary criticism are A. H. Gilbert and G. W. Allen, *Literary Criticism, Plato to Croce* (2 vols.; 1940–41); W. J. Bate, *Criticism: The Major Texts* (1952); Walter Sutton and Richard Foster, *Modern Criticism: Theory and Practice* (1963); Lionel Trilling, *Literary Criticism: An Introductory Reader* (1970); and for current views, Vassilis Lambropoulos and David Neal Miller, eds., *Twentieth-Century Literary Theory: An Introductory Anthology* (1986) and Hazard Adams and Leroy Searle, eds., *Critical Theory since 1965* (1986). Suggested readings in recent critical "theories" are listed in the essays of the *Glossary* in the section "Modern Theories of Literature and Criticism," which begins on p. 201.

Decorum, as applied to literature, is the propriety or fitness with which a literary *genre,* its subject matter, characters, and actions, and the style of its narration and its dialogue are matched to each other. The doctrine had its roots in classical theory, especially in the versified essay *Art of Poetry* by the Roman Horace in the first century B.C., and it achieved a highly elaborate form in the criticism and practice of literature in the Renaissance and the *Neoclassic* age, when (as Milton put it in his essay *Of Education,* 1644) decorum became "the grand masterpiece to observe." In the strictest application of this concept, literary forms, characters, and style were all ordered in hierarchies, or "levels," from high through middle to low, and had to be matched to one another. Thus comedy must not be mixed with tragedy, and the highest and most serious genres (epic and tragedy) must represent characters of the highest social classes (kings and nobility) acting in a way appropriate to their status and speaking in the *high style.* A number of critics in this period, however, especially in England, maintained the theory of decorum only in a qualified form.

See *neoclassic and romantic, poetic diction,* and *style,* and refer to Vernon Hall, *Renaissance Literary Criticism: A Study of Its Social Content* (1945). Erich Auerbach's *Mimesis* (1953) describes the sustained conflict in postclassical Europe between the doctrines of literary decorum and the example of the Bible; in the Bible the highest and most serious matters, including the sublime tragedy of Christ, are intermingled with base characters and humble narrative detail, and are treated with what seemed to a strict neoclassic taste a blatant indecorum of style. For Wordsworth's deliberate inversion of traditional poetic decorum at the beginning of the nineteenth century, by investing the common, the lowly, and the trivial with high dignity and sublimity, see M. H. Abrams, *Natural Supernaturalism* (1971), pp. 390–408.

Deus ex Machina is Latin for "a god from a machine." It describes the practice of some Greek playwrights (especially Euripides) to end a drama with a god who was lowered to the stage by a mechanical apparatus and, by his judgment and commands, solved the problems of the human characters. The phrase is now used for a forced and improbable device—a telltale birthmark, an unexpected inheritance, the discovery of a lost will or letter—by which a hard-pressed author makes shift to resolve a plot. Notorious examples occur even in major novels like Dickens' *Oliver Twist* (1837–38) and Hardy's *Tess of the D'Urbervilles* (1891). The German playwright Bertolt Brecht *parodies* the abuse of such devices in the madcap conclusion of his *Threepenny Opera* (1928). See *plot.*

Didactic Literature. The adjective "didactic" (from the Greek word meaning "skilled in teaching") is applied not only to a work that is designed to expound, systematically, a branch of theoretical, moral, or practical knowledge, but also to literary works which embody, in a persuasive imaginative or fictional form, a moral, religious, or philosophical *theme* or doctrine. Such works are distinguished from essentially imaginative works (sometimes called "mimetic," or "representational") in which the materials are organized and rendered, not for the sake of presenting and enforcing knowledge or doctrine, but primarily to maximize their human interest and their capacity to move and give artistic pleasure to their audience. In the first century B.C. the Roman Lucretius wrote his didactic poem *De Rerum Natura* ("On the Nature of Things") to expound and make persuasive his naturalistic philosophy and ethics, and in the same era Virgil wrote his *Georgics* on the practical subject of how to manage a farm. Most medieval and much Renaissance literature was didactic in intention. In the eighteenth century, a number of poets wrote **georgics** (on the model of Virgil) on such utilitarian arts as sheep-herding, running a sugar plantation, and making cider. Alexander Pope's *Essay on Criticism* and his *Essay on Man* are also eighteenth-century didactic poems.

Such works for the most part directly expound a branch of knowledge or art, or else argue an explicit doctrine by proofs and examples. Didactic literature, however, may also take on the aspect and attributes of imaginative works, by embodying the doctrine in a narrative or dramatic form in order to add a dimension of aesthetic pleasure and to enhance its interest and force. In the various forms of *allegory*, for example, including Spenser's *The Faerie Queene* and Bunyan's *The Pilgrim's Progress,* the incorporated doctrines are primary determinants of the choice of characters and the development of the plot. The various forms of *satire* are didactic in that they are designed, by various devices of ridicule, to alter the reader's attitudes toward certain types of people, institutions, and modes of conduct. Dante's *Letter to Can Grande* tells us that he designed his fourteenth-century *Divine Comedy* to represent, in the mode of a visionary narrative, the major Christian truths and the way to avoid damnation and achieve salvation. And Milton's *Paradise Lost* (1667) can also be called didactic to the extent that the narrative is in fact organized, as Milton claimed in his opening invocation, around his "great argument" to "assert Eternal Providence,/And justify the ways of God to men." It will be seen from these examples that "didactic literature," as here defined, is a technical distinction and not a derogatory term. Some literary masterpieces are didactic and others (Shakespeare's *King Lear*, Jane Austen's *Emma*, Joyce's *Ulysses*), even though the plots involve moral concerns and imply criteria for moral judgments, are essentially, to adopt a phrase by Coleridge, works "of pure imagination."

The term **propagandist literature** is sometimes used as the equivalent of didactic literature, but it is much more useful to reserve the term for that species of didactic work which patently undertakes to move the reader to assume a point of view toward, or to take direct action on, a particular and pressing social, political, or religious issue of the time at which the work is written. Prominent and effective examples of such works are Harriet Beecher Stowe's *Uncle Tom's Cabin* (1852; on slavery in the South), Upton Sinclair's *The Jungle* (on the horrors of the unregulated slaughtering and meat-packing industry in Chicago in 1906), and Clifford Odets' *Waiting for Lefty* (1935; a play directed against the strong-arm tactics used to suppress a taxicab drivers' union).

See *fiction*, and refer to John Chalker, *The English Georgic: A Study in the Development of a Form* (1969). On the distinction between didactic and purely imaginative, or "mimetic," literature, see R. S. Crane, ed., *Critics and Criticism* (1952), especially pp. 63–68 and 589–94.

Dissociation of Sensibility is a phrase introduced by T. S. Eliot in his essay "The Metaphysical Poets" (1921). Eliot's claim was that the *metaphysical poets* of the earlier seventeenth century, like the Elizabethan and Jacobean dramatists, "possessed a mechanism of sensibility which could devour any kind of experience." They manifested "a direct sensuous apprehension of thought," and felt "their thought as immediately as the odour of a rose." "A thought to Donne was an experience; it modified his sensibility." But "in the seventeenth century a dissociation of sensibility set in, from which we have never recovered." This dissociation, according to Eliot, was greatly aggravated by the influence of Milton and Dryden; and most later poets in English either thought or felt, but did not think and feel as an act of unified sensibility.

Eliot's vaguely defined distinction had a great vogue, especially among American *New Critics;* it was taken to be the characteristic feature of most poetry between Milton and the later Yeats, and was attributed to a variety of causes, but particularly to the development in the seventeenth century of the scientific view of the world as a material universe stripped of human values and feeling. (See, for example, Basil Willey, *The Seventeenth Century Background,* 1934.) Especially since 1950, however, Eliot's doctrine of a sudden but persisting dissociation of sensibility has come in for strong criticism, as an unjustified claim which was contrived both to support Eliot's disapproval of the course of English intellectual and religious history after the Civil War of 1642 and to justify Eliot's particular poetic preferences.

See T. S. Eliot, "The Metaphysical Poets," *Selected Essays* (2d ed., 1960), and "Milton II," *On Poetry and Poets* (1957). Attacks on the validity of the doctrine are Leonard Unger, *Donne's Poetry and Modern Criticism* (1950); F. W. Bateson, "Dissociation of Sensibility," in the journal *Essays in Criticism*, 1 (1951) and 2 (1952); and Frank Kermode, *Romantic Image* (1957), Chap. 8.

Distance and Involvement. In his *Critique of Aesthetic Judgment* (1790), Immanuel Kant analyzed our experience of an aesthetic object as an act of "contemplation" which is "disinterested" (that is, independent of our personal interests) and free from all reference to its reality, moral effect, or utility. Various philosophers of art developed this concept into attempts to distinguish aesthetic experience from all other kinds of experience in terms of the impersonality and disinterestedness with which we contemplate an object or work of art. Writing in 1912, Edward Bullough introduced the term "distance" into this type of theory. He points, for example, to the difference between our ordinary experience of a dense fog at sea, with its strains, anxiety, and fear of invisible dangers, and the aesthetic experience, in which we attend with delight to the "objective" features and sensuous qualities of the fog itself. He accounts for this aesthetic mode of experiencing the fog as the effect of "psychical distance," which "is obtained by separating the object and its appeal from one's own self, by putting it out of gear with practical needs and ends." The extent of this psychical distance varies according to the nature of the artistic object which we contemplate, and also in accordance with an "individual's capacity for maintaining a greater or lesser degree" of such distance.

In recent literary criticism the term **aesthetic distance,** or simply **distance,** is often used not only to define the nature of all literary and aesthetic experience, but also to analyze the many devices by which authors control the degree of a reader's distance, or "detachment"—in inverse relationship to the degree of **involvement,** or "concern"—with the actions and fortunes of one or another character represented within a work of literature. See, for example, Wayne C. Booth's detailed analysis of the control of distance in Jane Austen's *Emma*, in *The Rhetoric of Fiction* (1961), Chap. 9.

In his *epic theater* of the 1920s and later, the German dramatist Bertolt Brecht adapted the *Russian formalist* concept of "defamiliarization" into what he called **estrangement effects** (sometimes translated also as **alienation effects**), in order to make familiar aspects of reality seem strange, and so to prevent the emotional identification or involvement of the audience with the characters and subject matter of the play. His aim was to effect a critical attitude on the part of the audience so as to arouse them to take action against, rather than simply to accept, the social reality represented on the stage. (On Brecht, see *Marxist criticism*.)

See Edward Bullough, "Psychical Distance as a Factor in Art and an Aesthetic Principle," *British Journal of Psychology*, 5 (1912), reprinted in Melvin Rader, ed., *A Modern Book of Aesthetics* (rev., 1952), and partially reprinted in Eliseo Vivas and Murray Krieger, *The Problems of Aesthetics* (1963). A useful review of theories of the aesthetic attitude and of aesthetic distance is Jerome Stollnitz, *Aesthetics and the Philosophy of Art Criticism* (1960), Chap. 2.

For an opposed view that such theories are mistaken, see George Dickie, *Art and the Aesthetic* (1974), Chaps. 4 and 5.

Doggerel is a term applied to rough, heavy-footed, and jerky versification. It is usually the result of ineptitude on the part of the versifier, but is sometimes deliberately employed by poets for satiric, comic, or rollicking effect. John Skelton (1460?–1529) wrote in short lines of two or three stresses, rough and variable in meter, which have come to be called **Skeltonics;** as he described his own versification in *Colin Clout:*

> For though my rhyme be ragged,
> Tattered and jagged,
> Rudely rain-beaten,
> Rusty and moth-eaten,
> If ye take well therewith,
> It hath in it some pith.

The tumbling, broken, and comically grotesque *octosyllabic couplets,* often using double, triple, and imperfect rhyme, which were developed by Samuel Butler for his satiric poem *Hudibras* (1663–78) are a form of deliberate doggerel which came to be called **Hudibrastic verse:**

> Besides, he was a shrewd philosopher,
> And had read every text and gloss over;
> Whate'er the crabbed'st author hath,
> He understood b'implicit faith.

See *meter.*

Drama is the literary form designed for performance in the theater, in which actors take the roles of the characters, perform the indicated action, and utter the written dialogue. In **poetic drama** the dialogue is written in verse, which in English is usually *blank verse* and in French is the twelve-syllable line called an *Alexandrine;* almost all the *heroic dramas* of the English Restoration Period, however, were written in *heroic couplets* (iambic pentameter lines rhyming in pairs). A **closet drama** is written in the form of a drama, but is intended by the author to be read rather than to be performed in the theater; examples are Milton's *Samson Agonistes* (1671), Byron's *Manfred* (1817), Shelley's *Prometheus Unbound* (1820), and Hardy's *The Dynasts* (1904–08).

For the types and elements of dramas, see the Index under *drama.*

Dramatic Monologue. A **monologue** is a long speech by a single person; the dramatic device, in which a character in a play utters a monologue that expresses the character's private thoughts, is called a *soliloquy.* What is called a **dramatic monologue** is not an element in a play, but a type of *lyric poem* that was perfected by Robert Browning. In its fullest form, as represented in

Browning's "My Last Duchess," "The Bishop Orders His Tomb," "Andrea del Sarto," and many other poems, the dramatic monologue has the following features: (1) A single person, who is patently *not* the poet, utters the entire poem in a specific situation at a critical moment: the Duke is negotiating with an emissary for a second wife; the Bishop lies dying; Andrea once more attempts wistfully to believe his wife's lies. (2) This person addresses and interacts with one or more other people; but we know of the auditors' presence and what they say and do only from clues in the discourse of the single speaker. (3) The principle controlling the poet's selection and organization of what the lyric speaker says is the speaker's unintentional revelation of his or her temperament and character.

Even Browning, in monologues such as "Soliloquy of the Spanish Cloister" and "Caliban upon Setebos," omits the second attribute, the presence of a silent auditor; but attributes (1) and (3) are essential distinctions between the dramatic monologue and the **dramatic lyric,** which is also a monologue uttered in a specified situation at a dramatic moment. Thus John Donne's "The Canonization" and "The Flea" (1613) are dramatic lyrics that, although very close to the dramatic monologue, lack one essential feature: the focus of interest is primarily on the speaker's elaborately ingenious argument, rather than on the character he inadvertently reveals in the course of arguing. And although Wordsworth's "Tintern Abbey" (1798) is spoken by one person to a silent auditor (his sister) in a specific situation at a significant moment in his life, it is not properly a dramatic monologue, both because we are invited to identify the speaker with the poet himself, and because the organizing principle is not the revelation of the speaker's distinctive temperament so much as the evolution of his observation, thought, memory, and feelings.

Tennyson wrote "Ulysses" (1842) and other dramatic monologues, and the form has been used by Robert Frost, E. A. Robinson, Ezra Pound, Robert Lowell, and other poets of this century. The best-known modern instance is T. S. Eliot's "The Love Song of J. Alfred Prufrock" (1915).

See Benjamin Fuson, *Browning and His English Predecessors in the Dramatic Monologue* (1948); Robert Langbaum, *The Poetry of Experience: The Dramatic Monologue in Modern Literary Tradition* (1957); and Ralph W. Rader, "The Dramatic Monologue and Related Lyric Forms," *Critical Inquiry,* 3 (1976).

Dream Vision. A narrative mode widely employed by medieval poets: the narrator falls asleep, usually in a spring landscape, and dreams the events he goes on to relate; often he is led by a guide, human or animal, and the events which he dreams are at least in part an *allegory.* A very influential French example is the thirteenth-century poem *Roman de la Rose;* the greatest of medieval poems, Dante's *Divine Comedy,* is a dream vision; and in fourteenth-century England, Langland used the form in *Piers Plowman* and Chaucer in *The Book of the Duchess, The House of Fame,* and others of his earlier poems. After the Middle Ages the vogue of the dream allegory diminished, but it never died out, as Bunyan's prose *The Pilgrim's Progress* (1678) and Keats's verse *The Fall of Hy-*

perion: A Dream (1819) bear witness. Lewis Carroll's *Alice's Adventures in Wonderland* (1865) is in the mode of a dream vision, and James Joyce's *Finnegans Wake* (1939) is an immense cosmic dream on the part of an archetypal dreamer.

See C. S. Lewis, *The Allegory of Love* (1938).

Edwardian Period. The literary period between the death of Victoria (1901) and the beginning of World War I (1914); it is named for King Edward VII, who reigned from 1901 to 1910. Poets writing at the time were Thomas Hardy, Alfred Noyes, W. B. Yeats, and Rudyard Kipling; dramatists included James Barrie, John Galsworthy, G. B. Shaw, and playwrights of the *Celtic Revival* such as Lady Gregory, Yeats, and J. M. Synge. Many of the major achievements were in prose fiction—works by Joseph Conrad, Ford Madox Ford, John Galsworthy, H. G. Wells, Rudyard Kipling, and Henry James, who published his three great final novels, *The Wings of the Dove, The Ambassadors,* and *The Golden Bowl,* between 1902 and 1904.

Elegy. In Greek and Roman literature, the term "elegy" was used to denote any poem written in **elegiac meter** (alternating *hexameter* and *pentameter* lines), and also to denote the subjects and moods frequently expressed in that verse form, especially complaints about love. In Europe and England the word continued to have a variable usage through the Renaissance; John Donne's *Elegies,* for example, are love poems. In the course of the seventeenth century, however, the term began to be limited to its present usage: a formal and sustained lament (and usually consolation) for the death of a particular person. Examples are Tennyson's *In Memoriam* (1850) on the death of Arthur Hallam and W. H. Auden's "In Memory of W. B. Yeats" (1940). Sometimes the term is more broadly used for somber meditations such as the *Old English* "elegies" ("The Wanderer," "The Seafarer") and Gray's "Elegy Written in a Country Churchyard" (1751), which deal generally with the passing of men and the things they value, and the *Duino Elegies* (1912–22) of the German poet Rainer Maria Rilke, whose subject is the transience of mortal poets and of the earthly objects which they write about in their poems.

The **dirge** also expresses grief on the occasion of someone's death, but differs from the elegy in that it is short, is less formal, and is usually represented as a text to be sung; examples are Shakespeare's "Full Fathom Five Thy Father Lies" and William Collins' "A Song from Shakespeare's *Cymbeline*" (1749). **Threnody** is now used mainly as an equivalent for "dirge," and **monody** for an elegy or dirge which is presented as the utterance of a single person. Milton describes his "Lycidas" (1638), in the subtitle, as a "monody" in which "the Author bewails a learned Friend," and Matthew Arnold called his elegy on A. H. Clough "Thyrsis: A Monody" (1866).

An important subspecies of the elegy is the **pastoral elegy,** which represents both the mourner and the one he mourns—who is usually also a poet—as shepherds (the Latin word for shepherd is "pastor"). This poetic form was originated by the Sicilian Greek poet Theocritus, was continued by the Roman Virgil, was developed in various European countries during the Renaissance, and remained current in English poetry throughout the nineteenth century. Notable English pastoral elegies are Milton's "Lycidas" (1638), Shelley's "Adonais" (1821), and in the Victorian age, Arnold's "Thyrsis." The pastoral elegists, from the Greeks through the Renaissance, developed elaborate *conventions*, which are illustrated here by reference to "Lycidas." In addition to the fictional representation of both mourner and subject as shepherds tending their flocks (lines 23–36 and elsewhere), we find these conventions:

(1) The lyric speaker begins by invoking the muses, and goes on to make frequent reference to other figures from classical mythology (lines 15–22, and later).

(2) All nature joins in mourning the shepherd's death (lines 37–49). (Recent critics who stress the mythic and ritual origins of poetic genres claim that this feature is a survival from primitive laments for the death of Thammuz, Adonis, or other vegetational deities who died in the autumn to be reborn in the spring.)

(3) The mourner charges with negligence the nymphs or other guardians of the dead shepherd (lines 50–63).

(4) There is a procession of appropriate mourners (lines 88–111).

(5) The poet raises questions about the justice of Providence and adverts to the corrupt conditions of his own times (lines 64–84, 113–31). Such passages, though sometimes called "digressions," are entirely integral to the evolution of the mourner's thought in "Lycidas."

(6) Post-Renaissance elegies often include an elaborate passage in which appropriate flowers are brought to deck the hearse (lines 133–51).

(7) There is a closing consolation. In Christian elegies, the lyric reversal from grief and despair to joy and assurance occurs when the elegist suddenly realizes that death in this world is the entry to a higher life (lines 165–85).

In his *Life of Milton* (1779), Samuel Johnson, who disapproved both of pastoralism and mythology in modern poetry, decried "Lycidas" for "its inherent improbability," but in Milton and other major writers the ancient rituals are structural elements on which they play variations with originality and power. Some of the pastoral conventions, although adapted to an industrial age and a non-Christian worldview, continue to be manifest in Walt Whitman's great elegy on Lincoln, "When Lilacs Last in the Dooryard Bloom'd" (1866).

See *conventions* and *pastoral*. On the elegy: Mary Lloyd, *Elegies, Ancient and Modern* (1903); T. P. Harrison, Jr., and H. J. Leon, eds., *The Pastoral Elegy: An Anthology* (1939); Peter Sacks, *The English Elegy: Studies in the Genre from Spenser to Yeats* (1985). On "Lycidas": C. A. Patrides, ed., *Milton's "Lycidas": The Tradition and the Poem* (1961), which is an anthology of recent critical essays; and Scott Elledge, ed., *Milton's "Lycidas"* (1966).

Elizabethan Age denotes the period of Queen Elizabeth's reign, 1558–1603. This was a time of rapid development in English commerce, maritime power, and nationalist feeling—the defeat of the Spanish Armada occurred in 1588. It was a great (in drama the greatest) age of English literature—the age of Sidney, Marlowe, Spenser, Shakespeare, Raleigh, Bacon, Ben Jonson, and many other extraordinary writers of prose and of dramatic, lyric, and narrative poetry. See *Renaissance.*

Empathy and Sympathy. German theorists in the nineteenth century developed the concept of "Einfühlung" ("feeling into"), which has been translated as **empathy.** It signifies an identification with a perceived person or object, in which one seems to participate in the posture, motion, and sensations that one perceives. Empathy is often described as "an involuntary projection of ourselves into an object," and is commonly explained as the result of an "inner mimicry" on the part of the observer; that is, the observer undergoes incipient muscular movements which he does not experience as his own sensations, but as if they were attributes of an outer object. The object may be human, or nonhuman, or even inanimate. In thoroughly absorbed contemplation we seem empathically to pirouette with a ballet dancer, soar with a hawk, bend with the movements of a tree in the wind, and even share the strength, ease, and grace with which a well-proportioned arch appears to support a bridge. When Keats said that he became "a part of all I see," and that "if a sparrow comes before my window I take part in its existence and pick about the gravel," he was describing an habitual experience of his intensely empathic nature, long before the word was coined.

In literature we call "empathic" a passage which conspicuously evokes from the reader this sense of participation with the pose, movements, and physical sensations of the object that the passage describes. An example is Shakespeare's description, in his narrative poem *Venus and Adonis,* of

> the snail, whose tender horns being hit,
> Shrinks backward in his shelly cave with pain.

Another is the description of the motion of a wave in Keats's *Endymion* (1818),

> when heav'd anew
> Old ocean rolls a lengthen'd wave to the shore,
> Down whose green back the short-liv'd foam, all hoar,
> Bursts gradual, with a wayward indolence.

Sympathy, as distinguished from empathy, denotes fellow-feeling—not feeling-into the physical state, but feeling-along-with the mental state and emotions of another human being, or of nonhuman beings to whom we attribute human emotions. We "sympathize," for example, with the emotional experience of a child in his first attempt to recite a piece in public; we may also "empathize" as he falters in his speaking or makes an awkward gesture. Robert Burns's "To a Mouse" (1786) is an engaging expression of his quick sympathy with the terror of the "wee, sleekit, cow'rin, tim'rous beastie" whose nest he has turned up with his plow.

The engagement and control of a reader's sympathy with certain characters, and the establishment of "antipathy" toward others, is essential to the traditional literary artist. In Shakespeare's *King Lear,* we sympathize with Cordelia, for example, and progressively with King Lear, but feel horror and antipathy to his "pelican daughters," Goneril and Regan. Our attitude in the same play toward the villainous Edmund, the bastard son of Gloucester, as managed by Shakespeare, is more complex—antipathetic, yet with some element of sympathetic understanding of his distorted personality. (See *distance and involvement.*) Bertolt Brecht's *estrangement effects* were designed to inhibit the sympathy of an audience with the protagonists of his plays, in order to encourage a critical attitude to the social realities that the plays represent.

Refer to H. S. Langfeld, *The Aesthetic Attitude* (1920)—the section on empathy is reprinted in *Problems of Aesthetics* (1963), eds. Eliseo Vivas and Murray Krieger. For discussion and detailed analyses of empathic passages in literature, see Richard H. Fogle, *The Imagery of Keats and Shelley* (1949), Chap. 4.

Enlightenment. The name applied to an intellectual movement and cultural ambience which developed in western Europe during the seventeenth century and reached its height in the eighteenth. The common element was a trust in man's reason as adequate to solve the important problems and to establish the essential norms in life, together with the belief that the application of reason was rapidly dissipating the darkness of superstition, prejudice, and barbarity, was freeing man from his earlier reliance on mere authority and unexamined tradition, and was preparing him to achieve an ideal existence in this world. For some thinkers the model of "reason" was the inductive procedure of science, which develops by reasoning from the facts of experience to general laws; for others (especially Descartes and his followers), the model of "reason" was primarily geometrical—the deduction of particular truths from clear and distinct ideas which are known intuitively, by "the light of reason." Many thinkers relied on reason in both these senses.

In England, the thought and the world outlook of the Enlightenment are usually traced from Francis Bacon (1561–1626) through John Locke (1632–1704) to late-eighteenth-century thinkers such as William Godwin; in France, from Descartes (1596–1650) through Voltaire (1694–1778) to Diderot and other editors of the great twenty-volume *Encyclopédie* (1751–72); in Germany, from Leibniz (1646–1716) to what is often described as the highest product of the Enlightenment, the "critical philosophy" of Immanuel Kant (1724–1804). In the famous essay, written in 1784, "What Is Enlightenment?" Kant defined it as "the liberation of mankind from his self-caused state of minority" and the achievement of a stage of maturity which is exemplified in his "determination and courage to use [his understanding] without the assistance of another."

A typical manifestation of the Enlightenment was the widespread mode of religious thought known as **deism.** Many thinkers assimilated elements of deism but remained professing Christians. The thoroughgoing deist, however, renounced, as violating reason, all "revealed religion"—that is, all particular religions, including Christianity, which are based on faith in the truths and mysteries revealed in special scriptures at a certain time and place and to a particular individual or group. The deist instead relied on those truths which, it was claimed, prove their accord with universal human reason by the fact that they are to be found in all religions, everywhere, at all times. Therefore, the basic tenets of deism—for example, that there is a deity, discoverable by reasoning from the creation to the creator, who deserves our worship and sanctions all moral values—were in theory the common denominator of all particular, or "positive," religions. Alexander Pope, without renouncing his Catholicism, expressed succinctly the basic tenets of deism in his poem "The Universal Prayer" (1738), which begins

> Father of all! in every age,
>   In every clime adored,
> By saint, by savage, and by sage,
>   Jehovah, Jove, or Lord!

See *neoclassicism and romanticism;* and refer to Ernst Cassirer, *The Philosophy of the Enlightenment* (1932); A. O. Lovejoy, *Essays in the History of Ideas* (1948); Basil Willey, *The Eighteenth Century Background* (1950); Peter Gay, *The Enlightenment: An Interpretation* (1966).

Epic. In its strict use the term **epic** or **heroic poem** is applied to a work that meets at least the following criteria: it is a long narrative poem on a great and serious subject, told in an elevated style, and centered on a heroic or quasi-divine figure on whose actions depends the fate of a tribe, a nation, or the human race. The "traditional epics" (also called "primary epics" or "folk epics") were shaped by a literary artist from historical and legendary materials which had developed in the oral traditions of his people during a period of expansion and warfare. To this class of poems are ascribed the *Iliad* and *Odyssey* of the Greek Homer, and the Anglo-Saxon epic *Beowulf.* The "literary" or "secondary" epics were composed by sophisticated craftsmen in deliberate imitation of the traditional form. Of this kind is Virgil's Latin poem the *Aeneid,* which later served as the chief model for Milton's literary epic *Paradise Lost* (1667); and *Paradise Lost* in turn became, in the *Romantic Period,* a model for Keats's fragmentary epic *Hyperion,* as well as for Blake's several epics, or "prophetic books" (*The Four Zoas, Milton, Jerusalem*), which translated into Blake's own mythic terms the biblical design and materials which had served as Milton's subject matter.

The epic was ranked by the Greek theorist Aristotle as second only to tragedy, and by many Renaissance critics as the highest of all *genres.* The literary epic is certainly the most ambitious of poetic types, making immense demands on a poet's knowledge, invention, and skill to sustain the scope, grandeur, and variety of a poem that tends to encompass the world of its day and a large portion of its learning. Despite numerous attempts in many languages over nearly three thousand years, we possess no more than a half-dozen epic poems of indubitable greatness. Literary epics are highly conventional poems which commonly share the following features, derived ultimately from the traditional epics of Homer:

(1) The hero is a figure of great national or even cosmic importance. In the *Iliad* he is the Greek warrior Achilles, who is the son of the sea-nymph Thetis; and Virgil's Aeneas is the son of the goddess Aphrodite. In *Paradise Lost,* Adam represents the entire human race, or if we regard Christ as the hero, He is both God and man. Blake's primal figure is "the Universal Man" Albion, who incorporates, before his fall, man and God and the cosmos as well.

(2) The setting of the poem is ample in scale, and may be worldwide, or even larger. Odysseus wanders over the Mediterranean basin (the whole of the world known to Homer), and in Book XI he descends into the underworld (as does Vergil's Aeneas). The scope of *Paradise Lost* is cosmic, for it takes place in heaven, on earth, and in hell.

(3) The action involves superhuman deeds in battle, such as Achilles' feats in the Trojan War, or a long and arduous journey intrepidly accomplished, such as the wanderings of Odysseus on his way back to his homeland, despite the opposition of some of the gods. *Paradise Lost* includes the revolt in heaven by the rebel angels against God, the journey of Satan through chaos to discover the newly created world, and his desperately audacious attempt to outwit God by corrupting mankind, in which his success is ultimately frustrated by the sacrificial action of Christ.

(4) In these great actions the gods and other supernatural beings take an interest or an active part—the Olympian gods in Homer, and Jehovah, Christ, and the angels in *Paradise Lost.* These supernatural agents were in the *Neoclassic Age* called the **machinery,** in the sense that they were part of the literary contrivances of the epic.

(5) An epic poem is a ceremonial performance, and is narrated in a ceremonial style which is deliberately distanced from ordinary speech and proportioned to the grandeur and formality of the heroic subject and epic architecture. Hence Milton's **grand style**—his Latinate diction and elaborate and stylized syntax, his sonorous lists of names and wide-ranging *allusions,* and his imitation of Homer's *epic similes* and *epithets.*

There are also widely used epic *conventions* in the choice and ordering of episodes in the narrative; prominent among them are these features:

(1) The narrator begins by stating his **argument,** or epic theme, invokes a muse or guiding spirit to inspire him in his great undertaking, then addresses to the muse the **epic question,** the answer to which inaugurates the narrative proper (*Paradise Lost,* I, 1–49).

(2) The narrative proper starts **in medias res,** that is, "in the middle of things," at a critical point in the action. *Paradise Lost* opens with the fallen angels in hell, gathering their forces and determining on revenge. Not until Books V–VII does the angel Raphael relate to Adam the events in heaven which

led to this situation; while in Books XI–XII, after the fall, Michael foretells to Adam future events up to Christ's second coming. Thus Milton's epic, although its action focuses on the temptation and fall of man, encompasses all time from the creation to the end of the world.

(3) There are catalogues of some of the principal characters, introduced in formal detail, as in Milton's description of the procession of fallen angels in Book I of *Paradise Lost.* These characters are often given set speeches which reveal their diverse temperaments; an example is the debate in Pandemonium, Book II.

The term "epic" is often applied, by extension, to works which differ in many respects from this model but manifest the epic spirit in the scale, the scope, and the profound human importance of their subjects. In this broad sense Dante's fourteenth-century *Divine Comedy* and Spenser's late-sixteenth-century *The Faerie Queene* (1590–96) are often called epics, as are conspicuously large-scale and wide-ranging works of prose fiction such as Melville's *Moby-Dick* (1851) and Tolstoy's *War and Peace* (1863–69). In a still more extended application, the *Marxist critic* Georg Lukács uses the term **bourgeois epic** for all novels which, in his view, reflect social reality on a broad scale; and in the 1920s the German playwright Bertolt Brecht identified his plays as **epic theater.** By this Brecht signified primarily his attempt to emulate on the stage the objectivity of epic narrative; his aim was to prevent the spectators' emotional involvement with the characters and their actions, and so to encourage them to criticize, rather than passively to accept, the social conditions that the play represents (see *estrangement effects*).

See *mock epic* and refer to H. T. Swedenborg, *The Theory of the Epic in England, 1650–1800* (1944); C. M. Bowra, *From Vergil to Milton* (1945), and *Heroic Poetry* (1952); E. M. W. Tillyard, *The English Epic and Its Background* (1954); C. S. Lewis, *A Preface to "Paradise Lost"* (1942); Brian Wilkie, *Romantic Poets and Epic Tradition* (1965). For an *archetypal* theory of the epic, see Northrop Frye, *Anatomy of Criticism* (1957), pp. 315–26.

Epic Similes are formal and sustained similes in which the secondary subject, or "vehicle," is developed far beyond its specific points of close parallel to the primary subject, or "tenor," to which it is compared (see *figurative language*). This figure was imitated from Homer by Virgil, Milton, and other writers of literary epics, who employed it to enhance the ceremonial quality and wide range of reference of the epic style. So in *Paradise Lost,* I, lines 768 ff., Milton describes the fallen angels thronging toward their new-built palace of Pandemonium by an elaborate simile to the swarming of bees:

As Bees
In spring time, when the Sun with Taurus rides,
Pour forth their populous youth about the Hive
In clusters; they among fresh dews and flowers
Fly to and fro, or on the smoothèd Plank,

The suburb of their Straw-built Citadel,
New rubb'd with Balm, expatiate and confer
Their State affairs. So thick the aery crowd
Swarm'd and were strait'n'd; . . .

Epigram originally meant, in Greek, an inscription, but was extended to include any very short poem—whether amorous, elegiac, meditative, complimentary, anecdotal, or satiric—which is polished, terse, and pointed; often an epigram ends with a surprising or witty turn of thought. Martial, the Roman epigrammatist, established the enduring model for the caustically satiric epigram.

The epigram is a species of *light verse* which was much cultivated in England in the late sixteenth and seventeenth centuries by such poets as Donne, Jonson, and Herrick. The form flourished especially in the eighteenth century, during the time that Austin Dobson described as the age "of wit, of polish, and of Pope." Matthew Prior is one of the best English epigrammatists, and many of Alexander Pope's closed couplets are detachable epigrams. In the same century, when the exiled Stuarts were still pretenders to the English throne, John Byrom proposed this epigrammatic toast:

God bless the King—I mean the Faith's defender!
God bless (no harm in blessing) the Pretender!
But who pretender is or who is king—
God bless us all! that's quite another thing.

And here is one of Coleridge's epigrams, to show that Romanticism did not preclude wit:

On A Volunteer Singer

Swans sing before they die—'twere no bad thing
Should certain people die before they sing!

Many of the short poems of Walter Savage Landor (1775–1864) were fine examples of the nonsatirical epigram. Boileau and Voltaire excelled in the epigram in France, as did Lessing, Goethe, and Schiller in Germany. The form has continued to be cultivated by W. B. Yeats, Ezra Pound, Roy Campbell, Ogden Nash, and other poets in our own time.

Since approximately the end of the eighteenth century, the term "epigram" has come to be applied to neat and witty statements in prose as well as verse; for prose examples see *wit, humor, and the comic.* The deliberately witty epigram in prose is to be distinguished from the **aphorism:** the pithy statement of a serious maxim, opinion, or general truth. Refer to T. K. Whipple, *Martial and the English Epigram* (1925); E. B. Osborn, ed., *The Hundred Best Epigrams* (1928); Kingsley Amis, ed., *The New Oxford Book of Light Verse* (1978); Russell Baker, ed., *The Norton Book of Light Verse* (1986).

Epiphany means "a manifestation," and by Christian thinkers was used to signify a manifestation of God's presence in the created world. In the early draft of

A Portrait of the Artist as a Young Man, entitled *Stephen Hero* (published posthumously in 1944), James Joyce adapted the term to secular experience, to signify a sense of sudden radiance and revelation while observing a commonplace object. "By an epiphany [Stephen] meant a sudden spiritual manifestation." "Its soul, its whatness, leaps to us from the vestment of its appearance. The soul of the commonest object . . . seems to us radiant. The object achieves its epiphany." Joyce's short stories and novels include a number of epiphanies; a climactic one is the revelation Stephen experiences at sight of the young girl wading on the strand in *A Portrait of the Artist,* Chap. 4.

"Epiphany" has become the standard term for the description, frequent in modern poetry and prose fiction, of the sudden flare into revelation of an ordinary object or scene. Joyce, however, merely substituted this word for what earlier authors had called "the **moment.**" Thus Shelley, in his *Defense of Poetry* (1821), described the "best and happiest moments . . . arising unforeseen and departing unbidden," "visitations of the divinity" which poetry "redeems from decay." William Wordsworth was a preeminent poet of what he called "moments," or in more elaborate instances, "spots of time." For instances of his short poems which represent a moment of revelation, see Wordsworth's "The Two April Mornings" and "The Solitary Reaper." Wordsworth's *Prelude,* like Joyce's narratives, is constructed as a sequence of such visionary encounters. Thus in Book VIII, lines 539–59, Wordsworth describes the "moment" when he for the first time passed in a stagecoach over the "threshold" of London and the "trivial forms/Of houses, pavement, streets" suddenly manifested a profound power and significance:

> 'twas a moment's pause,—
> All that took place within me came and went
> As in a moment; yet with Time it dwells,
> And grateful memory, as a thing divine.

See Irene H. Chayes, "Joyce's Epiphanies," reprinted in *Joyce's "Portrait": Criticisms and Critiques,* ed. T. E. Connolly (1962); Robert Scholes, "Joyce and the Epiphany," *Sewanee Review,* 62 (1964); Morris Beja, *Epiphany in the Modern Novel* (1971). On both the traditional "moment" and the modern epiphany see M. H. Abrams, *Natural Supernaturalism: Tradition and Revolution in Romantic Literature* (1971), Chaps. 7–8.

Epithalamion, or in the Latin form, "epithalamium," is a poem written to celebrate a marriage; among its classical practitioners were the Greeks Sappho and Theocritus and the Romans Ovid and Catullus. The term in Greek means "at the bridal chamber," for the verses were originally written to be sung outside the bedroom of a newly married couple. Sir Philip Sidney wrote the first English instance in about 1580, and fifteen years later Spenser wrote his great lyric "Epithalamion," a celebration of his own marriage composed as a wedding gift to his bride. Spenser's poem follows, in elaborately contrived numbers of stanzas and lines, the sequence of the hours during his wedding day and night and combines, with unfailing grace and dignity, the inherited pagan topics and mythology, Christian ritual and beliefs, and the local Irish setting. Donne, Jonson, Herrick, and many other Renaissance poets composed wedding poems, solemn or ribald, according to the intended audience and the poet's temperament. Sir John Suckling's "A Ballad upon a Wedding" is an engaging *parody* of this upper-class poetic form applied to a lower-class wedding. The tradition persists. Shelley composed an "Epithalamium"; Tennyson's *In Memoriam,* although it opens with a funeral, closes with an epithalamion; A. E. Housman spoke in the antique idiom of the bridal song in "He Is Here, Urania's Son"; and W. H. Auden wrote an "Epithalamion" in 1939.

See Robert H. Case, *English Epithalamies* (1896); Virginia J. Tufte, *The Poetry of Marriage* (1970); and (on the elaborate construction of Spenser's "Epithalamion" to correspond with the passage of time) A. Kent Hieatt, *Short Time's Endless Monument* (1960).

Epithet is derived from the Greek "epitheton," signifying "something added." As a term in criticism, it denotes an adjective or adjectival phrase used to define a distinctive quality of a person or thing (Keats's "*silver snarling* trumpets"). The term is also applied to an identifying phrase that stands in place of a noun (Pope's "the *glittering forfex*" is a heroic epithet for the scissors with which the Baron performs his heinous act in *The Rape of the Lock,* 1714). The frequent use of derogatory adjectives and phrases in *invective* has led to the mistaken notion that an "epithet" is always uncomplimentary.

Homeric epithets are adjectival terms—usually a compound of two words—like those which Homer used as formulas in referring to someone or something: "*fleet-footed* Achilles," "*bolt-hurling* Zeus," "the *wine-dark* sea." Buck Mulligan in Joyce's *Ulysses* parodied the formula in his reference to "the snot-green sea." We often use fixed, or "conventional," epithets in identifying historical or legendary figures; for example, Charles *the Great,* Lorenzo *the Magnificent, Patient* Griselda.

Essay. Any short composition in prose that undertakes to discuss a matter, express a point of view, or persuade us to accept a thesis on any subject whatever. The essay differs from a "treatise" or "dissertation" in its lack of pretension to be a systematic and complete exposition, and in being addressed to a general rather than a specialized audience; as a consequence, the essay discusses its subject in nontechnical fashion, and often with a liberal use of such devices as anecdote, striking illustration, and humor to augment its appeal.

A useful distinction is that between the formal and informal essay. The **formal essay** is relatively impersonal: the author writes as an authority, or at least as highly knowledgeable, and expounds the subject in an orderly way. Examples will be found among the serious articles on current topics and issues in any of the magazines addressed to a thoughtful audience—*Harper's, Commentary, Scientific American,* and so on. In the **informal essay** (or "familiar" or "personal essay"), the author assumes a tone of intimacy with his audience, tends to deal with everyday things rather than with public affairs or specialized topics, and writes in a relaxed, self-revelatory, and often whimsical fashion. Accessible modern examples are to be found in *The New Yorker.*

The Greeks Theophrastus and Plutarch and the Romans Cicero and Seneca wrote essays long before the genre was given its standard name by Montaigne's great French *Essais* in 1580. The title signifies "attempts," and was meant to indicate the tentative and unsystematic nature of Montaigne's discussions, in contrast to formal and technical treatises on the same subjects. Francis Bacon, late in the sixteenth century, inaugurated the English use of the term in his own *Essays;* most of his essays are short comments with titles such as "Of Truth," "Of Adversity," "Of Marriage and the Single Life." Alexander Pope adopted the term for his expository compositions in verse, the *Essay on Criticism* (1711) and the *Essay on Man* (1733), but the verse essay has had few exponents after the eighteenth century. In the early eighteenth century Addison and Steele's *Tatler* and *Spectator,* with their many successors, gave to the prose essay its standard modern vehicle, the literary periodical (earlier essays had been published in books). In the early nineteenth century the founding of new types of magazines, and their steady proliferation, gave great impetus to the writing of essays and made them a major department of literature. This was the age when Hazlitt, De Quincey, and Charles Lamb brought the essay—and especially the personal essay—to a level that has remained unsurpassed. Major American essayists in the nineteenth century include Washington Irving, Ralph Waldo Emerson, James Russell Lowell, and Mark Twain. In our own time the many periodicals pour out scores of essays every week. Most of them are formal in type; George Orwell, E. M. Forster, James Thurber, and E. B. White, however, are notable recent practitioners of the informal essay.

Hugh Walker, *The English Essay and Essayists* (1915); W. F. Bryan and R. S. Crane, eds., *The English Familiar Essay* (1916), has an excellent introduction to this literary form.

Euphemism (from the Greek "to speak well") is the use, in place of the blunt term for something disagreeable, terrifying, or offensive, of a term that is vaguer, more roundabout, or less colloquial. Euphemisms are frequently used in reference to death ("to pass away," "mortician"); in irreligious references to God (the Elizabethan "Zounds!" for "God's wounds!" and the American "Gosh darn!" for "God damn!"); to soften moral opprobrium ("rip off" for "rob," "get high" for "use a drug"); and in discreet allusions to parts of the body, the bodily functions, and sex ("comfort station," the Victorian use of "limb" for leg and "friend" for a sexual partner, and the traditional, but now diminishing, use in mixed company, and in literature, of Latinate terms in place of the Anglo-Saxon four-letter words). On sexual euphemisms see Eric Partridge, *Shakespeare's Bawdy* (1960).

Euphony and Cacophony. **Euphony** is a term applied to language which seems to the ear to be smooth, pleasant, and musical, as in Keats's lines from *The Eve of St. Agnes* (1820),

> And lucent syrops, tinct with cinnamon;
> Manna and dates, in argosy transferred
> From Fez; and spicèd dainties, every one,
> From silken Samarcand to cedar'd Lebanon.

Analysis of the passage, however, will show that what strikes us as a purely auditory agreeableness is due more to the meaning of the words, and to the ease of articulating the sound combinations, than to the inherent melodiousness of the speech sounds. The American critic John Crowe Ransom demonstrated this fact by altering Tennyson's euphonious "The murmur of innumerable bees" to "The murder of innumerable beeves"; the euphony is destroyed, not by the change in two of the speech sounds, but by the change in reference.

Similarly, in **cacophony**, or **dissonance**—language which seems harsh, rough, and unmusical—the discordancy is the aggregate effect of difficulty in pronunciation, of sense, and of sound. Cacophony may be inadvertent, through a lapse in the writer's attention or skill, as in the unfortunate line of Arnold's "Dover Beach" (1867) "Lay like the folds of a bright girdle furled." But cacophony may also be deliberate and functional: for humor, as in Browning's "Pied Piper" (1842),

> Rats!
> They fought the dogs and killed the cats . . .
> Split open the kegs of salted sprats,
> Made nests inside men's Sunday hats;

or else for other effects, as in Hardy's attempt, in "In Tenebris I," to mimic, as well as describe, dogged endurance, by the difficulty of articulating the transition from one stressed monosyllable to the next:

> I shall not lose old strength
> In the lone frost's black length.
> Strength long since fled!

For other sound effects see *alliteration* and *onomatopoeia;* and refer to G. R. Stewart, *The Technique of English Verse* (1930), and Northrop Frye, ed., *Sound and Poetry* (1957).

Euphuism was a conspicuously formal and elaborate prose style which had a vogue in the 1580s. It takes its name from the moralistic prose romance *Euphues: The Anatomy of Wit,* which John Lyly wrote in 1578. In the dialogues of this work and of *Euphues and His England* (1580), as well as in his stage comedies, Lyly exaggerated and used persistently a kind of prose which other writers had developed earlier. The style is sententious (that is, full of moral maxims), relies constantly on syntactical *balance* and *antithesis,* reinforces the structural parallels by heavy and elaborate patterns of *alliteration* and *assonance,* exploits the *rhetorical question,* and is addicted to long similes and learned allusions which are often drawn from mythology and the habits of legendary animals. Here is a brief example from *Euphues;* the character Philautus is speaking:

> I see now that as the fish *Scholopidus* in the flood Araris at the waxing of the Moon is as white as the driven snow, and at the waning as black as the burnt coal, so Eu-

phues, which at the first encreasing of our familiarity, was very zealous, is now at the last cast become most faithless.

Shakespeare good-humoredly *parodied* this self-consciously elegant style in *Love's Labour's Lost* and other plays, but he, like other authors of the day, profited from Lyly's explorations of the formal and rhetorical possibilities of English prose.

See *style;* also Jonas A. Barish, "The Prose Style of John Lyly," *English Literary History,* 23 (1956), and G. K. Hunter, *John Lyly* (1962).

Expressionism was a German movement in literature and the other arts (especially the visual arts) which was at its height between 1910 and 1925—that is, in the period just before, during, and after World War I. Its chief precursors were artists and writers who had in various ways departed from realistic depictions of life and the world, by expressing in their art visionary or powerfully emotional states of mind. Among these precursors, in painting, were Van Gogh, Paul Gauguin, and the Norwegian Edvard Munch—Munch's lithograph "The Cry" (1894) depicting, against a bleak background, a tense figure with distorted face uttering a scream of pure horror, is often taken to epitomize what became the expressionist mode. Prominent among the literary precursors of the movement in the nineteenth century were the poets Baudelaire and Rimbaud, the novelist Dostoevsky, the philosopher Nietzsche, and above all the Swedish dramatist August Strindberg.

Expressionism itself was never a concerted or well-defined movement. It can be said, however, that its central feature is a radical revolt against the artistic and literary tradition of *realism,* both in subject matter and in style. The expressionist artist or writer undertakes to express a personal vision—usually a profoundly troubled or intensely emotional vision—of human life and human society. This is done by violent exaggeration and distortion of what, according to the norms of artistic realism, are objective features of the outer world, and by embodying violent extremes of mood and feeling. Often the work implies that what is depicted or described represents a modern individual standing alone and afraid in an industrial, technological, and urban society which is disintegrating into chaos. Expressionists who were radical in their politics also projected utopian views of a coming type of humanity belonging to a human community in a regenerate world.

Expressionist painters tended to use jagged lines to depict contorted objects and forms, as well as to substitute expressive, often lurid colors, for natural hues; among these painters were Emil Nolde, Franz Marc, Oskar Kokoschka, and, for a time, Wassily Kandinsky. Expressionist poets (including the Germans Gottfried Benn and Georg Trakl) departed from standard meter, syntax, and poetic structure to organize their works around symbolic images. Expressionist writers of prose narratives (most eminently, Franz Kafka) abandoned standard modes of characterization and plot for symbolic figures involved in a dream world of nightmarish events.

Drama was a prominent and widely influential form of expressionist writing. Among the better-known playwrights were Georg Kaiser *(Gas, From Morn to Midnight),* Ernst Toller *(Mass Man),* and the early Bertolt Brecht. Expressionist dramatists tended to represent anonymous human types instead of individualized characters, to replace plot by episodic rendering of intense and rapidly oscillating emotional states, often to fragment the dialogue into exclamatory and seemingly incoherent sentences or phrases, and to employ masks and abstract or lopsided and sprawling stage sets. The producer Max Reinhardt, although not himself in the movement, directed a number of plays by Strindberg and by German expressionists; in them he inaugurated such modern devices as the revolving stage and special effects in lighting and sound. This mode of German drama had an important influence on the American theater. Eugene O'Neill's *The Emperor Jones* (1920) projected, in a sequence of symbolic episodes, the individual and racial memories of a terrified modern Black; and Elmer Rice's *The Adding Machine* (1923) used nonrealistic means to represent a mechanical, sterile, and frightening world as experienced by Mr. Zero, a tiny and helpless cog in the impersonal system of big business. The flexible possibility of the medium made the motion picture an important vehicle of German expressionism. Robert Wiene's early expressionist film *The Cabinet of Dr. Caligari* (1920)—representing, in ominously distorted settings, the machinations of the satanic head of an insane asylum—as well as Friedrich Murnau's *Nosferatu* (1922) and Fritz Lang's *Metropolis* (1926) are often shown in current revivals of films.

Expressionism had begun to flag by 1925 and was finally suppressed in Germany by the Nazis in the early 1930s, but it has continued to exert influence on English and American, as well as European, art and literature. We recognize its effects, direct or indirect, on the writing and staging of such plays as Thornton Wilder's *The Skin of Our Teeth* and Arthur Miller's *Death of a Salesman,* as well as on the theater of the *absurd;* on the poetry of Allen Ginsberg and other *Beat* writers; on the prose fiction of Samuel Beckett and Thomas Pynchon; and on a number of films, manifesting the distorted perceptions and fantasies of disturbed characters, by the directors Ingmar Bergman, Federico Fellini, and Michelangelo Antonioni.

Richard Samuel and R. H. Thomas, *Expressionism in German Life, Literature and the Theater, 1910–1924* (1939); Walter H. Sokel, *The Writer in Extremis: Expressionism in Twentieth-Century German Literature* (1959); John Willett, *Expressionism* (1970). On the expressionist cinema: Siegfried Kracauer, *From Caligari to Hitler: A Psychological History of the German Film* (1947); Lotte Eisner, *The Haunted Screen: Expressionism in the German Cinema and the Influence of Max Reinhardt* (1969).

Fabliau. The medieval fabliau was a short comic or satiric tale in verse dealing realistically with middle-class or lower-class characters and delighting in the ribald and the obscene; its favorite theme is the cuckolding of a stupid husband. (Professor Douglas Bush neatly characterized the type as "a short story broader than it is long.") The fabliau flourished in France in the twelfth and thirteenth centuries and became popular in England during the fourteenth century.

Chaucer, who wrote one of the greatest serious short stories in verse, the account of Death and the rioters in "The Pardoner's Tale," also wrote one of the best fabliaux, the hilarious "Miller's Tale."

See Joseph Bédier, *Les Fabliaux* (5th ed., 1928); *Fabliaux: Ribald Tales from the Old French*, transl. Robert Hellman and Richard O'Gorman (1976).

Fancy and Imagination. The distinction between fancy and imagination was a key element in Coleridge's theory of poetry, as well as in his general theory of the mental processes. In earlier discussions of literature, "fancy" and "imagination" had for the most part been used synonymously to denote a faculty of the mind which is distinguished from "reason" and "judgment," and which receives "images" from the senses and reorders them into new combinations. In the thirteenth chapter of *Biographia Literaria* (1817), Coleridge attributes this reordering function to the lower-order faculty he calls **fancy:** "Fancy . . . has no other counters to play with, but fixities and definites. The Fancy is indeed no other than a mode of Memory emancipated from the order of time and space." To Coleridge, that is, the fancy is a mechanical process which receives the elementary images—the "fixities and definities" which come to it ready-made from the senses—and, without altering the parts, reassembles them into a different spatial and temporal order from that in which they were originally perceived. The **imagination** operative in producing a higher order of poetry, however,

> dissolves, diffuses, dissipates, in order to re-create; or where this process is rendered impossible, yet still at all events it struggles to idealize and unify. It is essentially *vital*, even as all objects (*as* objects) are essentially fixed and dead.

The imagination, that is, is able to "create" rather than merely reassemble, by dissolving the fixities and definites—the mental pictures, or images, received from the senses—and unifying them into a new whole. And while the fancy is merely mechanical, the imagination is "vital": it is an organic faculty which operates not like a sorting machine, but like a living and growing plant. As Coleridge says elsewhere, the imagination "generates and produces a form of its own," while its rules are "the very powers of growth and production." And in the fourteenth chapter of the *Biographia* Coleridge adds his famous statement that the "synthetic" power which is the "imagination . . . reveals itself in the balance or reconciliation of opposite or discordant qualities: of sameness, with difference; of the general, with the concrete; the idea, with the image. . . ." The faculty of imagination, in other words, assimilates and synthesizes the most disparate elements into an organic whole—that is, a newly generated unity, constituted by a living interdependence of parts whose identity cannot survive their removal from the whole. (See *organic form.*)

Most critics after Coleridge who distinguished fancy from imagination tended to make fancy simply the faculty that produces a lesser, lighter, or humorous kind of poetry, and to make imagination the faculty that produces a higher, more serious, and more passionate poetry. And the concept of "imagination" itself is as various as the modes of psychology that critics have adopted (associationist, Gestalt, *Freudian, Jungian*), while its processes vary according to the way in which a critic conceives of the essential nature of a poem (as essentially realistic or essentially visionary, as "object" or as "myth," as "pure poetry" or as a work designed to produce effects on an audience).

See I. A. Richards, *Coleridge on Imagination* (1934); M. H. Abrams, *The Mirror and the Lamp* (1953), Chap. 7; Richard H. Fogle, *The Idea of Coleridge's Criticism* (1962).

Fiction and Narratology. **Fiction** is a term often used inclusively for any literary **narrative,** whether in prose or verse, which is feigned or invented, and does not purport to be historical truth. In most present-day discussion, however, fiction denotes primarily prose narratives (the *novel* and *short story*), and is sometimes used simply as a synonym for the novel. Literary forms in which fiction is to a prominent degree based on fact are often denoted by compound names such as "fictional biography," the *historical novel,* and the *nonfiction novel.*

In recent years there has been great critical interest in the theory, language, and techniques of narrative fiction, denominated "the poetics of fiction" or (in a term coming into widespread use) **narratology.** On the one side, this theory is indebted to traditional treatments of fictional narratives, from Aristotle's *Poetics* to Wayne Booth's *The Rhetoric of Fiction* (1961); on the other, it incorporates recent developments in Continental *formalism,* and especially of French structuralism (see under *structuralist criticism*) and of *semiotics.* A basic interest of narratology is in the way that narrative "discourse" fashions a "story" (a simple sequence of events in time) into the organized form of a "plot." Narratology may include in its scope a systematic treatment of matters treated in other discussions in this book (see *plot, characterization, point of view, style*); it does so, however, in the endeavor to formulate a "morphology" or "grammar" of storytelling as an ascending order of levels in the organization of narrative formulae, and to establish the system of shared "rules" that govern all possible forms of narration. See Seymour Chatman, *Story and Discourse: Narrative Structure in Fiction and Film* (1978); Gérard Genette, *Narrative Discourse* (1980), and *Figures of Literary Discourse* (1982); and Paul Ricoeur, *Time and Narrative,* vols. 1 and 2, transl. Kathleen McLaughlin and David Pellauer (1984).

Both philosophers and literary critics have concerned themselves with the logical analysis of the types of sentences which constitute a fictional text, and especially with the question of their "truth-value"—that is, whether, and in just what way, they are subject to the criterion of truth or falsity. Some thinkers have asserted that "fictional sentences"—which seem to refer to nonexistent persons, places, and events—are to be taken as references to a special world, "created" by the author, which is analogous to the real world, but contains its own setting, beings, and mode of coherence. (See M. H. Abrams, *The Mirror and the Lamp,* 1953, pp. 272–85, "The Poem as Heterocosm"; James Phelan, *Worlds from Words: A Theory of Language in Fiction,* 1981.) Others, especially I. A. Richards, have held that fiction is a form of **emotive language,** composed of **pseudostatements;** and that whereas a statement in "referential language" is "justified by its truth, i.e. its correspondence . . . with the fact to which it points," a pseudostatement "is justified entirely by its effect in releasing or organizing our attitudes" (I. A. Richards, *Science and Poetry*, 1926). Most current theorists, however, present an elaborated logical version of what Sir Philip Sidney long ago proposed in his *Apology for Poetry* (published 1595), that a poet "nothing affirmes, therefore never lyeth. For, as I take it, to lye is to affirm that to be true which is false." Current versions of this view hold that fictive sentences are meaningful according to the rules of ordinary, nonfictional discourse, but that, in accordance with conventions implicitly shared by the author and reader of a work of fiction, they are not put forward as assertions of fact, and therefore are not subject to the criterion of truth or falsity as these apply to sentences in nonfictional discourse. See, e.g., Margaret MacDonald, "The Language of Fiction" (1954), reprinted in W. E. Kennick, ed., *Art and Philosophy* (rev., 1979).

By *speech act theorists*, a related view takes the form that a writer of fiction only "pretends" to make assertions, or "imitates" the making of assertions, and so suspends the "normal illocutionary commitment" of the speaker or writer of such utterances to the claim that what he asserts is true. See, e.g., John R. Searle, "The Logical Status of Fictional Discourse," *New Literary History*, 6 (1974–75). We find in a number of other theorists the attempt to extend the concept of "fictive utterances" to include all the genres of literature—poems, narratives, dramas, as well as novels; all these forms, it is proposed, are imitations, or fictive representations, of some type of "natural" discourse. A novel, for example, is itself a fictive utterance, in that it "*represents* the verbal action of a man [i.e., the narrator] reporting, describing, and referring." See Barbara Herrnstein Smith, "Poetry as Fiction," in *Margins of Discourse* (1978), and Richard Ohmann, "Speech Acts and the Definition of Literature," *Philosophy and Rhetoric*, 4 (1971). For a criticism of this widely held view, see Martha A. Woodmansee, "Speech Act Theory and the Perpetuation of the Dogma of Literary Autonomy," *Centrum*, 6 (1980).

Most modern theorists, whatever their persuasion, make an important distinction between the scenes, persons, events, and dialogue that an authoritative narrator reports or describes and generalizations inserted by the narrator about the world, human life, or the human situation; the central, or controlling, generalizations of the latter sort are said to be the *theme* or **thesis** of a work. These assertions by the narrator may be explicit (for example, Thomas Hardy's statement at the end of *Tess of the D'Urbervilles*, "The President of the immortals had had his sport with Tess"; or Tolstoy's philosophy of history at the end of *War and Peace*). Many such assertions, however, are said to be merely "implied," "suggested," or "inferrable" from the narrator's choice and control of the characters and plot of the narrative itself. It is often claimed that such generalizations by the narrator within a fictional work, whether expressed or implied, function as assertions that claim truth, and that they therefore serve to relate the fictional narrative to the factual and moral world of actual human experience. See John Hospers, "Implied Truths in Literature" (1960), reprinted in W. E. Kennick, ed., *Art and Philosophy* (rev., 1979).

A much-discussed topic, related to the question of an author's assertions and truth claims, is that of the role of the **beliefs** of the reader. The problem raised is the extent to which a reader's moral, religious, and social convictions, as they coincide with or diverge from those explicitly or implicitly put forth in a work, determine the interpretation, imaginative acceptability, and evaluation of that work by the reader. For the history and discussions of this problem in literary criticism, see William Joseph Rooney, *The Problem of "Poetry and Belief" in Contemporary Criticism* (1949); M. H. Abrams, editor and contributor, *Literature and Belief* (1957); Walter Benn Michaels, "Saving the Text: Reference and Belief," *Modern Language Notes*, 93 (1978).

A useful review of theories concerning the relevance of the criterion of truth to fiction is Monroe C. Beardsley's *Aesthetics: Problems in the Philosophy of Criticism* (1958), pp. 409–19. For a defense of the claim for propositional truth in poetry see Gerald Graff, *Poetic Statement and Critical Dogma* (1970), Chap. 6.

Figurative Language is a departure from what speakers of a particular language apprehend to be the standard meaning of words, or the standard order of words, in order to achieve some special meaning or effect. Such **figures** were long described as primarily "ornaments" of language, but they are integral to the functioning of language, and in fact indispensable not only to poetry, but to all modes of discourse.

Since classical times—the fullest and most influential treatment is the Roman Quintilian's *Institutes of Oratory* (first century), Books VIII and IX—figurative language has often been divided into two classes: (1) "Figures of thought," or **tropes** (meaning "turns," "conversions"), in which words or phrases are used in a way that effects a conspicuous change in what we take to be their standard meaning. The standard meaning, as opposed to its tropic meaning, is called the **literal meaning.** (For a philosophical analysis of standard, or literal, meaning, see John R. Searle, *Expression and Meaning*, 1979, Chap. 5, and "The Background of Meaning," in *Speech Act Theory and Pragmatics*, ed. John R. Searle, 1980.) (2) "Figures of speech," or "rhetorical figures," or **schemes** (from the Greek word for "form"), in which the departure from standard usage is not, primarily, in the meaning but in the order of the words. This distinction is not a sharp one, nor do all critics agree in its application. For convenience, however, the most common tropes are treated here, and the most common figures of speech are collected in the article *rhetorical figures.* A number of other deviations from the standard significance or order of words, treated in individual articles of the *Glossary* but often classified as tropes, are listed at the end of this essay.

In a **simile,** a comparison between two distinctly different things is indicated by the word "like" or "as." A simple example is Burns's "O my love's like a red, red rose." The following simile from Wordsworth's "Ode: Intimations of Immortality" differs from Burns's, in that it specifies the features in which custom is similar to frost ("heavy") and to life ("deep"):

And custom lie upon thee with a weight
Heavy as frost, and deep almost as life.

See also *epic similes*.

In a **metaphor,** a word or expression which in literal usage denotes one kind of thing or action is applied to a distinctly different kind of thing or action, without asserting a comparison. For example, if Burns had said "O my love is a red, red rose" he would have uttered, technically speaking, a metaphor instead of a simile. Here is a more complex metaphor, from the contemporary poet Stephen Spender:

Eye, gazelle, delicate wanderer,
Drinker of horizon's fluid line.*

For the distinction between metaphor and symbol, see *symbol*.

It should be noted that in these examples we can distinguish two elements, the metaphorical term, and its metaphorical signification or subject. In a widely adopted usage, I. A. Richards introduced the name **tenor** for the subject that the metaphor is applied to ("my love" in the altered line from Burns, and "eye" in Spender's lines), and the name **vehicle** for the metaphorical term itself ("rose" in Burns, and the three words "gazelle," "wanderer," and "drinker" in Spender). In an **implicit metaphor,** the tenor is not itself specified, but only implied; thus, if one were to say, in commenting about a death, "That reed was too frail to survive the storm of its sorrows," the situational and verbal context of the term "reed" indicates that it is the vehicle for an unspecified tenor, a human being, while "storm" is the vehicle for an aspect of a specified tenor, "sorrows." Those aspects, properties, or associations of a vehicle which, in a given context, apply to a tenor (specified or implicit) are called by Richards the **grounds** of a metaphor. (See I. A. Richards, *Philosophy of Rhetoric,* 1936, Chaps. 5–6.)

All the metaphoric terms, or vehicles, cited so far have been nouns, but other parts of speech may also be used metaphorically. The metaphoric use of a verb occurs in Shakespeare's *Merchant of Venice,* V. i. 54, "How sweet the moonlight *sleeps* upon this bank"; and the metaphoric use of an adjective occurs in Andrew Marvell's "The Garden" (1681):

Annihilating all that's made
To a *green* thought in a green shade.

Theories or explanations of metaphor fall roughly into two large classes. The most common, introduced by Aristotle in the fourth century B.C., maintains that a metaphor involves an implicit comparison or similarity between a literal object and a metaphoric object; in this view, a metaphor is an elliptical

*From "Not palaces, an era's crown." Reprinted from *Collected Poems, 1928–1953,* by Stephen Spender, by permission of Random House, Inc., and Faber and Faber Ltd.

form of simile. I. A. Richards proposed in 1936 the alternative view that the meaning of a metaphor is the product of an "interaction" between the meanings of the vehicle and the tenor of a metaphor. In an influential essay, the thesis that a metaphor involves an interaction between elements that involve not only individual words, but fields of associations, has been refined and expanded by the philosopher Max Black. Recently John Searle has rejected both the comparison and interaction views as inadequate, on the grounds that, at best, they serve to explain, and that only in part, how some metaphors get to be produced and to be understood. Searle, in consonance with his overall *speech act theory,* proposes that to explain metaphor, we must distinguish between "word, or sentence-meaning" (the literal meaning of the spoken or written expression) and "utterance meaning" (the metaphorical meaning that a speaker or writer uses the literal word or sentence to express). He goes on to present a set of principles, shared by the speaker and interpreter, to explain how we are able both to produce and to understand metaphorical utterances, as well as to clarify the variety of the relations that may obtain between a literal sentence meaning and the metaphorical utterance meaning of diverse figurative expressions. (For Black and Searle, see the list of readings below.)

A **mixed metaphor** combines two or more diverse metaphoric vehicles. When used inadvertently, without sensitivity to the possible incongruity of the vehicles, the effect can be ludicrous: "Girding up his loins, the chairman plowed through the mountainous agenda." Densely figurative poets such as Shakespeare, however, often mix metaphors in a functional way. Examples are Hamlet's expression of his troubled mind in his *soliloquy* (III. i. 59–60), "to take arms against a sea of troubles,/And by opposing end them," and the involvement of metaphor within metaphor in Shakespeare's Sonnet 65:

> O, how shall summer's honey breath hold out
> Against the wrackful siege of battering days?

A **dead metaphor** is one which, like "the leg of a table" or "the heart of the matter," has become so common that we have ceased to be aware of the discrepancy between vehicle and tenor. A dead metaphor, however, is only moribund, and can readily be brought back to life. Someone asked Groucho Marx, "Are you a man or a mouse?" He answered, "Throw me a piece of cheese and you'll find out." The history of language shows that most words that we now take to be literal were, in the distant past, metaphors.

Some tropes, sometimes classified as diverse species of metaphor, are more frequently given names of their own:

In **metonymy** (Greek for "a change of name"), the literal term for one thing is applied to another with which it has become closely associated. Thus "the crown" or "the scepter" can stand for a king and "the turf" for horse-racing; "Milton" can signify the writings of Milton ("I have read all of Milton"); and typical attire can signify the male and female sexes: "doublet and hose ought to show itself courageous to petticoat" (Shakespeare, *As You Like It,* II. iv. 6). (For the influential distinction by the linguist Roman Jakobson between the metaphoric, or "vertical," and the metonymic, or "horizontal," dimension and its application to many aspects of language, see under *linguistics in literary criticism.*)

In **synecdoche** (Greek for "taking together"), a part of something is used to signify the whole, or (more rarely) the whole is used to signify a part. We use the term "ten *hands*" for ten workmen, and Milton refers to the corrupt clergy in "Lycidas" as "blind *mouths.*"

Another figure related to metaphor is **personification,** or in the Greek term, **prosopopeia,** in which either an inanimate object or an abstract concept is spoken of as though it were endowed with life or with human attributes or feelings (compare *pathetic fallacy*). Milton wrote in *Paradise Lost* (IX, 1002–3), as Adam bit into the fatal apple,

> Sky lowered, and muttering thunder, some sad drops
> Wept at completing of the mortal sin.

The second stanza of Keats's "To Autumn" finely personifies the season, autumn, as a woman carrying on the rural chores of that time of year. The personification of abstract terms was standard in eighteenth-century *poetic diction,* where it sometimes became stereotyped. Coleridge cited an eighteenth-century ode celebrating the invention of inoculation against smallpox which began with this *apostrophe* to the personified subject of the poem:

> Inoculation! heavenly Maid, descend!

See Steven Knapp, *Personification and the Sublime* (1986).

A **kenning** is a descriptive phrase used in place of the ordinary name for a thing in *Beowulf* and other Old English poems; it is a type of *periphrasis* often used as a stereotyped expression in the highly formulaic poetry of the various old Germanic tongues. Some kennings are instances of *metonymy* ("the whale road" for the sea, and "the ring-giver" for a king); others of *synecdoche* ("the ringed prow" for a ship); still others describe salient or picturesque features of the object identified ("foamy-necked floater" for a ship under sail, "storm of swords" for a battle).

Other deviations from the standard use of words, sometimes classified as tropes, are treated elsewhere in this book: *aporia, conceit, epic similes, hyperbole, irony, litotes, paradox, periphrasis, pun, understatement.* In recent decades, especially in the *New Criticism, Russian formalism, deconstruction,* and Harold Bloom's theory of the *anxiety of influence,* there has been a strong interest in the nature and function of figurative language, which was once thought to be largely the province of rhetorical classifiers. Metaphor above all has become a focus of attention, by professional philosophers as well as by linguists and literary critics.

A clear summary of the standard classification of figures is Edward P. J. Corbett, *Classical Rhetoric for the Modern Student* (rev., 1971). Sister Miriam Joseph's *Shakespeare's Use of the Arts of Language* (1947) treats the conventional analysis of figures in the Renaissance. René Wellek and Austin Warren, in

Theory of Literature (rev., 1970), summarize, with bibliography, diverse treatments of figurative language; and Jonathan Culler, in *Structuralist Poetics* (1975) and *The Pursuit of Signs* (1981), discusses more recent developments. Influential philosophical analyses of metaphor, discussed above, are Max Black, "Metaphor," in *Models and Metaphor* (1962), and "More About Metaphor," in *Metaphor and Thought,* ed. Edward Ortney (1979); John R. Searle, *Expression and Meaning* (1979), Chap. 4, "Metaphor"; see also Paul Ricoeur, *The Rule of Metaphor* (1977); and Mark Johnson, ed., *Philosophical Perspectives on Metaphor* (1981). Sheldon Sacks, ed., *On Metaphor* (1979), includes recent essays by Black, Ricoeur, and other philosophers, as well as by literary critics. On the role of radical metaphors in philosophical systems, see Stephen C. Pepper, *World Hypotheses* (1942); and on constitutive metaphors in theories of criticism, M. H. Abrams, *The Mirror and the Lamp* (1953). A comprehensive bibliography of discussions of this trope up to the time of its publication is Warren A. Shibles, *Metaphor: An Annotated Bibliography and History* (1971).

Folklore, since the mid-nineteenth century, has been the collective name applied to verbal materials and social rituals that have been handed down solely, or at least primarily, by word of mouth and by example, rather than in written form. Folklore developed and continues to flourish most in communities where few if any people can read or write. It includes, among other things, legends, superstitions, songs, tales, proverbs, riddles, spells, and nursery rhymes; pseudoscientific lore about the weather, plants, and animals; customary activities at births, marriages, and deaths; and traditional dances and forms of drama which are performed on holidays or at communal gatherings. Elements of folklore have at all times entered into sophisticated written literature. For example, the choice among the three caskets in Shakespeare's *Merchant of Venice* (II. ix) and the superstition about a maiden's dream which is central to Keats's *Eve of St. Agnes* (1820) are both derived from folklore.

The following forms of folklore have been of special importance for written literature:

Folk drama originated in primitive rites of song and dance, especially in connection with agricultural activities, which centered on vegetational deities and goddesses of fertility. Some scholars maintain that Greek *tragedy* developed from such rites celebrating the life, death, and rebirth of the vegetational god Dionysus. Folk dramas survive in England in such forms as the St. George play and the **mummers' play** (a "mummer" is a masked actor). Thomas Hardy's *The Return of the Native* (Book II, Chap. 5) describes the performance of a mummers' play, and a form of this drama is still performed in America in the Kentucky mountains. See Edmund K. Chambers, *The English Folk-Play* (1933).

Folk songs include love songs, Christmas carols, work songs, sea chanties, religious songs, drinking songs, children's game-songs, and many other types of lyric, in addition to the narrative song, or traditional *ballad.* All forms of folk song have been assiduously collected since the late eighteenth century, and have inspired many imitations by major writers of lyric poetry. Robert Burns collected and edited Scottish folk songs, restored or rewrote them, and imitated them in his own songs. His "A Red, Red Rose" and "Auld Lang Syne," for example, both derive from one or more folk songs, and his "Green Grow the Rashes, O" is a tidied-up version of a bawdy folk song. See J. C. Dick, *The Songs of Robert Burns* (1903); Cecil J. Sharp, *Folk Songs of England* (5 vols.; 1908–12); and Alan Lomax, *The Folk Songs of North America* (1960).

The **folktale,** strictly defined, is a short narrative in prose, of unknown authorship, which has been transmitted orally. The term, however, is often extended to include stories by a known author (such as Robert Southey's story *The Three Bears* and Parson Mason L. Weems's story of George Washington and the cherry tree) which, after they were printed, have been adopted and transmitted orally. Folktales are found among peoples all over the world. They include *myths, fables,* tales of heroes (whether historical like Johnny Appleseed, or legendary like Paul Bunyan), and fairy tales. Many so-called fairy tales (the German word **Märchen** is frequently used for this type of folktale) are not stories of fairies, but of various kinds of marvels; examples are "Snow White" and "Jack and the Beanstalk." Another type of folktale, the set "joke," or comic (often bawdy) *anecdote,* is the most abundant and persistent of all; new jokes, or new versions of very old jokes, continue to be a staple of contemporary conversation, wherever people congregate in a relaxed mood.

The same, or closely similar, oral stories have turned up in Europe, the Orient, and even in Africa, and have been embodied in the narratives of many writers. Chaucer's *Canterbury Tales* includes a number of folktales; "The Pardoner's Tale" of Death and the three rioters, for example, was Oriental in its origin. See Benjamin A. Botkin, *A Treasury of American Folklore* (1944), and Vladimir Propp, *Morphology of the Folktale* (1970). The standard catalogue of the recurrent *motifs* in folktales throughout the world is Stith Thompson's *Motif-Index of Folk-Literature* (1932–37).

Form and Structure. "Form" is one of the most frequently used—and variously interpreted—terms in literary criticism. It is often used merely to designate a literary *genre* or type ("the lyric form," "the short story form"), or for patterns of meter, lines, and rhymes ("the verse form," "the stanza form"). It is also, however—in a usage descended from the Latin "forma" as an equivalent to the Greek "idea"—the term for a central critical concept. In this application, the **form** of a work is its principle of organization; but critics analyze the nature of this principle in diverse ways. All agree that "form" is not simply a fixed container, like a bottle, into which the "content" or "subject matter" of a work is poured; but beyond this, the definition of form varies according to a critic's particular premises and orientation (see *criticism*).

Many *neoclassic* critics, for example, thought of the form of a work as a combination of its component parts, put together according to the principle of *decorum,* or mutual fittingness. In the early nineteenth century, Coleridge, following the lead of the German critic A. W. Schlegel, distinguished between **mechanic form,** which is a preexistent shape such as we impose on wet clay by a mold, and **organic form,** which, as Coleridge says, "is innate; it shapes as it develops itself from within, and the fullness of its development is one and the same with the perfection of its outward form." To Coleridge, in other words, as to other **organicists** in literary criticism, a good poem is like a growing plant which evolves, by an internal energy, into the organic unity which constitutes its achieved form. (See *fancy and imagination.*) Many *New Critics* of our own time use the word **structure** interchangeably with "form," and regard it as primarily an equilibrium, or an interaction, or an ironic and paradoxical tension, of diverse words and images in an organized totality of "meanings." And various exponents of *archetypal* theory regard the form of a literary work as one of a limited number of plot-shapes which it shares with myths, rituals, dreams, and other elemental and recurrent patterns of human experience. See also *structuralist criticism,* which conceives a literary structure on the model of the systematic structure of language.

In an influential critical mode, R. S. Crane, a leader of the **Chicago School** of criticism, has revived and developed the concept of form in Aristotle's *Poetics.* Crane distinguishes between "form" and "structure." The form of a literary work is (in the Greek term) the "dynamis," the particular "working" or "emotional 'power' " that the work is designed to effect, which functions as its "shaping principle." This formal principle controls and synthesizes the "structure" of a work—that is, the order, emphasis, and rendering of all its component materials and parts—into "a beautiful and effective whole of a determinate kind." See R. S. Crane, *The Languages of Criticism and the Structure of Poetry* (1953), Chaps. 1 and 4; also Wayne C. Booth, "Between Two Generations: The Heritage of the Chicago School," in *Profession 82* (Modern Language Association, 1982).

Refer to René Wellek, "Concepts of Form and Structure in Twentieth-Century Criticism," in *Concepts of Criticism* (1963).

Format of a Book. **Format** signifies the size, shape, and other physical features of a book. The printer begins with a large "sheet"; if the sheet is folded once so as to form two "leaves" of four pages, the book is a **folio** (the Latin word for "leaf"). When we refer to "the first Shakespeare folio," for example, we mean a volume published in 1623, the first edition of Shakespeare's collected plays, the leaves of which were made by a single folding of the printer's sheets. A sheet folded twice into four leaves makes a **quarto;** a sheet folded a third time into eight leaves makes an **octavo.** In a **duodecimo** volume, a sheet is folded so as to make twelve leaves. The more leaves into which a single sheet is divided, the smaller the leaf, so that these terms indicate the dimensions of a book, but only approximately, because the size of the full sheet varies, especially in modern printing. It can be said, however, that a folio is a very large book; a quarto is the next in size, with a leaf that is nearly square. The third in size, the octavo, is the most frequently used in modern printing.

As this book is open in front of you, the page on the right is called a **recto,** and the page on the left is called a **verso.**

The **colophon** (Greek for "summit") in older books was a note at the end stating such facts as the title, author, printer, and date of issue. In modern books the colophon is ordinarily in the front, on the title page. With reference to modern books, "colophon" has come to mean, usually, the publisher's emblem, such as a torch (Harper), an owl (Holt), or a ship (Viking).

The term **incunabula** (Latin for "swaddling clothes"; the singular is "incunabulum") signifies books published in the infancy of printing. The terminal date is 1500, about fifty years after the German printer Johann Gutenberg invented movable printing type.

The word **edition** now designates the total copies of a book that are printed from a single setting of type; the various "printings" or "reprints" of this edition—sometimes with a few minor changes in the text—may be spaced over a period of years. We now identify as a "new edition" a printing in which substantial changes have been made in the text. A book may be revised and reprinted in this way many times, hence the terms "second edition," "third edition," etc.

A **variorum edition** designates either (1) an edition of a work that lists all the textual variants in authors' manuscripts and in their revised editions; a recent example is *The Variorum Edition of the Poems of W. B. Yeats*, eds. Peter Allt and Russell K. Alspach (1957); or (2) an edition of a text that includes a selection of annotations and commentaries on the text by earlier editors and critics. *The New Variorum Shakespeare*, still in process, is a variorum edition in both senses of the word.

See also *textual criticism*. The classic work on bookmaking and printing is Ronald B. McKerrow, *An Introduction to Bibliography* (rev., 1965). Also, Fredson Bowers, *Principles of Bibliographical Description* (1949), and Philip Gaskell, *A New Introduction to Bibliography* (1972).

Free Verse, also known as "open form" verse, or by the French term **vers libre,** is printed in short lines instead of with the continuity of prose, and has a more controlled rhythmic pattern than ordinary prose; but it lacks the regular syllabic stress pattern, organized into recurrent feet, of traditional *meter*. Most free verse also has irregular line lengths and lacks rhyme. Within these broad confines, there are a great variety of measures labeled as "free verse." Something close to one modern form is to be found in the King James translation (reflecting the original Hebrew parallelism and cadences) of the Psalms and the Song of Solomon; in the nineteenth century, Blake and Matthew Arnold experimented with free measures; and Walt Whitman startled the literary world with his *Leaves of Grass* (1855) by using lines of variable length which depended for their rhythmic effect on cadenced units and on the repetition, balance, and variation of words, phrases, clauses, and lines, instead of on recurrent metric feet.

The French Symbolist poets toward the end of the nineteenth century, and American and English poets of this century, especially after World War I, began the current era of the intensive use of free verse. It has been employed by Rainer Maria Rilke, Jules Laforgue, T. S. Eliot (see, for example, "Ash Wednesday"), Ezra Pound, William Carlos Williams, and numberless other poets; it is now the most common type of versification, both in the oracular, and sometimes biblical, mode of Whitman and Allen Ginsberg, and in quieter, more conversational or more ironic forms. The writer of free verse surrenders the regular rhythmic power and songlike effects of traditional versification in order to exploit other, often subtle features. The opening section of a poem by E. E. Cummings will illustrate the kind of effects, in the suspensions within syntactic units and the increased management of pace, pause, and time, that become available when the verse is released from a recurrent beat and regular line, but is controlled instead by the variable positioning, spacing, and length of words, phrases, and lines:

*Chanson Innocente**

in Just-
spring when the world is mud-
luscious the little
lame balloonman

whistles far and wee

and eddieandbill come
running from marbles and
piracies and it's
spring

See *meter;* and refer to Percy Mansell Jones, *The Background of Modern French Poetry* (1951); Donald Wesling, "The Prosodies of Free Verse," in *Twentieth-Century Literature in Retrospect,* ed. Reuben A. Brower (1971); Paul Fussell, *Poetic Meter and Poetic Form* (rev., 1979); Charles O. Hartman, *Free Verse: An Essay on Prosody* (1980).

Genre, a French term, in literary criticism denotes a type or species of literature, or as we now often call it, a "literary form." The genres into which literary works have been classified are numerous, and the criteria used for such classifications have been highly variable. There has endured, however, since the Greek theorist Aristotle, the tendency to order the total literary domain into three overall classes: *lyric* (uttered throughout in the first person); *epic* or *narrative* (in which the narrator speaks in the first person, then lets his characters speak for themselves); and *drama* (in which the characters do all the talking). A similar tripartite scheme was emphasized and elaborated by German critics in the late eighteenth and early nineteenth centuries, was echoed by James Joyce's *Portrait of the Artist as a Young Man* (1916), Chap. 5, and is still reflected in the common division of college courses into poetry, novels, and drama. Within, or crisscrossing, this overarching division, critics since classic times have specified a great number of more limited genres. The most common names are still ancient ones such as *epic, tragedy, comedy, satire,* and *lyric,* plus some relative newcomers like *biography, essay,* and *novel.* A glance at the articles listed in the Index under *genre* will indicate the variable criteria for such specifications, and the numerous subspecies into which each of these has in turn been divided.

*From *Poems 1923–1954.* Copyright 1923, 1951 by E. E. Cummings. Reprinted by permission of Harcourt, Brace & World, Inc., and Granada Publishing Limited.

From the Renaissance through much of the eighteenth century the recognized genres—or poetic "kinds" as they were then called—were widely thought to be fixed literary types, somewhat like species in the biological order of nature; many *neoclassic* critics insisted that each kind must remain "pure" (there must, for example, be no "mixing" of tragedy and comedy), and also proposed *rules* which specified the subject matter, structure, style, and emotional effect proper to each kind. At that time the genres were also commonly ranked in a hierarchy (closely related to the ranking of social classes from royalty and the nobility to peasants—see *decorum*), ranging from epic and tragedy at the top to the pastoral, short lyric, epigram, and other minor types at the bottom. Shakespeare satirized the rigid genre critics of his era in Polonius' catalogue (*Hamlet,* II. ii) of types of drama: "tragedy, comedy, history, pastoral, pastoral-comical, historical-pastoral, tragical-historical, tragical-comical-historical-pastoral . . ."

In the course of the eighteenth century the emergence of new literary types—such as the novel, and the poem which combined natural description, philosophy, and narrative (James Thomson's *Seasons,* 1726–30)—helped weaken neoclassic confidence in the fixity and stability of genres. And in the latter eighteenth and early nineteenth century, the extraordinary rise in the prominence and prestige of the short lyric poem, and the concurrent shift in the basis of critical theory to an *expressive* orientation, effected a drastic alteration both in the conception and ranking of literary genres, in which the lyric tended to replace epic and tragedy as the most normative of poetic types. From the Romantic Period until the recent past, genres have frequently been conceived as convenient but rather arbitrary ways to classify literature; consonantly, the major criteria for evaluating literature, unlike those in neoclassicism, have not been specific to one genre but applicable to all literary types: "sincerity," "intensity," "organic unity," "high seriousness," "maturity," "ironically qualified attitudes," and so on. In the *New Criticism* of the mid-twentieth century, the concept of genre all but ceased to play more than a superficial role in critical analysis and evaluation. For the evolution into the nineteenth century of the concept and hierarchy of genres, see M. H. Abrams, *The Mirror and the Lamp* (1953), especially Chaps. 1, 4, and 6; on the use and revision of traditional genres in the Romantic Period, see Stuart Curran, *Poetic Form and British Romanticism* (1986).

Since 1950 or so, genre theory has been revived by some critical theorists, although on various new principles of classification. R. S. Crane and other *Chicago critics* have defended the utility for practical criticism of a redefined distinction among genres; see Crane, ed., *Critics and Criticism* (1952), pp. 12–24, 546–63. Northrop Frye has proposed an *archetypal* theory in which the four major genres (comedy, romance, tragedy, and satire) are held to represent permanent forms of human imagination, as embodied in the archetypal myths correlated with the four seasons (*Anatomy of Criticism,* 1957, pp. 158–239). Other current theorists conceive genre on the model of evolving social institutions, such as the state or church, rather than on the model of biological species. By *structuralist critics* such as Roland Barthes, a genre is conceived as a set of constitutive conventions and codes, altering from age to age, but shared by a kind of implicit contract between writer and reader. These sets of conventions are what make possible the writing of a particular work of literature, though the writer may play against, as well as with, the prevailing generic conventions. For the reader, such conventions function as a set of expectations, which may be controverted rather than satisfied, but enable the reader to make the work intelligible—that is, to *naturalize* it, by relating it to the world as this is defined and ordered by the prevailing culture.

See the brief review of genre theory in René Wellek and Austin Warren, *Theory of Literature* (rev., 1970), Chap. 17; the survey and critique of diverse theories in Paul Hernadi, *Beyond Genre: New Directions in Literary Classification* (1972); also Alastair Fowler, *Kinds of Literature* (1982).

Georgian is a term applied both to the reigns in England of the four successive Georges (1714–1830) and to the reign of George V (1910–36). **Georgian poets** usually designates a group of writers in the latter era who loomed large in four anthologies entitled *Georgian Poetry,* which were published by Edward Marsh between 1912 and 1922. Marsh favored writers we now tend to regard as minor poets such as Rupert Brooke, Walter de la Mare, Ralph Hodgson, W. H. Davies, and John Masefield, and the term "Georgian poetry" has come to connote verse which is mainly rural in subject matter, deft and delicate rather than bold and passionate in manner, and traditional rather than experimental in technique and form.

Gothic Novel. "Gothic" originally referred to the Goths, a Germanic tribe, then came to signify "germanic," then "medieval." "Gothic architecture" now denotes the medieval type of architecture, characterized by the use of the pointed arch and vault, which spread through western Europe between the twelfth and sixteenth centuries. The **Gothic novel,** or *Gothic romance,* is a type of fiction which was inaugurated by Horace Walpole's *The Castle of Otranto: A Gothic Story* (1764)—the subtitle refers to its setting in the middle ages—and which flourished through the early nineteenth century. Following Walpole's example, authors of such novels set their stories in the medieval period, often in a gloomy castle replete with dungeons, subterranean passages, and sliding panels, and made bountiful use of ghosts, mysterious disappearances, and other sensational and supernatural occurrences (which in some writers turned out to have natural explanations); their principal aim was to evoke chilling terror by exploiting mystery and a variety of horrors. Many of the novels are now enjoyed mainly as period pieces, but the best of them opened up to fiction the realm of the irrational and of the perverse impulses and the nightmarish terrors that lie beneath the orderly surface of the civilized mind. Examples of Gothic novels are William Beckford's *Vathek* (1786)—of which the setting is both medieval and Oriental and the subject both erotic and sadistic—Ann Radcliffe's *The Mysteries of Udolpho* (1794) and other Gothic romances, and Matthew Gregory Lewis' *The Monk* (1797). Jane Austen made good-humored fun of this vogue in *Northanger Abbey* (written 1798, published 1818).

The term "Gothic" has also been extended to a type of fiction which lacks the medieval setting but develops a brooding atmosphere of gloom and terror, represents events which are uncanny or macabre or melodramatically violent, and often deals with aberrant psychological states. In this extended sense the term "Gothic" has been applied to William Godwin's *Caleb Williams* (1794), Mary Shelley's *Frankenstein* (1817), and the novels and tales of terror by the German E. T. A. Hoffmann, and still more loosely, to such later works as Dickens' *Bleak House* (for example, Chaps. 11, 16, 47) and *Great Expectations* (the Miss Havisham episodes). America, especially southern America, has been fertile in Gothic fiction in this extended sense, from the novels of Charles Brockden Brown (1771–1810) and the terror tales of Edgar Allan Poe to William Faulkner's *Sanctuary* and *Absalom, Absalom!* and some of the fiction of Truman Capote. The fantasied realm of uncanny terror and cruelty opened by the Gothic novel is now exploited especially in the vogue of horror movies.

See Eino Railo, *The Haunted Castle* (1927); Montagu Summers, *The Gothic Quest* (1938); Lowry Nelson, Jr., "Night Thoughts on the Gothic Novel," *Yale Review,* 52 (1963), reprinted in part in *Pastoral and Romance,* ed. Eleanor T. Lincoln (1969); G. R. Thompson, ed., *The Gothic Imagination: Essays in Dark Romanticism* (1974); and William Patrick Day, *In the Circles of Fear and Desire* (1985). On "American Gothic"—and especially the "southern Gothic"—see Chester E. Eisinger, "The Gothic Spirit in the Forties," *Fiction in the Forties* (1963).

Graveyard Poets. A term applied to eighteenth-century poets who wrote meditative poems, usually set in a graveyard, on the theme of human mortality, in moods which range from elegiac pensiveness to profound gloom. Examples are Thomas Parnell's "Night-Piece on Death" (1721), Edward Young's long *Night Thoughts* (1742), and Robert Blair's "The Grave" (1743). The vogue resulted in one masterpiece, Gray's "Elegy Written in a Country Churchyard" (1751). The writing of graveyard poems spread from England to Continental literature in the second part of the century.

See Amy Louise Reed, *The Background of Gray's Elegy* (1924). Edith M. Sickels, in *The Gloomy Egoist* (1932), follows the evolution of graveyard and other melancholy verse through the Romantic Period. For the vogue in Europe, refer to Paul Von Tieghem, *Le Pré-romantisme* (1924–47), 3 vols.

Great Chain of Being. The concept is grounded in ideas about the nature of God, or the first cause, in the Greek philosophers Plato, Aristotle, and Plotinus, and was developed by later thinkers into an inclusive worldview. This worldview was already prevalent in the Renaissance, but was given further philosophical refinement by the German philosopher Gottfried Leibniz early in the eighteenth century, and was adopted by a number of thinkers of the *Enlightenment.* In its comprehensive eighteenth-century form the Great Chain of Being was based on the concept that the essential "excellence" of God consists in His unlimited creativity, an unstinting overflow into the fullest possible variety of beings. From this premise were deduced three consequences:

(1) Plenitude. The universe is absolutely full of every possible kind and variety of life; no conceivable species of being remains unrealized.

(2) Continuity. Each species differs from the next by the least possible degree, and so merges all but imperceptibly into its nearest related kinds.

(3) Gradation. The existing species exhibit a hierarchy of status, and so compose a great chain, or ladder, of being, extending from the lowliest condition of the merest existence up to God Himself. In this chain human beings occupy the middle position between the animal kinds and the angels, or purely spiritual beings.

On these concepts Leibniz and other thinkers also grounded what is called the doctrine of **philosophical optimism**—the view that this is "the best of all possible worlds," but only in the special sense that this is the best world that is logically possible of being brought into existence. Since God's bountifulness consists in His creation of the greatest possible variety of graded beings, that which to a limited human point of view seems to be deficiency and evil is recognized, from an overall cosmic viewpoint, to follow necessarily from the very excellence of the divine nature, which logically entails that there be a progressive set of limitations, hence increasing "evils," as we move farther down along the chain of being. As Voltaire ironically summarized this mode of optimism: "This is the best of all possible worlds, and everything in it is a necessary evil."

With his incomparable precision and economy, Alexander Pope compressed the concepts that make up the Great Chain of Being into a half-dozen or so *heroic couplets*, in Epistle I of his *Essay on Man* (1732–34):

> Of systems possible, if 'tis confessed
> That Wisdom Infinite must form the best,
> Where all must full or not coherent be,
> And all that rises rise in due degree;
> Then in the scale of reasoning life, 'tis plain,
> There must be, somewhere, such a rank as man. . . .
> See, through this air, this ocean, and this earth,
> All matter quick, and bursting into birth. . . .
> Vast Chain of Being! which from God began,
> Natures ethereal, human, angel, man,
> Beast, bird, fish, insect, what no eye can see,
> No glass can reach! from Infinite to thee,
> From thee to nothing. . . .

Philosophical optimism is one form of what is known as a **theodicy.** This term, compounded of the Greek words for "God" and "right," designates any system of thought which sets out to reconcile the perfect goodness of God with the existence of evil in the world. Milton's "great argument" in *Paradise Lost,* by which he undertakes to "assert Eternal Providence/And justify the ways of God to men" (I. 24–26) is another example of theodicy.

See A. O. Lovejoy's classic work in the history of ideas *The Great Chain of Being* (1936); also E. M. W. Tillyard, *The Elizabethan World Picture* (1943), Chaps. 4–5.

Heroic Couplet. Lines of iambic pentameter (see *meter*) which rhyme in pairs: *aa, bb,* and so on. The adjective was applied in the latter seventeenth century, because of the frequent use of such couplets in "heroic" (that is, *epic*) poems and plays. This verse form was introduced into English poetry by Geoffrey Chaucer (in *The Legend of Good Women* and most of *The Canterbury Tales*), and has been used constantly ever since. From the age of Dryden through that of Samuel Johnson, the heroic couplet became the predominant English measure for all the poetic kinds; some poets, including Alexander Pope, used it almost to the exclusion of other meters.

In this *Neoclassic Period,* the poets wrote in **closed couplets;** that is, the end of each couplet tends to coincide with the end either of a sentence or of a self-sufficient unit of syntax. The sustained employment of the closed heroic couplet meant that two lines had to serve something of the function of a stanza. In order to maximize the interrelations of the component parts, neoclassic poets often used an end-stopped first line (that is, made the end of the line coincide with a pause in the syntax), and also broke many single lines into subunits by balancing the line around a strong *caesura,* or medial pause in the syntax.

The following passage from John Denham's *Cooper's Hill* (which he added in the version of 1655) is an early instance of the artful management of the closed couplet which fascinated later neoclassic poets; they quoted it and commented upon it again and again, and used it as a model for exploiting the possibilities of this verse form. Note how Denham achieves diversity within the straitness of his couplets by shifts in the position of the caesuras, by the use of rhetorical balance and *antithesis* between the single lines and between the two halves within a single line, and by the variable positioning of the adjectives in the second couplet. Note also the emphasis gained by inverting the iambic foot that begins the last line, and the manipulation of similar and contrasting vowel and consonant sounds. The poet is addressing the River Thames:

O could I flow like thee, and make thy stream
My great example, as it is my theme!
Though deep, yet clear; though gentle, yet not dull;
Strong without rage, without o'erflowing full.

And here is a passage from Alexander Pope, the greatest master of the metrical, syntactical, and rhetorical possibilities of the closed couplet ("Of the Characters of Women," 1735, lines 243–48):

See how the world its veterans rewards!
A youth of frolics, an old age of cards;
Fair to no purpose, artful to no end,
Young without lovers, old without a friend;
A fop their passion, but their prize a sot;
Alive, ridiculous, and dead, forgot!

Compare these closed neoclassic couplets with the "open couplets" quoted from Keats's *Endymion* in the entry on *meter,* in which the pattern of stresses varies often from the iambic norm, the syntax is unsymmetrical, and the couplets run on freely, with the rhyme serving to color rather than to stop the verse.

See George Williamson, "The Rhetorical Pattern of Neoclassical Wit," *Modern Philology,* 33 (1935); W. K. Wimsatt, "One Relation of Rhyme to Reason (Alexander Pope)," in *The Verbal Icon* (1954); William Bowman Piper, *The Heroic Couplet* (1969).

Heroic Drama was a form mainly specific to the *Restoration Period,* though instances continued to be written in the earlier eighteenth century. As Dryden defined it: "An heroic play ought to be an imitation, in little, of an heroic poem; and consequently . . . love and valour ought to be the subject of it" (Preface to *The Conquest of Granada,* 1672). By "heroic poem" he meant *epic,* and the plays attempted to emulate the epic by including a large-scale warrior as hero, an action involving the fate of an empire, and an elevated and elaborate style, usually cast in the epigrammatic form of the closed *heroic couplet.* A noble hero and heroine are typically represented in a situation in which their passionate love conflicts with the demands of honor and the hero's patriotic duty to his country; if the conflict ends in disaster, the play is called an **heroic tragedy.** Often the central dilemma is patently contrived and the characters are statuesque and unconvincing, while the attempt to sustain a high epic style swells sometimes into *bombast,* as in Dryden's *Love Triumphant* (1693): "What woods are these? I feel my vital heat/Forsake my limbs, my curdled blood retreat."

Dryden's *Conquest of Granada* is one of the better heroic tragedies, but his highest achievement is his adaptation (which he called *All for Love,* 1678) of Shakespeare's *Antony and Cleopatra* to the heroic formula. Other heroic dramatists were Nathaniel Lee (*The Rival Queens*) and Thomas Otway, whose *Venice Preserved* is a fine tragedy that transcends the usual limitations of the form. We also owe indirectly to heroic tragedy two very amusing *parodies* of the type: the Duke of Buckingham's *The Rehearsal* and Henry Fielding's *The Tragedy of Tragedies, or the Life and Death of Tom Thumb the Great.*

See Bonamy Dobrée, *Restoration Tragedy* (1929); Allardyce Nicoll, *Restoration Drama* (1955); Arthur C. Kirsch, *Dryden's Heroic Drama* (1965).

Humanism. In the sixteenth century the word **humanist** was coined to signify one who taught or worked in the "studia humanitatis," or **humanities**—that is, grammar, rhetoric, history, poetry, and moral philosophy, as distinguished from fields less concerned with the moral and imaginative aspects and activities of man, such as mathematics, natural philosophy, and theology. Scholarly humanists recovered, edited, and expounded many ancient texts in Greek and Latin, and so contributed greatly to the store of materials and ideas of the European *Renaissance.* These humanists also wrote many works concerned with educational, moral, and political problems, based largely on classical writers such as Aristotle, Plato, and above all, Cicero. In the nineteenth century a new word, **humanism,** came to be applied to the view of human nature, the general values, and the educational ideas common to many Renaissance humanists, as well as to later writers in the same tradition.

Typically, Renaissance humanism assumed the dignity and central position of man in the universe; emphasized the importance of the study of classical imaginative and philosophical literature, but with emphasis on its moral and practical rather than aesthetic values; and insisted on the primacy of reason (considered the distinctively human faculty), as opposed to the instinctual appetites and the "animal" passions, in ordering human life. Many humanists also stressed the need for a rounded development of people's diverse powers, physical and mental, artistic and moral, as opposed to merely technical or specialized training.

In our time, "humanist" often connotes a person who bases truth on human experience and bases values on human nature and culture, as distinct from the truths and sanctions based on a supernatural creed. With few exceptions, however, Renaissance humanists were pious Christians who incorporated the concepts and ideals inherited from pagan antiquity into the frame of the Christian creed. The result was that they tended to emphasize the values achievable by human beings in this world, and minimized the earlier Christian emphasis on innate corruption and on the ideals of extreme asceticism and of withdrawal from this world in a preoccupation with the world hereafter. It has recently become standard to refer to this structure of classical and Christian views, typical of writers such as Sir Philip Sidney, Spenser, and Milton, as **Christian humanism.**

The rapid advance in the achievements and prestige of natural science and technology after the Renaissance sharpened, in later heirs of the humanistic tradition, the need to defend the role of the humanities in a liberal education against the encroachments of natural philosophy and the practical arts. As Samuel Johnson, the eighteenth-century humanist who had once been a schoolmaster, wrote in his *Life of Milton:*

> The truth is, that the knowledge of external nature, and the sciences which that knowledge requires or includes, are not the great or the frequent business of the human mind. . . . We are perpetually moralists, but we are geometricians only by chance. . . . Socrates was rather of opinion that what we had to learn was, how to do good, and avoid evil.

Matthew Arnold, the notable proponent of humanism in the *Victorian Period,* strongly defended the central role of humane studies in general education. Many of Arnold's leading ideas are adaptations of the tenets of the older humanism—his view, for example, that culture is a perfection "of our humanity proper, as distinguished from our animality," and consists of "a harmonious expansion of *all* the powers which make the beauty and worth of human nature"; his emphasis on knowing "the best that is known and thought in the world" and his assumption that much of what is best is in the classical writers; and his conception of poetry as essentially "a criticism of life."

In our own century the American movement of 1910–33 known as the **New Humanism,** under the leadership of Irving Babbitt and Paul Elmer More, argued strongly for a return to a primarily humanistic education, and for a conservative view of moral, political, and literary values based largely on classical literature. But in the present age of proliferating demands for specialists in the sciences, technology, and the practical arts, the broad humanistic base for a general education has been greatly eroded. In most colleges the earlier humanistic theory of education survives mainly in the requirement that all students in the liberal arts must take at least six hours in "the humanities."

It is noteworthy that much recent *structuralist* and *poststructuralist* theory is deliberately antihumanistic, in the radical sense that it undertakes to dissolve or eliminate the traditional concept of humanity. Structuralism tends to conceive a human being as simply a "space" in which the diverse cultural conventions and codes of an era come together, and poststructuralism tends to reduce the human subject to an illusion, or "effect," engendered by the differential play of language. "Man," as Michel Foucault puts it, is "a simple fold in our language" who is destined to "disappear as soon as that knowledge has found a new form"; and Jacques Derrida remarks of his *deconstruction* that it "attempts to pass beyond man and humanism." See M. H. Abrams, "How to Do Things with Texts," *Partisan Review*, 46 (1979), and Charles Altieri, *Act and Quality: A Theory of Literary Meaning and Humanistic Understanding* (1981).

Douglas Bush, *The Renaissance and English Humanism* (1939); P. O. Kristeller, *The Classics and Renaissance Thought* (1955); H. I. Marrou, *A History of Education in Antiquity* (1956); R. S. Crane, *The Idea of the Humanities* (2 vols.; 1967). For the New Humanism see Irving Babbitt, *Literature and the American College* (1908); Norman Foerster, ed., *Humanism and America* (1930); and Claes G. Ryn, *Will, Imagination and Reason: Irving Babbitt and the Problem of Reality* (1986).

Hyperbole and Understatement. The figure, or *trope,* called **hyperbole** (Greek for "overshooting") is bold overstatement, or extravagant exaggeration of fact, used either for serious or comic effect. Iago says gloatingly of Othello (III. iii. 330 ff.):

> Not poppy nor mandragora,
> Nor all the drowsy syrups of the world,
> Shall ever medicine thee to that sweet sleep
> Which thou ow'dst yesterday.

See also, in seventeenth-century writers, Ben Jonson's gallantly hyperbolic compliments to his lady in "Drink to me only with thine eyes," and the ironic hyperboles in "To His Coy Mistress," by which Marvell attests how slow his "vegetable love should grow"—if he had "but world enough and time." The "tall talk" or "tall tale" of the American West is a form of mainly comic hyperbole. (There is the story of a cowboy in an eastern restaurant who ordered a steak well done. "Do you call this well done?" he roared at the waitress. "I've seen critters hurt worse than that get well!")

The contrary figure is **understatement** (the Greek term is **meiosis,** "lessening"), which deliberately represents something as much less in magnitude or importance than it really is, or is ordinarily considered to be. The effect is usually ironic—savagely ironic in Jonathan Swift's *A Tale of a Tub,* "Last week I saw a woman flayed, and you will hardly believe how much it altered her person for the worse," and comically ironic in Mark Twain's comment "Thc rcports of my death are greatly exaggerated." (See *irony.*) Some critics extend "meiosis" to the use in literature of an utterly simple, unemphatic statement to enhance the effect of a pathetic or tragic event; an example is the line at the close of the narrative in Wordsworth's *Michael* (1800): "And never lifted up a single stone."

A special form of understatement is **litotes** (Greek for "plain" or "simple"), which is the assertion of an affirmative by negating its contrary: "He's not the brightest man in the world" meaning "He is stupid." The figure is very frequent in Anglo-Saxon poetry, where the effect is usually one of grim irony. In *Beowulf,* after Hrothgar has described the ghastly mere where dwells the monster Grendel, he comments, "That is not a pleasant place."

Imagery. This term is one of the most common in modern criticism, and one of the most variable in meaning. Its applications range all the way from the "mental pictures" which, it is sometimes claimed, are experienced by the reader of a poem, to the totality of elements which make up a poem. An example of this range of usage is C. Day Lewis' statement, in his *Poetic Image* (1948), pp. 17–18, that an image "is a picture made out of words," and that "a poem may itself be an image composed from a multiplicity of images." Three uses of the word, however, are especially frequent; in all these senses, imagery is said to make poetry *concrete,* as opposed to abstract:

(1) "Imagery" (that is, "images" taken collectively) is used to signify all the objects and qualities of sense perception referred to in a poem or other work of literature, whether by literal description, by allusion, or in the analogues (the *vehicles*) used in its similes and metaphors. In Wordsworth's "She Dwelt among the Untrodden Ways" (1800), the imagery in this broad sense includes the literal objects the poem refers to ("ways," "maid," "grave"), as well as the "violet" and "stone" of the metaphor and the "star" and "sky" of the simile in the second stanza. The term "image" should not be taken to imply a visual reproduction of the object referred to; some readers of the passage experience visual images and some do not; and among those who do, the explicitness and detail of the mind-pictures vary greatly. Also, imagery includes auditory, tactile (touch), thermal (heat and cold), olfactory (smell), gustatory (taste), or kinesthetic (sensations of movement), as well as visual qualities. In his *In Memoriam* (1850), No. 101, for example, Tennyson's imagery encompasses not only things that are visible, but also qualities of smell and hearing, together with a suggestion, in the adjective "summer," of warmth:

> Unloved, that beech will gather brown, . . .
> And many a rose-carnation feed
> With summer spice the humming air. . . .

(2) Imagery is used, more narrowly, to signify only descriptions of visible

objects and scenes, especially if the description is vivid and particularized, as in Coleridge's "The Rime of the Ancient Mariner" (1798):

> The rock shone bright, the kirk no less,
> That stands above the rock:
> The moonlight steeped in silentness
> The steady weathercock.

(3) Most commonly in current usage, imagery signifies *figurative language*, especially the vehicles of metaphors and similes. Criticism after the 1930s, and notably the *New Criticism*, has gone far beyond older criticism in stressing imagery, in this sense, as the essential component in poetry, and as a major clue to poetic meaning, structure, and effect.

Caroline Spurgeon, in *Shakespeare's Imagery and What It Tells Us* (1935), made statistical counts of the subjects of this type of imagery in Shakespeare, and used the results as clues to Shakespeare's personal experience, interests, and temperament. Following the lead of several earlier critics, she also pointed out the frequent occurrence in Shakespeare's plays of **image-clusters** (recurrent groupings of metaphors and similes), and presented evidence that a number of the individual plays have characteristic image motifs (for example, animal imagery in *King Lear*, and the figures of disease, corruption, and death in *Hamlet*); these elements she viewed as establishing the overall tonality of a play. Many critics joined Spurgeon in the search for images, image patterns, and "thematic imagery" in works of literature. By some New Critics the implicit interaction of the imagery, rather than explicit statements, or than the overt speeches and actions of the characters, was held to constitute the working out of the primary subject, or "theme," of many plays, poems, and novels. See, for example, the critical writings of G. Wilson Knight, Cleanth Brooks on *Macbeth* in *The Well Wrought Urn* (1947), Chap. 2, and Robert B. Heilman, *This Great Stage: Image and Structure in "King Lear"* (1948).

On imagery in general see H. W. Wells, *Poetic Imagery* (1924); Owen Barfield, *Poetic Diction* (1928); June E. Downey, *Creative Imagination* (1929); Richard H. Fogle, *The Imagery of Keats and Shelley* (1949); Norman Friedman, "Imagery: From Sensation to Symbol," *Journal of Aesthetics and Art Criticism*, 12 (1953).

Imagism was a poetic vogue that flourished in England and, even more vigorously, in America between the years 1912 and 1917. It was organized by a group of English and American writers in London, partly under the influence of the poetic theory of T. E. Hulme, as a revolt against what Ezra Pound called the "rather blurry, messy . . . sentimentalistic mannerish" poetry at the turn of the century. Pound, the first leader of the movement, was soon succeeded by Amy Lowell; other leading participants, for a time, were H.D. (Hilda Doolittle), D. H. Lawrence, William Carlos Williams, John Gould Fletcher, and Richard Aldington. The Imagist claims, as voiced by Amy Lowell in her Preface to the first of three anthologies called *Some Imagist Poets* (1915–17), were for a poetry which, abandoning conventional poetic materials and versification, is free to choose any subject and to create its own rhythms, is expressed in common speech, and presents an image that is hard, clear, and concentrated.

The typical Imagist poem is written in *free verse,* and undertakes to render as precisely and tersely as possible, and without comment or generalization, the writer's response to a visual object or scene; often the impression is rendered by means of metaphor, or by juxtaposing a description of one object with that of a second and diverse object. This famed example by Ezra Pound exceeds all other Imagist poems in the degree of its concentration:

In a Station of the Metro

The apparition of these faces in the crowd,
Petals on a wet, black bough.*

In this poem Pound, like a number of other Imagists, was influenced by the Japanese **haiku** (or **hokku**), a lyric form that represents the poet's impression of a natural object or scene, viewed at a particular season or month, in exactly seventeen syllables. See Earl R. Miner, *The Japanese Tradition in British and American Literature* (1958).

Imagism was too restrictive to endure long as a concerted movement, but it proved to be the beginning of modern poetry. Almost every major poet up to this day, including W. B. Yeats, T. S. Eliot, and Wallace Stevens, has felt the influence of the Imagist experiments with precise, clear images, juxtaposed without specifying their interconnection.

See T. E. Hulme, *Speculations,* ed. Herbert Read (1924); Stanley K. Coffman, *Imagism* (1951); *The Imagist Poem,* introduction by William Pratt (1963).

Imitation. In literary criticism the word **imitation** has two diverse applications: (1) to define the nature of literature and the other arts, and (2) to indicate the relation of one literary work to another literary work which served as its model.

(1) In his *Poetics,* Aristotle defines poetry as an imitation (in Greek, **mimesis**) of human actions. By "imitation" he means something like "representation," in its root sense: the poem imitates by taking some kind of human action and re-presenting it in a new "medium," or material—that of words. By distinguishing differences in the artistic media, in the kind of actions imitated, and in the manner of imitation (for example, dramatic or narrative), Aristotle first discriminates poetry from other arts, and then discriminates among the various poetic kinds, such as drama and epic, tragedy and comedy. The term "imitation" continued to be an indispensable word in discussing the nature of poetry through the eighteenth century; critics differed radically, however, in their con-

*Ezra Pound, *Personae.* Copyright 1926 by Ezra Pound. Reprinted by permission of New Directions Publishing Corporation, and Faber and Faber Ltd.

cept of the nature of the mimetic relationship, and of the kinds of things in the external world that works of literature imitate, or ought to imitate. With the emergence in the early nineteenth century of the romantic view that poetry is essentially an expression of the poet's feelings or imaginative process, imitation tended to drop out of its central place in literary theory (see *criticism*). In recent decades, however, the use of the term has been revived, especially by R. S. Crane and other *Chicago critics*, who ground their theory on the analytic method and basic distinctions of Aristotle's *Poetics.* Many *Marxist critics* also hold a view of literature as an imitation, or, in their preferred term, "reflection," of reality.

(2) Ancient rhetoricians and critics often recommended that a poet should "imitate" the established models, or "classic" works, in a particular literary genre. The notion that the proper procedure for poets, with the rare exception of an "original genius," was to imitate the normative forms and styles of the ancient masters continued to be influential through the eighteenth century; yet all the major critics also insisted that mere copying was not enough—that a good work imitated the form and spirit rather than the detail of the classic models, and could be achieved only by a poet who possessed an innate individual talent.

In a specialized use of the term in this second sense, "imitation" was also used to describe a literary work which deliberately echoed an older work but adapted it to subject matter in the writer's own age. In the poems that Alexander Pope called *Imitations of Horace* (1733 and following), for example, an important part of the intended effect depends on the reader's recognition of the resourcefulness, wit, and subtlety with which Pope accommodated to contemporary circumstances the structure, details, and even the wording of one or another of Horace's Roman satires.

On "imitation" as a term used to define literature see R. S. Crane, ed., *Critics and Criticism* (1952), and M. H. Abrams, *The Mirror and the Lamp* (1953), Chaps. 1–2. On Pope's "imitations" of Horace and other ancient masters see R. A. Brower, *Alexander Pope: The Poetry of Allusion* (1959).

For other ways of dealing with the concept of the relation between literature and reality see *fiction* and *speech act theory;* for denials, on various grounds, that literature can be said to imitate reality, see *Russian formalism, structuralist criticism, deconstruction,* and *text and writing* (*écriture*). Among modern defenses of the view that literature is mimetic, in the broad sense that it has reference to the world of human experience, see Gerald Graff, *Literature against Itself* (1979); A. D. Nuttall, *A New Mimesis: Shakespeare and the Representation of Reality* (1983); and Robert Alter, "Mimesis and the Motives for Fiction," in his *Motives for Fiction* (1984).

Intentional Fallacy identifies what is claimed to be the error of interpreting a literary work by reference to evidence, outside the text itself, for the intention—the design and purposes—of its author. The term was proposed by W. K. Wimsatt and Monroe C. Beardsley in "The Intentional Fallacy" (1946), reprinted in Wimsatt's *The Verbal Icon* (1964). They asserted that whether an author has expressly stated what his or her intended aims and meanings were in writing a literary work, or whether these are merely inferred from what we know about the author's life and opinions, such intentions are irrelevant to the literary critic, because the meaning and value of a text are inherent within the finished, freestanding, and public work of literature itself. Reference to the author's supposed purposes or state of mind in writing a text is held to be a harmful mistake, because it distracts us to such "external" matters as the author's biography, or psychological condition, or creative process, which we substitute for the proper critical concern with the "internal" constitution of the literary product.

This claim, which was central in the *New Criticism,* has been strenuously debated, and has been reformulated by both of its original proponents. A reasonable view, acceptable to many critics, is that in the exceptional instances—for example, in Henry James's prefaces to his novels—where we possess an author's express statement about his artistic intentions in a literary work, that statement should constitute evidence for an interpretive hypothesis, but should not in itself be determinative. If the author's stated intentions do not accord with the text itself, it should be qualified or rejected in favor of an alternative interpretation that conforms more closely to the shared, or "public," conventions, both of the language and of the literary mode, which are relevant to the text.

For diverse views of the role of authorial intention in interpreting a text, see *interpretation and hermeneutics,* below; compare also *affective fallacy.* A strongly argued objection to Wimsatt and Beardsley's original essay is E. D. Hirsch's "Objective Interpretation" (1960), reprinted as an appendix to his *Validity in Interpretation* (1967). For a consideration of such objections and a reformulation of his original claim see W. K. Wimsatt, "Genesis: An Argument Resumed," in his *Day of the Leopards* (1976); also the defense of the concept of the "intentional fallacy" by Monroe C. Beardsley, *Aesthetics* (1958), pp. 457–61, and *The Possibility of Criticism* (1970), pp. 16–37. An anthology of discussions of this topic in criticism is David Newton-de Molina, *On Literary Intention* (1976).

Interpretation and Hermeneutics. In the narrow sense, to interpret a work of literature is to specify the meanings of its language by analysis, paraphrase, and commentary; usually such **interpretation** focuses on especially obscure, ambiguous, or figurative passages. In the broad sense, to interpret is to make clear the artistic purport of the overall literary work of which language is the medium; interpretation in this sense includes the *explication* of such aspects as the work's genre, elements, structure, theme, and effects (see *criticism*). The term **hermeneutics** was originally used specifically to designate the interpretation of the Bible, and included both the formulation of rules governing a valid reading of the biblical text and **exegesis,** or commentary on the application of the meanings expressed in the text. Since the nineteenth century, however, "hermeneutics" has come to designate the general theory of interpretation; that is, a formulation of the procedures and principles involved in getting at the meaning of all written texts, including legal, expository, and literary, as well as biblical texts.

The German theologian Friedrich Schleiermacher, in a series of lectures in 1819, was the first to frame a theory of "general hermeneutics" as "the art of understanding" texts of every kind. Schleiermacher's views were developed in the 1890s by the influential philosopher Wilhelm Dilthey (1833–1911), who proposed a science of hermeneutics designed to serve as the basis for interpreting all forms of writing in the "human sciences": that is, in literature, the humanities, and the social sciences, as distinguished from the natural sciences. Dilthey regarded the human sciences as ways of dealing with temporal, concrete, "lived experience." He proposed that whereas the natural sciences aim merely at "explanation" by applying static, reductive categories, the aim of hermeneutics is to establish a general theory of "understanding." A specifically textual understanding consists in "the interpretation of *works*, works in which the texture of inner life comes fully to expression."

In formulating the way in which we come to understand the meaning of a text, Dilthey gave the name the **hermeneutic circle** to a procedure Schleiermacher had earlier described. That is, to understand the determinate meanings of the parts of any linguistic unit, we must approach them with a prior sense of the meaning of the whole; yet we can know the meaning of the whole only by knowing the meanings of its constituent parts. This circularity of the interpretive procedure applies to the relations between the meaning of the single words within any sentence and the meaning of the sentence as a whole, as well as to the relations between all the single sentences and the work as a whole. Dilthey maintained, however, that the hermeneutic circle is not a vicious circle, in that we can achieve a valid interpretation by a sustained, mutually qualifying interplay between our evolving sense of the whole and our retrospective understanding of its component parts.

Interest in the theory of interpretation strongly revived in the 1950s and 1960s, concomitantly with the conspicuous turn of philosophy to questions of the uses and meanings of language, and the turn of literary criticism—exemplified by the *New Criticism* in America—to the conception of a literary work as a linguistic object and to the view that the primary task of criticism is to interpret its verbal meanings and their interrelations. There have been two main lines of development in recent hermeneutics:

(1) One development, represented notably by the Italian theorist Emilio Betti and the American E. D. Hirsch, takes off from Dilthey's claim that a reader is able to achieve an objective interpretation of an author's expressed meaning. In his *Validity in Interpretation* (1967), followed by *The Aims of Interpretation* (1976), Hirsch asserts that "a text means what its author meant," specifies that this meaning is "the verbal meaning which an author intends," and undertakes to show that such verbal meaning is in principle determinate (even if in some instances determinately ambiguous, or multiply significant), that it remains stable through the passage of time, and that it is in principle reproducible by each competent reader. The author's verbal **intention** is not the author's total state of mind at the time of writing, but only that aspect which, by making use of the potentialities of linguistic conventions and norms, gets expressed in words, and so may be shared by readers who know how to apply the same conventions and norms in their interpretive practice. If a text is read independently of the author's intentions, it remains indeterminate—that is, capable of an

indefinite diversity of meanings. A reader arrives at a determinate interpretation by using an implicit logic of validation (capable of being made explicit by the hermeneutic theorist), which serves to specify the author's intention, not only by reference to the general norms of language, but also by reference to all evidence, whether internal or external to the text, concerning "relevant aspects in the author's outlook," or "horizon." Relevant external references include the author's cultural milieu and personal prepossessions, as well as the literary and generic conventions that were available to the author at the time when the work was composed.

Hirsch reformulates Dilthey's concept of the hermeneutic circle as follows: a competent reader forms an "hypothesis" as to the meaning of a part or whole of a text which is "corrigible"—that is, the hypothesis can be either confirmed or disconfirmed by continued reference to the text; if disconfirmed, it is replaced by an alternative hypothesis which conforms more closely to all the components of the text. Since the interpreted meanings of the components of a text are to some degree constituted by the hypotheses one brings to their interpretation, such a procedure can never achieve total certainty as to a text's correct meaning. The most a reader can do is to arrive at the most probable meaning of a text; but this logic of highest probability, Hirsch insists, is adequate to yield objective knowledge, confirmable by other competent readers, concerning the determinate and stable meanings both of the component passages and of the artistic whole in a work of literature.

Hirsch follows traditional hermeneutics in making an essential distinction between verbal meaning and significance. The **significance** of a text is the relation of its verbal meaning to other matters, such as the personal situation, beliefs, and responses of an individual reader, or to the prevailing cultural milieu of the reader's own era, or to a particular set of concepts or values, and so on. The **verbal meaning** of a text, Hirsch asserts, is determinate and stable; its significance, however—what makes the text alive and resonant for diverse readers in diverse times—is indeterminate and ever changing. Verbal meaning is the particular concern of hermeneutics; textual significance, in its many aspects, is the particular concern of literary criticism.

(2) The second line of development takes off from Dilthey's view that the genuine understanding of literary and other humanistic texts consists in the reexperiencing by the reader of the "inner life" that the texts express. The primary thinker in this development is Martin Heidegger, whose *Being and Time* (1927, transl. 1962) incorporated the act of interpretation into an **existential philosophy**—that is, a philosophy centered on "Dasein," or what it is to-be-in-the-world. Heidegger's student, Hans Georg Gadamer, adapted Heidegger's philosophy into an influential theory of textual interpretation, *Truth and Method* (1960, transl. 1975). The philosophical premise is that temporality and historicality—a stance in one's present that looks back to the past and anticipates the future—is inseparably a part of each individual's being; that to understand something involves an act of interpretation, not only in the reading of a text but in all individual experience; and that language, like temporality, pervades all aspects of that experience. In applying these philosophical assumptions to the under-

standing of a literary text, Gadamer translates the traditional hermeneutic circle into the metaphors of dialogue and fusion. A reader inescapably brings to a text a "pre-understanding" which is constituted by his own temporal and personal "horizons." He should not, as a "subject," attempt to analyze and dissect the text as an autonomous "object." Instead he, as an "I," addresses questions to it as a "Thou," but with a receptive openness that simply allows the matter of the text—by means of their common heritage of language—to speak in responsive dialogue with the reader, and to readdress its own questions to him. The understood meaning of the text is an event which is inevitably the product of a "fusion of the horizons" which a reader brings to the text and which the text brings to the reader.

Gadamer insists that his hermeneutics is not an attempt to establish norms for a correct interpretation, but an attempt simply to describe how we in fact succeed in understanding texts. Nonetheless his theory has the practical consequence that the search for a determinate meaning of a text which remains stable through the passage of time becomes a will-o'-the-wisp. For since the meaning of a text "is always codetermined" by the particular temporal and personal horizon of the individual reader, there cannot be one stable "right interpretation"; the meaning of a text is always to an important extent its meaning here, now, for me. To Gadamer's view of the historical and personal relativity of meaning, Hirsch replies that a reader in the present, by reconstructing the linguistic, literary, and cultural conditions of its author, is able to determine the original and unchanging verbal meaning of a text written in the past; and that insofar as Gadamer is right about the unbridgeable gap between the meaning of a text then and its meaning now, he is referring to the ever-alterable "significance" attributed by each reader, in his or her time and personal and social circumstances, to the text's stable verbal meaning.

Traditional critics had tacitly assumed that to interpret a text correctly is to approximate the meaning intended by its author, long before theorists such as Hirsch undertook to define and justify this view. Even the *New Critics* assumed that the meaning of a text is the meaning that the author intended; what some of these critics called the *intentional fallacy* merely designates the supposed error, in interpreting a text, of employing clues concerning an author's intention which are "external" to the "internal" realization of that intention in the language of the text itself. Most traditional philosophers, including current "ordinary language philosophers," have also assumed that to understand an utterance involves reference to the speaker's or writer's intention. H. P. Grice, for example, proposed in the 1950s an influential account of meaning as a speaker's intention in an utterance to produce some effect in a hearer, by means of the hearer's recognition of the speaker's intention in making that utterance. In *Speech Acts* (1970), John Searle accepted this definition of meaning, with the qualification that the speaker can express, and so enable the hearer to recognize, his intention only insofar as he conforms to the conventions or rules of their common language. In a later refinement of this view, Searle makes a distinction between the speaker's intention which determines the kind and meaning of a speech act, and the speaker's intention to communicate that meaning to a hearer; see his *Intentionality* (1983), Chap. 6.

A radical departure from this traditional author-oriented theory of meaning is found in a variety of recent reader-oriented theories. Each of these theories severs a text from any control by reference to the intentions of the author, rejects the possibility of a determinate meaning and of a correct interpretation, and makes the meanings of the text either "undecidable," or else relative to the particular "productive" or "creative" operation, or "strategy," which is brought into play by the individual reader. (See *reader-response criticism, structuralist criticism, deconstruction,* and *text and writing* [*écriture*]).

In addition to the titles listed above, refer to Richard E. Palmer, *Hermeneutics: Interpretation Theory in Schleiermacher, Dilthey, Heidegger, and Gadamer* (1969), which offers an informative review of the history and conflicting theories of interpretation from the standpoint of an adherent to Gadamer's theory; also, *The Conflict of Interpretations: Essays in Hermeneutics* (1974) by the French philosopher Paul Ricoeur; P. D. Juhl, *Interpretation: An Essay in the Philosophy of Literary Criticism* (1980); Tzvetan Todorov, *Symbolism and Interpretation* (1982).

Interpretation: Typological and Allegorical. The **typological** (or **figural**) mode of interpreting the Bible was inaugurated by St. Paul and developed by the early Church Fathers as a way of reconciling the Jewish history and laws of the Old Testament with the Christian revelation of the New Testament. As St. Augustine expressed its principle: "In the Old Testament the New Testament is concealed; in the New Testament the Old Testament is revealed." In typological theory the key persons, actions, and events narrated in the Old Testament are viewed as "figurae" (Latin for "figures") which are historically real themselves, but also "prefigure" those later persons, actions, and events in the New Testament that are similar to them; alternatively, the Old Testament figures are called **types** and their New Testament correlatives are called **antitypes.** The Old Testament figure or type is held to be a prophecy or promise of the higher truth that is "fulfilled" in the New Testament, according to a plan which is eternally and completely present in the mind of God but manifests itself to human beings only in scriptural revelations over a span of time. For example, Adam is said to be a figure (or in alternative terms, a "type," "image," or "shadow") of Christ; one of the analogies cited between prefiguration and fulfillment is that between the creation of Eve from Adam's rib and the flow of blood from the side of the crucified Christ; another is the analogy between the tree that bore the fruit occasioning Adam's original sin and the cross which bore as its fruit Christ, the Redeemer of that sin. In a similar fashion the manna provided the children of Israel in the wilderness (Exodus 16) was said to prefigure the Eucharist, and the relation between the Egyptian servant girl Hagar and Sarah (Genesis 16) was said to prefigure the relation between the earthly Jerusalem of the Old Testament and the heavenly Jerusalem of the New Testament. By some interpreters, elements of New Testament history were represented as in their turn prefiguring the events that will be fulfilled in "the last days" of Christ's Second Coming and Last Judgment.

The **allegorical interpretation** of the Bible had its roots in Greek and Roman thinkers who treated classical myths as allegorical representations of abstract cosmological, philosophical, or moral truths. (See *allegory.*) The method was applied to Old Testament narrative by the Jewish philosopher Philo (died A.D. 50) and was adapted to Christian interpretation by Origen in the third century. Typological interpretation is sometimes said to be horizontal, in that it relates items in two texts (the Old and New Testaments) separated in time; allegorical interpretation is said to be vertical, in that it uncovers multiple meanings expressed by a single textual item. The fundamental distinction in allegorical interpretation is between the "literal" (or "historical," or "carnal") meaning of the text—the historical truth that it expressly signifies—and the "spiritual" or "mystical" or "allegoric" meaning that it signifies by analogy.

The spiritual aspect of a text's literal meaning was often in turn subdivided into two or three levels; by the twelfth century, biblical interpreters widely agreed in finding a **fourfold meaning** in many biblical passages. The definition of these four levels of meaning varied; a typical set of distinctions, as proposed by St. Thomas Aquinas and others, is that between: (1) the literal or historical meaning, which simply narrates what in fact happened; this is held to be the primary significance on which all the other levels are based; (2) the allegorical meaning proper, which is the New Testament truth, or else the prophetic reference to the Christian Church, that is signified by a passage in the Old Testament; (3) the tropological meaning, which is the moral truth or doctrine signified by the same passage; and (4) the anagogic meaning, or reference of the passage to Christian **eschatology,** that is, the events to come in the last days of Christ's judgment and the life after death of individual souls.

Typological and allegorical methods were often employed simultaneously, and sometimes fused, by biblical *exegetes;* they flourished through the seventeenth century and recur in later periods. They were employed in biblical allusions in sermons and in a great variety of writings on religious matters, and were adapted to **iconography**—that is, the symbolic significance in representations of biblical persons and events—in painting and sculpture. Medieval and later poets sometimes adopted typological and allegorical methods in constructing their own writings on religious subjects. Dante, for example, in a letter written in 1319 to his friend and patron Can Grande della Scala, announced that his *Divine Comedy* has a double subject, literal and allegorical, and that the allegorical subject can be subdivided into allegorical, moral, and anagogical meanings. Scholars have analyzed the use of typological and allegorical procedures by many later poets who wrote on religious themes, including Spenser, George Herbert, Milton, and (in a late revival of the mode) William Blake. The American scholar D. W. Robertson and others have recently proposed that, in addition, many seemingly secular poems of the Middle Ages, including the *Roman de la Rose,* the works of Chaucer and Chrétien de Troyes, and medieval love lyrics, were written to incorporate typological and allegorical modes of theological and moral references; however, the validity of extending these interpretive modes to secular literature is hotly disputed. In *The Genesis of Secrecy: On the Interpretation of Narrative* (1979), the English critic Frank Kermode adapted the ancient distinction between carnal and spiritual meanings to the analysis of recent works of prose fiction.

On the various modes of biblical interpretation, see F. W. Farrar, *History of Interpretation* (1886), and Beryl Smalley, *The Study of the Bible in the Middle Ages* (rev., 1952). A classic treatment of typological, or figural, interpretation is Erich Auerbach's "Figura," in his *Scenes from the Drama of European Literature* (1959). A surviving American application in the eighteenth century of the old interpretive modes is Jonathan Edwards' *Images or Shadows of Divine Things*, ed. Perry Miller (1948). For uses of typological and allegoric materials by various literary authors, see Rosemund Tuve, *A Reading of George Herbert* (1952), and *Allegorical Imagery* (1966); J. H. Hagstrum, *William Blake: Poet and Painter* (1964); P. J. Alpers, *The Poetry of "The Faerie Queene"* (1967); and the essays on a number of authors in Paul Miner, ed., *Literary Uses of Typology* (1977). For the extension of typological and allegoric methods to the analysis of secular medieval poems, see D. W. Robertson, Jr., "Historical Criticism," in *English Institute Essays, 1950,* ed. A. S. Downer (1951), and *A Preface to Chaucer: Studies in Medieval Perspectives* (1962). The validity of such an extension is debated by several scholars in *Critical Approaches to Medieval Literature,* ed. Dorothy Bethurum (1960). Sacvan Bercovitch showed the importance of such interpretive modes in early American thought and imagination in *The Puritan Origins of the American Self* (1975).

Irony. In Greek comedy the character called the *eiron* was a "dissembler," who characteristically spoke in understatement and deliberately pretended to be less intelligent than he was, yet triumphed over the *alazon*—the self-deceiving and stupid braggart. In most of the critical uses of the term "irony" there remains the root sense of dissembling or hiding what is actually the case; not, however, in order to deceive, but to achieve special rhetorical or artistic effects.

Verbal irony (which was traditionally classified as one of the *tropes*) is a statement in which the speaker's implicit meaning differs sharply from the meaning that is ostensibly expressed. Such an ironic statement usually involves the explicit expression of one attitude or evaluation, but with indications in the speech-situation that the speaker intends a very different, and often opposite, attitude or evaluation. Thus in Canto IV of Pope's *The Rape of the Lock* (1714) after Sir Plume, egged on by the ladies, has stammered out his incoherent request for the return of the stolen lock of hair, the Baron answers:

> "It grieves me much," replied the Peer again,
> "Who speaks so well should ever speak in vain."

This is a straightforward case of an ironic reversal of the surface statement, because there are patent clues in the circumstances established in the narrative that the Peer is not in the least aggrieved, and does not think that poor Sir Plume has spoken at all well. A more complex instance of irony is the famed opening sentence of Jane Austen's *Pride and Prejudice* (1813): "It is a truth universally acknowledged that a single man in possession of a good fortune must be in want of a wife"; part of the ironic implication is that a single woman is in want of a rich husband. Sometimes the use of irony by Pope and other masters is very complex; the meaning and evaluations may be subtly qualified rather than simply reversed, and the clues to the ironic counter-meaning under the surface statement may be indirect and unobtrusive. That is why recourse to irony by an author carries an implicit compliment to the intelligence of readers, who are invited to associate themselves with the author and the knowing minority who are not taken in by the ostensible meaning. That is also why many ironists are misinterpreted and sometimes (like Defoe and Swift) get into serious trouble with the obtuse authorities. Following the intricate and shifting maneuvers of great ironists like Plato, Swift, Austen, or Henry James is an ultimate test of skill in reading between the lines.

Some literary works exhibit **structural irony:** the author, instead of using an occasional verbal irony, introduces a structural feature which serves to sustain a duplicity of meaning and evaluation throughout the work. One common literary device of this sort is the invention of a **naive hero,** or else a naive narrator or spokesman, whose invincible simplicity or obtuseness leads him to persist in putting an interpretation on affairs which the knowing reader—who penetrates to, and shares, the implicit point of view of the authorial presence behind the naive *persona*—just as persistently is called on to alter and correct. (Note that verbal irony depends on knowledge of the speaker's ironic intention which is shared by the speaker and the reader; structural irony depends on a knowledge of the author's ironic intention which is shared by the reader, but is not intended by the speaker.) One example of the naive spokesman is Swift's well-meaning but insanely rational economist who writes the "Modest Proposal" (1729) to convert the excess children of the oppressed and poverty-stricken Irish into a financial and gastronomical asset. Other examples are Swift's stubbornly credulous Gulliver, the self-deceiving and paranoid monologuist in Browning's "Soliloquy of the Spanish Cloister" (1842), and the insane editor, Kinbote, in Vladimir Nabokov's *Pale Fire* (1962). A related device for sustaining ironic qualification is the use of the *fallible narrator,* in which the teller of the story is a participant in it; although such a narrator may be neither foolish nor demented, he nevertheless manifests a failure of insight, viewing and appraising his or her own motives, and the motives and actions of other characters, through what the reader is intended to recognize as the distorting perspective of the narrator's prejudices and private interests. (See *point of view.*)

In *A Rhetoric of Irony* (1965), Wayne Booth identifies as **stable irony** that in which the speaker or author offers the reader an assertion or position which, whether explicit or implied, serves as a solid ground for subverting the surface meaning. **Unstable irony,** on the other hand, offers no fixed standpoint which is not undercut by further ironies. The literature of the *absurd* typically presents such a regression of ironies. At an extreme, as in Samuel Beckett's drama *Waiting for Godot* (1955) or his novel *The Unnamable* (1960), there is an endless regress of ironic undercuttings; such works suggest a negation of any secure evaluative standpoint, or even of any rationale, in the human situation.

Irony can be discriminated from some related uses of language:

Invective is direct denunciation by the use of derogatory *epithets;* so Prince Hal, in *Henry IV, Part 1,* calls the rotund Falstaff "this sanguine coward, this bedpresser, this horseback-breaker, this huge hill of flesh." (In the context of the play, there is in this instance of invective an ironic undertone of affection, as often when friends, secure in an intimacy which guarantees that they will not be taken literally, resort to derogatory name-calling in the exuberance of their esteem.) In his *Discourse Concerning Satire* (1693), Dryden described the difference in efficacy between direct invective and the indirectness of irony, in which the ironist is able to maintain the advantage of seeming detachment by leaving it to the circumstances to convert his bland compliments into insults:

> How easy is it to call rogue and villain, and that wittily! But how hard to make a man appear a fool, a blockhead, or a knave, without using any of those opprobrious terms. . . . There is . . . a vast difference between the slovenly butchering of a man, and the fineness of a stroke that separates the head from the body, and leaves it standing in its place.

Sarcasm in ordinary parlance is sometimes used for all irony, but it is better to restrict it to the crude and taunting use of apparent praise for dispraise: "Oh, you're God's great gift to women, you are!" Sarcasm, in which an added clue is the inflection of the speaker's voice, is the common form of irony in dormitory persiflage.

The term "irony," qualified by an adjective, is also used in a number of specialized applications to literary devices and modes of organization:

Socratic irony takes its name from Socrates' characteristic assumption, in Plato's philosophical dialogues (fourth century B.C.), of the pose of ignorance, an eagerness to be instructed, and a modest readiness to entertain points of view which, upon his continued questioning, turn out to be ill-grounded or to lead to absurd consequences.

Dramatic irony involves a situation in a play or a narrative in which the audience or reader shares with the author knowledge of present or future circumstances of which a character is ignorant: the character acts in a way grossly inappropriate to the actual circumstances, or expects the opposite of what we know that fate holds in store, or says something that anticipates the actual outcome, but not at all in the way that the character intends. Writers of Greek tragedy, who based their plots on legends whose outcome was already known to their audience, made frequent use of this device. Sophocles' *Oedipus*, for example, is a complex instance of **tragic irony,** for the king ("I, Oedipus, whom all men call great") engages in a hunt for the evildoer who has brought a plague upon Thebes; the object of the hunt turns out (as the audience has known right along) to be the hunter himself, and the king, having achieved a vision of the terrible truth, penitently blinds himself. Dramatic irony occurs also in comedy. An example is the scene in *Twelfth Night* (II. v) in which Malvolio struts and preens in anticipation of a good fortune which the audience knows is based on a fake letter; the dramatic irony is heightened for the audience by Malvolio's ignorance of the presence of the hoaxers, who gleefully observe and comment on his ludicrously complacent speech and actions.

Cosmic irony (or "the irony of fate") is used in reference to literary works in which God, or destiny, or the process of the universe, is represented as though deliberately manipulating events so as to lead the protagonist to false hopes, only to frustrate and mock them. This is a favorite structural device of Thomas Hardy. In his *Tess of the D'Urbervilles* (1891) the heroine, having lost her virtue because of her innocence, then loses her happiness because of her honesty, finds it again only by murder, and having been briefly happy, is hanged. Hardy concludes: "The President of the Immortals, in Aeschylean phrase, had ended his sport with Tess."

Romantic irony is a term introduced by Friedrich Schlegel and other German writers of the late eighteenth and early nineteenth centuries to designate a mode of dramatic or narrative writing in which the author builds up artistic illusion, only to break it down by revealing that the author, as artist, is the arbitrary creator and manipulator of the characters and their actions. The concept owes much to Laurence Sterne's use of a self-conscious and willful narrator in his *Tristram Shandy* (1759–67). Byron's great narrative poem *Don Juan* (1819–24) persistently uses this device for ironic and comic effect, letting the reader into the narrator's confidence, and so revealing the latter to be an inventor who is often at a loss for matter to sustain his story and undecided about how to continue it. This type of irony, involving a *self-conscious narrator,* has become a standard mode in the modern form of *involuted fiction.*

A number of writers associated with the *New Criticism* used "irony," in a greatly extended sense, as a general criterion of literary value. This use is based largely on two literary theorists. T. S. Eliot praised a kind of "wit," absent in the romantic poets, which is an "internal equilibrium" that implies the "recognition," in dealing with any one kind of experience, "of other kinds of experience which are possible." ("Andrew Marvell," 1921, in *Selected Essays,* 1960.) And I. A. Richards defined irony in poetry as an equilibrium of opposing attitudes and evaluations (*Principles of Literary Criticism,* 1924, Chap. 32):

> Irony in this sense consists in the bringing in of the opposite, the complementary impulses; that is why poetry which is exposed to it is not of the highest order, and why irony itself is so constantly a characteristic of poetry which is.

Such observations were developed by Robert Penn Warren, Cleanth Brooks, and other New Critics into the claim that poems in which the writer commits himself unreservedly to an exclusive attitude or outlook, such as love or admiration or idealism, are of an inferior order because vulnerable to the reader's ironic skepticism; the greatest poems, on the other hand, are invulnerable to external irony because they incorporate the poet's own "ironic" awareness of opposite and complementary attitudes. See Robert Penn Warren, "Pure and Impure Poetry" (1943), in *Critiques and Essays in Criticism,* ed. Robert W. Stallman (1949); Cleanth Brooks, "Irony as a Principle of Structure" (1949), in *Literary Opinion in America,* ed. M. W. Zabel (1951).

J. A. K. Thomson, *Irony: An Historical Introduction* (1926); A. R. Thompson, *The Dry Mock: A Study of Irony in Drama* (1948); D. C. Muecke, *The Compass of Irony* (1969), and *Irony* (1970); A. E. Dyson, *The Crazy Fabric, Es-*

says in Irony (1965); Wayne C. Booth, *A Rhetoric of Irony* (1965). A suggestive and wide-ranging earlier treatment is Søren Kierkegaard's *The Concept of Irony* (1841), transl. Lee M. Capel (1965).

Ivory Tower is a phrase taken from the biblical Songs of Songs 7.4, in which it is said of the beloved woman, "Thy neck is as a tower of ivory." In the 1830s the French critic Sainte-Beuve applied the phrase "tour d'ivoire" to the stance of the poet Alfred de Vigny, to signify his isolation from everyday life and his exaltation of art above all practical concerns. Since then "ivory tower" has been frequently used (often in a derogatory way) as a term for an attitude or way of life which is indifferent or hostile to practical affairs and the everyday world, and especially for a theory and practice of art (see *Aestheticism*) which insulates it from all moral, political, and social concerns or effects.

Jacobean Age. The reign of James I (in Latin, "Jacobus"), 1603–25, which followed the Elizabethan Age. This was the period in prose writings of Bacon, Donne's sermons, Burton's *Anatomy of Melancholy*, and the King James translation of the Bible. It was also the period of Shakespeare's greatest tragedies and tragicomedies, and of major writings by other notable poets and playwrights including Donne, Ben Jonson, Drayton, Beaumont and Fletcher, Webster, Chapman, Middleton, and Massinger.

See Basil Willey, *The Seventeenth Century Background* (1934); Douglas Bush, *English Literature in the Earlier Seventeenth Century* (1945); C. V. Wedgewood, *Seventeenth Century English Literature* (1950).

Jeremiad is derived from the Old Testament prophet Jeremiah, who in the seventh century B.C. attributed the national calamities of Israel to its abandonment of the covenant with Jehovah and return to pagan idolatry, denounced with lurid and gloomy eloquence its religious and moral iniquities, and called on the people to repent and reform in order that Jehovah might restore them to His favor and renew the ancient covenant. As a literary term, **jeremiad** is applied to any work which, with a style emulating that of the Old Testament prophet (although it may be in secular rather than religious terms), explains the misfortunes of an era as a just penalty for great social and moral evils, but holds out hope for changes that will bring a happier future.

In the *Romantic Period*, powerful passages in William Blake's "prophetic poems" constitute short jeremiads, and the term is applicable to those of Thomas Carlyle's writings in which he uses a prophetic eloquence and rhetoric to denounce the social and economic misdeeds of the *Victorian Period* and to call for drastic reforms. The jeremiad, in its original religious mode, was a familiar genre in the sermons and writings of the *Colonial Period* in America, since it was then a commonplace that the colonies in New England were the "New Israel" with which God had covenanted a glorious future; their misfortunes were attributed to deviations from the divine commands and regarded as chastisements inflicted by God's providence on His chosen people for their own ultimate benefit. In the words of Increase Mather, "God does not punish . . . other

Nations until they have filled up the Measure of their sins, and then he utterly destroyeth them; but if our Nation forsake the God of their Fathers never so little," He punishes us in order "that so he may prevent our destruction" (*The Day of Trouble Is Near,* 1674). Since that era the prophetic stance and denunciatory rhetoric of the jeremiad has been manifested in many orators and writers, religious or secular, into the present time. See Sacvan Bercovitch, *The American Jeremiad* (1978), and George P. Landow, *Elegant Jeremiahs: The Sage from Carlyle to Mailer* (1986).

Lai. The term was originally applied to a variety of poems by medieval French writers in the latter twelfth and the thirteenth centuries. Some lais were lyric, but most of them were short romantic narratives written in *octosyllabic couplets.* Marie de France, who wrote in the French language although at the English court of King Henry II, composed a number of charming poems of this sort; they are called "Breton lais" because their narratives are drawn for the most part from Arthurian and other Celtic legends. ("Breton" refers to Brittany, which was a Celtic part of France; see *chivalric romance.*) The Anglicized term "Breton lay" was applied in the fourteenth century to English poems written on the model of the narratives of Marie de France; they included *Sir Orfeo,* the *Lay of Launfal,* and Chaucer's "The Franklin's Tale." Later still, the anglicized term **lay** was used by English poets simply as a synonym for song, or for a fairly short narrative poem (for example, Sir Walter Scott's *Lay of the Last Minstrel,* 1805).

See Roger S. Loomis, ed., *Arthurian Literature in the Middle Ages* (1959), and the Introduction by Charles W. Dunn to *Lays of Courtly Love,* transl. Patricia Terry (1963).

Light Verse uses an ordinary speaking voice and a relaxed manner to treat its subjects gaily, or comically, or whimsically, or with a good-natured satire. Its subjects may be serious as well as trivial; the defining quality is the *tone* of voice and the attitude of the lyric or narrative speaker toward the subject. Thomas Love Peacock's "The War Song of Dinas Vawr" (1829) begins

> The mountain sheep are sweeter,
> But the valley sheep are fatter;
> We therefore deemed it meeter
> To carry off the latter.

And it ends

> We brought away from battle,
> And much their land bemoaned them,
> Two thousand head of cattle,
> And the head of him who owned them:
> Ednyfed, king of Dyfed,
> His head was borne before us;
> His wine and beasts supplied our feasts,
> And his overthrow, our chorus.

The dispassionate attitude, brisk colloquialism, and pat rhymes convert what might have been matter for epic or tragedy into a comic narrative.

Vers de société ("society verse") is the subclass of light verse that deals with the relationships, concerns, and doings of polite society. It is often satiric, but in the mode of badinage rather than severity; and when it deals with love it does so as a sexual game, or flirtatiously, or in the mode of elegant and witty compliment, rather than with passion or high seriousness. The tone is urbane, the style deft, and the form polished and sometimes very elaborate; most poems using intricate French stanza forms, such as the *villanelle,* are society verse.

Nursery rhymes and other children's verses are another type of light verse. Edward Lear ("The Jumblies," "The Owl and the Pussy Cat") and Lewis Carroll ("Jabberwocky," *The Hunting of the Snark*) made children's nonsense verses into a Victorian specialty. Lear also popularized the five-line **limerick,** rhyming *aabba,* which is a form of light verse that everyone knows and many of us have practiced.

Some other fine artificers of light and society verse are the *Cavalier poets* of the early seventeenth century, and John Dryden, Matthew Prior, Alexander Pope, and W. S. Gilbert. Modern practitioners include Ezra Pound, W. H. Auden, E. E. Cummings, Ogden Nash, Edith Sitwell, Marianne Moore, Edna St. Vincent Millay, Dorothy Parker, Morris Bishop, John Betjeman, and Ishmael Reed.

See *epigram.* Refer to *Worldly Muse: An Anthology of Serious Light Verse,* ed. A. J. M. Smith (1951); *The New Oxford Book of Light Verse,* ed. Kingsley Amis (1978); *The Norton Book of Light Verse,* ed. Russell Baker (1986).

Local Color is the detailed representation in fiction of the setting, dialect, customs, dress, and ways of thinking and feeling which are distinctive of a particular region, such as Thomas Hardy's "Wessex" or Rudyard Kipling's India. After the Civil War a number of American writers exploited the possibilities of local color in various parts of America; for example, the West (Bret Harte), the Mississippi region (Mark Twain), the South (George Washington Cable), the Midwest (E. W. Howe, Hamlin Garland), and New England (Sarah Orne Jewett). The term "local color writing" is often applied to works which, like O. Henry's or Damon Runyon's stories set in New York City, rely for their interest mainly on a sentimental or comic representation of the surface peculiarities of a region, without penetrating to deeper and more general human characteristics and problems.

Lyric. Greek writers signified by "lyric" a song rendered to the accompaniment of a lyre. The term is now used for any fairly short, nonnarrative poem presenting a speaker who expresses a state of mind or a process of thought and feeling. Lyric speakers may be represented as musing in solitude; in a *dramatic lyric,* however, they are represented in a particular situation, addressing themselves to another person, as in Donne's "Canonization" and Wordsworth's "Tintern Abbey." Although the lyric is uttered in the first person, we should be wary about identifying the "I" in the poem with the poet. In some lyrics, such as

Milton's sonnet "When I consider how my light is spent" and Coleridge's "Frost at Midnight," the relation to the known circumstances of the author's life invites us to read the poem as the personal utterance of the writer. Even in such poems, however, the character of the lyric speaker is adapted to the particular lyric situation and effect, and the utterance is ordered so as to constitute an artistic whole. In many lyrics the speaker is clearly not the author but an invented character, and one who may be very different from the actual poet. (See *confessional poetry*, *persona*, and *dramatic monologue*.)

A lyric poem may be simply a brief expression of a mood or state of feeling; for example, Shelley's "To Night," or this fine medieval song:

> Fowles in the frith,
> The fisshes in the flood,
> And I mon waxe wood:
> Much sorwe I walke with
> For best of bone and blood.

But the genre also includes extended expressions of a complex evolution of mind, such as in the long elegy and the meditative ode. The process of observation, thought, memory, and feeling in a lyric may be organized in a variety of ways. For example, in "love lyrics" the speaker may simply express his state of mind in an ordered form, as in Robert Burns's "O my love's like a red, red rose"; or he may gallantly elaborate a compliment to his lady (Ben Jonson's "Drink to me only with thine eyes"); or he may deploy an argument to persuade his mistress to take advantage of opportunity and fleeting youth (Marvell's "To His Coy Mistress"). In other kinds of lyric the speaker manifests and justifies a particular disposition and set of values (Milton's "L'Allegro" and "Il Penseroso"); or expresses a sustained process of observation and meditation, in which he analyzes and tries to resolve an emotional problem (Wordsworth's "Intimations Ode," Arnold's "Dover Beach"); or is exhibited as making and justifying the choice of a way of life (Yeats's "Sailing to Byzantium").

For subclasses of the lyric see *aubade, dramatic monologue, elegy, epithalamion, ode,* and *sonnet.* Refer to Ernest Rhys, *Lyric Poetry* (1913); C. M. Ing, *Elizabethan Lyrics* (1951); Norman Maclean, "From Action to Image: Theories of the Lyric in the 18th Century," in *Critics and Criticism,* ed. R. S. Crane (1952); Don Geiger, *The Dramatic Impulse in Modern Poetics* (1967); William E. Rogers, *The Three Genres and the Interpretation of Lyric* (1983); W. R. Johnson, *The Idea of Lyric* (1985). In the present century the lyric has become by far the preponderant poetic form; see, for example, M. L. Rosenthal, *The Modern Poets* (1960), and *The New Poets* (1967).

Malapropism is that form of **solecism** (the conspicuous violation of standard usage in a language) which mistakenly uses a word in place of another that it resembles; the effect is usually comic. The term derives from Mrs. Malaprop in Richard Brinsley Sheridan's comedy *The Rivals* (1775), who in the attempt to display a copious vocabulary said things such as "a progeny of learning," "as headstrong as an allegory on the banks of the Nile," and "He is the very pineapple of politeness."

Masque. The masque was developed in Renaissance Italy and flourished in England during the reigns of Elizabeth, James I, and Charles I. It was an elaborate and costly form of court entertainment, combining poetic drama, music, song, dance, splendid costuming, and stage spectacle. A plot—often slight, and mainly mythological and allegorical—served to hold together these diverse elements. The speaking characters, who wore masks, were often played by amateurs. The play concluded with a dance, in which the players doffed their masks and were joined by the aristocratic audience.

In the early seventeenth century the masque drew upon the finest artistic talents of the day, including Ben Jonson for the poetic script (for example, *The Masque of Blacknesse* and *The Masque of Queens*) and Inigo Jones, the architect, for the elaborate stage sets, costumes, and machinery. Each lavish production cost a fortune; it was literally the sport of kings and queens until both court and drama were abruptly ended by the Puritan triumph of 1642. The two examples best known to modern readers are the masque-within-a-play in the fourth act of Shakespeare's *The Tempest*, and Milton's sage and serious revival of the form, *Comus*, which was presented at Ludlow Castle in 1634.

The **antimasque** was a form developed by Ben Jonson. In it the characters were grotesque and unruly, the action ludicrous, and the humor broad; it served as a foil to the elegance, order, and ceremony of the masque proper, to which it was juxtaposed.

See Enid Welsford, *The Court Masque* (1927); Allardyce Nicoll, *Stuart Masques and the Renaissance Stage* (1937). Stephen Orgel and Roy Strong, in *Inigo Jones: The Theatre of the Stuart Court* (2 vols.; 1973), discuss Jones's contributions to masques, with copious illustrations.

Melodrama. "Melos" is Greek for song, and the term "melodrama" was originally applied to all musical plays, including opera. In early-nineteenth-century London, many plays were put on using musical accompaniment (as in modern motion pictures) simply to fortify the emotional tone of the various scenes; the procedure was developed in part to circumvent the Licensing Act, which allowed "legitimate" plays only as a monopoly of the Drury Lane and Covent Garden theaters, but permitted musical entertainments elsewhere. "Melodrama" is now applied to some typical dramatic products written in that period; it can be said to bear the relation to tragedy that farce does to comedy. The protagonists are flat types; the hero and heroine are pure as the driven snow and the villain a monster of malignity (the good guys and bad guys of the movie western and many television dramas are modern derivatives of character types in the older melodramas). The plot revolves around malevolent intrigue and violent action, while credibility both of character and plot is sacrificed for violent effect and emotional opportunism. Nineteenth-century melodramas such as *Sweeney Todd, the Demon Barber of Fleet Street* (1842), *Under the Gaslight* (1867), and the temperance play *Ten Nights in a Barroom* (1858) are still sometimes produced—no longer for thrills, however, but for laughs. The adjective "melodramatic" is applied to any literary work or episode that relies on improbable events and sensational action.

See M. W. Disher, *Blood and Thunder: Mid-Victorian Melodrama and Its Origins* (1949), and *Plots That Thrilled* (1954); Frank Rahill, *The World of Melodrama* (1967); R. B. Heilman, *Tragedy and Melodrama* (1968); David Thorburn, "Television Melodrama," *Television as a Cultural Force*, ed. Douglas Cater (1976).

Metaphysical Poets. Dryden said in his *Discourse of Satire* (1693) that John Donne in his poetry "affects the metaphysics"; that is, he employs the terminology and abstruse arguments of the medieval Scholastic philosophers. In 1779 Samuel Johnson extended the term "metaphysical" from Donne to a school of poets, in the acute and balanced critique which he incorporated in his "Life of Cowley." The name is now applied to a group of seventeenth-century poets who, whether or not directly influenced by Donne, employ a similar poetic procedure and imagery, both in secular poetry (Cleveland, Marvell, Cowley) and in religious poetry (Herbert, Vaughan, Crashaw).

Attempts have been made to demonstrate that these poets had in common a philosophical worldview. The term "metaphysical," however, fits these very diverse writers only if it is used, as Johnson used it, to indicate a common poetic style and way of organizing the thought or poetic argument. Donne set the metaphysical pattern by writing poems which are sharply opposed to the rich mellifluousness, the sense of human dignity, and the idealized view of sexual love which had constituted a central tradition in Elizabethan poetry, especially in Spenser and the writers of *Petrarchan sonnets.* Instead, Donne wrote in a diction and meter modeled on the rough give-and-take of actual speech, and usually organized his poems in the dramatic and rhetorical form of an urgent or heated argument—with a reluctant mistress, or an intruding friend, or God, or death, or with himself. He employed a subtle and often deliberately outrageous logic; he was realistic, ironic, and sometimes cynical in his treatment of the complexity of human motives, especially in the sexual relation; and whether playful or serious, and whether writing the poetry of love or of intense religious experience, he was above all "witty," making ingenious use of *paradox, pun,* and startling parallels and distinctions in simile and metaphor (see *metaphysical conceit*). The beginnings of four of Donne's poems will illustrate the shock tactics, the dramatic form of direct address, the rough idiom, and the rhythms of the living voice which are characteristic of his metaphysical style:

> Go and catch a falling star,
> Get with child a mandrake root . . .
>
> For God's sake hold your tongue, and let me love.
>
> Busy old fool, unruly sun . . .
>
> Batter my heart, three-personed God . . .

The metaphysical poets have had some admirers in every age, but beginning with the *Neoclassic Period* of the later seventeenth century, they were for the most part regarded as interesting but perversely ingenious and obscure eccentrics, until a drastic revaluation after World War I elevated Donne, together with other poets in the mode, high in the *canon* of English poets. This reversal owed much to H. J. C. Grierson's Introduction to *Metaphysical Lyrics and Poems of the Seventeenth Century* (1912), was given strong impetus by T. S. Eliot's essays "The Metaphysical Poets" and "Andrew Marvell" (1921), and has been continued by a great number of commentators, including the *New Critics,* who tended to elevate the metaphysical style into the very model of the poetry of a "unified sensibility," irony, and paradox. See *dissociation of sensibility.*

George Williamson, *The Donne Tradition* (1930); Cleanth Brooks, *Modern Poetry and the Tradition* (1939); Rosemund Tuve, *Elizabethan and Metaphysical Imagery* (1947); J. E. Duncan, *The Revival of Metaphysical Poetry* (1959); F. J. Warnke, *European Metaphysical Poetry* (1961), which treats the continental vogue of this style; Helen Gardner, ed., *John Donne: A Collection of Critical Essays* (1962).

Meter. In all sustained spoken English we feel a **rhythm,** that is, a recognizable though variable pattern in the beat of the stresses in the stream of sound. If this rhythm of stresses is structured into a recurrence of regular—that is, approximately equivalent—units, we call it **meter.** Compositions written in meter are known as **verse.**

There is considerable dispute about the best way to analyze and classify English meters. This article will present a traditional stress-and-syllable analysis which has the virtue of being simple, widely accepted, and applicable to by far the greater part of English versification from Chaucer to the present day. Some major departures from this stress-and-syllable meter will be described at the end.

We attend, in reading verse, to the individual **line,** which is a separate entity on the printed page. The meter of a line is determined by the pattern of stronger and weaker stresses in its component syllables; often, the stronger stress is called the "stressed" and the weaker one the "unstressed" syllable. (What the ear detects as a strong stress is not an absolute quantity, but is relative to the degree of stress in the adjacent syllables; the degree of perceived stress is determined primarily by the relative loudness of the pronunciation of the syllable, and to a lesser extent by its relative pitch and duration.) There are three major factors that determine where the **stresses** (in the sense of the relatively stronger stresses, or "accents") will fall in a line of verse: (1) Most important is the "word accent" in polysyllabic words; in the noun "accent" itself, for example, the stress falls on the first syllable. (2) There are also many monosyllabic words in the language, and on which of these—in a sentence or a phrase—the stress will fall depends on the grammatical function of the word (we normally put stronger stress on nouns, verbs, and adjectives, for example, than on articles or prepositions), and also on the "rhetorical accent," or the emphasis we give a word because we want to enhance its importance in a particular utterance. (3) Another determinant of stress is the prevailing "metrical accent," which is an expected pulsation, in accordance with the stress pattern which was established earlier in the metrical line or passage.

If the prevailing stress pattern enforces a drastic alteration of the normal word accent, we get a **wrenched accent.** Wrenching may be the result of a lack of metrical skill; it was, however, conventional in the *folk ballad* (for example, "fair ladíe," "far countrée"), and is sometimes deliberately used, as in Byron's *Don Juan* (1819–24) and in the recent verses of Ogden Nash, for comic effects.

It is possible to distinguish a number of degrees of relative syllabic stress in English speech, but the most common and generally useful fashion of analyzing and classifying the standard English meters is to distinguish only two categories of stress in syllables—weak stress and strong stress—and to group the syllables into metric feet according to the patterning of these two stresses. A **foot** is the combination of a strong stress and the associated weak stress or stresses which make up the recurrent metric unit of a line. The relatively stronger-stressed syllable is called, for short, "stressed"; the relatively weaker-stressed syllables are called "light," or "slack," or simply "unstressed."

The four standard feet distinguished in English are:

(1) **Iambic** (the noun is "iamb"): a light followed by a stressed syllable.

Thĕ cúr'fĕw tólls'thĕ knéll'ŏf pár'tĭng dáy.'

(Gray, "Elegy in a Country Churchyard")

(2) **Anapestic** (the noun is "anapest"): two light syllables followed by a stressed syllable.

Thĕ Ăs sýr'iăn căme dówn'lĭke ă wólf'ŏn thĕ fóld.'

(Byron, "The Destruction of Sennacherib")

(3) **Trochaic** (the noun is "trochee"): a stressed followed by a light syllable.

Thére thĕy'áre, mÿ'fíf tÿ'mén ănd'wó mĕn.'

(Browning, "One Word More")

Most trochaic lines lack the final unstressed syllable—in the technical term, such lines are **catalectic.** So in Blake's "The Tiger":

Tí gĕr'! tí gĕr'! búrn ĭng' bríght'
Ín thĕ'fó rĕst óf thĕ'níght.'

(4) **Dactylic** (the noun is "dactyl"): a stressed syllable followed by two light syllables.

Éve, wĭth hĕr'bás kĕt, wăs'
Deép ĭn thĕ'béllş ănd grăss.'

(Ralph Hodgson, "Eve")

Iambs and anapests, since the strong stress is at the end, constitute a "rising meter"; trochees and dactyls, with the strong stress at the beginning, constitute a "falling meter." Iambs and trochees, having two syllables, are called "duple meter"; anapests and dactyls, having three syllables, are called "triple meter." It should be noted that the iamb is by far the commonest English foot.

Two other feet, often distinguished, occur only as occasional variants from standard feet:

(5) **Spondaic** (the noun is "spondee"): two successive syllables with approximately equal strong stresses, as in the first two feet of this line:

Goód stróng'thíck stú'pĕ fý'iňg ín'cĕnse smóke.'

(Browning, "The Bishop Orders His Tomb")

(6) **Pyrrhic** (the noun is also "pyrrhic"): two successive syllables with approximately equal light stresses, as in the second and fourth feet in this line:

Mý wăy'ĭs tŏ'bĕ gín'wĭth thĕ'bĕ gín nĭng'

(Byron, *Don Juan*)

(Some traditional metrists do not admit the existence of a true pyrrhic, on the grounds that the prevailing metrical accent—in this instance, iambic—always imposes a slightly stronger stress on one of the two syllables.)

A metric line is named according to the number of feet composing it:

monometer: one foot
dimeter: two feet
trimeter: three feet
tetrameter: four feet
pentameter: five feet
hexameter: six feet (an **Alexandrine** is a line of six iambic feet)
heptameter: seven feet (a **fourteener** is another term for a line of seven iambic feet—hence, of fourteen syllables; it tends to break into a unit of four feet followed by a unit of three feet)
octameter: eight feet

To describe the meter of a line we name (a) the predominant foot and (b) the number of feet it contains. In the illustrations above, for example, the line from Gray's "Elegy" is "iambic pentameter," and the line from Byron's "The Destruction of Sennacherib" is "anapestic tetrameter."

To **scan** a passage of verse is to go through it line by line, analyzing the component feet, and also indicating where any major pauses fall within a line. Here is a **scansion,** signified by conventional symbols, of the first five lines from Keats's *Endymion* (1818); the passage was chosen because it exemplifies a flexible and variable rather than a highly regular metrical pattern.

(1) Ă thíng'ŏf beáu'tў ís'ă jóy'fŏr é vĕr:'
(2) Ĭts lóve'lĭ nĕss' ĭn creás'ĕs; // ít'wĭll név ĕr'
(3) Páss ĭn'tŏ nóth'ĭng nĕss,' // bŭt stíll'wĭll keép'
(4) Ă bów'ĕr quí'ĕt fŏr'ŭs, // ánd'ă sleép'
(5) Fúll ŏf'swĕet dreáms,'ăňd heálth,'ăňd qúi'ĕt breáth iňg.'

The prevailing meter is clearly iambic, and the lines are iambic pentameter. As in all fluent verse, however, there are variations upon the basic iambic foot, which are sometimes called "substitutions":

(1) The closing feet of lines 1, 2, and 5 end with an extra light syllable, and are said to have a **feminine ending.** Lines 3 and 4, in which the closing feet, since they are standard iambs, end with a stressed syllable, are said to have **masculine endings.**

(2) In lines 3 and 5, the opening iambic feet have been "inverted" to form trochees. (These initial positions are the most common place for such inversions in iambic verse.)

(3) I have marked the second foot in line 2, and the third foot of line 3 and line 4, as pyrrhics (two light stresses); these help to give Keats's verses their rapid movement. This is a procedure in scansion with which competent readers often disagree: some will feel enough of a metric beat in all these feet to mark them as iambs; others will mark still other feet (for example, the third foot of line 1) as pyrrhics also. And some metric analysts prefer to use symbols measuring two degrees of strong stress, and will indicate a difference in the feet, as follows:

Ĭts lő̆ve'lĭ néss'ĭn crĕ́̋as'ĕs.

Notice, however, that these are differences in nuance rather than in essentials: the analysts agree that the prevailing pulse of Keats's versification is iambic throughout.

Two other elements are important in the metric movement of Keats's passage: (1) In lines 1 and 5, the pause in the reading—which occurs naturally at the end of a clause or other syntactic unit—coincides with the end of the line; such lines are called **end-stopped.** Lines 2 through 4, on the other hand, are called **run-on lines** (or in a French term, they exhibit **enjambement**—"a striding-over"), because the pressure of the incompleted syntactic unit toward closure carries on over the end of the verse-line. (2) When a strong phrasal pause falls within a line, as in lines 2, 3, and 4, it is called a **caesura**—indicated in the quoted passage by the conventional symbol, //. The management of these internal pauses is important for giving variety and for providing expressive emphases in the long pentameter line.

To understand the function of such an analysis, we must realize that scansion is an abstract scheme which deliberately omits notation of many aspects of the actual reading of a poem that contribute to its movement, rhythm, and total impression. It does not specify, for example, whether the component words in a metric line are short words or long words, or whether the strong stresses fall on short vowels or long vowels; it does not give any indication of the *intonation*—the overall rise and fall of the pitch and loudness of the voice—which we use to bring out the meaning and rhetorical effect of these poetic lines; nor does it indicate the rhythms of the varied phrasal structure of a sustained poetic passage. We deliberately omit such details in order to lay bare the essential metric skeleton; that is, the fall of the stronger stresses in the syllabic sequence of a verse-line. Moreover, an actual reading of a poem, if it is a skillful reading, will not accord mechanically with the scansion. That is, there is a difference between the scansion, as an abstract metrical norm, and the skilled oral reading, or **performance,** of a poem; and in fact, no two competent readers will perform the same lines in precisely the same way. But the metric norm indicated by the scansion is sensed as an implicit understructure of pulses, and the interplay of an expressive performance, sometimes with and sometimes against this underlying structural pattern, helps to give tension and vitality to our experience of verse.

We should note, finally, that various kinds of English versification differ from the syllable-and-stress type already described:

(1) **Strong-stress meters.** In this native English and Germanic meter only the strong stresses count in the scanning, and the number of intervening light syllables is highly variable. There are usually four strong-stressed syllables in a line. This was the meter of Old English poetry and of many Middle English poems, until Chaucer popularized the syllable-and-stress meter. In the opening passage, for example, of *Piers Plowman* (later fourteenth century) the four strong stresses (always divided by a medial caesura) are often reinforced by alliteration (see *alliterative meter*); the light syllables, which vary in number, are recessive and do not assert their individual presence:

> In a sómer séson, // whan sóft was the sónne,
> I shópe me in shroúdes, // as Í a shépe were,
> In hábits like an héremite, // unhóly of wórkes,
> Went wýde in this wórld, // wónders to hére.

Strong-stress meter still survives in traditional children's rhymes such as "Hickory, dickory, dock," and was revived as an artful literary meter by Coleridge in *Christabel* (1816), in which each line has four strong stresses but the number of syllables within a line varies from four to twelve.

What G. M. Hopkins in the later nineteenth century called his **sprung rhythm** is a variant of strong-stress meter: each foot, as he describes it, begins with a stressed syllable, which may either stand alone or be associated with from one to three (occasionally even more) light syllables. Two six-stress lines from Hopkins' "The Wreck of the *Deutschland*" indicate the variety of the rhythms in this meter, and also exemplify its most striking feature: the great weight of the strong stresses, and the frequent juxtaposition of strong stresses at any point in the line. The stresses in the second line were marked in a manuscript by Hopkins himself; they indicate that in complex instances, his metric decisions may seem arbitrary:

> The'soúr'scýthe'crínge, and the'bleár'sháre'cóme.'
> Our'heárts' charity's'heárth's'fíre, our'thoúghts' chivalry's'
>   thróng's'Lórd.'

(See Elisabeth Schneider, "Sprung Rhythm," *PMLA*, Vol. 80, 1965.) A number of modern metrists, such as T. S. Eliot and Ezra Pound, skillfully interweave both strong-stress and syllable-and-stress meters in some of their versification.

(2) **Quantitative meters** in English are written in imitation of Greek and Latin versification, in which the metrical pattern is not determined by the stress but by the "quantity" (duration of pronunciation) of a syllable, and the foot consists of a combination of "long" and "short" syllables. Sidney, Spenser, and other Elizabethan poets experimented with this meter in English, as did Coleridge, Tennyson, Longfellow, and Robert Bridges later on. The strong accentual character of English, however, as well as the indeterminateness of the syllabic duration, makes it impossible to sustain for any length a purely quantitative meter.

(3) In *free verse* (discussed in a separate essay), the component lines have no (or at least only occasional) units of uniform stress-patterns.

George Saintsbury, *Historical Manual of English Prosody* (1910), and R. M. Alden, *English Verse* (1930), are well-illustrated treatments of traditional syllable-and-stress metrics. For later discussions of this and alternative metric theories see George R. Stewart, *The Technique of English Verse* (1930); Seymour Chatman, *A Theory of Meter* (1965); and W. K. Wimsatt and Monroe C. Beardsley, "The Concept of Meter" (1959). This last essay is reprinted in W. K. Wimsatt, *Hateful Contraries* (1965), and in Harvey Gross, ed., *The Structure of Verse* (1966)—an anthology which reprints other essays, including Northrop Frye, "The Rhythm of Recurrence," and Yvor Winters, "The Audible Reading of Poetry." See also W. K. Wimsatt, ed., *Versification: Major Language Types* (1972); John Hollander, *Vision and Resonance* (1975); Paul Fussell, *Poetic Meter and Poetic Form* (rev., 1979).

Middle English Period. The four and a half centuries between the Norman Conquest in 1066, which effected radical changes in the language, life, and culture of England, and about 1500, when the standard literary language (deriving from the dialect of the London area) had become recognizably "modern English"—that is, very similar to the language we speak and write today.

The span from 1100 to 1350 is sometimes discriminated as the **Anglo-Norman Period,** because the non-Latin literature of that time was written mainly in Anglo-Norman, the French dialect spoken by the new ruling class of England. When the native vernacular, descended from Anglo-Saxon and known as "Middle English," came into general literary use, it was at first the vehicle mainly for religious and homiletic writings. The first great age of primarily secular literature was the second half of the fourteenth century—the age of Chaucer and John Gower, of William Langland's great religious and satirical poem *Piers Plowman*, and of the anonymous master who wrote four fine poems in complex *alliterative meter*, including the elegy *Pearl* and *Gawain and the Green Knight*. This last work is the best of the English *chivalric romances;* the best prose romance was Thomas Malory's *Morte d'Arthur*, written a century later. The outstanding poets of the fifteenth century were the "Scottish Chaucerians," who included King James I of Scotland and Robert Henryson. The fifteenth century was more important for popular literature than for the artful literature written for the upper classes: it was the age of many excellent songs, secular and religious, and of many of the best *folk ballads*, as well as the flowering time of the medieval drama, the *miracle* and *morality plays*, which were written and produced for the general public.

See W. L. Renwick and H. Orton, *The Beginnings of English Literature to Skelton* (rev., 1952); H. S. Bennett, *Chaucer and the Fifteenth Century* (1947); Edward Vasta, ed., *Middle English Survey: Critical Essays* (1965).

Miracle Plays, Morality Plays, and Interludes were types of late-medieval drama, written in a variety of verse forms.

The **miracle play** had as its subject either a story from the Scriptures, or else the life and martyrdom of a saint. (In the usage of some historians, however, "miracle play" denotes only dramas based on saints' lives, and the term **mystery play**—"mystery" in the archaic sense of the "trade" of the medieval guilds who sponsored these plays—is applied to dramas based on the Old and New Testaments.) The biblical plays originated within the church in about the tenth century, in dramatizations of brief parts of the Latin liturgical service, called "tropes," especially the "Quem quaeritis" ("Whom are you seeking") trope representing the visit of the three Marys to the tomb of Christ. Gradually these evolved into complete plays which were written in English instead of in Latin, produced under the auspices of the various trade guilds, and acted on stages set outside the church. The miracle plays written in England are of unknown authorship. In the fourteenth century there developed the practice, on the feast of Corpus Christi (sixty days after Easter), of putting on great "cycles" of such plays, representing in chronological order crucial events in the biblical history of mankind, from the Creation and Fall of man, through the Nativity, Crucifixion, and Resurrection of Christ, to the Last Judgment. Each scene was played on a separate "pageant wagon," which was drawn, in its proper sequence, to one after another of the fixed "stations" in a city, at each of which the entire cycle was enacted. The biblical texts were greatly expanded in these plays, and the author often added comic scenes of his own invention. For examples of the variety, vitality, and power of these dramas, see the Wakefield "Noah" and "Second Shepherd's Play," and the Brome "Abraham and Isaac."

Morality plays were dramatized *allegories* of the representative Christian life, in the mode of a quest for salvation in which the crucial events are temptation, sin, and the confrontation with death. The protagonist represents Mankind, or Everyman; among the other characters are personifications of virtues, vices, and Death, as well as angels and demons who contest for the prize of the soul of Mankind. A character known as the **Vice** often played the role of the tempter in a fashion both sinister and comic; he is regarded by some literary historians as a precursor both of the cynical and ironic villain and of some of the comic figures in Elizabethan drama, including Falstaff. The best-known morality play is the fifteenth-century *Everyman;* another fine example, written early in the same century, is *The Castle of Perseverance.*

Interlude (Latin, "between the play") is a term applied to a variety of short stage entertainments, including secular farces and witty dialogues with a religious or political point. In the late fifteenth and early sixteenth centuries, these little dramas were performed by bands of professional actors; it is believed that they were often put on between the courses of a feast or between the acts of a longer play. Among the better-known interludes are John Heywood's farces of the first half of the sixteenth century, especially *The Four PP* (that is, the Palmer, the Pardoner, the 'Pothecary, and the Peddler, who engage in a lying contest), and *Johan Johan the Husband, Tyb His Wife, and Sir John the Priest.*

See Karl Young, *The Drama of the Medieval Church* (1933), 2 vols.; A. P. Rossiter, *English Drama from Early Times to the Elizabethans* (1950); Hardin Craig, *English Religious Drama of the Middle Ages* (1955); Arnold Williams, *The Drama of Medieval England* (1961); T. W. Craik, *The Tudor Interlude* (1962); V. A. Kolve, *The Play Called Corpus Christi* (1966); Rosemary Woolf, *The English Mystery Plays* (1972). On the relation of the "Vice" in the morality plays to figures in Shakespearean drama, see Bernard Spivak, *Shakespeare and the Allegory of Evil* (1958).

Modern Period. The term "modern" is, of course, variable in its temporal reference, but it is frequently applied specifically to the literature in English written since the beginning of World War I in 1914. This period has been marked by persistent and multidimensioned experiments in subject matter and form, and has produced major achievements in all the literary genres. The poets include Yeats, Frost, Eliot, Wallace Stevens, Auden, Robert Graves, Robert Lowell, and Dylan Thomas; the novelists, Conrad, Joyce, Lawrence, Virginia Woolf, E. M. Forster, Ernest Hemingway, F. Scott Fitzgerald, William Faulkner, Vladimir Nabokov, and Doris Lessing; the dramatists, G. B. Shaw, Sean O'Casey, Eugene O'Neill, Tennessee Williams, and Samuel Beckett; and the critics, T. S. Eliot, I. A. Richards, F. R. Leavis, Lionel Trilling, and the *New Critics.* The term **Contemporary Period** is sometimes applied to the time after World War II (1939–45), or else to the last quarter-century or so of the Modern Period. See *modernism and postmodernism.*

Modernism and Postmodernism. The term **modernism** is often used to identify what are considered to be distinctive features in the concepts, sensibility, form, and style of literature and art since World War I (1914–1918). The specific features signified by "modernism" vary with the user, but most critics agree that it involves a deliberate and radical break with some of the traditional bases both of Western culture and of Western art. Important intellectual precursors of modernism, in this sense, are thinkers who questioned the certainties that had provided a support for traditional modes of social organization, religion, morality, and the conception of the human self—thinkers such as Friedrich Nietzsche (1844–1900), Karl Marx, Sigmund Freud, and James G. Frazer, whose *The Golden Bough* (1890–1915) stressed the correspondence between central Christian tenets and pagan, often barbaric myths and rituals.

The modernist revolt against traditional literary forms and subjects manifested itself strongly after the catastrophe of World War I shook men's faith in the foundations and continuity of Western civilization and culture. As T. S. Eliot wrote in a review of Joyce's *Ulysses* in 1923, the inherited mode of ordering a literary work, which assumed a relatively coherent and stable social order, could not accord with "the immense panorama of futility and anarchy which is contemporary history." Like Joyce and Ezra Pound, Eliot experimented with new forms and a new style that would render contemporary disorder, often contrasting it to a lost order that had been based on the religion and myths of the cultural past. In *The Waste Land* (1922), for example, Eliot replaces the standard flow of poetic language by fragmented utterances, and substitutes for the traditional coherence of poetic structure a dislocation of parts, in which remote components are related by connections which are left to the reader to discover, or invent. Major works of modernist fiction, following Joyce's *Ulysses* (1922) and his even more radical *Finnegans Wake* (1939), subvert the basic conventions of earlier prose fiction by breaking up the narrative continuity, departing from the standard ways of representing characters, and violating the traditional syntax and coherence of narrative language by the use of *stream of consciousness* and other innovative modes of narration. Such new forms of lyric and narrative construction were emulated and carried further by many poets and novelists; they have obvious parallels in the violation of representational conventions in *expressionism* and *surrealism,* in the modernist paintings of Cubism, Futurism, and Abstract Expressionism, and in the violations of standard conventions of melody, harmony, and rhythm by the modernist musical composers Stravinsky, Schoenberg, and their radical followers.

A prominent feature of modernism is the phenomenon of an **avant-garde** (a military metaphor: "advance-guard"); that is, a small, self-conscious group of artists and authors who undertake, in Ezra Pound's phrase, to "make it new." By violating accepted conventions and decorums, they undertake to create ever-new artistic forms and styles and to introduce hitherto neglected, and sometimes forbidden, subject matters. Frequently avant-garde artists represent themselves as "alienated" from the established order, against which they assert their own autonomy; their aim is to shock the sensibilities of the conventional reader and to challenge the norms and pieties of the dominant bourgeois culture. See Renato Poggioli, *The Theory of the Avant-Garde* (1968).

The term **postmodernism** is sometimes applied to the literature and art after World War II (1939–45), when the disastrous effects on Western morale of the first war were greatly exacerbated by the experience of Nazi totalitarianism and mass extermination, the threat of total destruction by the atomic bomb, the progressive devastation of the natural environment, and the ominous fact of overpopulation and the threat of starvation. Postmodernism involves not only a continuation, carried to an extreme, of the countertraditional experiments of modernism, but also diverse attempts to break away from modernist forms which had, inevitably, become in their turn conventional. A familiar undertaking in postmodernist writings is to subvert the foundations of our accepted modes of thought and experience so as to reveal the "meaninglessness" of existence and the underlying "abyss," or "void," or "nothingness" on which our supposed security is precariously suspended. In recent developments in linguistic and literary theory, there is an effort to subvert the foundations of language itself, so as to show that its seeming meaningfulness dissipates, for an unillusioned inquirer, into a play of unresolvable though conflicting indeterminacies.

For some of the radical postmodernist developments in literature, see literature of the *absurd, antihero, antinovel, Beat writers, concrete poetry, new novel;* and in critical theory, see *anxiety of influence, deconstruction, reader-response criticism, structuralism, text and writing (écriture)*. On modernism and postmodernism, refer to Richard Ellmann and Charles Feidelson, eds., *The Modern Tradition: Backgrounds of Modern Literature* (1965); Erich Heller, *The Artist's Journey into the Interior, and Other Essays* (1965); Robert M. Adams, *Nil: Episodes in the Literary Conquest of Void during the Nineteenth Century* (1966); Irving Howe, ed., *The Idea of the Modern in Literature and the Arts* (1967); Lionel Trilling, *Beyond Culture* (1968), and *Sincerity and Authenticity* (1972); David Perkins, *A History of Modern Poetry: From the 1890s to the High Modernist Mode* (1976); Christopher Lasch, *The Culture of Narcissism* (1978); Charles Altieri, *Enlarging the Temple: New Directions in American Poetry* (1979); Gerald Graff, *Literature Against Itself: Literary Ideas in Modern Society* (1979); Helen Vendler, *Part of Nature: Part of Us: Modern American Poets* (1981).

Motif and Theme. A **motif** is an element—a type of incident, device, reference, or formula—which recurs frequently in literature. The "loathly lady" who turns out to be a beautiful princess is a common motif in *folklore*. The man fatally bewitched by a fairy lady is a motif adopted from folklore in Keats's "La Belle Dame sans Merci" (1820). Common in lyric poems is the **ubi sunt motif,** or "where-are" formula for lamenting the vanished past ("Where are the snows of yesteryear?"); another is the *carpe diem* motif, whose nature is sufficiently indicated by Robert Herrick's title "To the Virgins, to Make Much of Time." An **aubade**—from the Old French word "alba," meaning dawn—is an early-morning song, whose usual motif is an urgent request to a beloved to wake up. A familiar example is Shakespeare's "Hark, hark, the lark at heaven's gate sings."

An older term for recurrent poetic concepts or formulas is the **topos** (Greek for "a commonplace"); Ernst R. Curtius, *European Literature and the Latin Middle Ages* (1953), treats many of the ancient literary topoi. The term "motif," or the German **leitmotif** (a guiding motif), is also applied to the frequent repetition of a significant phrase, or set description, or complex of images, in a single work, as in the operas of Richard Wagner, or in novels by Thomas Mann, James Joyce, Virginia Woolf, and William Faulkner. See *imagery;* and for a *deconstructive* treatment of recurrent elements or motifs in the novel, J. Hillis Miller, *Repetition and Fiction* (1982).

Theme is sometimes used interchangeably with "motif," but the term is more usefully applied to a general claim, or doctrine, whether implicit or asserted, which an imaginative work is designed to incorporate and make persuasive to the reader. Milton states as the explicit theme of *Paradise Lost* to "assert Eternal Providence,/And justify the ways of God to men"; see *didactic literature* and *fiction*. Some critics claim that all nontrivial works of literature, including lyric poems, involve an implicit theme which is embodied and dramatized in the evolving meanings and imagery; see, for example, Cleanth Brooks, *The Well Wrought Urn* (1947). For a discussion of the uses of the critical terms "subject," "theme," and "thesis" see Monroe C. Beardsley, *Aesthetics* (1958), pp. 401–11.

Myth. In classical Greek, "mythos" signified any story or plot, whether true or invented. In its central modern significance, however, a myth is one story in a **mythology**—a system of hereditary stories which were once believed to be true by a particular cultural group, and which served to explain (in terms of the intentions and actions of supernatural beings) why the world is as it is and things happen as they do, as well as to establish the rationale for social customs and observances, and the sanctions for the rules by which people conduct their lives. Most myths involve **rituals**—set forms and procedures in sacred ceremonies—but social anthropologists disagree as to whether rituals generated myths or myths generated rituals. If the protagonist is a person rather than a supernatural being, the story is usually not called myth but **legend;** if the story concerns supernatural beings, but is not part of a systematic mythology, it is usually classified as a *folktale*.

Recently the French structuralist Claude Lévi-Strauss has departed from the traditional views just described, to treat the myths of a particular culture as signifying systems whose true meanings are unknown to their proponents. He analyzes myths as composed of *signs* which are to be identified and interpreted on the model of the linguistic theory of Ferdinand de Saussure. See Lévi-Strauss, "The Structural Study of Myth," in *Structural Anthropology* (1968); and refer to *structuralist criticism* and *semiotics*.

A mythology, we can say, is a religion in which we no longer believe. Poets, however, long after having ceased to believe in them, have persisted in using the myths of Jupiter, Venus, Prometheus, Wotan, Adam and Eve, and Jonah for their plots, episodes, or allusions; as Coleridge said, "still doth the old instinct bring back the old names." The term has also been extended to denote supernatural tales which are deliberately invented by their authors. Plato in the fourth century B.C. used such invented myths in order to project philosophical speculation beyond the point at which certain knowledge is possible; see, for example, his "Myth of Er" in Book X of *The Republic*. The German romantic authors F. W. J. Schelling and Friedrich Schlegel proposed that to write great literature, modern poets must develop a new unifying mythology which will synthesize the insights of the myths of the Western past with the new discoveries of philosophy and physical science. In the same period in England, William Blake, who felt "I must create a system or be enslaved by another man's," incorporated in his poems a system of mythology he had himself created by fusing hereditary myths and biblical history and prophecy with his own intuitions, visions, and intellection. A number of modern writers have also asserted that an integrative mythology, whether inherited or invented, is essential to literature. Joyce in *Ulysses* and *Finnegans Wake,* Eliot in *The Waste Land,* O'Neill in *Mourning Becomes Electra,* and many other writers have deliberately woven their modern materials on the pattern of ancient myths, while Yeats, like his admired predecessor Blake, undertook to construct his own systematic mythology, which he expounded in *A Vision* (1926) and embodied in a number of great lyric poems.

Myth has become one of the most prominent terms in literary analysis. A large group of writers, the **myth critics**—including Robert Graves, Francis Fergusson, Maud Bodkin, Richard Chase, and (the most influential) Northrop Frye—view the genres and individual plot-patterns of much (or almost all) literature, including what on the surface are highly sophisticated and realistic works, as recurrences of certain **archetypes** and basic mythic formulas. As Northrop Frye puts it, "the typical forms of myth become the conventions and genres of literature." According to Frye's theory, there are four main narrative genres—comedy, romance, tragedy, and irony (satire)—and these are "displaced" modes of the four elemental forms of myth, associated with the seasonal cycle of spring, summer, autumn, and winter. (See *archetypal criticism* and *genre.*)

The student should be alert to the bewildering variety of applications of the term "myth" in contemporary criticism. In addition to the meanings already described, its uses range all the way from signifying any widely held fallacy ("the myth of progress," "the American success myth") to denoting the solidly imagined realm in which a work of fiction is enacted ("Faulkner's myth of Yoknapatawpha County," "the mythical world of *Moby-Dick*").

On classical mythology see H. J. Rose, *A Handbook of Greek Mythology* (1939), and G. M. Kirkwood, *A Short Guide to Classical Mythology* (1959). Among studies of myths especially influential for modern literature and criticism are James G. Frazer, *The Golden Bough* (rev., 1911); Jessie Weston, *From Ritual to Romance* (1920); Jane E. Harrison, *Themis* (2d ed., 1927); F. R. R. S. Raglan, *The Hero* (1936). For instances of the theory and practice of myth criticism see Francis Fergusson, *The Idea of a Theater* (1949); Richard Chase, *Quest for Myth* (1949); Philip Wheelwright, *The Burning Fountain* (1954); Leslie Fiedler, *Love and Death in the American Novel* (1960); Northrop Frye, *Anatomy of Criticism* (1957), and "Literature and Myth" in *Relations of Literary Study,* ed. James Thorpe (1967). This last essay has a useful bibliography of the theory and history of myths, as well as of major exponents of myth criticism.

Negative Capability. The poet John Keats introduced this term in a letter written December 1817 to define a literary quality "which Shakespeare possessed so enormously—I mean *Negative Capability,* that is, when man is capable of being in uncertainties, mysteries, doubts, without any irritable reaching after fact and reason." Keats contrasted to this quality the writings of Coleridge, who "would let go by a fine isolated verisimilitude . . . from being incapable of remaining content with half knowledge," and went on to express the general principle "that with a great poet the sense of beauty overcomes every other consideration, or rather obliterates all consideration."

The elusive term has entered critical circulation and has accumulated a large body of commentary. When conjoined to observations in other letters of Keats, "negative capability" can be taken (1) to characterize an impersonal, or objective, author who maintains *aesthetic distance,* as opposed to a subjective author who is personally involved in a work of literature, or to an author who writes in order to make persuasive his or her personal beliefs; and (2) to suggest that, when embodied in a beautiful artistic form, the literary subject matter, concepts, and characters are not subject to the ordinary standards of evidence, truth, and morality, as we apply these standards in our practical experience.

See *distance and involvement,* and *objective and subjective;* and on the interpretations of Keats's "negative capability," W. J. Bate, *John Keats* (1963).

Neoclassic and Romantic. The simplest use of these extremely variable terms is as noncommittal names for periods of literature. In this application, the "Neoclassic Period" in England spans the 140 years or so after the Restoration (1660), and the "Romantic Period" extends from the outbreak of the French Revolution in 1789—or alternatively, from the publication of *Lyrical Ballads* in 1798—through the first three decades of the nineteenth century. With reference to American literature, the term "neoclassic" is rarely applied to eighteenth-century writers; on the other hand, 1830–65, the era of Emerson, Thoreau, Poe, Melville, and Hawthorne, is sometimes called "the American Romantic Period." See *periods of English literature* and *periods of American literature.* (The same terms are applied to periods of German, French, and other Continental literatures, but with differences in the historical spans they identify.)

Historians have often tried to "define" neoclassicism or romanticism, as though each term denoted a single essence which was shared, to varying degrees, by all the major writings of an age. But the course of literary events has not formed itself around such simple entities, and the numerous and conflicting single definitions of neoclassicism and romanticism are either so vague as to be next to meaningless or so specific as to fall far short of equating with the great range and variety of the literary facts. A more useful undertaking is to specify a number of salient attributes of literary theory and practice, common to a number of the important writers of the Neoclassic Period in England, which serve to distinguish them from many major writers of the Romantic Period. The following list of ideas and characteristics, largely shared by such authors as Dryden, Pope, Addison, Swift, Johnson, Goldsmith, and Edmund Burke, may serve as an introductory sketch of distinctive features of **neoclassic** literature:

(1) These authors manifested a strong traditionalism, which was often joined to a distrust of radical innovation, and was evidenced above all in their

immense respect for **classical** writers—that is, the writers of ancient Greece and Rome—who were thought to have established the enduring models, and to have achieved a supreme level of excellence, in most of the major literary *genres.* Hence the term "neoclassic." (It is from this high estimate of the literary achievements of classical antiquity that the term **classic** has come to be applied to any later literary work which is considered to have achieved high excellence, and to set a standard in its literary kind.)

(2) Literature was conceived to be primarily an "art"; one which, though it requires innate talents, must be perfected by long study and practice, and consists mainly in the deliberate adaptation of known and tested means to the achievement of foreseen ends upon the audience of readers. The neoclassic ideal, founded especially on Horace's Roman *Ars Poetica* (first century B.C.), is the craftsman's ideal, demanding the utmost finish, correction, and attention to detail. Special allowances were often made for the unerring freedom of "natural geniuses," and also for happy strokes, available even to some less gifted poets, which occur without premeditation and achieve, as Alexander Pope said in his *Essay on Criticism* (1711), "a grace beyond the reach of art." But a natural genius such as Homer or Shakespeare is a rarity, and probably a thing of the past, and to even the best of artful poets, literary "graces" come only occasionally. The neoclassic writer strove, therefore, for "correctness," was careful to observe the complex demands of stylistic *decorum,* and for the most part respected the established "rules" of his art. The neoclassic **rules of poetry** were, in theory, the essential properties of the various genres (such as epic, tragedy, comedy, pastoral) that have been abstracted from classical works whose long survival has proved their excellence. These properties, such as the *three unities* in drama, a number of critics believed, must be embodied in modern works if they too are to be excellent and to survive.

(3) Human beings, and especially human beings as an integral part of an organized society, were regarded as the primary subject matter of literature. Poetry was held to be an *imitation* of human life—in a common phrase, "a mirror held up to nature." And by the human actions it imitates, and the artistic form it gives to the imitation, poetry is designed to yield both instruction and aesthetic pleasure to the people who read it. Not art for art's sake, but art for humanity's sake, was the ideal of neoclassic *humanism.*

(4) Both in the subject matter and the appeal of art, emphasis was placed on what human beings possess in common—representative characteristics, and widely shared experiences, thoughts, feelings, and tastes. "True wit," Pope said in a much-quoted passage of his *Essay on Criticism,* is "what oft was thought but ne'er so well expressed." That is, a primary aim of poetry is to give new and perfect expression to the great commonplaces of human wisdom, whose prevalence and durability are the best warrant of their importance and truth. There was also insistence, it should be noted, on the need to balance or enhance the typical and the familiar with the opposing qualities of novelty, particularity, and invention. Samuel Johnson substituted for Pope's definition of true wit the statement that wit "is at once natural and *new,*" and praised Shakespeare because, while his characters are species, they are all "discriminated" and "distinct." But there was wide agreement that the general nature and shared values of humanity are the

basic source and test of art, and also that the fact of universal agreement, everywhere and always, is the best test of moral and religious truths, as well as of aesthetic values. (See *deism.*)

(5) Neoclassic writers, like the philosophers of the time, viewed an individual as a limited being who ought to undertake accessible goals. Many of the great works of the period, satiric and didactic, attack humanity's "pride," or presumption beyond the natural limits of the species, and enforce the lesson of the golden mean (the avoidance of extremes) and of humanity's need to submit to its restricted position in the natural order—an order sometimes envisioned as a natural hierarchy, or *Great Chain of Being.* In art, as in life, there prevailed the law of measure and the acceptance of strict limits upon one's freedom. The poets admired extremely the great genres of epic and tragedy, but wrote their own masterpieces in admittedly lesser and less demanding forms such as the essay in verse and prose, the comedy of manners, and especially satire, in which they felt they had more chance to equal or surpass their classical and English predecessors. They uncomplainingly submitted to at least some "rules" and other limiting conventions in literary subjects, structure, and diction. Typical was their election, in many poems, to write within the extremely tight restrictions of the *closed couplet.* But the distinctive quality of the urbane and civilized poetry of the Neoclassic Period was, in the phrase often quoted from Horace, "the art that hides art"; that is, the seeming freedom and triumphant ease with which, at its best, it meets the challenge set by traditional and drastically restrictive patterns.

Here are some aspects in which **romantic** aims and achievements, in the major and most innovative writers during the first three decades of the nineteenth century, differ most conspicuously from the neoclassic:

(1) The prevailing attitude favored innovation instead of traditionalism in the materials, forms, and style of literature. English romantic poetry began with a kind of "manifesto," or statement of revolutionary aims, in the Preface to the second edition of Wordsworth and Coleridge's *Lyrical Ballads* (1800). This Preface, written by Wordsworth, denounced the *poetic diction* of the preceding century and proposed to deal with materials from "common life" in "a selection of language really used by men." The serious or tragic treatment of lowly subjects in common language violated the basic neoclassic rule of *decorum,* which asserted that the serious genres should deal with high subjects in an appropriately elevated style. Other innovations in the period were the exploitation by Coleridge, Keats, and others of the realm of the supernatural and of "the far away and the long ago"; the assumption by Blake, Wordsworth, and Shelley of the persona of a poet-prophet who writes a visionary mode of poetry; and the use of poetic *symbolism* (especially by Blake and Shelley) deriving from a world-view in which objects are charged with a significance beyond their physical qualities. "I always seek in what I see," as Shelley said, "the likeness of something beyond the present and tangible object."

(2) In his Preface to *Lyrical Ballads* Wordsworth repeatedly described good poetry as "the spontaneous overflow of powerful feelings." According to

this point of view poetry is not primarily a mirror of men in action; its essential element, on the contrary, is the poet's own feelings, while the process of composition, since it is "spontaneous," is the opposite of the artful manipulation of means to foreseen ends stressed by the neoclassic critics. (See *expressive criticism.*) Wordsworth carefully qualified this radical doctrine by describing his poetry as "emotion recollected in tranquillity," and by specifying that a proper spontaneity is the result of a prior process of deep reflection, and may be followed by second thoughts and revisions. But the immediate act of composition, if a poem is to be genuine, must be spontaneous—that is, unforced, and free of what Wordsworth decried as the "artificial" rules and conventions of his neoclassic predecessors. "If poetry comes not as naturally as the leaves to a tree," Keats wrote, "it had better not come at all." The philosophical-minded Coleridge substituted for neoclassic "rules," which are imposed by the poet from without, the concept of the inherent organic "laws" of the poet's *imagination:* each poetic work, like a growing plant, evolves according to its internal principles into its final organic form.

(3) To a remarkable degree external nature—the landscape, together with its flora and fauna—became a persistent subject of poetry, and was described with an accuracy and sensuous nuance unprecedented in earlier writers. It is a mistake, however, to describe the romantic poets as simply "nature poets." While many major poems by Wordsworth and Coleridge—and to a great extent by Shelley and Keats—set out from and return to an aspect or change of aspect in the landscape, the outer scene is not presented for its own sake, but only as a stimulus for the poet to engage in the most characteristic human activity, that of thinking. The important romantic poems are in fact poems of feelingful meditation which, though often stimulated by a natural phenomenon, are concerned with central human problems. Wordsworth asserted that it is "the Mind of Man" which is "my haunt, and the main region of my song."

(4) Neoclassic poetry was about other people, but much of romantic poetry represented the poets themselves, either directly, as in Wordsworth's *Prelude* (1805; revised 1850) and a number of romantic lyric poems, or in altered but recognizable form, as in Byron's *Childe Harold* (1812–18). In prose we find a parallel vogue in the revealingly personal essays of Lamb and Hazlitt and in a number of spiritual and intellectual autobiographies—De Quincey's *Confessions of an English Opium Eater* (1822), Coleridge's *Biographia Literaria* (1817), and Carlyle's fictionalized *Sartor Resartus* (1833–34). And whether romantic subjects were the poets themselves or someone else, they were no longer part of an organized society but, typically, solitary figures engaged in a long—and sometimes infinitely elusive—quest; often they were also social nonconformists or outcasts. Many important romantic works had as protagonist the isolated rebel, whether for good or ill: Prometheus, Cain, the Wandering Jew, the Satanic hero-villain, or the great outlaw.

(5) What seemed the infinite promise of the French Revolution, in the early 1790s, fostered the sense in writers of the Romantic Period that theirs was a great age of new beginnings and high possibilities. Many writers viewed a human being as endowed with limitless aspiration toward the infinite good envisioned by the faculty of imagination. "Our destiny," Wordsworth says in a vi-

sionary moment in *The Prelude*, "our being's heart and home,/Is with infinitude, and only there," and our desire is for "something evermore about to be." "Less than everything," Blake announced, "cannot satisfy man." Humanity's unquenchable aspirations beyond its assigned limits, which to the neoclassic moralist had been its tragic error, now became humanity's glory and a mode of triumph, even in failure, over the pettiness of circumstance. In a parallel way, the earlier judgment that the highest art is the perfect achievement of limited aims gave way to a dissatisfaction with rules and inherited restrictions. According to a number of romantic writers, the highest art consists in an endeavor beyond finite human possibility; as a result, neoclassical satisfaction in the perfectly accomplished, because limited, enterprise was replaced by a preference for the glory of the imperfect, in which the artist's very failure attests the grandeur of his aim. Romantic writers once more entered into competition with their greatest predecessors in audacious long poems in the most exacting genres: Wordsworth's *Prelude* (a rerendering, at epic length and in the form of a spiritual autobiography, of the central themes of Milton's *Paradise Lost*); Blake's visionary and prophetic epics; Shelley's *Prometheus Unbound* (emulating Greek drama); Keats's Miltonic epic *Hyperion;* and Byron's ironic conspectus of all modern European civilization, *Don Juan*.

See *Enlightenment*, and refer to R. S. Crane, "Neoclassical Criticism," in *Dictionary of World Literature*, ed. Joseph T. Shipley (rev., 1970); A. O. Lovejoy, *Essays in the History of Ideas* (1948); James Sutherland, *A Preface to Eighteenth Century Poetry* (1948); W. J. Bate, *From Classic to Romantic* (1948); Harold Bloom, *The Visionary Company: A Reading of English Romantic Poetry* (1961); René Wellek, "The Concept of Romanticism in Literary History" and "Romanticism Re-examined," in *Concepts of Criticism* (1963); Northrop Frye, ed., *Romanticism Reconsidered* (1963), and *A Study of English Romanticism* (1968); M. H. Abrams, *The Mirror and the Lamp: Romantic Theory and the Critical Tradition* (1953), and *Natural Supernaturalism: Tradition and Revolution in Romantic Literature* (1971); Thomas McFarland, *Romanticism and the Forms of Ruin* (1981); Jerome McGann, *The Romantic Ideology* (1983). Hugh Honour, in *Neo-classicism* (1969) and *Romanticism* (1979), stresses the visual arts. A useful collection of essays that define or discuss romanticism is Robert F. Gleckner and Gerald E. Enscoe, eds., *Romanticism: Points of View* (rev., 1975). In *Poetic Form and British Romanticism* (1986), Stuart Curran stresses the continuity, as well as innovation, in romantic uses of traditional poetic genres.

Novel. The term "novel" is now applied to a great variety of writings that have in common only the attribute of being extended works of *fiction* written in prose. As an extended narrative, the novel is distinguished from the *short story* and from the work of middle length called the *novelette;* its magnitude permits a greater variety of characters, greater complication of plot (or plots), ampler development of milieu, and more sustained and subtle exploration of character and motives than do the shorter, more concentrated modes. As a prose narrative, the novel is distinguished from the long narratives in verse of Chaucer, Spenser, and Milton which, beginning with the eighteenth century, it has increasingly supplanted. Within these limits the novel includes such diverse works as Richardson's *Pamela* and Sterne's *Tristram Shandy;* Dickens' *Pickwick Papers* and Henry James's *The Wings of the Dove;* Tolstoy's *War and Peace* and Kafka's *The Trial;* Hemingway's *The Sun Also Rises* and Joyce's *Ulysses;* C. P. Snow's *Strangers and Brothers* and Nabokov's *Ada or Ardor.*

The term for the novel in most European languages is **roman,** which is a derivative from the medieval *romance.* The English name for the form, on the other hand, is derived from the Italian **novella** (meaning "a little new thing"), which was a short tale in prose. In fourteenth-century Italy there was a vogue for collections of such tales, some serious and some scandalous; the best-known of these collections is Boccaccio's *Decameron,* which is still available in English translation at any well-stocked bookstore. Currently, the term "novella" (or in the German form, **Novelle**) is often used as an equivalent for *novelette:* a prose fiction of middle length, such as Joseph Conrad's *Heart of Darkness* or Thomas Mann's *Death in Venice.* (See under *short story.*)

Another important predecessor of the novel was the **picaresque narrative,** which emerged in sixteenth-century Spain, although the most popular instance, *Gil Blas* (1715), was written by the Frenchman Le Sage. "Picaro" is Spanish for "rogue," and the subject of a typical story is the escapades of an insouciant rascal who lives by his wits and shows little if any alteration of character through the long succession of his adventures; picaresque fiction is realistic in manner, **episodic** in structure (as opposed to the sustained development of a single *plot*), and often satiric in aim. We recognize the survival of the type in many later novels such as Mark Twain's *The Adventures of Tom Sawyer* (1876), Thomas Mann's *Felix Krull* (1954), and Saul Bellow's *The Adventures of Augie March* (1953). The development of the novel owes much to prose works which, like the picaresque story, were written to deflate romantic or idealized fictional forms. Cervantes' great quasi-picaresque narrative *Don Quixote* (1605)—in which an engaging madman who tries to live by the ideals of chivalric romance is used to explore the role of illusion and reality in life—was the single most important progenitor of the modern novel.

After these precedents and many others, including the seventeenth-century *character* (a brief sketch of a typical personality or way of life) and French romances such as Madame de La Fayette's *La Princesse de Clèves* (1678), the novel as we now think of it emerged in England in the early eighteenth century. In 1719 Daniel Defoe wrote *Robinson Crusoe,* and in 1722 *Moll Flanders.* Both of these are picaresque in type, in the sense that they are a sequence of episodes held together largely because they happened to one person; and Moll is herself a colorful female version of the old picaro—"twelve Year a Whore, five times a Wife (whereof once to her own Brother), Twelve Year a Thief, Eight Year a Transported Felon in Virginia," as the title page resoundingly informs us. But *Robinson Crusoe* is given an enforced unity of action by its focus on the problem of surviving on an uninhabited island, while both stories present so convincing a central character, set in so solid and factually realized a world, that Defoe is often credited with writing the first true "novel of incident."

The credit for having written the first English "novel of character," or "psychological novel," is almost unanimously given to Samuel Richardson for his

Pamela; or, Virtue Rewarded (1740). *Pamela* is the story of a sentimental but shrewd young woman who, by prudently safeguarding her beleaguered chastity, succeeds in becoming the wife of a wild young gentleman instead of his debauched servant girl. The distinction between the novel of incident and the novel of character cannot be drawn sharply; but in the novel of incident the greater interest is in what the *protagonist* will do next and on how the story will turn out; in the novel of character, it is on the protagonist's motives for what he or she does, and on how the protagonist as a person will turn out. On twentieth-century developments in the novel of character see Leon Edel, *The Modern Psychological Novel* (rev., 1965).

Pamela, like its greater and tragic successor, Richardson's *Clarissa* (1747–48), is an **epistolary novel;** that is, the narrative is conveyed entirely by an exchange of letters. Later novelists have preferred alternative devices for limiting the narrative *point of view* to one or another single character, but the epistolary technique is still occasionally revived—for example, in Mark Harris' hilarious novel *Wake Up, Stupid* (1959).

Novels may have any kind of plot form—tragic, comic, satiric, or romantic. A distinction—which was employed by Hawthorne, in his Preface to *The House of the Seven Gables* (1851) and elsewhere, and has been adopted and expanded by a number of recent critics—is that between two basic types of prose fiction: the novel proper and the "romance." The novel is characterized as the fictional attempt to give the effect of *realism,* by representing complex characters with mixed motives who are rooted in a social class, operate in a highly developed social structure, interact with many other characters, and undergo plausible and everyday modes of experience. The **prose romance** has as its ancestors the *chivalric romance* of the Middle Ages and the *Gothic novel* of the latter eighteenth century. It often deploys characters who are sharply discriminated as heroes and villains, masters and victims; the protagonist is often solitary, and relatively isolated from a social context; it is often set in the historical past, and the *atmosphere* is such as to suspend our expectations based on everyday experience; the plot emphasizes adventure, and is frequently cast in the form of the quest for an ideal, or the pursuit of an enemy; and the nonrealistic and occasionally melodramatic events are sometimes claimed to project in symbolic form the primal desires, hopes, and terrors in the depths of the human mind, and to be therefore analogous to the materials of dream, myth, ritual, and folklore. Examples of romance novels (as distinct from the realistic novels of Jane Austen, George Eliot, or Henry James) are Walter Scott's *Rob Roy* (1817), Alexandre Dumas' *The Three Musketeers* (1844–45), Emily Brontë's *Wuthering Heights* (1847), and an important mode of American fiction, from Poe, Cooper, Hawthorne, and Melville to some of the writings of William Faulkner and Saul Bellow. See Richard Chase, *The American Novel and Its Tradition* (1957); Northrop Frye, "The Mythos of Summer: Romance," in *Anatomy of Criticism* (1957); and the essays on romance in *Pastoral and Romance,* ed. Eleanor T. Lincoln (1969).

Other common subclasses of novelistic types are based on differences in subject matter, emphasis, and artistic purpose:

Bildungsroman and **Erziehungsroman** are German terms signifying "novel of formation" or "novel of education." The subject of these novels is the development of the protagonist's mind and character, in the passage from childhood through varied experiences—and usually through a spiritual crisis—into maturity and the recognition of his or her identity and role in the world. The mode was begun by K. P. Moritz's *Anton Reiser* (1785–90) and Goethe's *Wilhelm Meister's Apprenticeship* (1795–96) and includes Dickens' *Great Expectations* (1861), George Eliot's *The Mill on the Floss* (1860), Thomas Mann's *The Magic Mountain* (1924), and Somerset Maugham's *Of Human Bondage* (1915). An important subtype of the Bildungsroman is the **Künstlerroman** ("artist-novel"), which represents the growth of a novelist or other artist into the stage of maturity that signalizes the recognition of artistic destiny and mastery of artistic craft. Instances of this type include some of the major twentieth-century novels: Proust's *Remembrance of Things Past* (1913–27), Joyce's *A Portrait of the Artist as a Young Man* (1914–15), Mann's *Tonio Kröger* (1903) and *Dr. Faustus* (1947), and Gide's *The Counterfeiters* (1926). See Susanne Howe, *Wilhelm Meister and His English Kinsmen* (1930); Lionel Trilling, "The Princess Casamassima," in *The Liberal Imagination* (1950); Maurice Beebe, *Ivory Towers and Sacred Founts: The Artist as Hero in Fiction* (1964); Jerome H. Buckley, *Season of Youth: The Bildungsroman from Dickens to Golding* (1974); Martin Swales, *The German Bildungsroman from Wieland to Hesse* (1978).

The **social novel** emphasizes the influence of the social and economic conditions of an era on characters and events; often it also embodies an implicit or explicit thesis recommending social reform: Harriet Beecher Stowe's *Uncle Tom's Cabin* (1852), Upton Sinclair's *The Jungle* (1906), John Steinbeck's *The Grapes of Wrath* (1939).

Many romances and all realistic novels are set in a particular time and place, and some make use of historical events and personages by way of background. What is specified as the **historical novel** not only takes its setting and at least some of its chief characters and events from history, but develops these elements with careful attention to the known facts, and also makes the historical events and issues important to the central narrative, even when the protagonists are fictional rather than historical characters. Examples are Scott's *Ivanhoe* (1819), set in the period of Norman domination of the Saxons at the time of Richard I; Dickens' *A Tale of Two Cities* (1859), in Paris and London during the French Revolution; Tolstoy's *War and Peace* (1869), during Napoleon's invasion of Russia; and Margaret Mitchell's *Gone with the Wind* (1936), in Georgia during the Civil War and Reconstruction. See Georg Lukács, *The Historical Novel* (1962), and Harry Shaw, *The Forms of Historical Fiction: Sir Walter Scott and His Successors* (1983). For the recent emergence of "fabulative" historical novels that interweave history with fantasy—such as John Barth, *The Sot-Weed Factor* (1960, rev. 1967), Kurt Vonnegut, Jr., *Slaughterhouse-Five* (1969), Thomas Pynchon, *Gravity's Rainbow* (1973), and E. L. Doctorow, *Ragtime* (1975)—see Robert Scholes, *Fabulation and Metafiction* (1979).

A recent offshoot of the historical novel is the form that one of its innovators, Truman Capote, named the **nonfiction novel.** This uses a variety of novelistic techniques to give a graphic rendering of recent historical characters and events, and is based not only on historical records but often on personal interviews with the chief agents. Truman Capote's *In Cold Blood* (1965) and Norman Mailer's *The Executioner's Song* (1979) are instances of this mode; both these books offer a detailed rendering of the life, personality, and actions of murderers, based on a sustained series of prison interviews with the protagonists themselves. A related form, the **new journalism,** renders contemporary events by means of techniques earlier developed in the realistic novel; an example is Tom Wolfe's *The Electric Kool-Aid Acid Test* (1968), which deals with the "hippie" life-style of the novelist Ken Kesey and his group of drug-inspired "Merry Pranksters." See John Hollowell, *Fact and Fiction: The New Journalism and the Nonfiction Novel* (1977). Cushing Strout, in *The Veracious Imagination* (1981), studies other recent developments in novels, as well as in **documentary drama,** which combine fiction with history and biography.

The **regional novel** emphasizes the setting, speech, and social structure and customs of a particular locality, not merely as *local color,* but as important conditions affecting the temperament of the characters and their ways of thinking, feeling, and interacting; instances of such localities are "Wessex" in Hardy's novels, and "Yoknapatawpha County," Mississippi, in Faulkner's.

Since the second half of the nineteenth century, the novel has displaced all other literary forms in popularity, and has replaced long verse narratives almost entirely. The novelistic art has received the devoted attention of some of the supreme craftsmen of modern literature—Flaubert, Henry James, Proust, Mann, Joyce, and Virginia Woolf. There has been constant experimentation with new fictional methods, such as management of the *point of view* so as to minimize the apparent role of the author-narrator, the use of *symbolist* and *expressionist* techniques and of devices adopted from the art of the cinema, the dislocation of time sequence, the adaptation of forms and motifs from myths and dreams, and the exploitation of *stream of consciousness* narration in a way that converts the story of outer action and events into a drama of the life of the mind. Henry James's prefaces, gathered into one volume as *The Art of the Novel* (1934), exemplify the care and subtlety that have been lavished on the craft of fiction.

In recent decades such experimentation has reached a radical extreme (see *postmodernism*). Vladimir Nabokov is a supreme technician who writes *involuted novels* (a work whose subject incorporates an account of its own genesis and development—for example, his *Pale Fire*), employs multilingual puns and jokes, incorporates strategies from chess, crossword puzzles, and other games, parodies other novels (and his own as well), and sets elaborate traps for the unwary reader. This is also the era of what is sometimes called the **antinovel**—that is, a work which is deliberately constructed in a negative fashion, relying for its effects on deleting traditional elements, on violating traditional norms, and on playing against the expectations established in the reader by the novelistic methods and conventions of the past. Thus Alain Robbe-Grillet, a leader among the exponents of the **nouveau roman,** the **new novel,** in France—other new novelists are Natalie Sarraute and Philippe Sollers—has written a work, *Jealousy* (1957), in which he leaves out such standard novelistic elements as plot, characterization, descriptions of states of mind, normal relations of time and space, and a frame of reference to the world in which the work is set. We are simply presented in this novel with a sequence of perceptions, mainly visual, which we may *naturalize* (that is, make intelligible on the model of standard narrative procedures) by postulating that we are occupying the physical space and sharing the hyperacute observations of a jealous husband, from which we may infer also the tortured state of his disintegrating mind. See Roland Barthes, *Writing Degree Zero* (transl., 1967), and Stephen Heath, *The Nouveau Roman: A Study in the Practice of Writing* (1972).

The term **magic realism** has been applied to the prose fiction of Jorge Luis Borges in Argentina, as well as to the work of writers such as García Márquez in Colombia, Günter Grass in Germany, and John Fowles in England; they interweave, in an ever-shifting pattern, a sharply etched realism with fantastic and dreamlike elements. Robert Scholes has popularized the term **fabulation** to describe the large and growing class of such recent novels, which do not fit the traditional categories either of realism or of romance. These violate, in a variety of ways, standard novelistic expectations by drastic—and sometimes highly successful—experiments with subject matter, form, style, temporal sequence, and fusions of the everyday, the fantastic, the mythical, and the nightmarish, in renderings that blur traditional distinctions between what is serious or trivial, horrible or ludicrous, tragic or comic. Recent fabulators include Thomas Pynchon, John Barth, Donald Barthelme, William Gass, Robert Coover, and Ishmael Reed. See Robert Scholes, *Fabulation and Metafiction* (1979)—an expansion of his *The Fabulators* (1967)—and James M. Mellard, *The Exploded Form: The Modernist Novel in America* (1980); refer also to the essays above on literature of the *absurd* and *black humor.*

See *fiction,* and in addition to the books already mentioned, refer to the following. Histories of the novel: E. A. Baker, *History of the English Novel* (12 vols.; 1924 ff.); Arnold Kettle's *Marxist* survey, *An Introduction to the English Novel* (2 vols.; 1951); Dorothy Van Ghent, *The English Novel: Form and Function* (1953); Walter Allen, *The English Novel* (1954); Ian Watt, *The Rise of the Novel* (1957). On the art of the novel: Percy Lubbock, *The Craft of Fiction* (1921); E. M. Forster, *Aspects of the Novel* (1927); and two recent and influential books, Wayne C. Booth, *The Rhetoric of Fiction* (1961), and Frank Kermode, *The Sense of an Ending* (1968). Philip Stevick, ed., *The Theory of the Novel* (1967) is a collection of important essays by various critics, and Daniel Schwarz, *The Humanistic Heritage* (1986), reviews theories of prose fiction from 1900 to the present.

Objective and Subjective. John Ruskin complained in 1856 that "German dullness and English affectation have of late much multiplied among us the use of two of the most objectionable words that were ever coined by the troublesomeness of metaphysicians—namely, 'objective' and 'subjective.' " Ruskin was at least in part right. The words were imported into English criticism from the post-Kantian German critics of the late eighteenth and early nineteenth centuries, and they have certainly been troublesome. Amid the great variety of ways in which this opposition has been applied, one is sufficiently widespread to be worth specifying. A subjective work is one in which the author incorporates personal experiences, or projects into the narrative his or her personal disposition, judgments, values, and feelings. An objective work is one in which the author simply presents the invented situation or the fictional characters and their thoughts, feelings, and actions and seems to remain detached and noncommittal. Thus a subjective *lyric* is one in which we are invited to associate the "I," or lyric speaker, with the poet (Coleridge's "Frost at Midnight," Wordsworth's "Tintern Abbey," Shelley's "Ode to the West Wind," Sylvia Plath's "Daddy"); in an objective lyric the speaker is obviously an invented character (Browning's "My Last Duchess," Eliot's "Love Song of J. Alfred Prufrock," Wallace Stevens' "Sunday Morning"). A subjective novel is one in which the author (or at any rate the narrator) intervenes to comment and deliver judgments about the characters and actions represented; an objective novel is one in which the author is self-effacing and seemingly leaves the story to tell itself. See *confessional poetry, distance and involvement, negative capability, persona,* and *point of view.*

On the introduction of the terms "objective" and "subjective" into English criticism and the variousness of their application, see M. H. Abrams, *The Mirror and the Lamp* (1953), pp. 235–44. For their application to modern criticism of the novel, see Wayne C. Booth, *The Rhetoric of Fiction* (1961), Chap. 3.

Objective Correlative is a term rather casually introduced by T. S. Eliot, in the essay "Hamlet and His Problems" (1919), whose subsequent vogue in literary criticism, Eliot has confessed, astonished its inventor. "The only way of expressing emotion in the form of art is by finding an 'objective correlative'; in other words, a set of objects, a situation, a chain of events which shall be the formula of that *particular* emotion," and which will evoke the same emotion from the reader. Eliot's formulation has been often criticized for falsifying the way a poet actually composes, since no object or situation is in itself a "formula" for an emotion, but depends for its emotional significance and effect on the way it is rendered by the poet. The vogue of Eliot's concept was due in part to its accord with the reaction of the *New Criticism* against vagueness of description and the direct statement of feelings in poetry—an oft-cited example was Shelley's "Indian Serenade": "I die, I faint, I fail"—in favor of definiteness, impersonality, and descriptive concreteness.

See Eliseo Vivas, "The Objective Correlative of T. S. Eliot," reprinted in *Critiques and Essays in Criticism,* ed. Robert W. Stallman (1949).

Occasional Poems are written to celebrate or memorialize a specific occasion, such as a birthday, a marriage, a death, a military engagement or victory, the dedication of a public building, or the opening performance of a play. Spenser's "Epithalamion," Milton's "Lycidas," Marvell's "An Horatian Ode upon Cromwell's Return from Ireland," and Tennyson's "The Charge of the Light Brigade" are poems that have long survived their original occasions, and Yeats's "Easter, 1916" and Auden's "September 1, 1939" are notable modern examples. The English poet laureate is often called on to meet the emergency of royal anniversaries and important public events with an appropriate literary effort.

Ode. A long lyric poem that is serious in subject, elevated in style, and elaborate in its stanzaic structure. As Norman Maclean has said, the term now calls to mind a *lyric* which is "massive, public in its proclamations, and Pindaric in its classical prototype" ("From Action to Image," in *Critics and Criticism,* ed. R. S. Crane, 1952). The prototype was established by the Greek poet Pindar, whose odes were modeled on the songs by the *chorus* in Greek drama. His complex stanzas were patterned in sets of three: moving in a dance rhythm to the left, the chorus chanted the **strophe;** moving to the right, the **antistrophe;** then, standing still, the **epode.**

The **regular** or **Pindaric ode** in English is a close imitation of Pindar's form, with all the strophes and antistrophes written in one *stanza* pattern, and all the epodes in another; the typical construction may be conveniently studied in Thomas Gray's "The Progress of Poesy" (1757). The **irregular ode** was introduced in 1656 by Abraham Cowley, who imitated the Pindaric style and matter but disregarded the recurrent strophic triad, allowing each stanza to establish its own pattern of variable line lengths, number of lines, and rhyme scheme. This type of irregular stanzaic structure, which is free to alter in accordance with shifts in subject and mood, has been the most common for the English ode ever since; Wordsworth's great "Ode: Intimations of Immortality" (1807) is representative.

Pindar's odes were **encomiastic,** or written to praise and glorify someone—in his instance, a victorious athlete in the Olympic games. The earlier English odes, and many later ones, were also written to eulogize something: either a person (Dryden's "Anne Killigrew"), or the arts of music or poetry (Dryden's "Alexander's Feast"), or a time of day (Collins' "Ode to Evening"), or abstract concepts (Gray's "Hymn to Adversity" and Wordsworth's "Ode to Duty"). Romantic poets perfected the personal ode of description and passionate meditation, which is stimulated by (and sometimes reverts to) an aspect of the outer scene and turns on the attempt to solve either a personal emotional problem or a generally human one (Wordsworth's "Intimations" ode, Coleridge's "Dejection: An Ode," Shelley's "Ode to the West Wind"). Recent examples of this type are Allen Tate's "Ode to the Confederate Dead" and Wallace Stevens' "The Idea of Order at Key West." See M. H. Abrams, "Structure and Style in the Greater Romantic Lyric," in *The Correspondent Breeze,* 1984.

The **Horatian ode** was originally modeled on the matter, tone, and form of the odes of the Roman Horace. In contrast to the passion and visionary boldness of Pindar's odes, Horatian odes are calm, meditative, and restrained, and they are usually **homostrophic**—that is, written in a single repeated stanza form—as well as shorter than the Pindaric ode. Examples are Marvell's "An Horatian Ode upon Cromwell's Return from Ireland" (1650) and Keats's ode "To Autumn" (1820).

See Robert Shafer, *The English Ode to 1660* (1918); G. N. Shuster, *The English Ode from Milton to Keats* (1940); Carol Maddison, *Apollo and the Nine: A History of the Ode* (1960)—this book includes a discussion of the odes of Pindar and Horace (Chap. 2); Paul H. Fry, *The Poet's Calling in the English Ode* (1980).

Old English Period, or the **Anglo-Saxon Period,** extended from the invasion of Celtic England by Germanic tribes (the Angles, Saxons, and Jutes) in the first half of the fifth century to the conquest of England in 1066 by the Norman French, under the leadership of William the Conqueror. Only after they had been converted to Christianity in the seventh century did the Anglo-Saxons, whose earlier literature had been oral, begin to develop a written literature. A high level of culture and learning was soon achieved in various monasteries; the eighth-century churchmen Bede and Alcuin were both major scholars who wrote in Latin, the standard language of international scholarship. The poetry written in the vernacular Anglo-Saxon, known also as Old English, included *Beowulf* (eighth century), the greatest of Germanic epic poems, and such lyric laments as "The Wanderer," "The Seafarer," and "Deor," all of which, though composed by Christian writers, reflect the conditions of life in the pagan past. Caedmon and Cynewulf were poets who wrote on biblical and religious themes, and there survive a number of Old English lives of saints, sermons, and paraphrases of books of the Bible. Alfred the Great, a West Saxon king (871–99) who for a time united all the kingdoms of southern England against a new wave of Germanic invaders, the Vikings, was no less important as a patron of literature than as a warrior. He himself translated into Old English various books of Latin prose, supervised translations by other hands, and instituted the Anglo-Saxon Chronicle, a continuous record, year by year, of important events in England.

See H. M. Chadwick, *The Heroic Age* (1912); S. B. Greenfield, *A Critical History of Old English Literature* (1965); C. L. Wrenn, *A Study of Old English Literature* (1966).

Onomatopoeia, sometimes called **echoism,** is used both in a narrow and in a broad sense.

(1) In the narrow, and more common, sense onomatopoeia is applied to a word, or a combination of words, whose sound seems to resemble closely the sound it denotes: "hiss," "buzz," "rattle," "bang." There is no exact duplication, however, of nonverbal by verbal sounds; the seeming similarity is due as much to the meaning, and to the feel of articulating the words, as to their sounds. Two lines from Tennyson's "Come Down, O Maid" (1847) are often cited as a skillful instance of onomatopoeia:

> The moan of doves in immemorial elms,
> And murmuring of innumerable bees.

John Crowe Ransom has remarked that by making only two changes in the consonants of the last line, we lose the echoic effect because we change the meaning drastically: "And murdering of innumerable beeves."

The sounds seemingly mimicked by onomatopoeic words need not be pleasant ones. Browning liked squishy and scratchy effects, as in "Meeting at Night" (1845):

As I gain the cove with pushing prow,
And quench its speed i' the slushy sand.

A tap at the pane, the quick sharp scratch
And blue spurt of a lighted match. . . .

Compare *euphony and cacophony.*

(2) In the broad sense, "onomatopoeia" is applied to words or passages which seem to correspond to what they denote in any way whatever—in size, movement, or force, as well as sound (see *sound-symbolism*). Alexander Pope recommends such extended verbal mimicry in his *Essay on Criticism* (1711) when he says that "the sound should seem an echo of the sense," and goes on to illustrate his maxim by mimicking two different kinds of action or motion by the words, metrical movement, and the difficulty or ease of utterance of his lines:

When Ajax strives some rock's vast weight to throw,
The line too labors, and the words move slow;
Not so when swift Camilla scours the plain,
Flies o'er th' unbending corn, and skims along the main.

Pantomime and Dumb Show. **Pantomime** is acting without speech, using only posture, gesture, bodily movement, and exaggerated facial expression to **mime** ("mimic") a character's actions and to express a character's feelings. Elaborate pantomimes, halfway between drama and dance, were put on in ancient Greece and Rome, and the form was revived, usually for comic purposes, in Renaissance Europe. Mimed dramas enjoyed a vogue in eighteenth-century England, and in the present century the silent movies encouraged a brief revival of the art and produced a superlative pantomimist in Charlie Chaplin. Miming survives in French masters such as Marcel Marceau in the theater and Jacques Tati in the cinema, and England still retains the institution of the Christmas pantomime. In America, circus clowns are expert pantomimists, and miming has recently been revived in the theater for the deaf.

A **dumb show** is an episode of pantomime introduced into a spoken play. It was a common device in *Elizabethan* drama, in imitation of its use by Seneca, the Roman writer of tragedies. Two well-known dumb shows are the preliminary episode, summarizing the action to come, of the play-within-a-play in *Hamlet* (III. ii) and the miming of the banishment of the Duchess and her family in John Webster's *The Duchess of Malfi* (III. iv).

See R. J. Broadbent, *A History of Pantomime* (1901).

Paradox. A paradox is a statement which seems on its face to be self-contradictory or absurd, yet turns out to make good sense. So in the conclusion to Donne's sonnet "Death, Be Not Proud":

One short sleep past, we wake eternally
And death shall be no more; *Death, thou shalt die.*

The paradox is used occasionally by almost all poets, but was a central device in seventeenth-century *metaphysical poetry,* both in its religious and secular forms. John Donne, who wrote a prose collection titled *Problems and Paradoxes,* exploited the figure in his poetry. "The Canonization," for example, is organized as an extended proof, full of local paradoxes, of the paradoxical thesis that sexual lovers are saints.

If the paradoxical utterance conjoins two terms that in ordinary usage are contraries, it is called an **oxymoron;** an example is Tennyson's "O *Death in life,* the days that are no more." The oxymoron was a familiar type of *Petrarchan conceit* in Elizabethan love poetry, in phrases like "pleasing pains," "I burn and freeze," "loving hate." It is also a frequent figure in devotional prose and religious poetry as a way of expressing the Christian mysteries, which transcend human sense and logic. So Milton describes the appearance of God, in *Paradise Lost* (III, 380):

> Dark with excessive bright thy skirts appear.

Paradox was a prominent concern of many *New Critics,* who, however, extended the application of the term from the rhetorical figure to encompass all surprising deviations from, or qualifications of, common perceptions or commonplace opinions. It is only in this greatly expanded sense of the term that Cleanth Brooks is able to claim, with some plausibility, that "the language of poetry is the language of paradox," in *The Well Wrought Urn* (1947). See also the recent theory called *deconstruction* for the claim that all uses of language involve the unresolvable paradox called an *aporia.*

Pastoral. The originator of the pastoral was Theocritus, a Greek of the third century B.C. who wrote poems that represented the life of Sicilian shepherds. ("Pastor" is Latin for "shepherd.") Virgil later imitated Theocritus in his Latin *Eclogues* and established the enduring model for the traditional **pastoral:** an elaborately conventional poem expressing an urban poet's nostalgic image of the peace and simplicity of the life of shepherds and other rural folk in an idealized natural setting. The *conventions* that hundreds of later poets imitated from Virgil's imitations of Theocritus include a shepherd reclining under a spreading beech and meditating the rural muse, or piping as though he would ne'er grow old, or engaging in a friendly singing contest, or expressing his good or bad fortune with his beloved, or grieving over the death of a fellow shepherd. From this last type developed the *pastoral elegy,* which persisted long after the other traditional types had ceased to be written. Other terms often used synonymously with pastoral are **idyll,** from the title of Theocritus' pastorals; **eclogue** (literally, "a selection"), from the title of Virgil's pastorals; and **bucolic poetry,** from the Greek word for "herdsman."

Classical poets often described the pastoral life in terms of the mythical **golden age.** This term derives from the mode of chronological *primitivism* that was propounded in the Greek Hesiod's *Work and Days* (eighth century B.C.) and by many later Greek and Roman writers. The earliest period of humanity was regarded as a time of felicity, and described figuratively as an age of gold; the continuous decline through time was expressed by the sequence "the age of silver," and "the brazen age," to the present sad condition of humanity, "the iron age." Christian pastoralists combined pagan allusions to the golden age with the biblical Garden of Eden, and also exploited the symbolism of "shepherd" (the ecclesiastical or parish "pastor," and the figure of Christ as the Good Shepherd) to give many pastoral poems a Christian range of reference. (See Harry Levin, *The Myth of the Golden Age in the Renaissance,* 1969.) In the Renaissance the traditional pastoral was also adapted to satirical and allegorical uses. Spenser's *Shepherd's Calendar* (1579), which popularized the mode in English poetry, included most of the varieties of pastoral poems current in that period.

Such was the vogue of the pastoral dream that Renaissance writers incorporated it into various other literary forms. Sidney's *Arcadia* (1581–84) was a long pastoral *romance* written in an elaborately artful prose. (**Arcadia** was a mountainous region of Greece which Virgil substituted for Theocritus' Sicily as his idealized pastoral milieu.) There was also the pastoral lyric (Marlowe's "The Passionate Shepherd to His Love"), and the pastoral drama. John Fletcher's *The Faithful Shepherdess* is an example of this last type, and Shakespeare's *As You Like It,* based on a pastoral romance by Thomas Lodge, centers on the forest of Arden, a green refuge from the troubles and complications of ordinary life, where all enmities are reconciled, all problems resolved, and the course of true love made to run smooth.

The last important series of traditional pastorals, and an extreme instance of the calculated and graceful display of high artifice, was Alexander Pope's *Pastorals* (1709). Five years later John Gay's *Shepherd's Week* burlesqued the type by applying its elegant formulas to the crudity of actual rustic manners and language, and inadvertently showed the way to the seriously realistic treatment of rural life. In 1783 George Crabbe published *The Village* specifically in order to

> paint the cot
> As Truth will paint it and as bards will not.

How far the term then lost its traditional application is indicated by Wordsworth's title for his realistic rendering of a rural tragedy in 1800: "Michael, A Pastoral Poem."

In recent decades the term "pastoral" has been expanded in various special ways. William Empson, for example, identifies as pastoral any work which contrasts simple and complicated life, to the advantage of the former: the simple life may be that of the shepherd, the child, or the working man, and it is used as an oblique way to criticize the class structure of society. Empson thus applies the term to works ranging from Marvell's seventeenth-century poem "The Garden" to *Alice in Wonderland* and the modern proletarian novel. Other critics apply the term "pastoral" to any work which represents a withdrawal from ordinary life to a place apart, close to the elemental rhythms of nature, where a person achieves a new perspective on life in the complex social world.

W. W. Gregg, *Pastoral Poetry and Pastoral Drama* (1906); the Introduction to *English Pastoral Poetry from the Beginnings to Marvell*, ed. Frank Kermode (1952); Andrew V. Ettin, *Literature and the Pastoral* (1985). For modern expansions of the concept, see William Empson, *Some Versions of Pastoral* (1950), and Eleanor T. Lincoln, ed., *Pastoral and Romance: Modern Essays in Criticism* (1969).

Pathetic Fallacy was a phrase invented by John Ruskin in 1856 to signify the attribution to natural objects of human capabilities and feelings (*Modern Painters*, Vol. 3, Chap. 12). As used by Ruskin—for whom "truth" was a primary artistic criterion—the term was derogatory; for, he said, it applies to descriptions, not of the "true appearances of things to us," but of "the extraordinary, or false appearances, when we are under the influence of emotion, or contemplative fancy." Two of Ruskin's examples are the lines

> The spendthrift crocus, bursting through the mould
> Naked and shivering, with his cup of gold,

and Coleridge's description in "Christabel"of

> The one red leaf, the last of its clan,
> That dances as often as dance it can.

These passages, Ruskin says, however beautiful, are false and "morbid"; only in the greatest poets is the use of the pathetic fallacy valid, and then only at those rare times when it would be inhuman to resist the pressure of powerful feelings to humanize the perceived fact.

Ruskin's contention would make not only his *romantic* predecessors but even Shakespeare "morbid." His term is now used, for the most part, as a neutral name for a common phenomenon in descriptive poetry, in which the ascription of human traits to inanimate nature is less formally managed than in the figure called *personification.*

See Josephine Miles, *Pathetic Fallacy in the Nineteenth Century* (1942); Harold Bloom, ed., *The Literary Criticism of John Ruskin* (1965), Introduction and pp. 62–78.

Pathos in Greek meant the passions, or suffering, or deep feeling generally, as distinguished from **ethos,** a person's overall disposition or character. In modern criticism, however, pathos is attributed to a scene or passage designed to evoke the feelings of tenderness, pity, or sympathetic sorrow from the audience. In the Victorian era a number of prominent writers exploited pathos beyond the endurance of most readers today—examples are the rendering of the death of Little Nell in Dickens' *The Old Curiosity Shop* and of the death of Little Eva in Harriet Beecher Stowe's *Uncle Tom's Cabin.* (See *sentimentalism.*) To the modern sensibility, the greatest passages of literary pathos do not dwell on the pathetic details but achieve the effect by understatement and suggestion; for example, the speech of King Lear when he is briefly reunited with Cordelia (IV. vii. 59ff.), beginning

> Pray, do not mock me.
> I am a very foolish fond old man,

or Wordsworth's terse summation of the grief of the old man in *Michael* (1800), ll. 464–66:

> Many and many a day he thither went,
> And never lifted up a single stone.

Periods of American Literature. The division of American literature into convenient historical segments, or "periods," lacks the relatively clear consensus that we find for English literature; the many college syllabi of surveys of American literature reprinted in *Reconstructing American Literature* (ed. Paul Lauter, 1983) demonstrate how variable are the divisions, especially since the recent efforts to do greater justice to literature written by women and by ethnic minorities. A number of recent historians, anthologists, and teachers of American literature now divide their survey simply into dated segments, without affixing period names. A clear tendency, however, is to recognize the importance of major wars in marking significant changes in literature; as a scholar of American culture, Cushing Strout, has remarked, this tendency "suggests that there is an order in American political history more visible and compelling than that indicated by specifically literary or intellectual categories." The following temporal divisions recognize the importance assigned by literary historians to the Revolutionary War (1775–81), the Civil War (1861–65), World War I (1914–18), and World War II (1939–45); under these broad divisions are listed some of the more widely used terms for periods and subperiods of American literature. These terms, it will be noted, are diverse in kind; some name a time span or a form of political organization, others a prominent intellectual or imaginative mode, and others still a predominant form of literature.

1607–1775. This era, from the founding of the first settlement at Jamestown to the outbreak of the Revolution, is often called the **Colonial Period.** Writings were for the most part religious, practical, or historical. Notable among the seventeenth-century writers of journals and narratives concerning the founding and early history of some of the colonies were William Bradford, John Winthrop, and the theologian Cotton Mather. In the following century Jonathan Edwards was a major philosopher as well as theologian, and Benjamin Franklin an early American master of lucid and cogent prose. Not until Edward Taylor's writings were first published from manuscript in 1937 was he discovered to have been an able religious poet in the *metaphysical* style of the English devotional poets Herbert and Crashaw; Anne Bradstreet was the chief poet of secular and domestic as well as religious subjects. The publication in 1773 of *Poems on Various Subjects* by Phillis Wheatley, then a nineteen-year-old slave who had been born in Africa, inaugurated the long, but until recently neglected, line of **Black**

writers in America. See J. Saunders Redding, *To Make a Poet Black* (1939; reissued 1986); Houston A. Baker, Jr., *Black Literature in America* (1971); Henry L. Gates, Jr., ed., *Black Literature and Literary Theory* (1984).

The period between the Stamp Act of 1765 and 1790 is sometimes distinguished as the **Revolutionary Age;** it was the time of Thomas Paine's influential revolutionary tracts; of Thomas Jefferson's "Statute of Virginia for Religious Freedom" and "Declaration of Independence"; of *The Federalist Papers* in support of the Constitution, most notably those by Alexander Hamilton and James Madison; and of the patriotic and satiric poems by Philip Freneau and Joel Barlow.

1775–1865. The years 1775–1828, the **Early National Period** ending with the triumph of Jacksonian democracy in 1828, signalized the emergence of a national imaginative literature, including the first American comedy (Royall Tyler's *The Contrast,* 1787), the earliest American novel (William Hill Brown's *The Power of Sympathy,* 1789), and the establishment in 1815 of the first enduring American magazine, *The North American Review.* Washington Irving achieved international fame with his essays and stories; Charles Brockden Brown wrote authentic American versions of the *Gothic novel* of mystery and terror; the career of James Fenimore Cooper, the first major American novelist, was well launched; and William Cullen Bryant and Edgar Allan Poe wrote poetry that was relatively independent of English precursors.

The span 1828–1865, from the Jacksonian era to the Civil War, and often identified as the **Romantic Period in America** (see *neoclassic and romantic*), marks the full coming of age of a native American literature. This period is sometimes known also as the **American Renaissance,** the title of F. O. Matthiessen's influential book (1941) about its outstanding writers, Emerson, Thoreau, Poe, Melville, and Hawthorne (see also *symbolism*), or else as the **Age of Transcendentalism,** after the philosophical and literary movement, centered on Emerson, that was dominant in New England (see *Transcendentalism*). In all the major literary genres except drama, writers produced works of an originality and quality not exceeded in later American history. Emerson, Thoreau, and the early feminist Margaret Fuller shaped the ideas, ideals, and literary aims of many contemporary and later American writers. It was the age not only of continuing work by Bryant, Irving, and Cooper, but also of the novels and short stories of Poe, Hawthorne, Melville, Harriet Beecher Stowe, and the southern novelist William Gilmore Simms; of the poetry of Poe, Whittier, Emerson, Longfellow, and the most innovative and influential of American poets, Walt Whitman; and of the beginning of distinguished American criticism in the essays of Poe, Simms, and James Russell Lowell.

1865–1914. The cataclysm of the bloody Civil War and of the Reconstruction, followed by a burgeoning industrialism and urbanization in the North, profoundly altered the American sense of itself, as well as American literary modes. 1865–1900 is often known as the **Realistic Period,** in accord with the works by the major novelists Mark Twain, William Dean Howells, and Henry James, as well as by John W. DeForest, Harold Frederic, and the Black novelist Charles W. Chesnutt. These works, though diverse, are often labeled "realistic" in contrast to the "romances" of their predecessors in prose fiction, Poe, Hawthorne, and Melville (see *prose romance* and *realism*). Other authors wrote *regional,* or *local color*, forms of realistic fiction; these include (in addition to Mark Twain's novels on the Mississippi region) Bret Harte in California, Sarah Orne Jewett in Maine, Mary Wilkins Freeman in Massachusetts, and George W. Cable and Kate Chopin in Louisiana—the last is now viewed as an early and major *feminist* novelist. Whitman continued writing poetry up to the last decade of the century, and (unknown to him and almost everyone else) was joined by Emily Dickinson; although only seven of Dickinson's more than a thousand short poems were published in her lifetime, she is now widely recognized as one of the most original and eminent of American poets. Sidney Lanier published his experiments in versification based on the meters of music; and in the 1890s Stephen Crane, although he was only twenty-nine when he died, published short poems in free verse that anticipate the experiments of Ezra Pound and the *Imagists,* as well as the brilliantly innovative short stories and short novels that look forward to two later narrative modes, naturalism and impressionism. The years 1900–1914, although James, Howells, and Mark Twain were still writing, are discriminated as the **Naturalistic Period,** in recognition of the powerful though sometimes crudely wrought novels by Frank Norris, Jack London, and Theodore Dreiser, which typically represent characters who are joint victims of their instinctual drives and of external sociological forces; see *naturalism.*

1914–1939. The era between the profound dislocations of the two world wars, marked also by the trauma of the great economic depression beginning in 1929, was that of the emergence of what is still known as "modern literature," which in America reached an eminence rivaling that of the American Renaissance of the mid-nineteenth century, and unlike most of the literature of that earlier period, also achieved great international recognition and influence. *Poetry* magazine, founded in Chicago by Harriet Monroe in 1912, published many of the experimental authors. Among the notable poets were Edgar Lee Masters, Edwin Arlington Robinson, Robert Frost, Carl Sandburg, Wallace Stevens, William Carlos Williams, Ezra Pound, Robinson Jeffers, Marianne Moore, T. S. Eliot, Edna St. Vincent Millay, and E. E. Cummings—authors who wrote in an unexampled variety of poetic modes. These included the *Imagism* of Amy Lowell, H.D. (Hilda Doolittle), and others, the metric poems by Frost and the free-verse poems by Williams in the American vernacular, the formal and typographic experiments of Cummings, the poetic naturalism of Jeffers, and the assimilation to their own distinctive uses by Pound and Eliot of the forms and procedures of French *symbolism* together with the intellectual and figurative methods of the English *metaphysical poets.* Among the major writers of prose fiction were Edith Wharton, Sinclair Lewis, Ellen Glasgow, Willa Cather, Gertrude Stein, Sherwood Anderson, John Dos Passos, F. Scott Fitzgerald, William Faulkner, Ernest Hemingway, Thomas Wolfe, John Steinbeck. America produced in this period its first great dramatist in Eugene O'Neill, as well as a group of distinguished literary critics that included Van Wyck Brooks, Malcolm Cowley, T. S. Eliot, Edmund Wilson, and the irreverent and caustic H. L. Mencken.

The writers of this era are often subclassified in a variety of ways. The flamboyant and pleasure-seeking 1920s are called the **Jazz Age,** a title popularized by F. Scott Fitzgerald's *Tales of the Jazz Age* (1922). The same decade was also the early period of the **Harlem Renaissance.** After World War I, the area of upper Manhattan known as Harlem came to have an almost exclusively Black population and became the national center of Black culture, including the arts of theater, music, and dance. Distinguished Black writers—poets, novelists, playwrights, and essayists—who lived in Harlem or wrote about Harlem include James Weldon Johnson, Claude McKay, Jean Toomer, Langston Hughes, Countée Cullen, W. E. B. DuBois, and (in later decades) James Baldwin.

Many prominent American writers of the decade following the end of World War I, disillusioned by their war experiences and alienated by what they perceived as the crassness of American culture and its "puritanical" repressions, are often tagged (in a term first applied by Gertrude Stein to young Frenchmen of the time) as the **Lost Generation.** A number of these writers became "expatriates," moving abroad in their quest for a richer literary and artistic milieu and a freer way of life, either to London or to Paris; Ezra Pound, Gertrude Stein, and T. S. Eliot lived out their lives abroad, but most of the younger "exiles," as Malcolm Cowley called them (*Exile's Return*, 1934), came back to America in the 1930s. Hemingway's *The Sun Also Rises* and Fitzgerald's *Tender Is the Night* are novels that represent the mood and way of life of two groups of American expatriates. In "the radical '30s," the period of the great depression and of the economic and social reforms in "the New Deal" inaugurated by President Franklin Delano Roosevelt, some authors joined radical political movements, and many others dealt in their literary works with pressing social issues—including, in their novels, William Faulkner, John Dos Passos, James T. Farrell, Thomas Wolfe, and John Steinbeck, and in the drama, Eugene O'Neill, Clifford Odets, and Maxwell Anderson.

1939 to the Present, "the *contemporary period.*" World War II, and especially the disillusionment with Soviet Communism attending the Moscow trials for alleged treason and Stalin's signing of the Russo-German pact with Hitler in 1939, largely ended the literary radicalism of the 1930s. For several decades the *New Criticism*—dominated by southern writers, the **Agrarians,** who in the 1930s had championed a return from an industrial to an agricultural economy—typified the prevailing critical tendency to isolate literature from the life of the author and from society, and to conceive a work of literature, in formal terms, as an organic and autonomous entity (see John L. Stewart, *The Burden of Time: The Fugitives and Agrarians,* 1965). The eminent and influential critics Edmund Wilson and Lionel Trilling, however—as well as other critics grouped with them as "the New York Intellectuals," including Philip Rahv, Alfred Kazin, and Irving Howe—continued through the 1960s to deal with a work of literature humanistically and historically, in the context of its author's life, temperament, and social milieu, and in terms of its moral and imaginative qualities and its consequences for society. Since the latter 1970s, American criticism has come to be dominated by various forms of *postmodern* theory, derived in large part from French and European thinkers. (See the Index under *criticism.*)

The 1950s, while often regarded in retrospect as a period of cultural conformity and complacency, saw the emergence of vigorous antiestablishment and antitraditional literary movements: the *Beat writers* such as Allen Ginsberg and Jack Kerouac; the American exemplars of the literature of the *absurd;* the "Black Mountain Poets," Charles Olson and Robert Creeley; and the "New York Poets," John Ashbery, Kenneth Koch, and Frank O'Hara. It was also a time of *confessional poetry* and the literature of extreme sexual candor, marked by the emergence of Henry Miller as a notable author (his autobiographical and fictional works, begun in the 1930s, had earlier been available only under the counter) and the writings of Norman Mailer, William Burroughs, and Vladimir Nabokov (*Lolita* was published in 1955). The **counterculture** of the 1960s and early '70s continued some of these modes, but in a fashion made violent and fevered by the rebellious youth movement and the vehement and growing opposition to the war in Vietnam; for an approving treatment of this movement, see Theodore Roszak, *The Making of a Counter Culture* (1969), and for a later retrospect, Morris Dickstein, *Gates of Eden: American Culture in the Sixties* (1978).

Important American writers after World War II include, in prose fiction, Vladimir Nabokov (who emigrated to America in 1940), Eudora Welty, Robert Penn Warren, Bernard Malamud, James Gould Cozzens, Saul Bellow, Mary McCarthy, Norman Mailer, John Updike, Kurt Vonnegut, Jr., Thomas Pynchon, John Barth, and E. L. Doctorow; in poetry, Marianne Moore, Robert Penn Warren, Theodore Roethke, Elizabeth Bishop, Robert Lowell, Allen Ginsberg, Adrienne Rich, Sylvia Plath, A. R. Ammons, and John Ashbery; and in drama, Thornton Wilder, Arthur Miller, Tennessee Williams, and Edward Albee. *Black writers* such as Ralph Ellison, James Baldwin, Richard Wright, Gwendolyn Brooks, and Imamu Amiri Baraka (LeRoi Jones) achieved prominence in a variety of literary forms; and there are a large and increasing number of Black women who are notable novelists, including Zora Neale Hurston, Alice Walker, and Toni Morrison. (See *Modern Black Writers,* ed. Michael Popkin, 1978.) The contemporary literary scene in America is crowded and varied, and these lists could readily be expanded; we must await the passage of time to determine which writers now active will emerge as major figures in the *canon* of American literature.

Periods of English Literature. For convenience of discussion, historians divide the continuity of English literature into segments of time which are called "periods." The exact number, names, and dates of these periods vary, but the following listing conforms to widespread practice. Each period is discussed in a separate entry in this book.

450–1066 Old English (or Anglo-Saxon) Period
1066–1500 Middle English Period
1500–1660 The Renaissance
- 1558–1603 Elizabethan Age
- 1603–1625 Jacobean Age
- 1625–1649 Caroline Age
- 1649–1660 Commonwealth Period (or Puritan Interregnum)

1660–1798	The Neoclassical Period	
	1660–1700	The Restoration
	1700–1745	The Augustan Age (or Age of Pope)
	1745–1798	The Age of Sensibility (or Age of Johnson)
1798–1832	The Romantic Period	
1832–1901	The Victorian Period	
	1848–1860	The Pre-Raphaelites
	1880–1901	Aestheticism and Decadence
1901–1914	The Edwardian Period	
1910–1936	The Georgian Period	
1914–	The Modern Period	
	1939–	Postmodernism

Persona, Tone, and Voice. These terms, frequent in recent criticism, reflect the tendency to think of all works of literature, whether lyric or narrative, as a mode of speech. To conceive a work as an utterance suggests that there is a speaker who has determinate personal qualities, and who expresses attitudes both toward the characters and materials within the work and toward the audience to whom the work is addressed. In his *Rhetoric* (fourth century B.C.), Aristotle, followed by other Greek and Roman rhetoricians, long ago pointed out that an orator establishes in the course of his oration an *ethos,* that is, a personal character, which itself functions as a means of persuasion. For example, if the impression a speaker projects is that of a person of rectitude, intelligence, and goodwill, the audience is instinctively inclined to give credence to such a speaker's arguments. The current concern with the nature and function of the author's presence in a work of imaginative literature is related to this traditional concept, and is part of the strong rhetorical emphasis in modern criticism. (See *rhetoric, rhetorical criticism,* and *speech act theory.*)

The application of the terms "persona," "tone," and "voice" varies greatly from one critic to another, and involves difficult concepts in modern philosophy and social psychology—concepts such as "the self," "personal identity," "role-playing," "sincerity." This essay will merely sketch some central uses of these terms which have proved useful in analyzing our experience of diverse works of literature.

Persona was the Latin word for the mask used by actors in the classical theater, from which was derived the term **dramatis personae** for the list of characters who play a role in a drama, and ultimately the English word "person," a particular individual. In recent literary discussion "persona" is often applied to the first-person narrator, the "I," of a narrative poem or novel, or the lyric speaker whose voice we listen to in a lyric poem. Examples of personae are the visionary first-person narrator of Milton's *Paradise Lost* (who in the opening passages of various books discourses at some length about himself); the Gulliver who tells us about his misadventures in *Gulliver's Travels;* the "I" who carries on most of the conversation in Pope's satiric dialogue *Epistle to Dr. Arbuthnot;* the urbane and genial narrator of Fielding's *Tom Jones,* who pauses frequently for leisurely discourse with his reader; the speaker who talks first to himself, then to his sister, in Wordsworth's "Tintern Abbey"; the speaker who utters

Keats's "Ode to a Nightingale," from "My heart aches" at the beginning to the ending: "Fled is that music:—Do I wake or sleep?"; and the Duke who tells the emissary about his former wife in Browning's "My Last Duchess." By calling these speakers "personae" (some critics also call them **masks**) we stress the fact that they are all part of the fiction, characters invented for a particular artistic purpose. That the "I" in each of these works is not the author as he exists in his everyday life is obvious enough in the case of Swift's Gulliver and Browning's Duke, less obvious in the case of Milton, Pope, and Fielding, and does not seem obvious at all to an unsophisticated reader of the lyric poems of Wordsworth and Keats, in which we seem invited to identify the speaker with the poet himself. But even these lyric speakers exist at some remove from the men who wrote the poems, and were devised to play a role in a particular situation and to help achieve a particular effect. In each of the major lyricists the nature of the persona alters, sometimes subtly and sometimes radically, from one of his lyrics to the next. The speaker of Donne's "A Valediction: Forbidding Mourning" is very different from that of his "The Flea"; and the "I" in Wordsworth's "We Are Seven" is not identical with that of the "Intimations" ode, and neither of these with the speaker of his "Ode to Duty." (See *lyric.*)

The modern concern with **tone** dates mainly from I. A. Richards' definition of the term as expressing a literary speaker's "attitude to his listener." "The tone of his utterance reflects . . . his sense of how he stands toward those he is addressing" (*Practical Criticism*, 1929, Chaps. 1 and 3). The sense in which the word is used is indicated in the phrase "tone of voice"; the way one speaks subtly reveals one's conception of the social level, intelligence, and sensitivity of an auditor, and one's personal relation and attitude to that auditor. The tone of a speech can be formal or intimate, outspoken or reticent, abstruse or simple, solemn or playful, arrogant or prayerful, angry or loving, serious or ironic, condescending or obsequious, and so on through numberless possible nuances of relationship and attitude. We can describe the tone of the speeches of characters within a narrative or dramatic work, but most current discussions deal specifically with the tone of a narrative or lyric persona, in the process of telling a story, or of talking to oneself, or to a nightingale, or directly to the reader. And some critical uses of "tone" are broader and coincide in reference with what other critics prefer to call "voice."

Voice, in a recently evolved usage, signifies the equivalent in imaginative literature to Aristotle's "ethos" in a work of persuasive rhetoric, and suggests also the traditional rhetorician's concern with the importance of the physical voice in an oration. The term in criticism points to the fact that there is a voice beyond the fictitious voices that speak in a work, and a person behind all the dramatis personae, including even the first-person narrator. We have the sense of a pervasive presence, a determinate intelligence and moral sensibility, which has selected, ordered, rendered, and expressed these literary materials in just this way. The particular qualities of the author's ethos, or voice, in Fielding's novel *Tom Jones* (1749) manifest themselves, among other things, in the fact that he has chosen to create the wise, ironic, and worldly persona who ostensibly tells the story and talks to the reader about it. The sense of a distinctive authorial presence is no less evident in the work of recent writers who, unlike Fielding, pursue a strict policy of authorial noninterference, and by effacing themselves, try to give the impression that the story tells itself (see *point of view*). There is great diversity in the quality of the authorial mind, temperament, and sensibility which, by inventing, controlling, and rendering the fiction, pervades works, all of them "objective" in narrative technique, such as Joyce's *Ulysses,* Virginia Woolf's *Mrs. Dalloway,* Hemingway's "The Killers," and Faulkner's *The Sound and the Fury.* For a particular emphasis on the importance of the author's implicit presence in a work, see *critics of consciousness.*

Of the critics listed below who deal with this concept, Wayne C. Booth prefers the term **implied author** over "voice," in order better to indicate that the reader of a work of fiction has the sense not only of the timbre of a speaking voice, but of a total human presence. Booth's view is that this implied author is "an ideal, literary, created version of the real man"—that is, the implied author, no less than the specific narrative persona, is part of the total fiction, whom the author gradually brings into being in the course of his composition, and who plays an important role in the total effect of a work on the reader. Critics such as W. J. Ong, on the other hand, distinguish between the author's "false voice" and his "true voice," and regard the latter as the expression of the author's genuine self or identity; as they see it, for a writer to discover his true "voice" is to discover himself. All of these critics agree, however, that the sense of a convincing authorial voice and presence, whose values, beliefs, and moral vision are the implicit controlling forces throughout a work, serves to persuade the reader to yield to the work that unstinting imaginative consent without which a poem or novel would remain no more than an elaborate verbal game.

See Richard Ellmann, *Yeats: The Man and the Masks* (1948)—which discusses Yeats's theory of a poet's "masks" or "personae," both in his life and his art; Reuben Brower, "The Speaking Voice," in *Fields of Light* (1951); T. S. Eliot, "The Three Voices of Poetry," in *On Poetry and Poets* (1957); Wayne C. Booth, *The Rhetoric of Fiction* (1961), Chap. 3; W. J. Ong, *The Barbarian Within* (1962); J. O. Perry, ed., *Approaches to the Poem* (1965)—Sec. 3, "Tone, Voice, Sensibility," includes selections from I. A. Richards, Reuben Brower, and W. J. Ong; Don Geiger, *The Dramatic Impulse in Modern Poetics* (1967); Walter J. Slatoff, *With Respect to Readers* (1970); Lionel Trilling, *Sincerity and Authenticity* (1972); Robert C. Elliott, *The Literary Persona* (1982).

Platonic Love. In Plato's *Symposium* 210–212, Socrates recounts the doctrine of Eros (love) imparted to him by the wise woman Diotima. She bids us not to linger in the love evoked by the beauty in a single human body, but to mount up as by a stair, "from one going on to two, and from two to all fair forms," then up from the beauty of the body to the beauty of the mind, until we arrive at final contemplation of the Idea, or Form, of "beauty absolute, separate, simple, and everlasting." From this Ideal Beauty the human soul is in exile, and of it the beauties of the body and of the entire world of sense are only distant, distorted, and impermanent reflections. Plotinus and other **Neoplatonists** (the "new Platonists," a school of Platonic philosophers of the third to the fifth century) developed the view that all beauty—as well as all goodness and truth—in the sensible world is an "emanation" (radiation) from the One or Absolute, which is the source of all being and all value. From both Platonic and Neoplatonic sources Christian thinkers of the Italian Renaissance developed the theory that the true beauty of the body is only the outer manifestation of a moral and spiritual beauty of the soul, which in turn is rayed out from the absolute beauty of the one God Himself. The Platonic lover, irresistibly attracted to the bodily beauty of his beloved, reveres it as a sign of the spiritual beauty that she shares with all other beautiful women, and also regards it as the lowest rung on a ladder that leads up from sensual desire to the pure contemplation of Heavenly Beauty in God.

Highly developed versions of this conception of Platonic love are to be found in Dante, Petrarch, and other writers of the thirteenth and fourteenth centuries, and in many Italian, French, and English authors of sonnets and other love poems during the Renaissance. See, for example, the exposition in Book IV of Castiglione's *The Courtier* (1528), and in Spenser's "An Hymn in Honor of Beauty." As Spenser wrote in one of the sonnets he called *Amoretti* (1595):

> Men call you fayre, and you doe credit it. . . .
> But only that is permanent and free
> From frayle corruption, that doth flesh ensew.
> That is true beautie: that doth argue you
> To be divine and borne of heavenly seed:
> Derived from that fayre spirit, from whom al true
> And perfect beauty did at first proceed.

From this complex religious and philosophical doctrine, the modern notion that Platonic love is simply love divorced from sexual desire is a vulgarized abstraction.

The concept of Platonic love has fascinated some later poets, especially Shelley; see his "Epipsychidion" (1821). But his friend Byron took a skeptical view of such lofty claims for the human Eros-impulse. "Oh Plato! Plato!" Byron sighed,

> you have paved the way,
> With your confounded fantasies, to more
> Immoral conduct by the fancied sway
> Your system feigns o'er the controlless core
> Of human hearts, than all the long array
> Of poets and romancers. . . .
> (*Don Juan*, I. cxvi)

See Plato's *Symposium* and *Phaedrus*, and the exposition of Plato's doctrine of Eros in G. M. A. Grube, *Plato's Thought* (1935), Chap. 3. Refer to J. S. Harrison, *Platonism in English Poetry of the Sixteenth and Seventeenth Centuries* (1903); Paul Shorey, *Platonism Ancient and Modern* (1938); George Santayana, "Platonic Love in Some Italian Poets," in *Selected Critical Writings*, ed. Norman Henfrey (2 vols.; 1968), I, 41–59.

Plot. The plot in a dramatic or narrative work is the structure of its actions, as these are rendered and ordered toward achieving particular emotional and artistic effects. This definition is deceptively simple, because the actions (including verbal as well as physical actions) are performed by particular characters in a work, and are the means by which they exhibit their moral and dispositional qualities. Plot and *character* are therefore interdependent critical concepts—as Henry James has said, "What is character but the determination of incident? What is incident but the illustration of character?" Notice also that there is a difference between the plot and the "story"—that is, a mere synopsis of the temporal order of the events incorporated in a work of literature. As we usually summarize a work, we say that first this happens, then that, then that. . . . It is only when we say how this is related to that, and in what ways all these matters are rendered and organized so as to achieve their particular effects, that a synopsis begins to be adequate to the actual plot. (For the distinction between story and plot, see *fiction and narratology*.)

There are a great variety of plot forms. For example, some plots are designed to achieve tragic effects, and others to achieve the effects of comedy, romance, or satire (see *genre*). Each of these types in turn exhibits a multiplicity of plot patterns, and may be represented in the mode of drama or of narrative, and in verse or in prose. The following terms, widely current in criticism, are useful in analyzing the component elements of plots and in helping to discriminate among types of plots in traditional forms of narrative and dramatic literature.

The chief character in a work, on whom our interest centers, is called the **protagonist** (or alternatively, the **hero** or **heroine**), and if he or she is pitted against an important opponent, that character is called the **antagonist.** Elizabeth Bennett is the protagonist, or heroine, of Jane Austen's *Pride and Prejudice* (1813); Hamlet is the protagonist and King Claudius the antagonist in Shakespeare's play, and the relation between them is one of **conflict.** Many, but far from all, plots deal with a conflict; Thornton Wilder's play *Our Town* (1938), for example, does not. In addition to the conflict between individuals, there may be the conflict of a protagonist against fate, or against the circumstances that stand between him and a goal he has set himself; and in some works, the conflict is between opposing desires or values in the protagonist's own temperament.

If a character sets up a scheme which depends for its success on the ignorance or gullibility of the person or persons against whom it is directed, it is called an **intrigue.** Iago is a **villain** who intrigues against Othello and Cassio in Shakespeare's tragedy *Othello.* A number of comedies, including Ben Jonson's *Volpone* (1607) and many *Restoration* plays (for example, Congreve's *The Way of the World* and Wycherley's *The Country Wife*), have plots which turn largely on the success or failure of an intrigue.

As a plot progresses it arouses expectations in the audience or reader about the future course of events and how characters will respond to events. A concerned uncertainty about what is going to happen, especially to those characters whose qualities are such that we have established a bond of sympathy with them, is known as **suspense.** If what in fact happens violates our expectations, it is known as **surprise.** The interplay of suspense and surprise is a prime source of the vitality in a traditional plot. The most effective surprise, especially in realistic narratives, is one which turns out, in retrospect, to have been grounded in what has gone before, even though we have hitherto made the wrong inference from the given facts of circumstance and character. As E. M. Forster put it, the shock of the unexpected, "followed by the feeling, 'oh, that's all right,' is a sign that all is well with the plot." A "surprise ending" in the pejorative sense is one in which the author resolves the plot without adequate earlier grounds in characterization or events, often by the use of coincidence; there are numerous examples in the short stories of O. Henry. (For one type of manipulated ending, see *deus ex machina.*) *Dramatic irony* is a special kind of suspenseful expectation, when we foresee the oncoming disaster or triumph but the character does not.

A plot has **unity of action** (or is said to be "an artistic whole") if it is perceived by the reader as a complete and ordered structure of actions, directed toward the intended effect, in which none of the component parts, or **incidents,** is unnecessary; as Aristotle put it (*Poetics,* Sec. 8), all the parts are "so closely connected that the transposal or withdrawal of any one of them will disjoint and dislocate the whole." Aristotle claimed that it does not constitute a unified plot to present a series of episodes which are strung together because they happen to a single character. Many *picaresque narratives,* nevertheless, such as Defoe's *Moll Flanders* (1722), have held the interest of readers for centuries with such an *episodic* plot structure; while even so tightly integrated a plot as that of Fielding's *Tom Jones* (1749) introduces, for variety's sake, a long, digressive story by the Man of the Hill.

A successful development which Aristotle did not foresee is the type of structural unity that can be achieved with **double plots,** familiar in *Elizabethan* drama. In this structural form, a **subplot**—a second story that is complete and interesting in its own right—is introduced into the play; when it is skillfully managed, the subplot serves to broaden our perspective on the main plot and to enhance rather than diffuse the overall effect. This underplot may have either the relation of analogy to the main plot (the Gloucester story in *King Lear*) or of counterpoint against it (the comic subplot involving Falstaff in *Henry IV, Part 1*). Spenser's *The Faerie Queene* (1590–96) is an instance of a narrative romance which interweaves main plot and multiple subplots into an intricately controlled structure, in a way that the critic C. S. Lewis compares to the **polyphonic** art of contemporary Elizabethan music, in which two or more diverse melodies are sounded together.

The order of a unified plot, Aristotle pointed out, is a continuous sequence of beginning, middle, and end. The **beginning** initiates the main action in a way which makes us look forward to something more; the **middle** presumes what has gone before and requires something to follow; and the **end** follows from what has gone before but requires nothing more; we are satisfied that the plot is complete. The beginning (the "initiating action," or "point of attack") need not be the initial stage of the action that is brought to a climax in the narrative or play. The epic, for example, plunges *in medias res* (see *epic*), many short stories begin at the point of the climax itself, and the writer of a drama often captures our attention in the opening scene with a representative incident, related and close in sequence to the event which precipitates the central situation or conflict. Thus Shakespeare's *Romeo and Juliet* opens with a street fight between the servants of two great houses, and his *Hamlet* with the apparition of a ghost; the necessary **exposition** of essential prior matters—the feud between the Capulets and Montagues, or the posture of affairs in the Royal House of Denmark—Shakespeare weaves rapidly and skillfully into the dialogue and action of these startling initial scenes. In the novel, the modern drama, and especially the motion picture, such exposition is sometimes managed by **flashbacks:** interpolated narratives or scenes (often justified as a memory, a revery, or a confession by one of the characters) which represent events that happened before the time at which the work opened. Arthur Miller's play *Death of a Salesman* (1949) and Ingmar Bergman's film *Wild Strawberries* make persistent and skillful use of this device.

The German critic Gustav Freytag, in *Technique of the Drama* (1863), introduced what is known as **Freytag's Pyramid.** He characterized the typical plot of a five-act play as a pyramidal shape, consisting of a rising action, climax, and falling action. Although the total pattern that Freytag described applies only to a limited number of plays, various of his terms are frequently echoed by critics of prose fiction as well as drama. As applied to *Hamlet*, for example, the **rising action** (the section that Aristotle called the **complication**) begins, after the opening scene and exposition, with the ghost's telling Hamlet that he has been murdered by his brother Claudius; it continues with the developing conflict between Hamlet and Claudius, in which Hamlet, despite setbacks, succeeds in controlling the course of events. The rising action reaches the **climax** of the hero's fortunes with his proof of the King's guilt by the device of the play within a play (III. ii). Then comes the **crisis,** the reversal or "turning point" of the fortunes of the protagonist, in his failure to kill the King while he is at prayer. This inaugurates the **falling action;** from now on the antagonist, Claudius, largely controls the course of events, until the **catastrophe,** or outcome, which is decided by the death of the hero, as well as of Claudius, the Queen, and Laertes. "Catastrophe" is usually applied to tragedy only; a more general term for this precipitating final scene, which is applied to both comedy and tragedy, is the **denouement** (French for "unknotting"): the action or intrigue ends in success or failure for the protagonist, the mystery is solved, or the misunderstanding cleared away.

In many plots the denouement involves a **reversal,** or in Aristotle's term, **peripety,** in the hero's fortunes, whether to his failure or destruction, as in tragedy, or to his success, as in comic plots. The reversal frequently depends on a **discovery** (in Aristotle's Greek term, **anagnorisis**). This is the recognition by the protagonist of something of great importance hitherto unknown to him or to her: Cesario reveals to the Duke at the end of Shakespeare's *Twelfth Night* that he is really Viola; the fact of Iago's lying treachery dawns upon Othello; Fielding's Joseph Andrews, in his comic novel by that name (1742), discovers on the evidence of a birthmark—"as fine a strawberry as ever grew in a garden"—that he is in reality the son of Mr. and Mrs. Wilson.

The foregoing discussion has summarized traditional critical analyses of traditional plot forms. Recently the *archetypal critic* Northrop Frye has proposed that the four main plot forms reflect the myths corresponding to the four seasons; see *genre.* And structuralist critics, regarding plots as sets of alternative conventions for ordering a fiction, have undertaken to analyze and classify plot forms on the model of the analysis and classification of the elements and structures of language in the science of linguistics; see *structuralist criticism* and *narratology,* and refer to the discussion of plots in Jonathan Culler, *Structuralist Poetics* (1975), pp. 205–24. Furthermore, a number of innovative writers of narrative fiction and drama since the 1920s have deliberately designed their works to frustrate expectations that a reader has formed on traditional plots, or have even attempted to omit a recognizable plot altogether. See, for example, literature of the *absurd, modernism and postmodernism, antinovel,* the *new novel.*

Aristotle, *Poetics;* E. M. Forster, *Aspects of the Novel* (1927); R. S. Crane, "The Concept of Plot and the Plot of *Tom Jones,*" in *Critics and Criticism* (1952); Wayne C. Booth, *The Rhetoric of Fiction* (1961); Elder Olson, *Tragedy and the Theory of Drama* (1966); Robert Scholes and Robert Kellog, *The Nature of Narrative* (1966); Frank Kermode, *The Sense of an Ending: Studies in the Theory of Fiction* (1967); Eric S. Rabkin, *Narrative Suspense* (1974); Seymour Chatman, *Story and Discourse: Narrative Structure in Fiction and Film* (1980). For structuralist treatments of plot by V. I. Propp and others, see the bibliography under *structuralist criticism.*

Poetic Diction. The term **diction** signifies the kinds of words, phrases, sentence structures, and figurative language in a work of literature. A writer's diction can be analyzed under a great variety of categories, such as the degree to which the vocabulary and phrasing is abstract or concrete, Latinate or Anglo-Saxon in origin, colloquial or formal, technical or common, literal or figurative.

The poetry of almost all ages has been written in a distinctive language, a "poetic diction," which includes words, phrasing, and figures not current in the ordinary discourse of the time. In modern discussion, however, the term **poetic diction** is usually applied to poets who, like Spenser in the Elizabethan age or G. M. Hopkins in the Victorian age, deliberately employed a diction which deviated markedly even from other poets of their era. In particular, "poetic diction," as a period term, is used to denote the special procedures of *neoclassic* writers of the eighteenth century who, like Thomas Gray, believed that "the language of the age is never the language of poetry" (letter to West, 1742). This neoclassic diction was in part derived from the characteristic usage of admired earlier poets such as Virgil, Spenser, and Milton, but was in part based on the reigning principle of *decorum,* according to which a poet must adapt the "level" and type of his diction to the mode and status of a particular genre (see *style*). Formal satire, such as Pope's *Epistle to Dr. Arbuthnot* (1735), because it represented a poet's direct commentary on everyday matters, permitted—indeed required—the use of language really spoken by urbane and cultivated people of the time. But other genres, such as epic, tragedy, and ode, required a refined and elevated poetic diction to raise the style to the level of the form, while pastoral and descriptive poems employed a special diction to make possible the management of lowly materials with what was considered appropriate dignity and elegance.

Prominent characteristics of eighteenth-century poetic diction were its *archaism* and its use of recurrent *epithets;* its Latinity ("refulgent," "irriguous," "umbrageous"); the frequent *invocations* to, and *personifications* of, abstractions or inanimate objects; and the use of circumlocution, or **periphrasis,** to avoid low, technical, or commonplace terms through a roundabout, but more decorous, substitute. Periphrases in James Thomson's *The Seasons* (1726–30) are "the finny tribe" for "fish," "the bleating kind" for "sheep," and "from the snowy leg . . . the inverted silk she drew" instead of "she took off her silk stocking."

The following stanza from Thomas Gray's excellent period piece "Ode on a Distant Prospect of Eton College" (1747) demonstrates all these devices of poetic diction. Contemporary readers took special pleasure in the ingenious periphrases by which, to achieve the stylistic elevation appropriate to an ode in describing schoolboys at play, Gray evaded the use of common or lowly words such as "swim," "cage," "boys," "hoop," and "bat":

Say, Father Thames, for thou hast seen
Full many a sprightly race
Disporting on thy margent green
The paths of pleasure trace;
Who foremost now delight to cleave
With pliant arm thy glassy wave?
The captive linnet which enthrall?
What idle progeny succeed
To chase the rolling circle's speed,
Or urge the flying ball?

In his famed attack on the doctrine of a special language for poetry, in the Preface of 1800 to *Lyrical Ballads,* Wordsworth claimed that there is no "*essential* difference between the language of prose and metrical composition"; decried the poetic diction of eighteenth-century writers as "artificial," "vicious," and "unnatural"; set up as the criterion for a valid poetic language that it be, not a matter of artful contrivance, but the "spontaneous overflow of powerful feelings"; and, by a drastic reversal of the hierarchy of linguistic decorum, claimed that the best model for such a natural expression of feeling is not upper-class speech, but the speech of "humble and rustic life."

See Thomas Quayle, *Poetic Diction: A Study of Eighteenth-Century Verse* (1924); Geoffrey Tillotson, "Eighteenth-Century Poetic Diction" (1942), reprinted in *Eighteenth-Century English Literature,* ed. James L. Clifford (1959); J. Arthos, *The Language of Natural Description in Eighteenth-Century Poetry* (1949); M. H. Abrams, "Wordsworth and Coleridge on Diction and Figures," in *The Correspondent Breeze* (1984); and for a more general treatment, Owen Barfield, *Poetic Diction* (rev., 1973).

Poetic Justice was a term coined by Thomas Rymer, an English critic of the later seventeenth century, to signify the distribution, at the end of a literary work, of earthly rewards and punishments in proportion to the virtue or vice of the various characters. Rymer's view was that a poem (in a sense which includes dramatic tragedy) is a realm of its own, and should be governed by ideal principles of *decorum* and morality, and not by the random way things often work out in the real world. Few important critics or literary writers since Rymer's day have acceded to his recommendation of poetic justice; it would, for example, destroy the possibility of tragic suffering, which exceeds what the protagonist has deserved because of his *tragic flaw*.

See Introduction to *The Critical Works of Thomas Rymer*, ed. Curt A. Zimansky (1956); M. A. Quinlan, *Poetic Justice in the Drama* (1912).

Poetic License. Dryden in the late seventeenth century defined poetic license as "the liberty which poets have assumed to themselves, in all ages, of speaking things in verse which are beyond the severity of prose." In its most common use the term is confined to *diction* alone, to justify the poet's departure from standard discourse and written prose in matters such as syntax, word order, the use of archaic or new-coined words, and the conventional use of *eye-rhymes* (wind-bind, daughter-laughter). The degree and kinds of freedom assumed by poets have varied according to the conventions of each age, but in every case the justification of the freedom lies in the success of the effect. The great opening sentence of Milton's *Paradise Lost* (1667), for example, departs radically from the colloquial prose of his time in the choice and order of words, in idiom and figurative construction, and in syntax, to achieve a distinction of language and grandeur of announcement commensurate with Milton's high subject and the epic form.

In a broader sense "poetic license" is applied to all the ways in which poets and other literary authors are held to be free to violate the ordinary norms both of speech and of literal truth, including the devices of meter and rhyme and the use of fiction and myth. A special case is **anachronism**—the placing of an event or person or thing outside of its historical era. Shakespeare dressed his Cleopatra in Elizabethan corsets, and in the Roman play *Julius Caesar*, he introduced a clock that strikes the hour. Another instance is the poet's departure from geographical or historical fact, whether from ignorance or design. It need not diminish our enjoyment of the work that Shakespeare attributed a seacoast to Bohemia in *The Winter's Tale*, or that Keats, in writing "On First Looking into Chapman's Homer" (1816), mistakenly made Cortez instead of Balboa the discoverer of the Pacific Ocean.

Point of View signifies the way a story gets told—the mode or perspective established by an author by means of which the reader is presented with the characters, actions, setting, and events which constitute the narrative in a work of fiction. The question of point of view has always been a practical concern of the novelist, and there have been scattered observations on the matter in critical writings since the emergence of the modern novel in the eighteenth century. After Henry James's Prefaces to his various novels, however—collected as *The Art of the Novel* in 1934—and Percy Lubbock's *The Craft of Fiction* (1926), which codified and expanded upon James's comments, point of view has become a prominent and persistent concern of modern theorists of the novelist's art.

Authors have developed many different ways to present a story, and many extended works employ several ways within the single narrative. The simplified classification below, however, is widely recognized and can serve as a preliminary frame of reference for analyzing traditional types of narration. It establishes a broad division between third-person and first-person narratives, then divides third-person narratives into subclasses according to the degree and kind of freedom or limitation which the author assumes in getting the matter of his story before the reader. In a **third-person narrative,** the **narrator** is someone outside the story proper, who refers to all the characters in the story by name, or as "he," "she," "they." Thus Fielding's narrator begins *Tom Jones* (1749): "In that part of the western division of this kingdom which is commonly called Somersetshire, there lately lived, and perhaps still lives, a gentleman whose name was Allworthy. . . ." In a **first-person narrative,** the narrator speaks as "I," and is himself a participant in the story. Salinger's *The Catcher in the Rye* (1951) begins: "If you really want to hear about it, the first thing you'll really want to know is where I was born, and what my lousy childhood was like, and how my parents were occupied and all before they had me, and all that David Copperfield kind of crap. . . ."

(I) Third-person points of view:

(1) The **omniscient point of view.** This is a common term for the *convention* in a work of fiction that the narrator knows everything that needs to be known about the agents and events; is free to move at will in time and place, to shift from character to character, and to report (or conceal) their speech and actions; and also that the narrator has privileged access to the characters' thoughts and feelings and motives, as well as to their overt speech and actions.

Within this mode, the **intrusive narrator** not only reports but freely comments on and evaluates the actions and motives of the characters, and sometimes expresses personal views about human life in general; ordinarily, the omniscient narrator's reports and judgments are intended to be taken as authoritative, hence to establish what counts as the facts and values within the fictional world. This is the fashion in which many of the greatest novelists have written, including Fielding, Jane Austen, Dickens, Thackeray, George Eliot, Hardy, Dostoevsky, and Tolstoy. (In Fielding's *Tom Jones* and Tolstoy's *War and Peace,* 1863–69, the intrusive narrator goes so far as to interpolate essays suggested by the subject matter of the novels.) On the other hand, the omniscient narrator may be **unintrusive** (alternative terms are **impersonal** or **objective**). Flaubert in *Madame Bovary* (1857), for example, for the most part describes, reports, or "shows" the action in dramatic scenes without introducing his own comments or judgments. More radical instances of the unintrusive narrator, who gives up even the privilege of access to inner feelings and motives, are to be found in a number of Ernest Hemingway's short stories; for example, "The Killers," and "A Clean, Well-Lighted Place." (See *showing and telling*, under *character*.) For an extreme use of impersonal showing, see the comment on Robbe-Grillet's *Jealousy*, under *novel*.

(2) The **limited point of view.** The narrator tells the story in the third person, but within the confines of what is experienced, thought, and felt by a single character (or at most by very few characters) within the story. Henry James, who refined this narrative mode, described such a selected character as his "focus," or "mirror," or "center of consciousness." In a number of James's later works all the events and actions are represented as they unfold before, and filter to the reader through, the particular awareness of one of his characters; for example, Strether in *The Ambassadors* (1903) or Maisie in *What Maisie Knew* (1897).

Later writers developed this technique into *stream-of-consciousness* narration, in which we are presented with outer observations only as they impinge on the current of thought, memory, feelings, and associations which constitute the observer's total awareness. The limitation of point of view represented both by James's "center of consciousness" narration and by the "stream-of-consciousness" narration sometimes used by Joyce, Virginia Woolf, Faulkner, and others, is often said to exemplify the "self-effacing author," or "objective narration," more effectively than does the use of an unintrusive but omniscient narrator. In the latter instance, it is said, the reader remains aware that someone, or some outside voice, is telling us about what is going on; the alternative mode, in which the point of view is limited to the consciousness of a character within the story itself, gives readers the illusion of experiencing events that evolve before their own eyes. For a subtle analysis, however, of the way even an author who restricts the narrative center of consciousness to a single character nonetheless manifests authorial judgments on people and events, and also controls the judgments of the reader, see Ian Watt, "The First Paragraph of *The Ambassadors;* An Explication," reprinted in James's *The Ambassadors*, ed. S. P. Rosenbaum, 1964. See also *persona, tone, and voice*, above.

(II) First-person points of view:

This mode, insofar as it is consistently carried out, naturally limits the point of view to what the first-person narrator knows, experiences, infers, or can find out by talking to other characters. We distinguish between the narrative "I" who is a fortuitous witness of the matters he relates (Marlow in *Heart of Darkness* and other works by Conrad); or who is a minor or peripheral participant in the story (Ishmael in Melville's *Moby-Dick*, Nick in F. Scott Fitzgerald's *The Great Gatsby*); or who is himself or herself the central character in the story (Defoe's *Moll Flanders*, Dickens' *Great Expectations*, Mark Twain's *The Adventures of Huckleberry Finn*, Salinger's *The Catcher in the Rye*). For a special case of first-person narrative, see *epistolary novel*.

Two other frequently discussed narrative tactics, which cut across diverse points of view, need to be mentioned:

The **self-conscious narrator** reveals to the reader that the narration is a work of fictional art, or in some way flaunts the discrepancies between its fictionality and the reality it seems to represent. This can be done either seriously (Fielding's narrator in *Tom Jones* and Marcel in Proust's *Remembrance of Things Past,* 1913–27) or for primarily comic purposes (Tristram in Sterne's *Tristram Shandy,* 1759–67, and the narrator of Byron's versified *Don Juan,* 1819–24), or for purposes which are both serious and comic (Carlyle's *Sartor Resartus,* 1833–34). See Robert Alter, *Partial Magic: The Novel as a Self-Conscious Genre* (1975), and refer to *dramatic irony.*

One variety of self-conscious narrative, exploited in recent prose fiction, is called the **self-reflexive novel,** or the **involuted novel,** which incorporates into its narration reference to the composition of the fictional story itself. An early modern version, André Gide's *The Counterfeiters* (1926), is also one of the most intricate. As Harry Levin summarized its self-involution: it is "the diary of a novelist who is writing a novel [to be called *The Counterfeiters*] about a novelist who is keeping a diary about the novel he is writing"; the nest of Chinese boxes was further multiplied by Gide's publication, also in 1926, of his own *Journal of The Counterfeiters,* kept while he was composing the novel. Vladimir Nabokov is an ingenious exploiter of involuted fiction; for example, in *Pale Fire* (1962). See under *novel.*

The **fallible** or **unreliable narrator** is one whose perception, interpretation, and evaluation of the matters he narrates do not coincide with the implicit opinions and norms manifested by the author, and which the author expects the alert reader to share with him. Henry James made repeated use of the narrator whose excessive innocence, or oversophistication, or moral obtuseness, makes him a flawed and distorting "center of consciousness" in the work; the result is an elaborate structure of ironies. (See *irony.*) Examples of James's use of a fallible narrator are his short stories "The Aspern Papers" and "The Liar." *The Sacred Fount* and *The Turn of the Screw* are works by James in which, according to some critics, the clues for correcting the views of the fallible narrator are inadequate, so that the facts and evaluations intended by the author remain problematic. See, for example, the remarkably diverse critical interpretations collected in *A Casebook on Henry James's "The Turn of the Screw,"* ed. Gerald Willen (1960), and in *The Turn of the Screw,* ed. Robert Kimbrough (1966). The critic Tzvetan Todorov, on the other hand, has classified *The Turn of the Screw* as an instance of **fantastic literature,** which he defines as deliberately designed by the author to leave the reader in a state of uncertainty whether the events are to be explained by reference to natural or to supernatural causes. (*The Fantastic: A Structural Approach to a Literary Genre,* transl. Richard Howard, 1973.)

Drastic experimentation in recent prose fiction have complicated in many ways traditional renderings of point of view; see *fiction* and *persona, tone, and voice.* On point of view, in addition to the writings by James and Lubbock mentioned above, refer to Norman Friedman, "Point of View in Fiction," *PMLA,* 70

(1955); Leon Edel, *The Modern Psychological Novel* (rev., 1964), Chaps. 3–4; Wayne C. Booth, *The Rhetoric of Fiction* (1961); Franz Stanzel, *Narrative Situations in the Novel*, transl. James P. Pusack (1971); Seymour Chatman, *Story and Discourse: Narrative Structure in Fiction and Film* (1980).

Pre-Raphaelites. In 1848 a group of English artists, including Dante Gabriel Rossetti, William Holman Hunt, and John Millais, organized the "Pre-Raphaelite Brotherhood." The aim was to replace the reigning academic style of painting by a return to the truthfulness, simplicity, and spirit of devotion which these artists found in Italian painting before the time of Raphael (1483–1520) and the high Italian *Renaissance*. The ideals of this group were taken over by a literary movement which included D. G. Rossetti himself (who was a poet as well as a painter), his sister Christina Rossetti, William Morris, and Algernon Swinburne. Rossetti's poem "The Blessed Damozel" typifies the medievalism, the pictorial realism with symbolic overtones, and the union of flesh and spirit, sensuousness and religiousness, associated with the earlier writings of this school. See also William Morris' narrative in verse *The Earthly Paradise* (1868–70).

William Gaunt, *The Pre-Raphaelite Tragedy* (1942); Graham Hough, *The Last Romantics* (1949).

Primitivism and Progress. A **primitivist** is someone who prefers what is "natural" (in the sense of what exists prior to and independently of human reasoning and contrivance) to what is "artificial" (in the sense of what human beings achieve by thought, activities, laws and conventions, and the complex arrangements of a civilized society). A useful, although not mutually exclusive, distinction is made between two manifestations of primitivism:

(1) **Cultural primitivism** is the preference of "nature" and "the natural" over "art" and "the artificial" in any field of human culture and values. For example, in ethics a primitivist lauds the "natural," or innate, instincts and passions over the dictates of reason and prudential forethought; in social philosophy, the ideal is the simple and "natural" forms of social and political order in place of the anxieties and frustrations engendered by a complex and highly developed social organization; in milieu, a primitivist prefers outdoor "nature," unmodified by human intervention, to cities or artful gardens; and in literature and the other arts, the primitivist relies on spontaneity, the free expression of emotion, and the intuitive products of "natural genius," as against a reasoned adaptation of artistic means to foreseen ends and a conformity to "artificial" forms, rules, and conventions. Typically, the cultural primitivist asserts that in the modern world, the life, activities, and products of "primitive" people—who are considered to live in a way more accordant to "nature" because they are isolated from civilization—are preferable to the life, activities, and products of people living in a highly developed society, especially in cities. The eighteenth-century cult of the **Noble Savage,** and the concurrent vogue of "natural" poetry

written by supposedly uneducated peasants or simple working folk, were both aspects of primitivism. Cultural primitivism has played a prominent and persistent role in American thought and literature, where the "new world" was early identified both with the *golden age* of the distant past and the Christian millennium to come, the American Indian was sometimes identified with the legendary Noble Savage, and the American pioneer was often represented as a new Adam who had cut free from the artifice and corruptions of European civilization in order to begin a "natural" life of freedom, innocence, and simplicity. See Henry Nash Smith, *Virgin Land* (1950), and R. W. B. Lewis, *The American Adam* (1955).

(2) **Chronological primitivism** signifies the belief that the ideal stage of humanity's way of life lies in the very distant past, when men and women lived naturally, simply, and freely, and that the process of history has been a gradual "decline" from that happy stage into increasing artifice, complexity, inhibitions, prohibitions, and consequent anxieties and discontents in the psychological, social, and cultural order. In its extreme form, this ideal stage is postulated as having existed in "the state of nature," before even the beginning of society and civilization; more commonly, it is placed at a later time, and sometimes as late as the era of classical Greece. Many, but not all, cultural primitivists are also chronological primitivists.

The historical concept which is antithetic to chronological primitivism emerged in the seventeenth century and reached its height in the nineteenth century. This is the idea of **progress:** the doctrine that, by virtue of the development and exploitation of humanity's art, science and technology, and wisdom, the course of history represents an overall improvement in the life, morality, and happiness of human beings from early barbarity to the present stage of civilization; and also, that this historical progress will continue indefinitely—possibly to end in a final stage of social, rational, and moral perfection.

Primitivism is as old as humanity's recorded thought and imaginings, and is reflected in the myths of a vanished age of gold and a lost Garden of Eden. (See *golden age.*) It achieved a special vogue, however, in the eighteenth century, by way of reaction to the prevailing stress on artfulness and high civilization during the *Neoclassic Period,* in a European movement in which Jean-Jacques Rousseau (1712–78) was a central figure. D. H. Lawrence (1885–1930) was a recent example of a radically primitivistic thinker, in his laudation of the spontaneous instinctual life, his belief in an ancient, vanished condition of humanity's personal and social wholeness, his resort to "primitive" modes of life that survive outside the bounds of sophisticated societies, and his attacks on the disintegrative effects of the modern technological economy and culture. There are obvious strains of primitivism in the outlook and life-style of "hippie" and other subcultures in our day, and in the establishment of communes whose ideal is a radically simplified individual and social life close to the soil. But most men and women, and many writers of literature, are primitivists in some moods, longing to escape from the complications, fever, anxieties, and "alienation" of modern civilization into the elemental simplicities of a lost natural life. That life may be imagined as an individual's own childhood, as the prehistoric or classical or medieval past, or as some primitive, carefree, faraway place on earth.

See H. N. Fairchild, *The Noble Savage* (1928); J. B. Bury, *The Idea of Progress* (1932); Lois Whitney, *Primitivism and Ideas of Progress* (1934); A. O. Lovejoy and George Boas, *Primitivism and Related Ideas in Antiquity* (1948); A. O. Lovejoy, *Essays in the History of Ideas* (1948). Friedrich Nietzsche's *The Genealogy of Morals* (1887) and Sigmund Freud's *Civilization and Its Discontents* (1949—see *psychoanalysis*) involve aspects of cultural primitivism, in their stress on the compelling needs of the body and the elemental human instincts, especially sexuality, which require a complex and very difficult reconciliation with the repressions and inhibitions that are inescapable in a civilized society. A recent example of extreme cultural primitivism is Norman O. Brown's *Life Against Death* (1959).

Problem Play is a fairly recent dramatic type which was popularized by the great Norwegian playwright Henrik Ibsen. In problem plays, the situation of the protagonist is intended to represent a contemporary social problem; often the dramatist manages—by the use of a character who speaks for the author, or by the evolution of the plot, or both—to propose a solution to the problem which is at odds with prevailing opinion. The issue may be the inadequate autonomy and scope allowed to a woman in the middle-class nineteenth-century family (Henrik Ibsen's *A Doll's House*, 1879); or the morality of prostitution, regarded as a typical economic phenomenon in a capitalist society (George Bernard Shaw's *Mrs. Warren's Profession*, 1898); or the crisis in race relations in present-day America (in numerous current dramas and films). Compare *social novel.*

In a specialized application, derivative from the use of the term for the modern dramatic form, **problem play** is sometimes applied to a group of Shakespeare's plays, also called "bitter comedies"—especially *Troilus and Cressida, Measure for Measure,* and *All's Well That Ends Well*—which present a commingling of very dark aspects with nobler aspects of human nature, and in which the resolution of the plot seems to many readers to be problematic, in that it does not settle or solve, except superficially, the moral problems raised in the play. See A. P. Rossiter, "The Problem Plays," in *Shakespeare: Modern Essays in Criticism,* ed. Leonard F. Dean (rev., 1967).

One subtype of the modern problem play is the **discussion play,** in which the social issue is not incorporated into a plot, but expounded in the give and take of a sustained debate among the characters. See Shaw's *Getting Married* and Act III of his *Man and Superman;* also his book on Ibsen's plays, *The Quintessence of Ibsenism* (1891).

Prose is often used as an inclusive term for all discourse, spoken or written, which is not patterned into the lines and rhythms either of metric verse or of free verse. (See *meter.*) It is useful, however, to discriminate a great variety of nonmetric types of language, which can be placed along a spectrum according to the degree to which they exploit modes of formal organization. At one end is the irregular, and only occasionally formal, prose of ordinary discourse. Distinguished written discourse, in what John Dryden called "that other harmony of prose," is no less an art than distinguished verse; in all literatures, in fact, artfully written prose seems to have developed later than written verse. As written prose gets more "literary"—whether its function is descriptive, expository, narrative, or expressive—it manifests more patent, though highly diverse, modes of rhythm and other formal features. The prose translations of the poetic books of the Old Testament in the King James Bible, for example, have a repetition, balance, and contrast of clauses which approximate the form that in the nineteenth century was named the **prose poem:** densely compact, pronouncedly rhythmic, and highly sonorous compositions which are written as a continuous sequence of sentences without line breaks. Examples of prose poems are, in French, Baudelaire's *Little Poems in Prose* (1869) and Rimbaud's *Illuminations* (1886), and in English, excerptible passages in Walter Pater's prose essays, such as his famous meditation on Leonardo da Vinci's painting the *Mona Lisa,* in *The Renaissance* (1873). Farther along the formal spectrum comes the interruption of the continuity of prose by line breaks and the subtly controlled rhythms, pauses, syntactical suspensions, and cadences in *free verse.* At the far end of the spectrum we get the regular, recurrent units of weaker and stronger stressed syllables that constitute the meters of English verse.

See *linguistics in modern criticism, meter,* and *style;* and for a special form of self-consciously formal prose, *euphuism.* Refer to George Saintsbury, *A History of English Prose Rhythm* (1912); M. Boulton, *Anatomy of Prose* (1954); George L. Trager and Henry Lee Smith, Jr., *An Outline of English Structure* (1951). E. D. Hirsch discusses the development of English prose in *The Philosophy of Composition* (1977), pp. 51–72. Refer also to the bibliographical references under *style.*

Prosody signifies the systematic study of **versification,** that is, of the principles and practice of *meter, rhyme,* and *stanza* forms. Sometimes the term "prosody" is extended to include also the study of sound effects such as *alliteration, assonance, euphony,* and *onomatopoeia.*

Pun. A play on words that are either identical in sound ("homonyms") or very similar in sound, but are sharply diverse in meaning. Puns have had serious literary uses. The authority of the Pope goes back to the Greek pun uttered by Christ in Matthew XVI:18, "Thou art Peter [Petros] and upon this rock [petra] I will build my church." Shakespeare and other writers used puns seriously, as well as for comic purposes. In *Romeo and Juliet* (III. i. 101) Mercutio, bleeding to death, says, "Ask for me tomorrow and you shall find me a grave man"; and John Donne's solemn "Hymn to God the Father" (1633) puns throughout on his own name and the verb "done." In the eighteenth century and thereafter, however, the literary use of the pun has been almost exclusively comic. The great exception is James Joyce's *Finnegans Wake* (1939), which exploits puns throughout in order to help sustain its complex effect, at once serious and comic, of multiple levels of meaning; see *portmanteau word.*

A special type of pun, known as the **equivoque,** is the use of a single word or phrase which has two disparate meanings, in a context which makes both meanings equally relevant. An example is the epitaph suggested for a bank teller:

> He checked his cash, cashed in his checks,
> And left his window. Who is next?

Purple Patch is a translation of Horace's Latin phrase "purpureus . . . pannus" in his versified *Ars Poetica* (first century B.C.). It signifies a marked heightening of style in rhythm, diction, and figurative language that makes a section of verse or prose—especially a descriptive passage—stand out from its context. The term is sometimes applied without derogation to a set piece, separable and quotable, in which an author rises to an occasion. An example is the eulogy of England by the dying John of Gaunt in Shakespeare's *Richard II* (II. i. 40 ff.), beginning

> This royal throne of kings, this scept'red isle,
> This earth of majesty, this seat of Mars,
> This other Eden, demi-paradise. . . .

Other well-known examples are Byron's depiction of the Duchess of Richmond's ball on the eve of Waterloo in *Childe Harold's Pilgrimage,* Canto III, xxi–xxviii (1816), and Pater's prose description of the *Mona Lisa* in his essay on Leonardo da Vinci in *The Renaissance* (1873). Usually, however, "purple passage" connotes disparagement of an author who has self-consciously girded himself to perform a piece of fine writing.

Realism and Naturalism. Realism is used by literary critics in two chief ways: (1) to identify a literary movement of the nineteenth century, especially in prose fiction (beginning with Balzac in France, George Eliot in England, and William Dean Howells in America); and (2) to designate a recurrent mode, in various eras, of representing human life and experience in literature, which was especially exemplified by the writers of this historical movement.

Realistic fiction is often opposed to romantic fiction: the *romance* is said to present life as we would have it be, more picturesque, more adventurous, more heroic than the actual; realism, to present an accurate imitation of life as it is. This distinction is not invalid, but it is inadequate. Casanova, T. E. Lawrence, and Winston Churchill were people in real life, but their histories, as related by themselves or others, demonstrate that truth can be stranger than literary realism. The typical realist sets out to write a fiction which will give the illusion that it reflects life and the social world as it seems to the common reader. To achieve this effect the author prefers as protagonist an ordinary citizen of Middletown, living on Main Street, perhaps, and engaged in the real estate business. The realist, in other words, is deliberately selective in material and prefers the average, the commonplace, and the everyday over the rarer aspects of the social scene. The characters, therefore, are usually of the middle class or (less frequently) the working class—people without highly exceptional endowments, who live through ordinary experiences of childhood, adolescence, love, marriage, parenthood, infidelity, and death; who find life rather dull and often unhappy, though it may be brightened by touches of beauty and joy; but who may, under special circumstances, display something akin to heroism.

A thoroughgoing realism involves not only a selection of subject matter but, more important, a special literary manner as well: the subject is represented, or "rendered," in such a way as to give the reader the illusion of actual and ordinary experience. (*Structuralist critics* claim that the techniques used by a realistic author are in fact purely literary *conventions* and codes which the reader interprets, or *naturalizes,* so as to make the work seem a reflection of everyday reality.) Daniel Defoe, the first novelistic realist in the early eighteenth century, dealt with the extraordinary adventures of a shipwrecked mariner named Robinson Crusoe and with the extraordinary misadventures of Moll Flanders; but these novels are made to seem to the reader a mirror held up to real life by Defoe's reportorial manner of rendering the events, whether trivial or extraordinary, in a circumstantial, matter-of-fact, and seemingly unselective way.

In the broad sense of the term, authors of highly wrought prose fiction such as Fielding, Jane Austen, Balzac, George Eliot, and Tolstoy are realists, for they often render ordinary people and settings so richly and persuasively that they convince us that men and women really lived, talked, and acted in the way that they depict. Some critics, however, use the term "realist" more narrowly for writers who render a subject so as to make it seem a reflection of the casual order of experience, without too patently shaping it into a tightly wrought comic or ironic or tragic pattern (see *plot*). In this narrower sense, "realism" is applied more exclusively to works such as William Dean Howells' *The Rise of Silas Lapham* (1885), Arnold Bennet's novels about the "Five Towns" (1902 and following), and Sinclair Lewis' *Main Street* (1920). See also *magic realism.*

Naturalism is sometimes claimed to be an even more accurate picture of life than is realism. But naturalism is not only, like realism, a special selection of subject matter and a special literary manner; it is a mode of fiction that was developed by a school of writers in accordance with a particular philosophical thesis. This thesis, a product of post-Darwinian biology in the mid-nineteenth century, held that a human being belongs entirely in the order of nature and does not have a soul or any other mode of participation in a religious or spiritual world beyond nature; that such a being is therefore merely a higher-order animal whose character and fortunes are determined by two kinds of forces, heredity and environment. A person inherits personal traits and compulsive instincts, especially hunger, the accumulative drive, and sex, and is then subject to the social and economic forces in the family, the class, and the milieu into which that person is born. The French novelist Émile Zola, beginning in the 1870s, did much to develop this theory in what he called "le roman expérimental" (that is, the novel organized in the mode of a scientific experiment). Zola and later naturalistic writers, such as the Americans Frank Norris, Stephen Crane,

Theodore Dreiser, and James Farrell, try to present their subjects with an objective scientific attitude and with elaborate documentation, sometimes including an almost medical frankness about activities and bodily functions usually unmentioned in earlier literature. They tend to choose characters who exhibit strong animal drives such as greed and sexual desire, and who are victims both of their glandular secretions within and of sociological pressures without. The end of the naturalistic novel is usually "tragic," but not, as in classical and Elizabethan *tragedy*, because of a heroic but losing struggle of the individual mind and will against gods, enemies, and circumstance. Instead the protagonist of the naturalistic plot, a pawn to multiple compulsions, usually disintegrates, or is wiped out.

Aspects of the naturalistic selection and management of materials and its austere or harsh frankness of manner are apparent in many modern novels and dramas, such as Hardy's *Jude the Obscure*, 1895 (although Hardy largely substituted a cosmic determinism for biological and environmental determinism), various plays of Eugene O'Neill in the 1920s, and Norman Mailer's novel of World War II, *The Naked and the Dead*. An enlightening exercise is to distinguish how the relation between the sexes is represented in a romance (Richard Blackmore's *Lorna Doone*, 1869), an ironic comedy of manners (Jane Austen's *Pride and Prejudice*, 1813), a realistic novel (William Dean Howells' *A Modern Instance*, 1882), and a naturalistic novel (Émile Zola's *Nana*, 1880, or Theodore Dreiser's *An American Tragedy*, 1925). Movements originally opposed both to realism and naturalism (though some modern works, such as Joyce's *Ulysses*, 1922, combine aspects of all these novelistic modes) are *expressionism* and *symbolism* (see *Symbolist Movement*).

Socialist Realism is a term used by Marxist critics for novels which are held to embody or "reflect" some aspect of the Marxist view that the struggle between economic classes is the essential dynamic of society. Since the 1930s, "Socialist Realism" has been the official doctrine directing the work of authors in the Soviet Union. In its crude version, it is a term of approbation applied mainly to novels which adhere to the party line, emphasizing the oppressions by bourgeois capitalists, the virtues of the proletariat, and the felicities of life under Soviet Socialism. A flexible Marxist such as Georg Lukács, however, employs complex criteria of narrative realism to laud most of the classics of European realistic fiction. See *Marxist criticism*, and refer to Marc Slonim, *Soviet Russian Literature* (1967), and George Bisztray, *Marxist Models of Literary Realism* (1978).

On realism: Walter L. Myers, *The Later Realism* (1927); Erich Auerbach, *Mimesis: The Representation of Reality in Western Literature* (1953); Ernst Gombrich, *Art and Illusion* (1960); Harry Levin, *The Gates of Horn: A Study of Five French Realists* (1963); René Wellek, "The Concept of Realism in Literary Scholarship," in *Concepts of Criticism* (1963); Linda Nochlin, *Realism* (1971).

Refrain. A line, or part of a line, or a group of lines, which is repeated in the course of a poem, sometimes with slight changes, and usually at the end of each stanza. The refrain occurs in many ballads and work poems, and is a frequent element in Elizabethan songs, where it sometimes occurs in a nonsignificant form as mere carrier of the melodic line, as in Shakespeare's "It Was a Lover and His Lass": "With a hey, and a ho, and a hey nonino." A famous refrain is that which closes each stanza in Spenser's "Epithalamion" (1594)—"The woods shall to me answer, and my echo ring"—in which sequential changes indicate the altering sounds during the successive hours of the poet's wedding day. The refrain in Spenser's "Prothalamion"—"Sweet Thames, run softly, till I end my song"—is echoed ironically in Part III of T. S. Eliot's *The Waste Land* (1922), describing the Thames in our age of polluted rivers.

A refrain may consist of a single word—"Nevermore" as in Poe's "The Raven" (1845)—or a whole stanza. If the stanza-refrain occurs in a song as a part in which all the listeners join, it is called the **chorus;** for example, in "Auld Lang Syne" and many other songs by Robert Burns in the late eighteenth century.

Renaissance ("rebirth") is the name commonly applied to the period of European history following the Middle Ages; it is usually said to have begun in Italy in the late fourteenth century and to have continued in western Europe through the fifteenth and sixteenth centuries. In this period the arts of painting, sculpture, architecture, and literature reached an eminence not exceeded by any civilization in any age. The development came late to England in the sixteenth century, and did not have its flowering until the *Elizabethan* and *Jacobean* periods; sometimes, in fact, Milton (1608–74) is said to be the last great Renaissance poet.

Many attempts have been made to define "the Renaissance" in a brief predication, as though a single essence underlay the complex features of the culture of numerous countries over several hundred years. It has, for example, been described as the birth of the modern world out of the ashes of the Dark Ages; as the discovery of the world and the discovery of man; and as the era of untrammeled individualism in life, thought, religion, and art. Recently some historians, finding that similar attributes were present in various people and places in the Middle Ages, and also that many elements long held to be medieval survived into the Renaissance, have denied that the Renaissance ever existed. It is true that history is a continuous process, and that "periods" are invented not by God but by historians. Nonetheless, the division of the temporal continuum into segments called "periods" is a great convenience in discussing cultural history. In addition, during the temporal span called "the Renaissance," it is possible to identify a number of events and discoveries which, beginning approximately in the fifteenth century, undoubtedly effected radical and distinctive changes in the views, productions, and manner of life of at least the intellectual classes.

All these occurrences may be regarded as putting a strain on the relatively closed and stable world of the great civilization of the later Middle Ages, when most of the essential truths about man, the universe, God, and philosophy were held to be well known and permanently established. The full impact of many Renaissance developments did not make itself felt until the Enlightenment in the later seventeenth and the eighteenth centuries, but the fact that they occurred in this period indicates the vitality, the audacity, and the restless curiosity of many men of the Renaissance, whether scholars, thinkers, artists, or adventurers. Prominent developments in the Renaissance were:

(1) The new learning. Renaissance scholars of the classics, called *humanists*, revived the knowledge of the Greek language, discovered and disseminated a great number of Greek manuscripts, and added considerably to the number of Roman authors and works which had been known to the Middle Ages. The result was to enlarge immensely the stock of ideas, materials, literary forms, and styles available to Renaissance writers. In the mid-fifteenth century the invention of printing on paper from movable type made books for the first time cheap and plentiful, and floods of publications, ancient and modern, poured from the presses of Europe to satisfy the demands of the expanding audience who were taught to read. The speed of the inauguration and spread of ideas, discoveries, and types of literature in the Renaissance was made possible by this technological development of printing.

The humanistic revival sometimes resulted in pedantic scholarship, sterile imitations of ancient works and styles, and a rigid rhetoric and literary criticism. It also bred, however, the gracious and tolerant humanity of an Erasmus, and the high concept of a cultivated Renaissance aristocracy expressed in Baldassare Castiglione's *Il Cortegiano* ("The Courtier"), published in 1528. This was the most admired and widely translated of the many Renaissance **courtesy books,** or books on the character, obligations, and training of the man of the court. It presents the ideal of the completely rounded or "universal" man, developed in all his faculties and skills, physical, intellectual, and artistic. He is trained to be a warrior and statesman, but is capable also as athlete, philosopher, artist, conversationist, and man of society. His relations to women, and of women to men, are in accord with the quasi-religious code of *Platonic love,* and his activities are crowned by the grace of **sprezzatura**—the seeming ease and negligence with which he meets the demands of complex and exacting rules of behavior. Leonardo da Vinci in Italy and Sir Philip Sidney in England are often represented as embodying many aspects of the courtly ideal.

(2) The new religion. The **Reformation** led by Martin Luther (1483–1546) was a successful heresy which struck at the very basis of the institutionalism of the Roman Catholic Church. This early Protestantism was grounded on the individual's inner experience of spiritual struggle and salvation. Faith (based on the word of the Bible as interpreted by the individual) was alone thought competent to save, and salvation itself was regarded as a direct transaction with God in the theater of the individual soul, without the need of intermediation by Church, priest, or sacrament. For this reason Protestantism is sometimes said to have been an extreme manifestation of "Renaissance individualism" in northern Europe; it soon, however, developed its own institutionalism, in the theocracy proposed by John Calvin (1509–64) and his Puritan followers. England in characteristic fashion muddled its way into Protestantism under Henry VIII and Elizabeth I, empirically finding a middle way that minimized violence and hastened a stable new settlement.

(3) The new world. In 1492 Columbus, acting on the persisting belief in the old Greek idea that the world is a globe, sailed west to find a new commercial route to the East, only to be frustrated by the unexpected barrier of a new continent. The succeeding explorations of this continent gave new materials and stimulus to the literary imagination; the magic world of Shakespeare's *The Tempest,* for example, is based on a contemporary account of a shipwreck on Bermuda. More important for English literature, however, was the fact that economic exploitation of the new world put England at the center, rather than as heretofore at the edge, of the chief trade routes, and so helped establish the commercial prosperity that in England, as in Italy earlier, was a necessary though not sufficient condition for the development of a vigorous intellectual and artistic life.

(4) The new cosmos. The cosmos of medieval astronomy and theology was **Ptolemaic** (that is, based on the astronomy of Ptolemy, second century) and pictured a stationary earth around which rotated the successive spheres of the moon, the various planets, and the fixed stars; Heaven, or the Empyrean, was thought to be situated above the spheres, and Hell to be situated either at the center of the earth (as in Dante's *Inferno*) or else below the system of the spheres (as in Milton's *Paradise Lost*). In 1543 Copernicus published his new hypothesis concerning the system of the universe; this gave a much simpler and more coherent explanation of accumulating observations of the actual movements of the heavenly bodies, which had led to ever greater complications of the Ptolemaic world picture. The **Copernican theory** pictured a system in which the center is not the earth, but the sun, and in which the earth is not stationary, but one planet among the many planets which revolve around the sun.

Investigations have not borne out the earlier assumption of historians that the world picture of Copernicus and his followers delivered an immediate and profound shock to the theological and secular beliefs of thinking men. For example, in 1611, when Donne wrote in "The First Anniversary" that "new Philosophy calls all in doubt," for "the Sun is lost, and th' earth," he did so only to support the ancient theme, or literary *topos,* of the world's decay and to enforce a standard Christian "contemptus mundi" (contempt for the worldly). Still later, Milton in *Paradise Lost* (1667) expressed a suspension of judgment between the Ptolemaic and Copernican theories; he adopted as the cosmic setting for his own poem the older Ptolemaic scheme because it was more firmly traditional and better adapted to his narrative purposes.

Much more important, in the long run, was the effect on men's opinions of the general principles and methods of the **new science** of the great successors of Copernicus in the late sixteenth and early seventeenth centuries, such as the physicists Kepler and Galileo and the English physician and physiologist William Harvey. The cosmos of many Elizabethan writers remained not only Ptolemaic, and subject throughout to God's Providence; it remained also an animate universe, invested with occult powers, inhabited by demons and spirits, and often thought to control men's lives by stellar influences and to be itself subject to control by the powers of witchcraft and of magic. The cosmos that emerged in the course of the seventeenth century, as a product of the newly developed scientific procedure of constructing hypotheses capable of being tested by precisely measured observations, was the physical universe of René Descartes (1596–1650). "Give me extension and motion," Descartes wrote, "and I will construct the universe." This universe of Descartes and the new science consisted of extended particles of matter which moved in space according to fixed mathematical laws, free from interference by angels, demons, human prayer, or occult magical powers, and subject only to the limited manipulations of experimental scientists who, in Francis Bacon's phrase, had learned to obey nature in order to be her master. In this way the working hypotheses of the physical scientists were converted into a philosophical worldview, which was made current by many popular expositions, and—together with the methodological principle that controlled observation, rather than tradition or authority, is the only criterion of truth in all areas of knowledge of this world—helped constitute the climate of eighteenth-century opinion known as the *Enlightenment.*

Refer to J. Burckhardt, *Civilization of the Renaissance in Italy* (first published in 1860); H. O. Taylor, *Thought and Expression in the 16th Century* (1920); E. A. Burtt, *The Metaphysical Foundations of Modern Science* (rev., 1932); W. K. Ferguson, *The Renaissance in Historical Thought* (1948); C. S. Lewis, *English Literature in the 16th Century* (1954); Marjorie Nicolson, *Science and Imagination* (1956); Thomas S. Kuhn, *The Copernican Revolution* (1957); Paul O. Kristeller, *Renaissance Thought: The Classic, Scholastic, and Humanistic Strains* (rev., 1961); John R. Hale, *Renaissance* (1965).

Restoration. This period in England takes its name from the restoration of the Stuart line (Charles II) to the English throne in 1660, at the end of the *Commonwealth;* it is specified as lasting until 1700. The urbanity, wit, and licentiousness of the life centering on the court, in sharp contrast to the seriousness and sobriety of the earlier Puritan regime, is reflected in much of the literature of this age. The theaters came back to vigorous life after the revocation of the ban placed on them by the Puritans in 1642; Etherege, Wycherley, Congreve, and Dryden developed the distinctive comedy of manners called *Restoration comedy,* and Dryden, Otway, and other playwrights developed the even more distinctive form of tragedy called *heroic drama.* Dryden was the major poet and critic, as well as one of the major dramatists. Other poets were the satirists Samuel Butler and the Earl of Rochester; other notable writers in prose were Samuel Pepys, Sir William Temple, the religious writer John Bunyan, and the philosopher John Locke.

Basil Willey, *The Seventeenth Century Background* (1934); L. I. Bredvold, *The Intellectual Milieu of John Dryden* (1934). See also the entry *neoclassic and romantic.*

Rhetoric. In his *Poetics* the Greek philosopher Aristotle defined poetry as a mode of *imitation*—a fictional representation in words of human beings thinking, feeling, acting, and interacting—and focused his discussion on elements such as plot, character, thought, and diction within the work itself. In his *Rhetoric* Aristotle defined rhetorical discourse as the art of "discovering all the available means of persuasion in any given case," and focused his discussion on the means and devices that an orator uses in order to achieve the intellectual and emotional effects on an audiencc that will persuade them to accede to his point of view. Later classical rhetoricians (one of the most important and influential was the Roman Quintilian in the first century) concurred with this definition of rhetoric as the art of persuading an audience, discussed the role of memory and oral delivery, and (still following Aristotle's lead) analyzed the text of a persuasive rhetorical discourse as consisting of "invention" (the finding of arguments or proofs), "disposition" (the arrangement of such matters), and "style" (the choice of words, verbal patterns, and rhythms that will most effectively express this material); this last topic sometimes came to include extensive classifications and analyses of figures of speech. Rhetoricians also discriminated three main categories of oratory, each of which uses characteristic devices to achieve its persuasive aims:

(1) **Deliberative**—to persuade an audience (such as a legislative assembly) to approve or disapprove of a matter of public policy, and to act accordingly.

(2) **Forensic**—to achieve (for example, in a judicial trial) condemnation or approval of a person's actions.

(3) **Epideictic**—"display rhetoric," used on appropriate, usually ceremonial, occasions to enlarge upon the praiseworthiness (or sometimes, the blameworthiness) of a person or group of persons, and in so doing, to display the orator's own talents and skill at rising to the rhetorical needs of the occasion. Lincoln's "Gettysburg Address" is a famed instance of epideictic oratory; in America, it remains traditional for a chosen speaker to meet the challenge of the Fourth of July by appropriate epideictic oratory. The *ode* is a poetic form often used for epideictic purposes.

Figurative language, in classical and later traditional rhetorics, had been considered as only one element of style and subordinated to the overall aim of persuasion. In the present century, however (and especially in the last fifty years), the analysis of the types and functions of figurative language has been increasingly excerpted from this rhetorical context and made an independent and central concern, not only by critics of literature but also by language theorists and by philosophers, as well as by some *poststructuralist* analysts who regard all modes of discourse as composed primarily of figurative elements which are nonlogical or counterlogical (see *figurative language*).

Refer to *ethos* (the speaker's projected character as a means of persuasion) under *persona, tone, and voice;* also *rhetorical criticism.* See Aristotle's *Rhetoric*, ed. Lane Cooper (1932); M. L. Clarke, *Rhetoric at Rome: A Historical Survey* (1953); George Kennedy, *The Art of Persuasion in Greece* (1963); Edward P. J. Corbett, *Classical Rhetoric for the Modern Student* (rev., 1971).

Rhetorical Criticism. The Roman Horace in his versified *Art of Poetry* (first century B.C.) declared that the aim of a poet is either to instruct or delight a reader, or preferably to do both. Such *pragmatic criticism,* which breaks down

Aristotle's distinction between imitative poetry and persuasive rhetoric (see *rhetoric*), dominated literary theory and practice from late classical times through the eighteenth century. Discussions of poetry absorbed and expanded upon the terms of traditional rhetoric, and a poem was regarded mainly as a deployment of established artistic means for achieving particular effects upon the reader or audience. The triumph in the early nineteenth century of *expressive* theories of literature (which conceive a work primarily as the expression of the feelings, temperament, and mental powers of the author himself), followed by the dominance, beginning in the 1920s, of *objective* theories of literature (which maintain that a work must be considered as an object in itself, independently of the mental qualities of the author and the responses of a reader), served to diminish, and sometimes to eliminate, rhetorical considerations in literary criticism.

Since the late 1950s, however, there has been a revival of interest in literature as a verbal act involving communication between author and reader, and this has led to the development of a **rhetorical criticism** which, without departing from a primary focus on the work itself, undertakes to analyze those elements within a poem or a prose narrative which are there primarily for the reader's sake. As Wayne Booth has said in the Preface to his influential book *The Rhetoric of Fiction* (1961), his subject is "the rhetorical resources available to the writer of epic, novel, or short story as he tries, consciously or unconsciously, to impose his fictional world upon the reader." A number of recent critics of prose fiction and of narrative and nonnarrative poems have devoted special attention to an author's use of a variety of means—including the authorial presence or voice that he projects—in order to inform, to achieve imaginative consent, and to engage the interests and guide the emotional responses of the readers to whom, whether deliberately or not, his literary work is addressed. (See *persona, tone, and voice.*)

Since the 1960s there has also emerged a prominent mode of reader-response criticism which focuses upon a reader's complex interpretive responses to the sequence of words in a literary text; most of its spokesmen, however, either ignore or reject the rhetorical view that such responses are effected by literary devices contrived for that purpose by the author. See *reader-response criticism.*

For recent examples of the rhetorical criticism of poetry and fiction see (in addition to Wayne Booth) Kenneth Burke, *A Rhetoric of Motives* (1955); M. H. Nichols, *Rhetoric and Criticism* (1963); Donald C. Bryant, ed., *Papers in Rhetoric and Poetic* (1965); Edward P. J. Corbett, ed., *Rhetorical Analyses of Literary Works* (1969).

Rhetorical Figures. It is convenient to list under this heading some common "figures of speech" which depart from what is felt to be standard, or "literal," language mainly by the arrangement of their words to achieve special effects, and not, like metaphors and other *tropes,* by a radical change of meaning in the words themselves. See this distinction under *figurative language.*

An **apostrophe** is a direct and explicit address either to an absent person or to an abstract or inanimate entity. Often the effect is either of high formality or else of a sudden emotional impetus. Many *odes* are constituted throughout in this conventional form. So Keats begins his "Ode on a Grecian Urn" (1820) by apostrophizing the Urn—"Thou still unravished bride of quietness"—and addresses all the rest of the poem to the Urn. Coleridge's fine lyric "Recollections of Love" (1817) is addressed to an absent woman; at the end of the poem, Coleridge turns suddenly from thoughts of his beloved to apostrophize also the River Greta:

> But when those meek eyes first did seem
> To tell me, Love within you wrought—
> O Greta, dear domestic stream!
>
> Has not, since then, Love's prompture deep,
> Has not Love's whisper evermore
> Been ceaseless, as thy gentle roar?
> Sole voice, when other voices sleep,
> Dear under-song in clamor's hour.

Many apostrophes, like these examples from Keats and Coleridge, imply a *personification* of the object addressed. (See Jonathan Culler, "Apostrophe," in *The Pursuit of Signs*, 1981.)

If such an address is to a god or muse to assist the poet in his composition, it is called an **invocation;** so Milton invokes divine guidance at the opening of *Paradise Lost:*

> And chiefly Thou, O Spirit, that dost prefer
> Before all temples th' upright heart and pure,
> Instruct me. . . .

A **rhetorical question** is a question asked, not to evoke an actual reply, but to achieve an emphasis stronger than a direct statement, by inviting the auditor to supply an answer which the speaker presumes to be the obvious one. The figure is most used in persuasive discourse, and tends to impart an oratorical tone to any utterance. When "fierce Thalestris" in Pope's *The Rape of the Lock* (1714) asks Belinda,

> Gods! Shall the ravisher display your hair,
> While the fops envy, and the ladies stare?

she does not stay for an answer, which she obviously thinks should be "No!" (The most common rhetorical question is one that won't take "Yes" for an answer.) Shelley's "Ode to the West Wind" (1820) closes with the most famous rhetorical question in English:

> O, Wind,
> If Winter comes, can Spring be far behind?

Chiasmus (derived from the Greek term for the letter X, or a cross-over) is a sequence of two phrases or clauses which are parallel in syntax, but reverse the order of the corresponding words. So in this line from Pope the verb first precedes, then follows, the adverbial phrase:

> *Works* without show, and without pomp *presides*.

The effect is sometimes reinforced by alliteration and other similarities in sound, as in Pope's summary of the common fate of coquettes in marriage:

> A *fop* their *passion*, but their *prize* a *sot*.

In Yeats's "An Irish Airman Foresees His Death" (1919), the chiasmus consists in a reversal of the position of an entire phrase:

> The years to come seemed *waste of breath*,
> A *waste of breath* the years behind.*

And as a reminder that all these figures occur in prose as well as verse, here is an instance of chiasmus from Shelley's *Defence of Poetry* (1821): "Poetry is the record of the best and happiest moments of the happiest and best minds."

Zeugma in Greek means "yoking"; in the most common present usage, it is applied to expressions in which a single word stands in the same grammatical relation to two or more other words, but with some alteration in its idiomatic use or significance. Here are examples of zeugma in Pope:

> Or *stain* her honour, or her new brocade.

> *Obliged* by hunger, and request of friends.

Byron uses zeugma for grimly comic effects, in his description in *Don Juan* (1819–24) of a shipwreck:

> And the waves oozing through the port-hole *made*
> His berth a little damp, and him afraid.

> The loud tempests *raise*
> The waters, and repentance for past sinning.

To achieve the maximum of concentrated verbal effects within the tight limits of the *closed couplet*, Pope in the early eighteenth century exploited all these language patterns with supreme virtuosity. He is the English master of the rhetorical figures, as Shakespeare is of tropes.

Other linguistic patterns, sometimes classified as figures of speech, are treated elsewhere in this book; see *antithesis, alliteration, assonance*, rhetorical *climax* (under *bathos*), and *parallelism.* For concise definitions and examples of other figures of speech which are less commonly referred to in literary analyses, see Edward P. J. Corbett, *Classical Rhetoric for the Modern Student* (rev., 1971).

Rhyme. In English versification the standard rhyme consists in the identity, in rhyming words, of the last stressed vowel and of all the speech sounds following that vowel: láte-fáte; fóllow-hóllow.

End rhymes, by far the most frequent type, occur at the end of a verse-line. **Internal rhymes** occur within a verse-line, as in the Victorian poet Swinburne's

> Sister, my sister, O *fleet sweet* swallow.

A stanza from Coleridge's "The Rime of the Ancient Mariner" (1798) illustrates the patterned use both of internal rhymes (within lines 1 and 3) and of an end rhyme (lines 2 and 4):

> In mist or *cloud,* on mast or *shroud,*
> It perched for vespers *nine;*
> Whiles all the *night,* through fog-smoke *white,*
> Glimmered the white moon-*shine.*

The numbered lines in the following stanza of Wordsworth's "The Solitary Reaper" (1807) are followed by a column which, in the conventional way, marks the sequence of the terminal rhyme elements by a corresponding sequence and repetition of the letters of the alphabet:

(1) Whate'er her theme, the maiden sang	*a*
(2) As if her song could have no *ending;*	*b*
(3) I saw her singing at her work	*c*
(4) And o'er the sickle *bending*—	*b*
(5) I listened, motionless and *still;*	*d*
(6) And as I mounted up the *hill,*	*d*
(7) The music in my heart I *bore,*	*e*
(8) Long after it was heard no *more.*	*e*

Lines 1 and 3 do not rhyme with any other line. Both in lines 5 and 6 and lines 7 and 8 the rhyme consists of a single stressed syllable, and is called a **masculine rhyme;** stíll-híll, bóre-móre. In lines 2 and 4, the rhyme consists of a stressed syllable followed by an unstressed syllable, and is called a **feminine rhyme:** éndiňg-béndiňg. (On syllabic stress-patterns, see *meter.*)

A feminine rhyme, since it involves two syllables, is also known as a **double rhyme.** A rhyme involving three syllables is called a **triple rhyme;** such rhymes, since they coincide with surprising patness, usually have a comic quality. In *Don Juan* (1819–24) Byron often uses triple rhymes such as compárĭsŏngárrĭsŏn, and sometimes intensifies the comic effect by permitting the pressure of the rhyme to force a distortion of the pronunciation; thus he addresses the husbands of learned wives:

> But—Oh! ye lords of ladies intell*éctŭăl*
> Inform us truly, have they not hen-*pécked yoŭ ăll*?

This maltreatment of words, called **forced rhyme,** in which the poet seems to surrender helplessly to the exigencies of a triple rhyme, has been comically exploited by the modern poet Ogden Nash:

> Farewell, farewell, you old rhinocerous,
> I'll stare at something less prepocerous.*

If the correspondence of the rhymed sounds is exact, it is called **perfect rhyme,** or else "full" or "true rhyme." Until recently almost all English writers of serious poems have limited themselves to perfect rhymes, except for an occasional *poetic license* such as **eye-rhymes;** that is, words whose endings are spelled alike, and in most instances were once pronounced alike, but have in the course of time acquired a different pronunciation: prove-love, daughter-laughter. Many modern poets, however, deliberately supplement perfect rhyme with **imperfect rhyme** (also known as "partial," "near," or "slant" rhyme, or else as "pararhyme"). This effect is fairly common in folk poetry such as children's verses, and it was employed occasionally by various writers of art lyrics such as Thomas Vaughan in the seventeenth, William Blake in the late eighteenth, and Emily Dickinson in the nineteenth century. Hopkins and Yeats, however, were the first important poets fully to exploit partial rhymes, in which the vowels are either approximate or quite different, and occasionally even the rhymed consonants are similar rather than identical. Wilfred Owen, in 1917–18, constructed the following six-line stanza with two sets of partial rhymes, established at the ends of the first two lines:

> The centuries will burn rich loads
> With which we groaned,
> Whose warmth shall lull their dreamy lids,
> While songs are crooned.
> But they will not dream of us poor lads,
> Lost in the ground.†

In his poem "The Force That through the Green Fuse Drives the Flower" (1933), Dylan Thomas uses, most effectively, such distantly approximate rhymes

*Copyright, 1933, by Ogden Nash. From *Many Long Years Ago* by Ogden Nash, by permission of Little, Brown and Company, and J. M. Dent & Sons Ltd.

†From "Miners" by Wilfred Owen, *Collected Poems.* Copyright Chatto & Windus, Ltd., 1946, © 1963. Reprinted by permission of New Directions Publishing Corporation.

as (with masculine endings) trees-rose, rocks-wax, tomb-worm, and (with feminine endings) flower-destroyer-fever.

The passages quoted will illustrate some of the many effects of the device that has been called "making ends meet in verse"—the pleasure of the expected but varying chime; the reinforcement of syntax and rhetorical emphasis when a strong masculine rhyme concurs with the end of a clause, sentence, or stanza; the sudden grace of movement which may be lent by a feminine rhyme; the broadening of the comic by a pat coincidence of sound; the sometimes haunting effect of the limited *consonance* in partial rhymes. Cunning artificers in verse make rhyme more than an auxiliary sound effect; they use it to enhance or contribute to the significance of the words. When Pope in the earlier eighteenth century satirized two contemporary pedants in the lines

> Yet ne'er one sprig of laurel graced these ribalds,
> From slashing Bentley down to piddling Tibalds,

the rhyme on "Tibalds," as W. K. Wimsatt has said, demonstrates "what it means to have a name like that," with its implication that the scholar is as graceless as his appellation. And in one of its important functions, rhyme ties individual lines into the larger pattern of a *stanza.*

See George Saintsbury, *History of English Prosody* (3 vols.; 1906–10); H. C. K. Wyld, *Studies in English Rhymes* (1923); W. K. Wimsatt, "One Relation of Rhyme to Reason," in *The Verbal Icon* (1954). For an analysis of the complex interrelations between sound-repetitions and meaning, see Roman Jakobson, "Linguistics and Poetics," in *Style and Language,* ed. Thomas A. Sebeok (1960).

Roman à Clef (French for "novel with a key") is a novel in which the knowing reader is expected to identify within the fiction, and despite altered names, actual people of the time. One example is Thomas Love Peacock's *Nightmare Abbey* (1818), whose characters are entertaining *caricatures* of such contemporary literary figures as Coleridge, Byron, and Shelley. A more recent instance is Aldous Huxley's *Point Counter Point* (1928), in which we find, under fictional names, well-known English people of the twenties such as the novelist D. H. Lawrence, the critic Middleton Murry, and the right-wing political extremist Oswald Mosely.

Romantic Period. The Romantic Period in English literature is usually dated between 1789 (the outbreak of the French Revolution) or else 1798 (the publication of Wordsworth's and Coleridge's *Lyrical Ballads*), and 1832, when Sir Walter Scott died and the passage of the Reform Bill signaled the political preoccupations of the Victorian era. For some characteristics of the thought and writings of this great literary period, as well as for a list of suggested readings, see *neoclassic and romantic.* The term is applied to literary movements in European countries and America as well; see *periods of American literature.* It is usually held to have been manifested first in Germany and England in the 1790s, but to have been delayed in France and America for two or three decades. Major English writers of the time, in addition to Wordsworth and Coleridge, were the poets Blake, Byron, Shelley, Keats, and Landor, the essayists Lamb, Hazlitt, De Quincey, and Leigh Hunt, and the novelists Jane Austen and Sir Walter Scott.

Satire can be described as the literary art of diminishing or derogating a subject by making it ridiculous and evoking toward it attitudes of amusement, contempt, scorn, or indignation. It differs from the *comic* in that comedy evokes laughter mainly as an end in itself, while satire "derides"; that is, it uses laughter as a weapon, and against a butt existing outside the work itself. That butt may be an individual (in "personal satire"), or a type of person, a class, an institution, a nation, or even (as in Rochester's "A Satyr against Mankind," 1675, and much of Swift's *Gulliver's Travels*, 1726, especially Book IV) the whole human race. The distinction between the comic and the satiric, however, is a sharp one only at its extremes. Shakespeare's Falstaff is a comic creation, presented without derision for our unmitigated enjoyment; the puritanical Malvolio in Shakespeare's *Twelfth Night* is for the most part comic but has aspects of satire directed against the type of the fatuous and hypocritical Puritan; Jonson's *Volpone* (1607) clearly satirizes the type of man whose cleverness—or stupidity—is put at the service of his cupidity; and Dryden's *MacFlecknoe* (1682), while representing a permanent type of the pretentious *poetaster,* ridiculed specifically the living author Shadwell.

Satire has usually been justified by those who practice it as a corrective of human vice and folly; Pope remarked that "those who are ashamed of nothing else are so of being ridiculous." Its frequent claim (not always borne out in the practice) has been to ridicule the failing rather than the individual, and to limit its ridicule to corrigible faults, excluding those for which a person is not responsible. As Swift said, speaking of himself in his ironic "Verses on the Death of Dr. Swift" (1739):

> Yet malice never was his aim;
> He lashed the vice, but spared the name. . . .
> His satire points at no defect,
> But what all mortals may correct. . . .
> He spared a hump, or crooked nose,
> Whose owners set not up for beaux.

Satire occurs as an incidental element in many works whose overall mode is not satiric—in a certain character, or situation, or interpolated passage of ironic commentary on some aspect of the human condition or of contemporary society. But in many literary achievements, verse or prose, the attempt to diminish a subject by ridicule is the organizing principle of the whole, and these works constitute the formal *genre* of "satires." In discussing such writings the following distinctions are useful.

(1) Critics make a broad division between formal (or "direct") satire and indirect satire. In **formal satire** the satiric voice speaks out in the first person; this

"I" may address either the reader (as in Pope's *Moral Essays*, 1731–35; for example, Epistle II, "Of the characters of Women") or else a character within the work itself, who is called the **adversarius** and whose major function is to elicit and guide the satiric speaker's comments. (In Pope's "Epistle to Dr. Arbuthnot," 1735, Arbuthnot serves as adversarius.) Two types of formal satire are commonly distinguished, taking their names from the great Roman satirists Horace and Juvenal. The types are defined by the character of the *persona* whom the author presents as the first-person satiric speaker, and by the attitude and *tone* that such a persona manifests toward the subject matter and the readers of the work.

In **Horatian satire** the character of the speaker is that of an urbane, witty, and tolerant man of the world, who is moved more often to wry amusement than to indignation at the spectacle of human folly, pretentiousness, and hypocrisy, and who uses a relaxed and informal language to evoke from readers a smile at human follies and absurdities—sometimes including his own. Pope's *Moral Essays* and other formal satires for the most part sustain an Horatian stance.

In **Juvenalian satire** the character of the speaker is that of a serious moralist who uses a dignified and public style of utterance to decry modes of vice and error which are no less dangerous because they are ridiculous, and who undertakes to evoke from readers contempt, moral indignation, or an unillusioned sadness at the aberrations of humanity. Samuel Johnson's "London" (1738) and "The Vanity of Human Wishes" (1749) are distinguished instances of Juvenalian satire.

(2) **Indirect satire** is cast in another literary form than that of direct address. The most common indirect form is that of a fictional narrative, in which the objects of the satire are characters who make themselves and their opinions ridiculous by what they think, say, and do, and are sometimes made even more ridiculous by the author's comments and narrative style.

One type of indirect satire is **Menippean satire,** named for its Greek originator, the philosophical Cynic Menippus. It is sometimes called **Varronian satire,** after a Roman imitator, Varro; while Northrop Frye, in *Anatomy of Criticism*, pp. 308–12, suggests an alternative name, the **anatomy,** after a major English instance of the type, Burton's *Anatomy of Melancholy* (1621). Such satires are written in prose—though often with interpolated passages of verse—and constitute a miscellaneous form often held together by a loosely constructed narrative. Their major feature, however, is a series of extended dialogues and debates (often conducted at a banquet or party) in which a group of loquacious eccentrics, pedants, literary people, and representatives of various professions or philosophical points of view serve to make ludicrous the attitudes and viewpoints they typify by the arguments they urge in their support. Examples are Rabelais' *Gargantua and Pantagruel* (1564), Voltaire's *Candide* (1759), Thomas Love Peacock's *Nightmare Abbey* (1818) and other satiric fiction, and Huxley's *Point Counter Point* (1928), in which, as in Peacock, the central satiric scenes are discussions during a weekend at a country manor. Frye also classifies Lewis Carroll's two books about Alice in wonderland as "perfect Menippean satires."

It should be noted that any narrative or other literary vehicle can be adapted to the purposes of indirect satire. Dryden's *Absalom and Achitophel* turns Old Testament history into a satiric allegory on *Restoration* political maneuverings. In *Gulliver's Travels* Swift converts to satiric use the early-eighteenth-century literature of voyage and discovery, and his *Modest Proposal* is written in the form of a project in political economy. Many of Addison's *Spectator* papers are satiric essays; Byron's *Don Juan* is a versified satiric form of the old episodic *picaresque* fiction; Ben Jonson's *The Alchemist,* Molière's *The Misanthrope,* Wycherley's *The Country Wife,* and Shaw's *Arms and the Man* are satiric plays; and Gilbert and Sullivan's *Patience,* and other works such as Gay's eighteenth-century *Beggar's Opera* and its modern adaptation by Bertolt Brecht, *The Threepenny Opera* (1928), are satiric operettas. T. S. Eliot's *The Waste Land* (1922) employs motifs from myth in a work which can be considered a verse satire directed against the spiritual dearth in twentieth-century life. The greatest number of recent satires, however, are written in prose, and especially in novelistic form; for example, Evelyn Waugh's *The Loved One,* Joseph Heller's *Catch-22,* and Kurt Vonnegut, Jr.'s, *Player Piano* and *Cat's Cradle.* Much of the current vogue of *black humor* occurs in satiric works whose butt is the contemporary state of social chaos, cruelty, or inanity.

Good English satire has been written in every period beginning with the Middle Ages; pieces in the English *Punch* and the American *New Yorker* demonstrate that formal essayistic satire, no less than satiric novels and plays, still commands a wide audience; and W. H. Auden is a recent author who wrote excellent satiric poems. The proportioning of the examples in this article, however, indicates how large the Restoration and eighteenth century loom in satiric achievement: the best age of English, and probably of world, satire is the century and a half that included Dryden, the Earl of Rochester, Samuel Butler, Wycherley, Addison, Pope, Swift, Gay, Fielding, Johnson, Goldsmith, and (it should not be overlooked) the Robert Burns of "The Holy Fair" and "Holy Willie's Prayer" and the William Blake of *The Marriage of Heaven and Hell.* This was also the period in France of such excellent satirists as Boileau, La Fontaine, and Voltaire, as well as Molière, the greatest of satirists in drama.

The articles on *burlesque,* on *irony,* and on *wit, humor, and the comic* describe some of the forms and stylistic devices available to satirists. Consult David Worcester, *The Art of Satire* (1940); Ian Jack, *Augustan Satire* (1952); James Sutherland, *English Satire* (1958); R. C. Elliott, *The Power of Satire* (1960); Gilbert Highet, *The Anatomy of Satire* (1962); Alvin B. Kernan, *The Plot of Satire* (1965); Ronald Paulson, *Satire and the Novel in Eighteenth-Century England* (1967); Matthew Hodgart, *Satire* (1969); Charles Sanders, *The Scope of Satire* (1971); Raman Selden, *English Verse Satire, 1590–1765* (1978). Anthologies: Ronald Paulson, ed., *Satire: Modern Essays in Criticism* (1971); Ashley Brown and John L. Kimmey, eds., *Satire: An Anthology* (1977), which includes both satiric writings and critical essays on satire.

Sensibility, Age of. The period between the death of Alexander Pope (1744) and the publication of the *Lyrical Ballads* by Wordsworth and Coleridge (1798). The older and alternative name for this half-century, the **Age of Johnson,** stresses the dominant position of Samuel Johnson (1709–84) and his literary and intellectual circle, including Oliver Goldsmith, Edmund Burke, James Boswell, Edward Gibbon, and Hester Lynch Thrale. These authors on the whole represented a culmination of the literary and critical modes of *neoclassicism* and the worldview of the *Enlightenment.* The more recent name, "Age of Sensibility," instead puts its stress on the emergence, in other writers of the 1740s and later, of new cultural attitudes, theories of literature, and types of poetry—a growing sympathy for the Middle Ages, *cultural primitivism,* an awakening interest in ballads and other folk literature, a turn from neoclassic "correctness" and an emphasis on judgment and restraint to an emphasis on instinct and feeling, the development of a *literature of sensibility,* and above all the exaltation of "original genius" and a "bardic" poetry of the sublime and visionary imagination. Thomas Gray expressed the antineoclassic sensibility and values in his "Stanzas to Mr. Bentley" (1752):

> But not to one in this benighted age
> Is that diviner inspiration given,
> That burns in Shakespeare's or in Milton's page,
> The pomp and prodigality of Heaven.

Other poets manifesting similar shifts in thought and taste were William Collins and Joseph and Thomas Warton (poets who, together with Gray, began in the 1740s the vogue for what Johnson slightingly referred to as "ode, and elegy, and sonnet"), Christopher Smart, William Cowper, and Robert Burns. Thomas Percy published his influential *Reliques of Ancient English Poetry* (1765), which included many *folk ballads* and a few medieval metrical romances, and James Macpherson in the same decade published his greatly doctored versions of the poems of the Gaelic bard Ossian (Oisin), which had an immense vogue throughout Europe. In the last decade of the period William Blake signaled the arrival of a new era in his *Songs of Innocence and of Experience* and *The Marriage of Heaven and Hell,* and in his early books of visionary prophecy, written in what he called "the voice of the Bard," including *The Book of Los* and *Visions of the Daughters of Albion.*

See W. J. Bate, *From Classic to Romantic* (1946); Northrop Frye, "Towards Defining an Age of Sensibility," in *Fables of Identity* (1963), and ed., *Romanticism Reconsidered* (1965); F. W. Hilles and Harold Bloom, eds., *From Sensibility to Romanticism* (1965).

Sensibility, Literature of. When a modern critic talks of a poet's **sensibility,** the reference is to a characteristic way of responding, in sensation, thought, and feeling, to experience; and when T. S. Eliot claimed that a *dissociation of sensibility* set in with the poetry of Milton and Dryden, he signified that there occurred a division between a poet's sensuous, intellectual, and emotional modes of experience. When a literary historian, however, talks of the **literature of sensibility,** the reference is to a particular cultural phenomenon of the eighteenth century. The background of this type of literature was the moral philosophy that developed as a reaction against seventeenth-century Stoicism (which emphasized reason and the unemotional will as the sole motives to virtue), and even more important, as a reaction against Thomas Hobbes's theory, in *Leviathan* (1651), that a human being is innately selfish, and that the mainsprings of human behavior are self-interest and the drive for power and status. Many sermons, philosophical writings, and popular tracts and essays proclaimed that "benevolence"—wishing other persons well—is an innate human sentiment, and that central to moral experience are the feelings of sympathy and "sensibility"—that is, a hair-trigger responsiveness to another person's distresses and joys. "Sensibility" also connoted an intense emotional responsiveness to beauty and sublimity, whether in nature or in art, and such responsiveness was regarded as an index to a person's gentility. It became a commonplace in popular morality that readiness to shed a sympathetic tear is the sign both of polite breeding and a virtuous heart, and also that sympathy with another's grief, unlike personal grief, is a pleasurable emotion in itself. Common phrases in the cult of sensibility were the *oxymorons* "the luxury of grief," "pleasurable sorrows," and "the sadly pleasing tear." A late-eighteenth-century mortuary inscription in Dorchester Abbey says:

> Reader! If thou hast a Heart fam'd for Tenderness and Pity, Contemplate this Spot. In which are deposited the Remains of a Young Lady. . . . When Nerves were too delicately spun to bear the rude Shakes and Jostlings which we meet with in this transitory world, Nature gave way; She sunk and died a Martyr to Excessive Sensibility.

It is clear that much of what in that age was called, with approval, "sensibility" we now call, with disapproval, *sentimentalism.*

In literature these ideas and tendencies were reflected in the **drama of sensibility,** or **sentimental comedy,** which replaced the tough amorality and the comic or satiric representation of aristocratic sexual license in *Restoration comedy.* In the contemporary plays of sensibility, Oliver Goldsmith wrote in his "Comparison between Sentimental and Laughing Comedy" (1773), "the virtues of private life are exhibited rather than the vices exposed, and the distresses rather than the faults of mankind make our interest in the piece"; the characters, "though they want humor, have abundance of sentiment and feeling"; with the result, he added, that the audience "sit at a play as gloomy as at the tabernacle." Plays such as Richard Steele's *The Conscious Lovers* (1722) and Richard Cumberland's *The West Indian* (1771) present monumentally benevolent heroes and heroines of the middle class, whose dialogue abounds with elevating sentiments and who, prior to the manipulated happy ending, suffer tribulations designed to evoke the maximum in pleasurable tears from the audience.

The **novel of sensibility,** or **sentimental novel,** of the later eighteenth century similarly emphasized the tearful distresses of the virtuous, either at their own sorrows or at those of their friends, and sometimes an intensity of response to beauty or sublimity which also expressed itself in tears. Richardson's *Pamela, or Virtue Rewarded* (1740) exploits sensibility in some of its scenes; and Lawrence Sterne, in *Tristram Shandy* and *A Sentimental Journey*, published in the 1760s, gives us his own inimitable compound of sensibility, irony, and innuendo. The vogue of sensibility was international. Rousseau's novel *Julie, or* *the New Héloise* (1761) dealt with lovers of sensibility, and in his great autobiography, *The Confessions* (written 1764–70), Rousseau represented himself, in some circumstances and moods, as a man of extravagant sensibility. Goethe's novel *The Sorrows of Young Werther* (1774) is a famed presentation of the aesthetic sensibility and finespun emotional tribulations of a young man who, frustrated in his love for a woman betrothed to another, and in general unable to adapt his sensibility to the demands of ordinary life, finally shoots himself.

An extreme English instance of the sentimental novel is Henry MacKenzie's *The Man of Feeling* (1721), which represents a hero of such exquisite sensibility that he goes into a decline from excess of tenderness toward a young lady, and dies in the perturbation of finally declaring to her his emotion. "If all his tears had been tears of blood," declares an editor of the novel, Hamish Miles, "the poor man could hardly have been more debile." Jane Austen's gently satiric treatment of a young woman of sensibility in *Sense and Sensibility* (begun 1797, published 1811) marks the decline of the fashion; but the literary exploitation of the mode survives in such later novelistic episodes as the death of Little Nell in Dickens' *Old Curiosity Shop* (1841) and the death of Little Eva in Harriet Beecher Stowe's *Uncle Tom's Cabin* (1852).

Herbert Ross Brown, *The Sentimental Novel in America* (1940); C. A. Moore, *Backgrounds of English Literature, 1700–1760* (1953); Arthur Sherbo, *English Sentimental Drama* (1957); L. I. Bredvold, *The Natural History of Sensibility* (1962); R. P. Utter and G. B. Needham, *Pamela's Daughters* (1963); R. S. Crane, "Suggestions toward a Genealogy of the 'Man of Feeling,' " in *The Idea of the Humanities* (2 vols.; 1967); Jean H. Hagstrum, *Sex and Sensibility: Ideal and Erotic Love from Milton to Mozart* (1980).

Sentimentalism is now a pejorative term applied to what is perceived to be an excess of emotion to an occasion, or, in a more limited sense, to an overindulgence in the "tender" emotions of pathos and sympathy. Since what constitutes emotional excess or overindulgence is relative both to the judgment of the individual and to large-scale changes in culture and in literary fashion, what to the common reader of one age is a normal expression of humane feeling may seem sentimental to many later readers. The emotional responses that Shelley expresses and tries to evoke from the reader in his "Epipsychidion" (1821) seemed sentimental to the *New Critics* of the 1930s and later, who insisted on the need for an ironic counterpoise to intense feeling in poetry. Readers now find both the *drama* and *novel of sensibility* of the eighteenth century ludicrously sentimental, and also respond with jeers instead of tears to once celebrated episodes of pathos, such as many of the death scenes, especially that of a child, in Dickens and other Victorian writers. And a staple in current anthologies of bad poetry are poems which were no doubt written, and by some people read, with deep and sincere feeling. A useful distinction between sentimental and nonsentimental is one which does not depend on the intensity or type of the feeling expressed or evoked, but labels as sentimental a work or passage in which the feeling is rendered in commonplaces and *clichés*, instead of being freshly verbalized and sharply realized in the details of the representation.

See *pathos;* and refer to I. A. Richards, *Practical Criticism* (1929), Chap. 6;

Laurence Lerner, "A Note on Sentimentality," *The Truest Poetry* (1960); and the discussion of sentimentality by Monroe C. Beardsley, "Bad Poetry," in *The Possibility of Criticism* (1970).

Setting. The setting of a narrative or dramatic work is the general locale, historical time, and social circumstances in which its action occurs; the setting of an episode or scene within a work is the particular physical location in which it takes place. The general setting of *Macbeth,* for example, is medieval Scotland, and the setting for the scene in which Macbeth comes upon the witches is a blasted heath; the setting of Joyce's *Ulysses* is Dublin on June 16, 1904, and its opening episode is set in the Martello Tower overlooking Dublin Bay. The physical setting, in writers like Poe, Hardy, and Faulkner, is an important element in generating the *atmosphere* of their works. The Greek term **opsis** ("scene," or "spectacle") is now occasionally used to denote the visible or picturable setting in any work of literature, including a lyric poem.

When applied to a theatrical production, "setting" is synonymous with **décor** and **mise en scène,** French terms denoting both the scenery and the **properties,** or movable pieces of furniture, on the stage. The term "mise en scène" sometimes includes also the positioning of the actors in a particular scene.

Short Story. A short story is a work of prose fiction, and most of the terms for analyzing the component elements, the types, and the various narrative techniques of the *novel* are applicable to the short story as well. The short story differs from the **anecdote**—the simple and unelaborated narration of a single incident—in that it organizes the action, thought, and interactions of its characters into the artful pattern of a plot. As in the novel, the plot form may be comic, tragic, romantic, or satiric; the story is presented to us from one of many available *points of view;* and it may be written in the mode of fantasy, realism, or naturalism.

In the **tale,** or "story of incident," the focus of interest is on the course and outcome of the events, as in Poe's *The Gold Bug* (1843) and in other tales of detection, in many of the stories of O. Henry (1862–1910), and in the stock but sometimes well-contrived western story in the popular magazines. "Stories of character" focus instead on the state of mind and motivation, or on the moral qualities, in the protagonists. In some of the stories of character by the Russian master of the form Chekhov, nothing more happens than an encounter and conversation between two people. Ernest Hemingway's classic "A Clean, Well-Lighted Place" consists only of a curt conversation between two waiters about an old man who each day gets drunk and stays on in the café until it closes, followed by a brief meditation on the part of one of the waiters. Some stories achieve a balance of interest between external action and character. Hemingway's "The Short Happy Life of Francis Macomber" is as violent in its packed events as any sensational tale of adventure, but every detail of the action and dialogue is contrived to test and reveal, with a surprising set of *reversals,* the moral quality of all three protagonists.

The short story, however, is a story that is short; that is, it differs from the novel in the dimension which Aristotle calls "magnitude," and this limitation imposes differences both in the effects that can be achieved and in the choice and management of the elements to achieve those effects. Edgar Allan Poe, who is sometimes called the originator of the short story as a specific genre, was at any rate its first critical theorist. He defined what he called "the prose tale" as a narrative which can be read at one sitting of from half an hour to two hours, and is limited to "a certain unique or single effect," to which every detail is subordinate (Review of Hawthorne's *Twice-Told Tales,* 1842). Poe's comment applies to many short stories, and points to the economy of management which the tightness of the form always imposes in some degree. We can say that, by and large, the short story writer introduces a very limited number of persons, cannot afford the space for the leisurely analysis and sustained development of character, and cannot undertake to develop as dense and detailed a social milieu as does the novelist. The author often begins the story close to, or even on the verge of, the climax, minimizes both prior exposition and the details of the *setting*, keeps the complications down, and clears up the denouement quickly—sometimes in a few sentences. (See *plot.*) The central incident is often selected to be as revelatory as possible of the totality of the protagonist's life and character, and the details are devised to carry maximum significance. This spareness in the narrative often gives the artistry in a good short story higher visibility than the artistry in a well-constructed novel.

Many distinguished short stories, nonetheless, depart from this paradigm in various ways. It must be remembered that the name covers a great diversity of prose fiction, all the way from the **short short story,** which is a slightly elaborated anecdote of perhaps five hundred words, to such long and complex forms as Melville's *Billy Budd* (c. 1890), Henry James's *The Turn of the Screw* (1898), Conrad's *Heart of Darkness* (1902), and Thomas Mann's *Mario and the Magician* (1930). In such works, the status of middle length between the tautness of the short story and the expansiveness of the novel is sometimes indicated by the name **novelette,** or *novella.* This form has been especially exploited in Germany (where it is called the *Novelle*) after it was introduced by Goethe in 1795 and exploited by Heinrich von Kleist and many other writers; the genre has also been the subject of much critical attention by German theorists (see the list of readings below).

The short narrative, in both verse and prose, is one of the oldest and most widespread of literary forms. Some of the narrative types which preceded the short story, treated elsewhere in the *Glossary,* are the *fable,* the *exemplum,* the *folktale,* and the *fabliau.* Early in its history, there developed the device of the **frame-story:** a preliminary narrative within which one or more of the characters proceeds to tell a story. This device was widespread in the Orient, as in the collection of stories called *Arabian Nights Entertainments,* and was used by Boccaccio for his prose *Decameron* (1353) and by Chaucer for his versified *Canterbury Tales* (c. 1387). In the latter instance, Chaucer developed the frame-story of the journey, dialogue, and interactions of the Canterbury pilgrims to such a degree that the frame itself approximated the form of a plot: the stories that the individual pilgrims tell function both as a means of characterizing the tellers and as a vehicle for the quarrels and arguments en route, yet each story constitutes a complete and rounded narrative in its own right. In its more recent forms, the frame-story may enclose either a single narrative (James's *The Turn of the Screw*) or a sequence of narratives (Joel Chandler Harris' stories told by Uncle Remus, 1881 and later; see under *beast fable*).

The form of prose narrative which approximates the contemporary short story was developed in the nineteenth century by Washington Irving, Hawthorne, and Poe in America, Sir Walter Scott in England, E. T. A. Hoffmann in Germany, Balzac in France, and Gogol and Turgenev in Russia. The short story in English has flourished more in America than in England; Frank O'Connor has called it "the national art form," and its American masters include (in addition to those already mentioned) William Faulkner, Katherine Anne Porter, Eudora Welty, Flannery O'Connor, John O'Hara, J. F. Powers, John Cheever, and J. D. Salinger.

H. S. Canby, *The Short Story in English* (1909); Sean O'Faolain, *The Short Story* (1948); Frank O'Connor, *The Lonely Voice: A Study of the Short Story* (1962); R. L. Pattee, *The Development of the American Short Story* (rev., 1966). On the novella: E. K. Bennett, *History of the German Novelle, Goethe to Thomas Mann* (1934); Ronald Paulson, *The Novelette Before 1900* (1968); Mary Doyle Springer, *Forms of the Modern Novella* (1976); Martin Swales, *The German Novelle* (1977).

Sociology of Literature. Most literary historians and critics have taken some account of the relation of individual authors to the distinctive circumstances of the cultural era in which they live and write, as well as of the relation of a literary work to the segment of society that its fiction represents or to which the work is addressed. (For major recent exceptions see *Russian formalism, New Criticism, structuralism, deconstruction.*) The term "sociology of literature," however, is applied only to the writings of those historians and critics whose primary, and sometimes exclusive, interest is in the ways authors are affected by such circumstances of their time and place as their class status, gender, and interests, the ways of thinking and feeling characteristic of their era, the economic conditions of the writer's profession and of the publication and distribution of books, and the social class, conceptions, and values of the audience to which writers address themselves. Sociological critics treat a work of literature as inescapably conditioned—in its subject matter, the ways of thinking it incorporates, its evaluations of the modes of life it renders, and even in its form—by the social, political, and economic organization and forces of its age; they also tend to view the sensibility and preferences of the reading public as shaped by the circumstances specific to an era. The French historian Hippolyte Taine is sometimes considered the first modern sociologist of literature in his *History of English Literature* (1863), which analyzed a work as largely explicable by reference to three factors: its author's "race," geographical and social "milieu," and historical "moment."

For prominent sociological approaches to literature in recent critical writings, see *feminist criticism,* with its emphasis on "patriarchal" social assumptions as determinants of literary content, form, and values, and especially *Marxist criticism.* It should be noted that Marx's view of the economic basis of social organization, class ideologies, and class conflict have influenced the work of many critics who, although not committed to strictly Marxist doctrine, stress the sociological context and content of works of literature.

In addition to the items listed under *Marxist criticism*, see the pioneering study by Alexandre Beljame, *Men of Letters and the English Public*—i.e., in the eighteenth century (1883, transl. 1948); Levin Schücking, *The Sociology of Literary Taste* (rev., 1941); Harry Levin, "Literature as an Institution," in *The Gates of Horn* (1963); Hugh Dalziel Duncan, *Language and Literature in Society, with a Bibliographical Guide to the Sociology of Literature* (1953). Collections of essays in sociological criticism include Joseph P. Strelka, ed., *Literary Criticism and Sociology* (1973), and Elizabeth and Tom Burns, eds., *Sociology of Literature and Drama: Selected Readings* (1973).

Soliloquy is the act of talking to oneself, silently or aloud. In drama it denotes the *convention* by which a character, alone on the stage, utters his thoughts aloud; playwrights use this device as a convenient way to convey to the audience information about a character's thoughts, motives, and state of mind, as well as for purposes of general exposition. Marlowe's *Dr. Faustus* (first performed in 1594) opens with a long expository soliloquy, and concludes with another which expresses Faustus' frantic mental and emotional condition during his belated attempts to escape damnation. The best-known of all dramatic soliloquies is Hamlet's speech "To be or not to be." (Compare *monologue.*)

A related stage device is the **aside,** in which a character expresses his or her thought or intention in a short speech which, by convention, is inaudible to the other characters on the stage. Both devices, common in Elizabethan and later drama, fell into disuse in the later nineteenth century, when increasing demands that plays convey the illusion of real life forced the dramatists to exploit indirect means for conveying information and guidance to the audience. Eugene O'Neill, however, revived the aside and made it a central and persistent element in his play *Strange Interlude* (1928).

Sonnet. A lyric poem in a single *stanza* consisting of fourteen iambic pentameter lines linked by an intricate rhyme scheme. The *rhyme*, in English, usually follows one of two main patterns:

(1) The **Italian** or **Petrarchan sonnet** (named after the fourteenth-century Italian poet Petrarch) falls into two main parts: an **octave** (eight lines) rhyming *abbaabba* and a **sestet** (six lines) rhyming *cdecde* or some variant, such as *cdccdc.* Petrarch's sonnets were first imitated in England, both in form and in primary subject matter—an adoring male lover's hopes and pains—by Sir Thomas Wyatt in the early sixteenth century. The Petrarchan form was later used, for a variety of subjects, by Milton, Wordsworth, D. G. Rossetti, and other sonneteers, who sometimes made it technically easier in English (which does not have as many rhyming possibilities as Italian) by introducing a new pair of rhymes in the second four lines of the octave.

(2) The Earl of Surrey and other English experimenters in the sixteenth

century also developed a new form called the **English sonnet,** or else the **Shakespearean sonnet,** after the greatest practitioner. This stanza falls into three *quatrains* and a concluding *couplet: abab cdcd efef gg.* There was one especially important variant, the **Spenserian sonnet,** in which Spenser links each quatrain to the next by a continuing rhyme: *abab bcbc cdcd ee.*

John Donne shifted from the hitherto standard subject, secular love, to a variety of religious themes in his *Holy Sonnets,* written early in the seventeenth century, and Milton, in the latter part of that century, expanded the range of the sonnet to other matters of serious concern. The sonnet, except for a lapse in the English *Neoclassic Period,* has remained a popular form and includes among its distinguished practitioners, in the nineteenth century, Wordsworth, Keats, Elizabeth Barrett Browning, and D. G. Rossetti, and more recently, E. A. Robinson, Edna St. Vincent Millay, W. H. Auden, and Dylan Thomas. The stanza is just long enough to permit a fairly complex lyric development, yet so short and so exigent in its rhymes as to pose a standing challenge to the artistry of the poet. The rhyme pattern of the Petrarchan sonnet has on the whole favored a statement of problem, situation, or incident in the octave, with a resolution in the sestet. The English form sometimes uses a similar division of material, but often presents a repetition-with-variation of a statement in the three quatrains; the final couplet, however, usually imposes an *epigrammatic* turn at the end. In Drayton's fine Elizabethan sonnet in the English form "Since there's no help, come let us kiss and part," the lover brusquely declares in the first two quatrains that he is glad that the affair is cleanly broken off, pauses in the third quatrain as though at the threshold, and in the last couplet suddenly drops his swagger to make one last plea. Here are the concluding quatrain and couplet:

> Now at the last gasp of love's latest breath,
> When, his pulse failing, passion speechless lies,
> When faith is kneeling by his bed of death,
> And innocence is closing up his eyes;
> Now if thou wouldst, when all have given him over,
> From death to life thou mightst him yet recover.

Following Petrarch's early example, a number of Elizabethan poets wrote **sonnet sequences,** or **sonnet cycles,** in which a series of sonnets are linked together by exploring the varied aspects of a relationship between lovers, or by indicating a development in that relationship which constitutes a kind of implicit plot. Shakespeare wrote his sonnets in a sequence, as did Sidney in *Astrophel and Stella* (1580) and Spenser in *Amoretti* (1595). Later examples of the sonnet sequence on a variety of subjects are Wordsworth's *The River Duddon,* D. G. Rossetti's *House of Life,* Elizabeth Barrett Browning's *Sonnets from the Portuguese,* and William Ellery Leonard's *Two Lives.* Dylan Thomas' *Altarwise by Owl-light* (1936) is a sequence of ten sonnets which is a meditation on the poet's own life. George Meredith's *Modern Love* (1862) concerns a bitterly unhappy marriage; although it consists of poems written in sixteen lines, it is sometimes called a sonnet sequence.

See T. W. H. Crosland, *The English Sonnet* (1917); L. G. Sterner, *The Sonnet in American Literature* (1930); L. C. John, *The Elizabethan Sonnet Sequences* (1938); J. B. Leishman, *Themes and Variations in Shakespeare's Sonnets* (1963).

Stanza. A stanza (Italian for "stopping place") is a grouping of the verse-lines in a poem, set off by a space in the printed text. Usually the stanzas of a given poem are marked by the same recurrent rhyme scheme, and are also uniform in the number and lengths of the component lines. Some unrhymed poems, however, are divided into stanzaic units (for example, Collins' "Ode to Evening," 1747), and some rhymed poems are composed of variable stanzas (for example, the *irregular ode*).

Of the great variety of English stanza forms, many have no special names and must be described by specifying the number of lines, the type and number of *feet* in each line, and the pattern of the *rhyme*. Some stanzas, however, have been used so frequently that they have been given the convenience of a name, as follows:

A **couplet** is a pair of rhymed lines. The **octosyllabic couplet** has lines of eight syllables, usually consisting of four iambic feet. So in Marvell's "To His Coy Mistress" (1681):

> The grave's a fine and private place,
> But none, I think, do there embrace.

Iambic pentameter lines rhyming in pairs are called **decasyllabic** ("ten-syllable") **couplets,** and also *heroic couplets.*

The **tercet,** or **triplet,** is a stanza of three lines, usually with a single rhyme. The lines may be the same length (as in Robert Herrick's "Upon Julia's Clothes," 1648, written in tercets of iambic tetrameter), or else of varying lengths. In Richard Crashaw's "Wishes to His Supposed Mistress" (1646), the lines of each tercet are successively in *iambic dimeter, trimeter,* and *tetrameter:*

> Who e'er she be
> That not impossible she
> That shall command my heart and me.

Terza rima is composed of tercets which are interlinked, in that each is joined to the one following by a common rhyme: *aba, bcb, cdc,* and so on. Dante composed his *Divine Comedy* (early fourteenth century) in terza rima; but although Sir Thomas Wyatt introduced the form early in the sixteenth century, it has not been a common meter in English, in which rhymes are much harder to find than in Italian. Shelley, however, used it brilliantly in "Ode to the West Wind" (1820), and it occurs also in the poetry of Milton, Browning, and T. S. Eliot.

The **quatrain,** or four-line stanza, is the most common in English versification, and is employed with various meters and rhyme schemes. The *ballad* *stanza* (in alternating four- and three-foot lines rhyming *abcb,* or less frequently *abab*) is one common quatrain; when the same stanza occurs in hymns, it is called **common measure.** The **heroic quatrain,** in iambic pentameter rhyming *abab,* is the stanza of Gray's "Elegy Written in a Country Churchyard" (1751).

Rime royal was introduced by Chaucer in *Troilus and Criseyde* (the latter 1380s) and other narrative poems; it is believed to take its name, however, from its later use in the verses by King James I of Scotland. It is a seven-line, iambic pentameter stanza rhyming *ababbcc.*

Ottava rima, as the Italian name indicates, has eight lines; it rhymes *abababcc.* Like terza rima and the *sonnet,* it was brought from Italian into English by Sir Thomas Wyatt in the first half of the sixteenth century. Although employed by a number of earlier poets, it is notable especially as the stanza which helped Byron discover what he was born to write, the satiric poem *Don Juan* (1819–24). Note the comic effect of the *forced rhyme* in the concluding couplet:

> Juan was taught from out the best edition,
> Expurgated by learned men, who place,
> Judiciously, from out the schoolboy's vision,
> The grosser parts; but, fearful to deface
> Too much their modest bard by this omission,
> And pitying sore his mutilated case,
> They only add them all in an appendix,
> Which saves, in fact, the trouble of an index.

Spenserian stanza is a still longer form devised by Edmund Spenser for *The Faerie Queene* (1590–96)—nine lines, in which the first eight are iambic pentameter and the last iambic hexameter (an *Alexandrine*), rhyming *ababbcbcc.* Enchanted by Spenser's gracious movement and music, many poets have attempted the form in spite of its difficulties. Its greatest successes have been in poems which, like *The Faerie Queene,* move in a leisurely way, with ample time for unrolling the richly textured stanzas; for example, James Thomson's "The Castle of Indolence" (1748), Keats's "The Eve of St. Agnes" (1820), Shelley's "Adonais" (1821), and the narrative section of Tennyson's "The Lotus Eaters" (1832).

There are also various elaborate stanza forms imported from France, such as the rondeau, the villanelle, and the triolet, containing intricate repetitions of rhymes and lines, which have been used mainly, but not exclusively, for *light verse.* Their revival by W. H. Auden, William Empson, and other recent poets was a sign of renewed interest in high metrical artifice. Dylan Thomas' "Do not go gentle into that good night" is a **villanelle;** that is, it consists of five *tercets* and a *quatrain,* all on two rhymes, and with systematic later repetitions of lines 1 and 3 of the first tercet.

See *meter.* Stanzas discussed elsewhere in the *Glossary* are *ballad stanza, blank verse, heroic couplet,* and *sonnet.* The nature and history of the various stanzas are briefly described and exemplified in R. M. Alden, *English Verse* (1903), and in Paul Fussell, *Poetic Meter and Poetic Form* (rev., 1979).

Stock Characters are character types that recur repeatedly in a particular literary genre, and so are recognizable as part of the *conventions* of the form. The *Old Comedy* of the Greeks had three stock characters whose interactions constituted the standard plot: the **alazon,** or impostor and self-deceiving braggart; the **eiron,** or self-derogatory and understating character, whose contest with the alazon is central to the comic plot; and the **bomolochos,** buffoon, whose antics add an extra comic element. (See Lane Cooper, *An Aristotelian Theory of Comedy,* 1922.) In his *Anatomy of Criticism* (1957), Northrop Frye has revived these old terms, added a fourth, the **agroikos**—the rustic or easily deceived character—and identified the recurrence of these types (very broadly defined) in comic plots up to our own time.

Elizabethan *romantic comedy,* such as Shakespeare's *As You Like It* and *Twelfth Night,* often turned on a heroine disguised as a handsome young man; and a stock figure in the Elizabethan comedy of intrigue was the clever servant who, like Mosca in Jonson's *Volpone,* connives with his master to fleece another stock character, the stupid "gull." Nineteenth-century comedy, on stage and in fiction, exploited the stock Englishman with a monocle, an exaggerated Oxford accent, and a defective sense of humor. Western stories and films generated the tight-lipped sheriff who lets his gun do the talking; while a familiar figure in the fiction of the recent past was the stoical Hemingway hero, unillusioned but faithful to his primal code of honor and loyalty in a civilization grown effete and corrupt. The *Beat* or hipster or alienated intellectual who, with or without the help of drugs, has opted out of the Establishment is an even more recent stock character.

The artistic success of a character in literature does not depend on whether or not an author incorporates an established type, but on how well the type is re-created as a convincing individual. Two of Shakespeare's greatest characters are patently conventional. Falstaff is a re-rendering in part of the *Vice,* the comic tempter of the medieval morality play, and in part of the familiar braggart soldier, the **miles gloriosus** of Roman and Renaissance comedy, whose ancestry goes back to the Greek alazon; and Hamlet combines some stock attributes of the hero of Elizabethan *revenge tragedies* with those of the Elizabethan melancholic man. Jane Austen's fine character Elizabeth Bennet in *Pride and Prejudice* (1813) can be traced back through Restoration comedy to the intelligent, witty, and self-assured heroines of Shakespeare's romantic comedies.

Stock Response is an habitual and stereotyped reaction, in place of one which is genuinely and aptly responsive to a given object, situation, or text. The term may be applied to the response of authors themselves to characters, situations, or topics that they set forth in a work; usually, however, it is applied to the response of readers to a passage within a work; in either case, the connotation is derogatory. I. A. Richards, in his *Practical Criticism* (1929), Chap. 5, gave currency to this term by citing and analyzing stock responses by students who wrote critiques on unidentified poems presented for their inspection.

Stock Situations are the counterparts, in the events of a plot, to *stock characters;* that is, they are often-used incidents or sequences of actions in a drama or narrative. Instances range from single situations—the eavesdropper who is hidden behind a bush or under a table, or the suddenly discovered will or birthmark—to the overall pattern of a plot. The Horatio Alger books for boys, in mid-nineteenth-century America, were all variations on the rags-to-riches-by-pluck-and-luck plot, and we often recognize the stock boy-meets-girl story in the opening episode of popular fiction or motion pictures.

A number of modern critics distinguish certain recurrent character types and elements of plot, such as the sexually irresistible but fatal enchantress, the sacrificial scapegoat, and the underground journey, as "archetypal" components which are held to recur, not simply because they are functional literary conventions, but because, like dreams and myths, they express elemental and universal human impulses, anxieties, and needs. See *archetype.*

Stream of Consciousness was a phrase used by William James in his *Principles of Psychology* (1890) to describe the unbroken flow of thought and awareness in the waking mind; it has since been adopted to describe a narrative method in modern fiction. Long passages of **introspection,** describing in some detail what passes through a character's mind, are found in novelists from Samuel Richardson to Henry James, and as early as 1888 a minor French writer, Edouard Dujardin, wrote a short novel, *Les Lauriers sont coupés* ("The Laurels Have Been Cut"), which is a rather crude but sustained attempt to represent all the scenes and events of the story solely as they impinge upon the consciousness of the central character. The stream of consciousness, as it has been refined since the 1920s, is a special mode of narration that undertakes to capture the full spectrum and the continuous flow of a character's mental process, in which sense perceptions mingle with conscious and half-conscious thoughts, memories, expectations, feelings, and random associations. For a study of the linguistic modes for rendering in narrative fiction these states of consciousness, by such means as shifts in temporal perspective and alterations in the tenses of the verbs, see Käte Hamburger, *The Logic of Literature* (1973), Chap. 3.

Some critics use "stream of consciousness" interchangeably with the term **interior monologue.** It is useful, however, to employ the former as the inclusive term, denoting all the diverse techniques employed by authors to describe or to represent the overall state and process of consciousness in a character. "Interior monologue" can then be reserved for the technique that undertakes to reproduce the course and rhythm of consciousness just as it occurs in a character's mind. In interior monologue the author does not intervene, or at any rate intervenes minimally, as guide or commentator, and does not tidy the vagaries of the mental process into grammatical sentences or into a logical order. The interior monologue, in its radical form, is sometimes described as the exact reproduction of consciousness; but since sense perceptions, mental images, feelings, and some aspects of thought itself are nonverbal, it is clear that the author must convert these elements into some kind of verbal equivalent. Much of this conversion is a matter of narrative *conventions* rather than of unedited, point-for-point reproduction.

James Joyce developed various techniques of stream-of-consciousness narrative in *Ulysses* (1922). Here is a passage of interior monologue from the "Lestrygonian" episode, in which Leopold Bloom saunters through Dublin, observing and musing:

> Pineapple rock, lemon platt, butter scotch. A sugar-sticky girl shoveling scoopfuls of creams for a christian brother. Some school treat. Bad for their tummies. Lozenge and comfit manufacturer to His Majesty the King. God. Save. Our. Sitting on his throne, sucking red jujubes white.

Dorothy Richardson sustains a stream-of-consciousness narrative, focused exclusively on the mind of her heroine, throughout the twelve volumes of her novel *Pilgrimage* (1915–38); Virginia Woolf employs the procedure as a primary narrative mode in several novels, including *Mrs. Dalloway* (1925) and *To the Lighthouse* (1927); and William Faulkner exploits it brilliantly in the first three of the four parts of *The Sound and the Fury* (1929).

See *fiction and narrative*, and refer to Leon Edel, *The Modern Psychological Novel* (1955); Robert Humphrey, *Stream of Consciousness in the Modern Novel* (1954); Melvin Friedman, *Stream of Consciousness: A Study in Literary Method* (1955).

Style is the manner of linguistic expression in prose or verse—it is *how* speakers or writers say whatever it is that they say. The style of a particular work or writer may be analyzed in terms of the characteristic modes of its *diction*, or choice of words; its sentence structure and syntax; the density and types of its figurative language; the patterns of its rhythm, component sounds, and other formal features; and its rhetorical aims and devices.

In traditional theories of *rhetoric*, styles were classified into three main levels: the **high** (or grand), the **middle** (or mean), and the **low** (or base, or plain) **style.** The doctrine of *decorum* required that the level of style in a work be appropriate to the social class of the speaker, the occasion, and the dignity of its literary genre (see *poetic diction*). The modern critic Northrop Frye has introduced a variant of this long-persisting analysis of stylistic levels in literature. He makes a basic differentiation between the **demotic style** (which is modeled on the language, rhythms, and associations of ordinary speech) and the **hieratic style** (which employs a variety of formal elaborations that separate the literary language from ordinary speech). Frye then proceeds to distinguish a high, middle, and low level in each of these classes. See *The Well-Tempered Critic* (1963), Chap. 2.

In analyzing style, two types of sentence structure are often distinguished:

The **periodic sentence** is one in which the parts, or "members," are so composed that the completion of the sense—that is, the closure of the *syntax*—remains suspended until the end of the sentence; the effect tends to be formal or oratorical. An example is the eloquent opening sentence of Boswell's *Life of Samuel Johnson* (1791), in which the syntactic structure remains incomplete until we reach the final noun, "task":

> To write the life of him who excelled all mankind in writing the lives of others, and who, whether we consider his extraordinary endowments, or his various works, has been equalled by few in any age, is an arduous, and may be reckoned in me a presumptuous task.

In the **nonperiodic** (or **loose**) **sentence**—which is more relaxed and conversational in effect—the component members are continuous, but so loosely joined that the sentence would have been syntactically complete if a period had been inserted at one or more places before the actual close. So Addison's two sentences in *Spectator 105,* describing the limited topics in the conversation of a mere man-about-town, could each have closed at several points in the sequence of component clauses:

> He will tell you the names of the principal favourites, repeat the shrewd sayings of a man of quality, whisper an intrigue that is not yet blown upon by common fame; or, if the sphere of his observations is a little larger than ordinary, will perhaps enter into all the incidents, turns, and revolutions in a game of ombre. When he has gone thus far he has shown you the whole circle of his accomplishments, his parts are drained, and he is disabled from any farther conversation.

Another distinction made with increasing frequency in discussing prose style is that between parataxis and hypotaxis:

A **paratactic style** is one in which the members within a sentence, or else a sequence of complete sentences, are put one after the other without any expression of their connection or relations except (at most) the noncommittal connective "and." Hemingway's style is characteristically paratactic. The members in this sentence from his novel *The Sun Also Rises* (1926) are joined merely by "ands": "It was dim and dark and the pillars went high up, and there were people praying, and it smelt of incense, and there were some wonderful big buildings." And the curt sentences in his short story "Indian Camp" omit all connectives: "The sun was coming over the hills. A bass jumped, making a circle in the water. Nick trailed his hand in the water. It felt warm in the sharp chill of the morning."

A **hypotactic style** is one in which the temporal, logical, and syntactic relations between members and sentences are expressed by words (such as "when," "then," "because," "therefore") or by phrases (such as "in order to," "as a result") or by the use of subordinate phrases and clauses. The typical style in this article is hypotactic.

A very large number of descriptive terms are used to classify types of style, such as "pure," "ornate," "florid," "gay," "sober," "simple," "elaborate," and so on. Styles are also classified according to a literary period or tradition ("the *metaphysical* style," "Restoration prose style"); according to an influential work ("biblical style," *euphuism*); according to a type of use ("a scientific style," "journalese"); or according to the distinctive practice of an individual author (the "Shakespearean" or "Miltonic style"; "Johnsonese"). Historians of English prose style, especially in the seventeenth and eighteenth centuries, have distinguished between the vogue of the "Ciceronian style" (named after the characteristic practice of the Roman writer Cicero), which is elaborately constructed, highly periodic, and typically builds to a climax, and the opposing vogue of the clipped, concise, pointed, and uniformly stressed sentences in the "Attic" or "Senecan" styles (named after the practice of the Roman Seneca). See J. M. Patrick and others, eds., *Style, Rhetoric, and Rhythm: Essays by Morris W. Croll* (1966), and George Williamson, *The Senecan Amble: A Study in Prose Form from Bacon to Collier* (1951).

See *prose*, and for some recent developments in modes of analysis, *stylistics*. Among the more traditional treatments of style are Herbert Read, *English Prose Style* (1928); Bonamy Dobree, *Modern Prose Style* (1934); W. K. Wimsatt, *The Prose Style of Samuel Johnson* (1941); P. F. Baum, *The Other Harmony of Prose* (1952); Erich Auerbach, *Mimesis: The Representation of Reality in Western Literature* (1953); Josephine Miles, *Eras and Modes in English Poetry* (1957); James Phelan, *Worlds from Words: A Theory of Language in Fiction* (1981). For attempts to distinguish and analyze "mannerist," "*baroque*," and "rococo" styles in seventeenth-century and later poetry and prose, see Wylie Sypher, *Four Stages of Renaissance Style* (1955), and *Rococo to Cubism in Art and Literature* (1960).

Surrealism ("superrealism") was launched as a concerted movement in France by André Breton's *Manifesto on Surrealism* (1924). The expressed aim was a rebellion against all restraints on free artistic creativity; included among such restraints were logical reason, standard morality, social and artistic conventions and norms, and any control by forethought and intention. To ensure the unhampered operation of the "deep mind," which they regarded as the only source of valid knowledge and art, surrealists turned to **automatic writing** (writing delivered over entirely to the promptings of the unconscious mind), and to exploiting the material of dreams, of states of mind between sleep and waking, and of natural or artificially induced hallucinations.

Surrealism was a revolutionary movement in painting, sculpture, and the other arts, as well as literature; it often united briefly with one or another revolutionary political and social movement. It is more important, however, in its widespread influence in Europe and America than in the work of the relatively small group of its professed adherents such as André Breton, Louis Aragon, and the painter Salvador Dali. The influence, direct or indirect, of surrealist innovations can be found in many modern writers of prose and verse who have broken with conventional modes of artistic organization to experiment with free association, violated syntax, nonlogical and nonchronological order, dreamlike and nightmarish sequences, and the juxtaposition of bizarre, shocking, or seemingly unrelated images. In England and America such effects can be found in a wide range of writings, from the poetry of Dylan Thomas to the flights of fantasy, hallucinative writing, startling inconsequences, and *black humor* in the novels of Henry Miller, Thomas Pynchon *(V)*, and William Burroughs *(Naked Lunch)*.

See literature of the *absurd, antinovel*, and *postmodernism*, and refer to David Gascoyne, *A Short Survey of Surrealism* (1935); A. E. Balakian, *Literary*

Origins of Surrealism (1947); Herbert Read, *The Philosophy of Modern Art* (1955); M. Nadeau, *History of Surrealism* (1967); Paul C. Ray, *The Surrealist Movement in England* (1971).

Symbol. A symbol, in the broadest sense, is equivalent to a *sign*—that is, anything which signifies something else; in this sense all words are symbols. In discussing literature, however, the term **symbol** is applied only to a word or phrase that signifies an object or event which in turn signifies something, or has a range of reference, beyond itself. Some symbols are "conventional" or "public"; thus "the Cross," "the Red, White, and Blue," and "the Good Shepherd" are terms that signify symbolic objects of which the further significance is determinate within a particular culture. Poets, like all of us, use such conventional symbols; many poets, however, also use "private" or "personal symbols." Often they do so by exploiting widely shared associations of an object or event or action with a particular concept; for example, the general association of a peacock with pride and of an eagle with heroic endeavor, or the rising sun with birth and the setting sun with death, or climbing with effort or progress and descent with surrender or failure. Some poets, however, often use symbols whose significance they generate mainly for themselves, and these pose a more difficult problem in interpretation.

Take as an example the word "rose," which in its literal use is a kind of flower. In Burns's line "O my love's like a red, red rose," the word "rose" is used as a *simile;* and in the lines by Winthrop Mackworth Praed

> She was our queen, our rose, our star;
> And then she danced—O Heaven, her dancing!

the word "rose" is used as a *metaphor.* In *The Romance of the Rose,* a long medieval *dream vision,* we read about a half-opened rose to which the dreamer's access is aided by a character called "Fair Welcome," but impeded or forbidden by other characters called "Reason," "Shame," and "Jealousy." We readily recognize that the whole narrative is an *allegory* about an elaborate courtship, in which most of the agents are personified abstractions and the rose itself is an **emblem** (that is, an object whose significance is made determinate by its own qualities and by its role in the narrative context) which represents the lady's love, as well as her lovely body. Then we read William Blake's poem "The Sick Rose."

> O Rose, thou art sick.
> The invisible worm
> That flies in the night
> In the howling storm
>
> Has found out thy bed
> Of crimson joy,
> And his dark secret love
> Does thy life destroy.

This rose is not the vehicle for a simile or metaphor, because it lacks the paired subject—"my love," or the girl referred to as "she," in the examples just cited—which is an identifying feature of these figures. And it is not an allegorical rose, since, unlike the flower in *The Romance of the Rose,* it is not part of an obvious double order of correlated references, one literal and the second allegorical, in which the allegorical reference of the rose is made determinate by its role within the literal narrative. Blake's rose *is* a rose—yet it is also something more than a rose: words such as "bed," "joy," "love," which do not comport literally with an actual flower, together with the sinister tone and the intensity of the feeling, press the reader to infer that the described object has a further range of suggested but unspecified reference which makes it a symbol. But Blake's rose is a personal symbol and not—like the symbolic rose in the closing cantos of Dante's fourteenth-century *Paradiso* and other Christian poems—an element in a set of conventional and widely known religious symbols, in which concrete objects of this passing world are used to signify, in a relatively determinate way, the truths of a higher and eternal realm. (See Barbara Seward, *The Symbolic Rose,* 1960.) Only from the implicit suggestions in the words of Blake's poem itself—the sexual connotations of "bed" and "love," especially in conjunction with "joy" and "worm"—supplemented by our knowledge of related elements in Blake's other poems, as well as by our common associations with the objects described in this poem, are we led to infer that Blake's lament for a crimson rose which has been entered and sickened unto death by a dark and secret worm symbolizes the destruction wrought by furtiveness, deceit, and hypocrisy in what should be a frank and joyous relationship of physical love. Various critics of the poem, however, have proposed different interpretations of its symbolic significance. It is an attribute of many private symbols—the White Whale in Melville's *Moby-Dick* (1851) is another famous example—as well as one reason why they are an irreplaceable literary device, that they suggest a direction or a broad area of significance rather than, like an item in an allegorical narrative, a relatively determinate reference.

In the copious modern literature on the nature of the literary symbol, reference is often made to seminal passages, written early in the nineteenth century by Coleridge in England and Goethe in Germany, on the difference between an allegory and a symbol. Coleridge is in fact describing what he believes to be the uniquely symbolic nature of the Bible as a sacred text, but later commentators have taken his comment to define the general nature of a symbol in secular literature:

> Now an allegory is but a translation of abstract notions into a picture-language, which is itself nothing but an abstraction from objects of the senses. . . . On the other hand a symbol . . . is characterized by a translucence of the special [i.e., of the species] in the individual, or of the general [i.e., of the genus] in the special, or of the universal in the general; above all by the translucence of the eternal through and in the temporal. It always partakes of the reality which it renders intelligible; and while it enunciates the whole, abides itself as a living part in that unity of which it is the representative. [Allegories] are but empty echoes which the fancy arbitrarily associates with apparitions of matter. . . .
>
> (Coleridge, *The Statesman's Manual,* 1816)

Goethe had been speculating on the nature of the literary symbol since the 1790s, but gave his concept its clearest formulation in 1824:

> There is a great difference, whether the poet seeks the particular for the sake of the general or sees the general in the particular. From the former procedure there ensues allegory, in which the particular serves only as illustration, as example of the general. The latter procedure, however, is genuinely the nature of poetry; it expresses something particular, without thinking of the general or pointing to it.
>
> Allegory transforms the phenomenon into a concept, the concept into an image, but in such a way that the concept always remains bounded in the image, and is entirely to be kept and held in it, and to be expressed by it.
>
> Symbolism [however] transforms the phenomenon into idea, the idea into an image, and in such a way that the idea remains always infinitely active and unapproachable in the image, and even if expressed in all languages, still would remain inexpressible.
>
> (Goethe, *Maxims and Reflections*, Nos. 279, 1112, 1113)

It will be noted that both Coleridge and Goethe stress that an allegory presents a pair of subjects (an image and a concept) and a symbol only one (the image alone); that the allegory is specific in its reference, while the symbol remains indefinite, but richly—even infinitely—suggestive in its significance; and also that for this very reason, a symbol is the higher mode of literary expression. To all these claims, characteristic in the Romantic Period, critics until the recent past have for the most part agreed. For an elevation of allegory over symbol, in express opposition to romantic theory, on the ground that it is less "mystified" about its rhetorical and fictional status, see Paul de Man, "The Rhetoric of Temporality," in *Interpretation: Theory and Practice*, ed. C. S. Singleton (1969), and *Allegories of Reading* (1979).

W. B. Yeats, "The Symbolism of Poetry" (1900), in *Essays and Introductions* (1961); H. Flanders Dunbar, *Symbolism in Medieval Thought* (1929); C. S. Lewis, *The Allegory of Love: A Study in Medieval Tradition* (1936); Elder Olson, "A Dialogue on Symbolism," in R. S. Crane, ed., *Critics and Criticism* (1952); W. Y. Tindall, *The Literary Symbol* (1955); Harry Levin, "Symbolism and Fiction," in *Contexts of Criticism* (1957); Isabel C. Hungerland, *Poetic Discourse* (1958), Chap. 5; Maurice Beebe, ed., *Literary Symbolism* (1960).

Symbolist Movement. Various poets of the *Romantic Period,* such as Novalis and Hölderlin in Germany and Shelley in England, employed private *symbols* in their poetry; Shelley, for example, repeatedly made symbolic use of objects such as the morning and evening star, a boat moving upstream, winding caves, and the conflict between a serpent and an eagle. William Blake, however, exceeded all his romantic contemporaries in the use of a persistent and sustained **symbolism,** both in his lyric poems and prophetic epics. In the *Romantic Period in America,* a symbolist procedure was prominent in the novels of Hawthorne and Melville, the prose of Emerson and Thoreau, and the poetic theory and practice of Poe. (See Charles Feidelson, Jr., *Symbolism and American Literature,* 1953.) These writers derived the mode in large part from the native Puritan tradition of typology (see *interpretation: typological and allegorical*), and from the theory of correspondences of the Swedish theologian Emanuel Swedenborg (1688–1772). The **Symbolist Movement,** however, is a term applied by literary historians specifically to a group of French writers beginning with Baudelaire (*Fleurs du mal,* 1857) and continued by such major poets as Rimbaud, Verlaine, Mallarmé, and Valéry. Baudelaire based the symbolic mode of his poems on the writings of Poe, and especially on the ancient doctrine of **correspondences,** or inherent analogy, both between the mind and the outer world and between the natural and the spiritual world; as Baudelaire put it: "Everything, form, movement, number, color, perfume, in the *spiritual* as in the *natural* world, is significative, reciprocal, converse, *correspondent.*" The techniques of the French **Symbolists,** who exploited private symbols in a poetry of rich suggestiveness rather than explicit signification, had an immense influence throughout Europe, and (especially in the 1890s and later) also in England and America, on poets such as Arthur Symons, Ernest Dowson, Yeats, Pound, Dylan Thomas, Hart Crane, E. E. Cummings, and Wallace Stevens. Major symbolist poets in Germany are Stefan George and Rainer Maria Rilke.

The *Modern Period,* in the decades after World War I, was a notable era of symbolism in literature. Many of the major writers of the period exploit symbols which are in part drawn from religious and esoteric traditions and in part from their own invention. Some of the works of the age are symbolist throughout: in their settings, their agents, and their actions, as well as in their diction. Instances of a persistently symbolic procedure occur in lyrics (Yeats's "Byzantium" poems, Dylan Thomas' series of sonnets *Altarwise by Owl-light*), in longer poems (Hart Crane's *The Bridge,* Eliot's *The Waste Land,* Stevens' "The Comedian as the Letter C"), and in novels (Joyce's *Ulysses* and *Finnegans Wake,* Faulkner's *The Sound and the Fury*).

See Arthur Symons, *The Symbolist Movement in Literature* (rev., 1919); Edmund Wilson, *Axel's Castle* (1936); C. M. Bowra, *The Heritage of Symbolism* (1943); Kenneth Cornell, *The Symbolist Movement* (1951); Edward Engelberg, ed., *The Symbolist Poem* (1967); and Anna Balakian, ed., *The Symbolist Movement in the Literature of European Languages* (1982). For William Blake's complex symbolism, refer to S. Foster Damon, *A Blake Dictionary: The Ideas and Symbols of William Blake* (1965).

Synesthesia is the psychological term for experiencing two or more modes of sensation when only one sense is being stimulated. In literature the term is applied to descriptions of one kind of sensation in terms of another; color is attributed to sounds, odor to colors, sound to odors, and so on. A complex example, sometimes also called "sense transference" or "sense analogy," is this passage from Shelley's "The Sensitive Plant" (1820):

> And the hyacinth purple, and white, and blue,
> Which flung from its bells a sweet peal anew
> Of music so delicate, soft, and intense,
> It was felt like an odor within the sense.

The varicolored, bell-shaped flowers send out a peal of music which affects the sense as though it were (what in fact it is) the scent of the hyacinths. Keats, in the "Ode to a Nightingale" (1819), calls for a draught of cool wine

> Tasting of Flora and the country green,
> Dance, and Provençal song, and sunburnt mirth;

tasting, that is, of sight, color, motion, sound, and heat. Before the Romantic Period, occasional uses of synesthetic imagery had been made by poets ever since Homer. After that period, synesthesia was especially exploited by the French *Symbolists* of the middle and later nineteenth century; see Baudelaire's sonnet "Correspondances," and Rimbaud's sonnet on the color of vowel sounds "A black, E white, I red, U green, O blue."

Refer to June Downey, *Creative Imagination* (1929), and to the general discussion and detailed analyses of synesthesia in Richard H. Fogel, *The Imagery of Keats and Shelley* (1949), Chap. 3.

Tension is a common descriptive and evaluative word in literary criticism, especially since Allen Tate proposed it as a term to be made by "lopping the prefixes off the logical terms *ex*tension and *in*tension." In technical logic the "intension" of a word is the abstract set of attributes which must be possessed by any object to which the word can be literally applied, and the "extension" of a word is the class of individual objects to which it literally applies. The meaning of good poetry, according to Tate, "is its 'tension,' the full organized body of all the extension and intension that we can find in it." ("Tension in Poetry," 1938, in *On the Limits of Poetry*, 1948.) It would seem that by this statement Tate meant that a good poem incorporates both the abstract and the concrete, the general idea and the particular image, in an integral whole.

Other critics use "tension" to characterize poetry that manifests an equilibrium of the serious and the ironic, or "a pattern of resolved stresses," or a harmony of opponent tendencies, or any other mode of that stability-in-opposition which was the favorite way in the *New Criticism* for conceiving the organization of a good poem. And some critics, dubious perhaps about the validity of Tate's logical derivation of the term, simply apply "tension" to any poem in which the elements seem tightly rather than loosely interrelated.

Three Unities. In the sixteenth and seventeenth centuries, critics of the drama in Italy and France added to Aristotle's recommendation of *unity of action* two other unities, to constitute the rules of drama known as "the three unities." On the assumption that **verisimilitude**—the achievement of an illusion of reality in the audience—requires that the action represented in a play approximate the actual conditions of the staging of the play, they imposed the "unity of place" (that the action be limited to a single location) and the "unity of time" (that the time represented be limited to the two or three hours it takes to act the play, or at most to a single day of either twelve or twenty-four hours). In large part because of the strong influence of Shakespeare, whose plays involve frequent changes of place and the passage of many years, the rules of the unities of place and time were never so dominant in English *neoclassicism* as in Italy and France; a final blow was the famous attack against them in Samuel Johnson's "Preface to Shakespeare" (1765). Since the mid-eighteenth century in England, the unities of place and time (as distinguished from the unity of action) have been regarded as optional devices, available to the playwright for special effects of dramatic concentration.

See Joel Spingarn, *Literary Criticism in the Renaissance* (rev., 1924); J. W. H. Atkins, *English Literary Criticism: Seventeenth and Eighteenth Centuries* (1957); Bernard Weinberg, *A History of Literary Criticism in the Italian Renaissance* (1961).

Touchstone is a hard stone used to determine, by the streak left on it when rubbed by gold, whether a metal is pure gold or a gold alloy. The word was introduced into literary criticism by Matthew Arnold in "The Study of Poetry" (1880) to denote distinctive short passages selected from the greatest poets which he used to determine the excellence of passages or poems which are compared to them. Arnold proposed this method of evaluation as a corrective for what he called the "fallacious" estimates of poems according to their "historic" importance in the evolution of literature, or according to their "personal" appeal to an individual critic. As Arnold put it:

> There can be no more useful help for discovering what poetry belongs to the class of the truly excellent . . . than to have always in one's mind lines and expressions of the great masters, and to apply them as a touchstone to other poetry. . . . If we have any tact we shall find them . . . an infallible touchstone for detecting the presence or absence of high poetic quality, and also the degree of this quality, in all other poetry which we may place beside them.

The touchstones he proposed are single passages from Homer, Dante, and Milton and two from Shakespeare; they range in length from one to four lines. Two of his best-known touchstones are also the shortest: Dante's "In la sua volontade è nostra pace" ("In Thy will is our peace"), and the close of Milton's description of the loss to Ceres of her daughter Proserpine, ". . . which cost Ceres all that pain/To seek her through the world."

Tragedy. The term is broadly applied to literary, and especially to dramatic, representations of serious and important actions which turn out disastrously for the *protagonist*, or chief character. Detailed discussions of the tragic form properly begin—although they should not end—with Aristotle's classic analysis in the *Poetics* (fourth century B.C.). Aristotle based his theory on induction from the only examples available to him, the tragedies of Greek dramatists such as Aeschylus, Sophocles, and Euripides. In the subsequent two thousand years and more, many new and artistically effective types of serious plots ending in a catastrophe have been developed—types that Aristotle had no way of foreseeing. The many attempts to stretch Aristotle's analysis to apply to all later tragic forms serve merely to blur his critical categories and to obscure important differences among diverse types of plays. When flexibly managed, however, Aristotle's concepts apply in great part to many tragic plots, and they serve as a suggestive starting point for establishing the differentiae of various non-Aristotelian modes of tragic construction.

Aristotle defined tragedy as "the imitation of an action that is serious and also, as having magnitude, complete in itself," in the medium of poetic language, and in the manner of dramatic rather than narrative presentation, incorporating "incidents arousing pity and fear, wherewith to accomplish the catharsis of such emotions." (See *imitation.*) Precisely how to interpret Aristotle's **catharsis**—which in Greek signifies "purgation," or "purification," or both—is much disputed. On two matters, however, a number of commentators agree. Aristotle in the first place sets out to account for the undeniable, if extraordinary, fact that many tragic representations of suffering and defeat leave an audience feeling not depressed, but relieved, or even exalted. (One modern commentator, however, interprets Aristotle's "catharsis" as applying not to an effect on the audience, but to an element within the play itself: it signifies, he claims, the purgation of the guilt attached to the hero's tragic act, through the demonstration by the course of the drama that the hero performed this act without knowledge of its nature. See Gerald Else, *Aristotle's Poetics,* 1957, pp. 224–32, 423–47.) In the second place, Aristotle uses this distinctive effect on the reader, "the pleasure of pity and fear," as the basic way to distinguish the tragic from comic or other forms, and he regards the dramatist's aim to produce this effect in the highest degree as the principle which determines both the choice of the tragic protagonist and the organization of the tragic plot.

Accordingly, Aristotle says that the **tragic hero** will most effectively evoke both our pity and terror if he is neither thoroughly good nor thoroughly evil but a mixture of both; and also that the tragic effect will be stronger if the hero is "better than we are," in the sense that he is of higher than ordinary moral worth. Such a man is exhibited as suffering a change in fortune from happiness to misery because of a mistaken act, to which he is led by his **hamartia**—his "error of judgment" or, as it is often though less literally translated, his **tragic flaw.** (One common form of hamartia in Greek tragedies was **hubris,** that "pride" or overweening self-confidence which leads a protagonist to disregard a divine warning or to violate an important moral law.) The tragic hero moves us to pity because, since he is not an evil man, his misfortune is greater than he deserves; but he moves us also to fear, because we recognize similar possibilities of error in our own lesser and fallible selves. Aristotle grounds his analysis of "the very structure and incidents of the play" on the same principle; the plot, he says, which will most effectively evoke "tragic pity and fear" is one in which the events develop through complication to a *catastrophe* in which there occurs (often by a discovery of facts hitherto unknown to the hero) a sudden *reversal* in his fortune from happiness to disaster. See *plot.*

Authors in the Middle Ages lacked direct knowledge either of classical tragedies or of Aristotle's theory. **Medieval tragedies** are simply the story of an eminent person who, whether deservedly or not, is brought from prosperity to wretchedness by an unpredictable turn of the wheel of fortune. The short narratives in "The Monk's Tale" of *The Canterbury Tales* (late fourteenth century) are all, in Chaucer's own term, "tragedies" of this kind. With the Elizabethan era came both the beginning and the acme of dramatic tragedy in England. The tragedies of this period owed much to the native religious drama, the *miracle* and *morality plays,* which had developed independently of classical influence; but a most important contribution came from the Roman writer Seneca (first century), whose dramas got to be widely known earlier than those of the Greek tragedians.

Senecan tragedy was written to be recited, rather than acted; but to English playwrights, who thought that these tragedies had been intended for the stage, they provided the model for a fully developed five-act play with a complex plot and an elaborately formal style of dialogue. Senecan drama, in the Elizabethan Age, had two main lines of development. One of these consisted of academic tragedies written in close imitation of the Senecan models, including the use of a *chorus,* and usually constructed according to the rules of the *three unities,* which had been elaborated by Italian critics of the sixteenth century; the earliest English example was Sackville and Norton's *Gorboduc* (1562). The other and much more important development was written for the popular stage, and is called the **revenge tragedy,** or (in its most sensational form) the **tragedy of blood.** This type of play derived from Seneca's favorite materials of murder, revenge, ghosts, mutilation, and carnage, but while Seneca had relegated such matters to long reports of offstage actions by messengers, the Elizabethan writers had them acted out on stage to satisfy the audience's appetite for violence and horror. Thomas Kyd's *The Spanish Tragedy* (1586) established this popular form, based on a murder and the quest for vengeance and including a ghost, insanity, suicide, a play-within-a-play, sensational incidents, and a gruesomely bloody ending. Marlowe's *The Jew of Malta* (c. 1592) and Shakespeare's *Titus Andronicus* (c. 1590) are in this mode; and from this lively but unlikely prototype came one of the greatest of tragedies, *Hamlet,* as well as Webster's fine horror plays of 1612–13, *The Duchess of Malfi* and *The White Devil.*

Many major tragedies in the brief flowering time between 1585 and 1625, by Marlowe, Shakespeare, Chapman, Webster, Beaumont and Fletcher, and Massinger, deviate radically from the Aristotelian norm. Shakespeare's *Othello* is one of the few plays which accords entirely with Aristotle's basic concepts of the tragic hero and plot. The hero of *Macbeth,* however, is not a good man who commits a tragic error, but an ambitious man who knowingly turns great gifts to evil purposes and therefore, although he retains something of our sympathy by his courage and self-insight, deserves his destruction at the hands of his morally superior antagonists. Shakespeare's *Richard III* presents first the success, then the ruin, of a malign protagonist who nonetheless arouses in us a reluctant admiration by his intelligence and imaginative power and by the shameless candor of his ambition and malice. Most Shakespearean tragedies, like Elizabethan tragedies generally, also depart from Aristotle's paradigm by introducing humorous incidents or scenes, called *comic relief.* There developed also in this age the mixed mode of *tragicomedy,* a popular non-Aristotelian form which produced a number of artistic successes. And later in the seventeenth century the Restoration Period produced the curious form, a cross between epic and tragedy, called *heroic tragedy.*

Until the close of the seventeenth century almost all tragedies were written in verse and had as protagonists men of high rank, whose fate affected the fortunes of a state. A few minor Elizabethan tragedies, such as *A Yorkshire Tragedy* (of uncertain authorship), had as the chief character a man of the lower class, but it remained for eighteenth-century writers to popularize the **bourgeois** or **domestic tragedy,** which was written in prose and presented a protagonist from the middle or lower social ranks who suffers a commonplace or domestic disaster. George Lillo's *The London Merchant: or, The History of George Barnwell* (1731), about a merchant's apprentice who falls into the toils of a heartless courtesan and comes to a bad end by robbing his employer and murdering his uncle, is still read, at least in college courses.

Since that time most successful tragedies have been in prose, and represent middle-class, or occasionally even working-class, heroes and heroines. One of the more notable recent tragedies, Arthur Miller's *The Death of a Salesman* (1949), relies for its tragic seriousness on the degree to which Willy Loman, in his bewildered defeat by life, is representative of the ordinary man whose aspirations reflect the false values of a commercial society; the effect on the audience is one of compassionate understanding rather than of tragic pity and terror. A term sometimes applied to a recurrent protagonist in modern serious plays and prose fiction, to signify his discrepancy from the heroes of traditional tragedies, is the **antihero:** a person who, instead of manifesting largeness, dignity, power, and heroism in the face of fate, is petty, ignominious, ineffectual, or passive. Extreme instances are the characters who people the world stripped of certainties, values, or even meaning, in Samuel Beckett's dramas—the tramps Vladimir and Estragon in *Waiting for Godot,* or the blind and paralyzed old man, Hamm, who is the protagonist in *Endgame.* See literature of the *absurd.*

Tragedy since World War I has been innovative in many other ways, including experimentation with new versions of ancient types. Eugene O'Neill's *Mourning Becomes Electra* (1931), for example, is an adaptation of Aeschylus' *Oresteia,* with the locale shifted from Greece to New England, the poetry altered to rather flat prose, and the tragedy of fate converted into a tragedy of the psychological compulsions of a family trapped in a tangle of Freudian complexes (see *psychoanalysis*). T. S. Eliot's *Murder in the Cathedral* (1935) is a tragic drama written in verse which incorporates elements from two early forms, the medieval *miracle play* (dealing with the martyrdom of a saint) and the medieval *morality play.*

See *genre,* and refer to A. C. Bradley, *Shakespearean Tragedy* (1904); F. L. Lucas, *Tragedy: Serious Drama in Relation to Aristotle's Poetics* (1927); H. D. F. Kitto, *Greek Tragedy* (rev., 1954); H. J. Muller, *The Spirit of Tragedy* (1956); Elder Olson, *Tragedy and the Theory of Drama* (1961); R. B. Sewall, ed., *Tragedy: Modern Essays in Criticism* (1963).

Tragicomedy was a type of Elizabethan and Jacobean drama which mingled both the standard subject matters and the forms of tragedy and comedy: (1) Its important characters included both people of high degree and people of low degree, even though, according to the reigning critical theory, only upper-class characters were appropriate to tragedy, while members of the middle and lower classes were the proper subject of comedy; see *decorum.* (2) It represented a serious action which threatened a tragic disaster to the protagonist, yet, by an abrupt reversal of circumstance, ended happily. As John Fletcher wrote in his Preface to *The Faithful Shepherdess* (c. 1610), tragicomedy "wants deaths, which is enough to make it no tragedy, yet brings some near it, which is enough to make it no comedy, which must be a representation of familiar people. . . . A god is as lawful in [tragicomedy] as in a tragedy, and mean people as in a comedy."

Shakespeare's *Merchant of Venice* is by these criteria a tragicomedy, because it mingles people of high degree with lower-class characters (such as the Jewish merchant Shylock and the clown Launcelot Gobbo), and also because the developing threat of death to Antonio is suddenly reversed at the end by Portia's ingenious casuistry in the trial scene. Francis Beaumont and John Fletcher developed, in *Philaster* and numerous other plays written from about 1606 to 1613, a mode of tragicomedy which employs a romantic and fast-moving plot of love, jealousy, treachery, intrigue, and disguises, and ends in a melodramatic reversal of fortune for the protagonists, who had hitherto seemed headed for disaster. Shakespeare wrote his late plays *Cymbeline* and *The Winter's Tale,* between 1609 and 1611, in this very popular mode of the tragicomic *romance.* "Tragicomedy" is sometimes applied also to plays with *double plots,* one serious and the other comic.

See E. M. Waith, *The Pattern of Tragicomedy in Beaumont and Fletcher* (1952); M. T. Herrick, *Tragicomedy* (1955).

Transcendentalism in America was a philosophical and literary movement, centered in Concord and Boston, which was prominent in the intellectual and cultural life of New England from 1836 until just before the Civil War. The movement began in 1836 at George Ripley's house with a Unitarian discussion group which came to be called the Transcendental Club; in the seven years or so that the group met, it included at one time or another Ralph Waldo Emerson, Bronson Alcott, W. E. Channing and W. H. Channing, Theodore Parker, Margaret Fuller, Elizabeth Peabody, George Ripley, Nathaniel Hawthorne, Henry Thoreau, and Jones Very. A quarterly periodical, *The Dial* (1840–44), printed many of the early essays by the Transcendentalists.

Transcendentalism was neither a systematic nor a sharply definable philosophy, but rather an intellectual mode and emotional mood that was expressed by very diverse, and in some instances rather eccentric, voices. Modern historians of the movement tend to take as its central exponents Emerson (especially in *Nature, The American Scholar,* the Divinity School Address, "The Over-Soul," and "Self Reliance") and Thoreau (especially in *Walden* and his journals). The term "transcendental," as Emerson pointed out in his essay "The Transcendentalist" (1841–43), was taken from the German philosopher Immanuel Kant. Kant had confined the expression "transcendental knowledge" to the cognizance of those forms and categories imposed in perception by all human minds (such as space, time, quantity, causality), which he regarded as the constitutive conditions of all sense-experience; Emerson and others, however, extended the concept of transcendental knowledge, in a way whose validity Kant had specifically denied, to include an intuitive cognizance of moral and other truths that transcend the bounds of our sense-experience. The intellectual antecedents of American Transcendentalism were in fact very diverse, and included post-Kantian German Idealists, the English thinkers Coleridge and Carlyle (themselves exponents of forms of German Idealism), Plato and Neoplatonists, the occult Swedish theologian Emanuel Swedenborg, and some varieties of Oriental philosophy.

What the various Transcendentalists largely shared was an opposition to rigid rationalism; to the empirical philosophy of the school of John Locke, dominant in the eighteenth century, which derived all knowledge from sense impressions; to highly formalized religion, and especially the Calvinist orthodoxy of New England; and to the social conformity, materialism, and commercialism that they found increasingly dominant in American life. What was frequently affirmed, on the contrary, especially by Emerson, was confidence in the validity of knowledge that is grounded in human consciousness and intuition, and a consequent tendency to accept what, to strictly logical reasoning, might seem contradictions; an ethics of individualism that stressed self-trust, self-reliance, and self-sufficiency; a turn from modern society, with its getting and spending, to the scenes and objects of the natural world, regarded both as physical facts and as correspondences to the human spirit (see *correspondences*); and, in place of a formal or doctrinal religion, faith in an omnipresent divine "Principle," or "Spirit," or "Soul" (Emerson's "Over-Soul") which is shared by mankind and the cosmos. This omnipresent Spirit, as Emerson said, constitutes the "Unity within which every man's particular being is contained and made one with all other"; it manifests itself to human consciousness as influxes of inspired insights, and is the source of the profoundest truths and the necessary condition of all moral and spiritual development.

Walden (1854) records how Thoreau tested his distinctive and radically individualist version of Transcendental values by withdrawing from societal complexities and distractions to a life of solitude and complete self-reliance. He simplified his material wants to those he could satisfy by the bounty of the woods and lake or could provide by his own labor, attended minutely and passionately to natural objects in the material world for their inherent interest as well as correlatives to the mind of the observer, and devoted his leisure to reading and meditation; in his nonconformity, he chose a day in jail rather than pay his poll tax to a government that supported the Mexican War and slavery. Brooks Farm, on the other hand, was a short-lived experiment (1841–47) by more socially oriented Transcendentalists who established a commune on the principle of the equal sharing of work, pay, and cultural benefits; Hawthorne, who lived there for a while, later wrote about Brooks Farm, with considerable skepticism, in *The Blithedale Romance* (1852).

The Transcendental movement, with its optimism about the indwelling divinity, self-sufficiency, and high potentialities of human nature, did not survive the crisis of the Civil War and its aftermath, and Melville as well as Hawthorne satirized aspects of Transcendentalism in his fiction. Some of its basic concepts and values, however, were assimilated by Whitman, were echoed in writings by Henry James and other major American authors, and continue to reemerge in America—the voice of Thoreau, for example, however distorted, can be recognized in the *counterculture* of the 1960s and later.

See *periods of American literature,* and refer to: Harold C. Goddard, *Studies in New England Transcendentalism* (1908); F. O. Matthiessen, *American Renaissance* (1941); the anthology edited, together with commentary, by Perry Miller, *The Transcendentalists* (1950); Joel Porte, *Emerson and Thoreau: Transcendentalists in Conflict* (1965); Lawrence Buell, *Literary Transcendentalism: Style and Vision in the American Renaissance* (1973).

Utopias and Dystopias. *Utopia* was the title of a book about an imaginary commonwealth, written in Latin (1515–16) by the Renaissance *humanist* Sir Thomas More. The title plays on two Greek words, "outopia" (no place) and "eutopia" (good place); and the **utopia** has come to signify the class of fiction which represents an ideal, nonexistent political state and way of life. The first and greatest instance of the type was Plato's *Republic* (later fourth century B.C.), which sets forth, in dialogue form, the eternal Idea or Form of a commonwealth as a model that can be only approximated by political organizations in the actual world. Most utopias, beginning with that of Sir Thomas More, represent their ideal place under the fiction of a distant country reached by a venturesome traveler. There have been many utopias written since More gave impetus to the genre, some as mere Arcadian dreams, others as blueprints for social and technological progress in the actual world. They include Tommaso Campanella's *City of the Sun* (1623), Francis Bacon's *New Atlantis* (1627), Edward Bellamy's *Looking Backward* (1888), William Morris' *News from Nowhere* (1891), and James Hilton's *Lost Horizon* (1934).

The utopia can be distinguished from literary representations of imaginary places which, either because they are greatly superior to the real world or manifest exaggerated versions of some of its unsavory aspects, are used primarily as vehicles for *satire* on human life and society: Swift's *Gulliver's Travels* (1726), Samuel Butler's *Erewhon* (1872). Samuel Johnson's *Rasselas* (1759) presents the "Happy Valley," which functions as a gentle satire on humanity's stubborn dream of a utopia, on the ground that the realization of all human wishes will merely replace the unhappiness of frustrated desires with the unhappiness of boredom; see Chaps. 1–3. Another related but distinctive form is that of **science fiction,** represented by the works of H. G. Wells, Jules Verne, and many current writers, which explores the marvels of discovery and achievement that may result from future developments in science and technology. There are also diverse cross-forms; for example, an aspect or tendency of scientific research is attacked by imagining its disastrous conclusion, as in Kurt Vonnegut, Jr.'s, *Cat's Cradle* (1963) and the motion picture *Dr. Strangelove, or: How I Learned to Stop Worrying and Love the Bomb.*

The term **dystopia** ("bad place") has recently come to be applied to works of fiction which represent a very unpleasant imaginary world, in which ominous tendencies of our present social, political, and technological order are projected in some future culmination. Examples are Aldous Huxley's *Brave New World* (1932), George Orwell's *1984* (1949), and Ursula K. Le Guin's *The Dispossessed: An Ambiguous Utopia* (1974).

See J. O. Hertzler, *The History of Utopian Thought* (1923); Lewis Mumford, *The Story of Utopias* (1922); Karl Mannheim, *Ideology and Utopia* (1934); Chad Walsh, *From Utopia to Nightmare* (1962); Nell Eurich, *Science in Utopia* (1967); and the anthology *Utopian Literature: A Selection,* ed. J. W. Johnson (1960).

Victorian Period. The beginning of the Victorian Period is dated sometimes at 1832 (the passage of the first Reform Bill) and sometimes at 1837 (the accession of Queen Victoria); it extends to the death of Victoria in 1901. The year 1870 is often used to distinguish between "early Victorian" and "late Victorian." Much writing of the period, whether imaginative or didactic, in verse or in prose, dealt with or reflected contemporary social, economic, religious, and intellectual issues and problems. Among these were the industrial revolution and its effects on the economic and social structure; rapid urbanization and the deterioration of rural England; massive poverty, growing class tensions, and pressures toward political and social reform; what was often called "the woman question" (the *feminist* movement for equal status and rights); and the impact on philosophy and religious fundamentalism both of Darwin's theory of evolution and of the general extension of **positivism** (the method of empirical investigation and proof developed in the physical sciences) into all areas of speculation and inquiry. It was an age of immense, variegated, and often self-critical literary activity. The frequently derogatory connotations of the term "Victorian" in our time—sexual priggishness, narrow-mindedness, complacency, the stress on respectability—are indeed based on attitudes and values expressed by many members of the rapidly expanding Victorian middle class; but current attacks on such Victorian attributes merely echo the attacks by numerous men of letters within the age itself. The most eminent poets were Tennyson, Browning, and Arnold; the most prominent essayists were Carlyle, Ruskin, Arnold, and Pater; the most distinguished of many excellent novelists (this was a great age of English prose fiction) were Dickens, Thackeray, George Eliot, Meredith, Trollope, Hardy, and Samuel Butler.

For some prominent literary developments within the period see *Pre-Raphaelites* and *Aestheticism and Decadence;* and refer to G. M. Young, *Victorian England: Portrait of an Age* (2d ed., 1953); Jerome Buckley, *The Victorian Temper* (1951); W. E. Houghton, *The Victorian Frame of Mind* (1957). On aspects of love and sexuality in that age, see Steven Marcus, *The Other Vic-*

torians (1966), and Peter Gay, *The Bourgeois Experience, Victoria to Freud*, Vol. 1, *Education of the Senses* (1984), and Vol. 2, *The Tender Passion* (1986).

Wit, Humor, and the Comic. Both "wit" and "humor" now denote species of the **comic:** any element in literature that is designed to amuse or to excite mirth in the reader or audience. Wit and humor, however, had a variety of other meanings in earlier literary criticism, and a brief comment on their history will help to clarify the difference between them in present usage.

Wit once meant the human faculty of intelligence, inventiveness, and mental acuity, a sense it still retains in the term "half-wit." In the sixteenth and seventeenth centuries it came to be used also for ingenuity in literary invention, and especially for the ability to discover brilliant, surprising, and paradoxical figures of speech; hence "wit" was often applied to the style of poetry we now call *metaphysical*. And in the eighteenth century there were frequent attempts to distinguish the "false wit" of Cowley and other metaphysical stylists, who were said to aim at a merely superficial dazzlement, and "true wit," regarded as the apt phrasing of truths whose enduring validity is attested by their very commonplaceness. So Pope defined "true wit" in his *Essay on Criticism* (1711) as "What oft was thought, but ne'er so well expressed." (See under *neoclassic*.)

The most common present use of the term derives from its seventeenth-century application to a brilliant and paradoxical style. "Wit," that is, now denotes a kind of verbal expression which is brief, deft, and intentionally contrived to produce a shock of comic surprise. The surprise is usually the result of an unforeseen connection or distinction between words or concepts, which frustrates the listener's expectation only to satisfy it in a different way. Philip Guedalla wittily said: "History repeats itself. Historians repeat each other." Thus the historians' trite comment about history turns out to be unexpectedly appropriate, with an unlooked-for turn of meaning, to the writers of history as well. "The only sure way to double your money," remarked the American comedian Abe Martin, "is to fold it and put it in your hip pocket." The resulting laughter, in a famous phrase of the German philosopher Immanuel Kant, arises "from the sudden transformation of a strained expectation into nothing"; it might be more accurate to say, however, "from the sudden satisfaction of an expectation, but in a way we did not in the least expect."

Abe Martin's remark is what the *psychoanalyst* Sigmund Freud called "harmless wit," which evokes a laugh or smile that is without malice. What Freud distinguished as "tendency wit" is aggressive; it is a derisive turn of phrase, directing the laugh at a particular object or butt. "Mr. James Payn," in Oscar Wilde's barbed comment on a contemporary novelist of the 1890s, "hunts down the obvious with the enthusiasm of a short-sighted detective. As one turns over the pages, the suspense of the author becomes almost unbearable." As Wilde's comment demonstrates, wit often is couched in the form of an *epigram*.

Repartee is a term aptly taken from fencing to signify a contest of wit, in which each person tries to cap the remark of the other, or to turn it to his or her own purpose. Attacking Disraeli in Parliament, Gladstone remarked that "the honorable gentleman will either end on the gallows or die of some loathsome disease." To which Disraeli rejoined: "That depends on whether I embrace the honorable gentleman's principles or his mistresses." *Restoration comedies* usually included episodes of sustained repartee; a classic example is the discussion of their coming marriage by Mirabel and Millamant in Act IV of Congreve's *The Way of the World* (1700).

Humor derives from the ancient theory of the *four humours* as determining types of personality, and from the derivative application of the term "humorous" to one of the comically eccentric characters in the Elizabethan *comedy of humours.* As we now use the word, "humor" may be ascribed both to a comic speech and to a comic appearance or mode of behavior. A humorous speech differs from a witty speech in one or both of two ways: (1) wit, as we saw, is always intended by the speaker to be comic, but many speeches that we find comically humorous are intended by the speakers themselves to be serious; and (2) a humorous saying is not cast in the neat, epigrammatic form of a witty saying. For example, the chatter of the old Nurse in Shakespeare's *Romeo and Juliet* is humorous only to the audience, not to the speaker; similarly, the discussion of the mode of life of the goldfish in Central Park by the inarticulate and irascible taxi driver in Salinger's *The Catcher in the Rye* (1951) is unintentionally but superbly humorous, and is not cast in the form of a witty turn of phrase.

More important still is the difference that wit is exclusively verbal, while humor has a much broader range of reference. We find humor, for example, in the way Charlie Chaplin looks, dresses, and acts, and also in the sometimes wordless cartoons in *The New Yorker.* In a thoroughly humorous situation, the sources of the fun are complex. In Act III, Scene iv of Shakespeare's *Twelfth Night,* Malvolio's appearance and actions, and his speech as well, are humorous, but all despite his own very solemn intentions; and our comic enjoyment is increased by our knowledge of the hilarity of the hidden auditors onstage. One source of the greatness of a comic creation like Shakespeare's Falstaff is that he exploits the full gamut of comic possibilities. Falstaff is humorous in the way he looks and in what he does; what he says is sometimes witty, and at almost all other times humorous; while his actions and speech are sometimes unintentionally humorous, sometimes intentionally humorous, and not infrequently—as in his whimsical account to his skeptical auditors of how he bore himself in the highway robbery, in the second act of *Henry IV, Part 1*—they are humorous even beyond his intention.

One other point needs to be made about humor and the comic. In the normal use, the term "humor" refers to what is purely comic: it evokes, as it is sometimes said, sympathetic laughter, or else laughter which is an end in itself. If we extend Freud's distinction between harmless and tendency wit, we can say that humor is a "harmless" form of the comic. There is, however, another mode of the comic, "tendency comedy," in which we are made to laugh at a person not merely because he is ridiculous, but because he is being ridiculed—the laughter is derisive, with some element of contempt or malice, and serves as a weapon against its ridiculous subject. Tendency comedy and tendency wit, but not humor, are among the devices that a writer employs in *satire,* the literary art of derogating by deriding a subject.

On the alternative use of "comic" to define formal features of a type of dramatic or narrative plot, see *comedy;* for a frequent modern literary form of humor-in-horror, see *black humor.* For theories, the history, and examples of wit, humor, and the comic, refer to Sigmund Freud, *Wit and Its Relation to the Unconscious* (1916); Max Eastman, *Enjoyment of Laughter* (1936); D. H. Monro, *The Argument of Laughter* (1951); Louis Kronenberger, *The Thread of Laughter* (1952); Stuart M. Tave, *The Amiable Humorist* (1960); George Williamson, *The Proper Wit of Poetry* (1961).

Modern Theories of Literature and Criticism

The essay on *criticism* in the preceding section of the *Glossary* describes the diverse types of literary criticism and practice from Aristotle to the recent past. The following section contains essays on the innovative literary theories and methods of critical analysis of the last half-century, including recently revised and amplified versions of *Marxist criticism* and of *psychological and psychoanalytic criticism.* The arrangement of the essays is in the alphabetic order of their titles. The chronological order in which the major new forms of theory and critical methods became prominent is approximately as follows:

1920s and 1930s:	*Russian formalism.*
1930s and 1940s:	*archetypal criticism.*
1940s and 1950s:	*New Criticism; phenomenology* (as applied to literary criticism); *stylistics.*
1960s:	*structuralist criticism;* modern forms of *feminist criticism.*
1970s:	theory of the *anxiety of influence; deconstruction;* forms of *reader-response criticism; reception-theory; semiotics; speech act theory.*

Archetypal Criticism. On one side the literary theory of the archetype derives from the school of comparative anthropology at Cambridge University, of which the basic work is J. G. Frazer's *The Golden Bough* (1890–1915); this book traced elemental patterns of myth and ritual which, it claimed, recur in the legends and ceremonials of many diverse cultures. On the other side the theory derives from the depth psychology of C. G. Jung, who applied the term "archetype" to "primordial images," the "psychic residue" of repeated types of experience in the lives of our very ancient ancestors which, Jung maintained, survive in the "collective unconscious" of the human race and are expressed in myths, religion, dreams, and private fantasies, as well as in works of literature (see Jung under *psychoanalytic criticism*).

The term has been often used in literary criticism, especially since the appearance of Maud Bodkin's *Archetypal Patterns in Poetry* (1934). In criticism "archetype" signifies narrative designs, character types, or images which are said to be identifiable in a wide variety of works of literature, as well as in myths, dreams, and even ritualized modes of social behavior. The archetypal similarities within these diverse phenomena are held to reflect a set of universal, primitive, and elemental patterns, whose effective embodiment in a literary work evokes a profound response from the reader. Some archetypal critics have dropped Jung's theory of the collective unconscious as the deep source of these patterns; in the words of Northrop Frye, this theory is "an unnecessary hypothesis," and the recurrent archetypal patterns are simply there, "however they got there."

Among the prominent practitioners of various forms of **archetypal criticism,** in addition to Maud Bodkin, are G. Wilson Knight, Robert Graves, Philip Wheelwright, Richard Chase, and Joseph Campbell. All these critics tend to emphasize mythical patterns in literature, on the assumption that myths are closer to the elemental archetype than the artful products of sophisticated writers (see *myth critics*). The death-rebirth theme is often said to be the archetype of archetypes, and is held to be grounded in the cycle of the seasons and the organic cycle of human life; this archetype, it has been claimed, informs primitive rituals of the sacrificial king, myths of the god who dies to be reborn, and a multitude of diverse literary works, including the Bible, Dante's *Divine Comedy* in the early fourteenth century, and Coleridge's "Rime of the Ancient Mariner" in 1798. Among other archetypal themes, images, and characters which have been frequently traced in literature are the journey underground, the heavenly ascent, the search for the father, the paradise-Hades image, the Promethean rebel-hero, the scapegoat, the earth goddess, and the fatal woman.

In the remarkable and influential book *The Anatomy of Criticism* (1957), Northrop Frye developed the archetypal approach—which he combined with the *typological interpretation* of the Bible and the concept of the literary imagination in the writings of the poet and painter William Blake (1757–1827)—into a radical and comprehensive revision of traditional grounds both of the theory of literature and the practice of literary criticism. Frye proposes that, as opposed to the natural universe, the total structure of literature is a "self-contained literary universe" which has been created over the ages by the human imagination so as to incorporate the alien and indifferent world of nature into persisting archetypal forms that serve to satisfy enduring human desires and needs. In this literary universe, four radical **mythoi** (that is, plot forms, or organizing structural principles), correspondent to the four seasons in the cycle of the natural world, constitute the four major *genres* of comedy, romance, tragedy, and satire. Within the overall archetypal mythos of each of these genres, individual works of literature also play variations upon a number of more limited archetypes—that is, of conventional forms and types that literature shares with social rituals as well as with theology, history, law, and in fact all other "discursive verbal structures." Viewed archetypally, according to Frye, literature turns out to play an essential role in remaking the physical universe into an alternative verbal universe that is humanly intelligible and viable, because adapted to essential human needs and concerns. Frye has continued, in a long series of later writings, to expand his archetypal theory and to apply it to the elucidation of documents ranging from the Bible to contemporary poets and novelists.

Consult, in addition to the works mentioned above, C. G. Jung, "On the Relation of Analytical Psychology to Poetic Art" (1922), in *Contributions to Analytical Psychology* (1928), and "Psychology and Literature," in *Modern Man in Search of a Soul* (1933); G. Wilson Knight, *The Starlit Dome* (1941); Robert Graves, *The White Goddess* (1948); Richard Chase, *Quest for Myth* (1949); Philip Wheelwright, *The Burning Fountain* (1954), and *Metaphor and Reality* (1962); Northrop Frye, "The Archetypes of Literature," in *Fables of Identity* (1963). For discussions and critiques of archetypal theory and practice see H. M. Block, "Cultural Anthropology and Contemporary Literary Criticism," *Journal of Aesthetics and Art Criticism,* 11 (1952); Murray Krieger, ed., *Northrop Frye in Modern Criticism* (1966); Robert Denham, *Northrop Frye and Critical Method* (1978); Frank Lentricchia, *After the New Criticism* (1980), Chap. 1.

Deconstruction is the term applied to a theory of reading which undertakes to "subvert" or "undermine" the implicit claim of a textual work to possess adequate grounds, in the system of language that it uses, to establish its own boundaries, its coherence or unity, and the determinate meanings of its verbal elements. According to this theory, therefore, no text is capable of representing determinately, far less of demonstrating, the "truth" about any subject. Deconstruction, together with the neo-Freudian theory of Jacques Lacan and the literary criticism of Roland Barthes after about 1973, is frequently called **poststructuralist** because it employs the Saussurean linguistic concepts and other aspects of structuralism in a way that undermines the grounds both of Ferdinand de Saussure's linguistic system and of structuralism itself, and results in the claim that the meaning of any text remains radically "open" to contradictory readings. (See *structuralist criticism;* also *semiotics.*)

The originator and namer of deconstruction is the French thinker Jacques Derrida, whose major precursors were Friedrich Nietzsche (1844–1900) and Martin Heidegger (1889–1976)—German philosophers who put to radical question the validity of key philosophical concepts such as "knowledge," "truth," and "identity"—as well as Sigmund Freud (1856–1939), whose *psychoanalysis* violated traditional concepts of a coherent "consciousness" and a unitary "self." Derrida presented his basic views in three books, all published in 1967, *Of Grammatology, Writing and Difference,* and *Speech and Phenomena;* since then, he has been reiterating, expanding, and applying those views in a rapid sequence of publications.

Derrida's writings are complex and elusive; the summary here can provide only an indication of some of their main tendencies. His point of vantage is what, in *Of Grammatology,* he calls "the axial proposition that there is nothing outside the text" ("il n'y a rien hors du texte," or alternatively, "il n'y a pas de hors-texte"). Like all Derrida's key terms and statements, this has multiple significations; but a primary significance is that one cannot get beyond the sequence of verbal signs to anything that stands outside of, and independent of, the language system that constitutes a text—for example, its referents, or else the intention of its speaker or writer to express a determinate signification. Derrida's reiterated claim is that not only all Western philosophies or theories of language but all Western uses of language—hence all Western culture—are **logocentric** (that is, grounded on a "logos," or in a phrase he adopts from Heidegger, on "the metaphysics of presence"), and that they are logocentric in large part because they are **phonocentric** (that is, they grant, implicitly or explicitly, logical "priority," or "privilege," to speech over writing, as the model for analyzing all discourse). By logos or **presence** Derrida signifies what he also calls an "ultimate referent"—a self-certifying absolute, or ground, or foundation, directly present to our awareness outside the play of language itself, which is adequate to "center" (that is, to anchor and organize) the linguistic system and to fix the determinate meaning of any spoken or written utterance within that system. Historical instances of claims for such an absolute ground are God as the guarantor of the validity of language, or a Platonic Form of the true reference of a term that is accessible to one's mental vision, or an intention to signify something determinate that is directly known to the person who initiates an utterance. Derrida undertakes to show that all philosophical attempts to demonstrate an absolute ground in presence, and all implicit reliance on such a ground in using language, are illusory; especially, he directs his skeptical arguments against the phonocentric assumption—which he regards as central in modern theories of language—that at the instant of speaking, the "intention" of a speaker, which determines the significance of what he or she says, is immediately and fully present in the speaker's consciousness, and communicable to an auditor. (See *intention,* under *interpretation and hermeneutics.*)

Derrida derives his alternative conception of the radically "undecidable" play of linguistic meanings primarily from Saussure's view that in a linguistic sign-system, both the *signifiers* (the material elements of a language, whether spoken or written) and the *signifieds* (their conceptual meanings) owe their seeming identity, not to their own "positive" or inherent features, but to their *differences* from other speech-sounds, written marks, or conceptual significations. (See Saussure, in *linguistics in modern criticism* and in *semiotics,* below.) From this view Derrida evolves his own radical claim that the features that would strictly establish a signified meaning—since this significance is nothing other than a network of differences from other signified meanings—are never "present" to us in their own identity. On the other hand, neither can these identifying features be said to be strictly "absent"; instead, in any spoken or written utterance, the seeming signification is the result only of a "self-effacing" **trace**—self-effacing because one is not aware of it —which consists of all the nonpresent meanings whose differences from the present instance are the sole factor which invest the utterance with its "effect" of having a meaning in itself. The consequence, according to Derrida, is that we can never have a determinate, or decidable, present meaning; he asserts, however, that the differential play of language does produce illusory "effects" of determinable meanings.

In a characteristic move, Derrida coins the *portmanteau* term **différance,** in which, he says, he uses the spelling "-ance" instead of "-ence" in the noun to indicate a fusion of two senses of the French verb "différer": to be different, and to defer. The point of this double sense is that on the one hand there is indeed an "effect" of meaning in an utterance which is produced by its difference from other meanings, but that on the other hand, since this meaning can never come to rest in an actual presence, or "transcendental signified," its determinate specification is deferred from one substitutive linguistic interpretation to another, in a movement, or "play," without end. The meaning of any spoken or written utterance, as Derrida puts it in another of his coinages, is **disseminated**—a term which includes, among its deliberately contradictory significations, that of having an effect of meaning (a "semantic" effect), of dispersing meanings among innumerable alternatives, and of negating any specific meaning. There is thus no ground, in the incessant play of différance that constitutes language, for attributing a decidable meaning, or even a finite set of determinately multiple meanings (which he calls "polysemism"), to any utterance that we speak or write. As Derrida puts it in *Writing and Difference*, p. 280: "The absence of a transcendental signified extends the domain and the play of signification infinitely."

Two others of Derrida's skeptical operations have been especially important for deconstructive literary criticism. One is his undertaking to show that we cannot establish a determinate bound, or limit, or margin, to a textual work so as to differentiate what is "inside" from what is "outside" the work. Another is his analysis of the inherent nonlogicality, or rhetoricity—the inescapable reliance on *rhetorical figures* and *figurative language*—in all uses of language, including in the purportedly logical arguments of philosophy. Derrida, for example, emphasizes the indispensable role in all modes of discourse of metaphors that are assumed to be merely convenient substitutes for *literal*, or "proper" meanings; he undertakes to show, however, that metaphors cannot be reduced to literal meanings, but on the other hand that supposedly literal terms are metaphors whose metaphoric nature has been forgotten.

Derrida's characteristic procedure is not to expound his deconstructive concepts and operations in a systematic exposition, but to allow them to emerge in a sequence of exemplary close readings of passages from writings that range from Plato through Rousseau to the present era—writings that, by standard classification, are mainly philosophical, although occasionally literary. He describes his procedure as a "double reading." Initially, that is, he interprets a text as, in the standard fashion, "lisible" (readable or intelligible), since it engenders "effects" of having determinate meanings. But this reading, Derrida says, is only "provisional," as a stage toward a second, or deconstructive, "critical reading," which disseminates the provisional meaning into an indefinite range of significations that, Derrida claims, always involve (in a term taken from rhetoric) an **aporia**—a deadlock, or "double bind," between incompatible or contradictory meanings which are "undecidable," in that we lack any solid ground for choosing among them. The result is that each text deconstructs itself, by undermining its own supposed grounds and dispersing itself into incoherent meanings, in a way, Derrida claims, that the deconstructive reader does not engender, but merely exposes. Derrida is aware, furthermore, that he has no option except to express and attempt to communicate his own deconstructive readings in the inherited logocentric language, hence that his own interpretive texts deconstruct themselves in the very act of deconstructing the texts to which they are applied. He insists, however, that "deconstruction has nothing to do with destruction," and that all the standard uses of language will inevitably go on; what he does, he says, is merely to "situate" or "reinscribe" all such texts in a system of différance which shows that, though they seem to function intelligibly, they do so only by means of "effects" that turn out to lack an adequate ground.

Derrida did not propose deconstruction as a mode of literary criticism, but as a way of reading texts in all uses of language without exception. His views and procedures, however, have been taken up by literary critics, especially in America, who adapt Derrida's elaborate mode of "critical reading" to the kind of "close reading" of particular literary texts which had earlier been the familiar procedure of the *New Criticism;* they do so, however, as Paul de Man has said, in a way which shows that new-critical close readings "were not nearly close enough." The end results of the two kinds of close reading are utterly diverse. The new-critical explications of texts had undertaken to show that a great literary work, in the tight internal relations of its figurative and often paradoxical meanings, constitutes a freestanding, strictly bounded, and thoroughly organic entity of multiple yet determinate meanings. On the contrary, a radically deconstructive close reading undertakes to show that, in the last analysis, a literary text turns out to have no "totalized" boundary that makes it an entity, much less an organic unity, and no adequate ground for its own linguistic procedures, and therefore that its seemingly determinate meanings disseminate into an indefinite range of aporias, or self-conflicting significations. The claim is sometimes made by deconstructive critics that a literary text is in fact superior to, and less self-delusive than, nonliterary texts, because it shows itself, in its self-reference, to be more aware of features that all texts inescapably share: its fictionality, its lack of a genuine ground, and especially its "rhetoricity" (unavoidable figurative procedures)—features that deconstruct any seeming reference, logicality, or possibility of proof, and so make any "right reading" or "correct reading" of a text impossible.

Prominent exponents of deconstructive close reading in America include Paul de Man, J. Hillis Miller, Joseph Riddell, Barbara Johnson, and Cynthia Chase. Their interests are varied and their individual procedures and aims are diverse. One can, however, use a concise and inclusive statement by J. Hillis Miller, who has published readings of texts by numerous poets and novelists, to indicate the radical result of applying to the analysis of literary works Derrida's procedures for deconstructing the metaphysical foundations of Western thought and writing:

> Deconstruction as a mode of interpretation works by a careful and circumspect entering of each textual labyrinth. . . . The deconstructive critic seeks to find, by this process of retracing, the element in the system studied which is alogical, the thread in the text in question which will unravel it all, or the loose stone which will pull down the whole building. The deconstruction, rather, annihilates the ground on which the building stands by showing that the text has already annihilated the ground, knowingly or unknowingly. Deconstruction is not a dismantling of the structure of a text but a demonstration that it has already dismantled itself.

Miller's conclusion is that any literary text, as a ceaseless play of "irreconcilable" and "contradictory" meanings, or aporias, is "indeterminable" or "undecidable";

hence, that "all reading is misreading." ("Stevens' Rock and Criticism as Cure, II," *Georgia Review*, vol. 30, 1976, and "Walter Pater: A Partial Portrait," *Daedalus*, vol. 105, 1976.)

Some of the central books by Jacques Derrida available in English, with the dates of translation, are *Of Grammatology*, translated and introduced by Gayatri C. Spivak, 1976; *Writing and Difference* (1978); *Dissemination* (1981). See also Derrida's essay on the ordinary-language philosopher John Austin, "Signature, Event, Context," and John R. Searle's critical reply, "Reiterating the Differences," in *Glyph*, 1 (1977). Books exemplifying types of deconstructive literary criticism: Paul de Man, *Blindness and Insight* (1971), and *Allegories of Reading* (1979); Joseph N. Riddell, *The Inverted Bell: Modernism and the Counterpoetics of William Carlos Williams* (1974); Barbara Johnson, *The Critical Difference: Essays in the Contemporary Rhetoric of Reading* (1980); J. Hillis Miller, *Fiction and Repetition: Seven English Novels* (1982), and *The Linguistic Moment: From Wordsworth to Stevens* (1985); Cynthia Chase, *Decomposing Figures: Rhetorical Readings in the Romantic Tradition* (1986).

Expositions of Derrida's deconstruction and of its applications to literary criticism are Jonathan Culler's *On Deconstruction* (1982) and Vincent B. Leitsch, *Deconstructive Criticism: An Advanced Introduction* (1983). Among many critiques of Derrida and various practitioners of deconstructive criticism are M. H. Abrams, "The Deconstructive Angel," *Critical Enquiry*, 3 (1977), "How to Do Things with Texts," *Partisan Review* (1979), and "Construing and Deconstructing" in *Romanticism and Contemporary Criticism*, ed. Morris Eaves and Michael Fischer (1986); Gerald Graff, *Literature Against Itself* (1979); Frank Lentricchia, *After the New Criticism* (1980), Chap. 5; Charles Altieri, *Act and Quality: A Theory of Literary Meaning and Humanistic Understanding* (1981); Robert Scholes, *Textual Power: Literary Theory and the Teaching of English* (1985).

Feminist Criticism. As a concerted and self-conscious approach to literature, feminist criticism was not inaugurated until late in the 1960s. Behind it, however, lie two centuries of struggle for women's rights, marked by such books as Mary Wollstonecraft's *A Vindication of the Rights of Woman* (1792), John Stuart Mill's *The Subjection of Women* (1869), and the American Margaret Fuller's *Woman in the Nineteenth Century* (1845); feminist criticism continues to be interrelated with contemporary movements for women's social, economic, and cultural freedom and equality.

An important precursor in literary criticism was Virginia Woolf, in *A Room of One's Own* (1929) and in numerous essays on women authors and on the cultural and economic disabilities, in what she called a "patriarchal" society, which have hindered or prevented women from realizing their creative possibilities. A much more radical critical mode was launched in France by Simone de Beauvoir's *The Second Sex* (1949), a wide-ranging critique of woman's cultural identification as merely the negative object, or "Other," to man as the defining and dominating "Subject"; the book dealt also with "the great collective myths" of women in various male writers, including Stendhal and D. H. Lawrence. In

America modern feminist criticism began with Mary Ellman's deft and witty treatment, in *Thinking about Women* (1968), of the derogatory stereotypes of women in literature by men and of the subversive perspectives in some writings by women; even more influential was Kate Millett's polemical and hard-hitting *Sexual Politics*, published the following year. By "politics" Millett signifies the mechanisms of power relations; she represents Western social arrangements and institutions as covert ways of manipulating power so as to establish and perpetuate the dominance of men and subordination of women, attacks the male bias in Freud's psychoanalytic theory, and analyzes selected passages by D. H. Lawrence, Henry Miller, and Norman Mailer as revealing, from the vantage of someone who reads as a woman, the ways in which their authors, in fictional fantasy, exploit sexuality in order to aggrandize their aggressive phallic selves or to master and degrade women as submissive sexual objects.

Since 1969 there has been an explosion of feminist writings without close parallel in the history of previous critical innovations, in a movement that, as Elaine Showalter has remarked, displays something of the urgency and excitement of a religious awakening. This current criticism, in America, England, France, and other countries, is not a unitary theory or procedure; it manifests, among those who practice it, a great variety of critical vantage points and procedures, including adaptations of *psychoanalytic*, *Marxist*, and *poststructuralist* theories, and its vitality is marked by the vigor of the debates within the ranks of professed feminists themselves. The various feminisms, however, share certain assumptions and concepts that constitute a common ground for the diverse ways that individual critics explore the factor of sexual difference in the production, the form and content, the reception, and the analysis and evaluation of works of literature:

(1) The basic view is that our civilization is pervasively **patriarchal** (ruled by the father)—that is, it is male-centered and controlled, and is organized and conducted in such a way as to subordinate women to men in all cultural domains, religious, familial, political, economic, social, legal, and artistic. The female tends to be defined by negative reference to the male as the human norm, hence as a kind of non-man, by her lack of the identifying male organ, of male powers, and of the male character traits that are presumed to have achieved the most important inventions and works of civilization. In Marxist terms, the order of women is conceived as a subordinate class of social classes, or as a lower caste that cuts across all economic classes. Women themselves are said, in the process of their being socialized, to internalize the reigning patriarchal *ideology* (that is, the set of conscious and unconscious presuppositions about male superiority), and so are conditioned to derogate their own sex and to cooperate in their own subordination.

(2) It is widely held that while one's sex is determined by anatomy, the concepts of "gender"—of the traits that constitute masculinity and femininity—are largely, if not entirely, cultural constructs, effected by the omnipresent patriarchal biases of our civilization. As Simone de Beauvoir put it, "One is not born, but rather becomes, a woman. . . . It is civilization as a whole that pro-

duces this creature . . . which is described as feminine." The masculine in this fashion has come to be identified as active, dominating, adventurous, rational, creative; the feminine, by systematic opposition to such traits, has come to be identified as passive, acquiescent, timid, emotional, and conventional.

(3) The further claim is that this patriarchal ideology also pervades those writings which, in our culture, have been considered great literature, and which until recently have been written almost entirely by men for men. Typically, the most highly regarded literary works focus on male protagonists—Oedipus, Ulysses, Hamlet, Captain Ahab, Huck Finn—who embody masculine traits and ways of feeling and pursue masculine interests in specifically masculine fields of action; to these, the female characters, when they play a role, are marginal and subordinate, and are represented as complementary, or else as in opposition, to masculine desires and enterprises. Such works, lacking autonomous female role models, and implicitly addressed to male readers, either leave the woman reader an alien outsider or else solicit her to identify against herself by assuming male values and ways of perceiving, feeling, and acting. It is often held, in addition, that the traditional aesthetic categories and *criteria* for analyzing and appraising literary works, although presented as objective, disinterested, and universal, are in fact infused with male assumptions, interests, and ways of reasoning, so that standard critical treatments of literary texts have been tacitly but thoroughly gender-biased.

A major interest of feminist critics in English-speaking countries has been to reconstitute all our dealings with literature so as to do justice to female points of view, concerns, and values. An emphasis has been to alter the way a woman reads our inherited literature, so as to make her not an acquiescent but, in the title of Judith Fetterley's book of 1978, *The Resisting Reader*, that is, one who resists the author's intentions and design in order, by a "revisionary rereading," to bring to light and to counter the covert sexual biases written into a literary work. Another prominent procedure of applied feminist criticism in America and England has been to identify recurrent "images of women," especially in novels and poems written by men. These are often represented as falling into antithetic patterns; on the one side we find idealized projections of men's desires (the Madonna, the Muse, Dante's Beatrice, the pure and innocent virgin, the Victorian Coventry Patmore's "the Angel in the House"); on the other side are demonic projections of men's sexual resentments and terrors (Eve and Pandora as the source of all evil, destructive sensual temptresses such as Delilah and Circe, the malign witch, the castrating mother). While feminist critics have decried much of the literature written by men for its depiction of women as marginal, docile, and subservient to men's interests and emotional needs, a number of them have also praised male writers who, in their view, have managed to rise above the sexual prejudices of their time sufficiently to understand and represent the cultural pressures that have shaped the characters of women and forced upon them their negative or subsidiary social roles; the latter class is said to include, in selected works, such authors as Chaucer, Shakespeare, Samuel Richardson, Ibsen, and Shaw.

Many feminists have concentrated on what Elaine Showalter calls **gynocriticism**—that is, a criticism which concerns itself specifically with writings by women, in all aspects of their production, psychological motivation, analysis, and interpretation, and in all literary forms, including journals and letters. Notable books in this mode include Patricia Meyer Spacks, *The Female Imagination* (1975), on English and American novels of the past three hundred years; Ellen Moers, *Literary Women* (1976), on major women novelists and poets in England, America, and France; Elaine Showalter, *A Literature of Their Own: British Women Novelists from Brontë to Lessing* (1977); and Sandra Gilbert and Susan Gubar, *The Madwoman in the Attic* (1979). This last book stresses especially the psychodynamics of women writers in the nineteenth century. Its authors propose that the "anxiety of authorship," inflicted on nineteenth-century women writers by stereotypes of literary creativity as an exclusively male prerogative, effected in them a psychological duplicity that they projected in the form of a monstrous counterfigure to the heroine, such as Bertha Rochester, the madwoman in Charlotte Brontë's *Jane Eyre;* this figure is "usually in some sense the *author's* double, an image of her own anxiety and rage."

One concern of gynocritics is to define a specifically feminine subject matter in literature written by women—the world of domesticity, for example, or the special experiences of gestation, giving birth, and nurturing, or mother-daughter and woman-woman relations—in which personal and affectional matters, and not external activism, are the primary interest; some critics have attended especially to the literature of lesbian relationships in a heterosexual culture. Another concern is to uncover in literary history a female tradition, expressed by a subcommunity of women writers who are aware of, emulate, and find support in earlier women writers, and who in turn offer models and emotional support to their women readers. A third undertaking is to establish the existence of a distinctively feminine mode of experience, or "subjectivity," in thinking, feeling, valuing, and perceiving oneself and the outer world. Related to this is the attempt (thus far, without widespread agreement about details) to specify the traits of a "woman's language," or distinctively feminine *style* of speech and writing, in sentence structure, types of relations between the elements of a discourse, and characteristic figures and imagery. Some feminists have turned their critical attention to the large body of women's domestic and "sentimental" novels, which are noted perfunctorily and in derogatory fashion in standard literary histories, yet which dominated the market for fiction in the nineteenth century and produced most of the best-sellers of the time; instances are Elaine Showalter's *A Literature of Their Own* (1977) on British writers, and Nina Baym's *Woman's Fiction: A Guide to Novels by and about Women in America, 1820–1870* (1978).

The often professed goal of feminist critics has been to reopen, reorder, and enlarge the literary *canon*—that is, the set of works which, by a cumulative consensus in the past, have come to be considered "major" and to serve as the persistent subjects of literary history, criticism, and scholarship. Feminist studies have served to reveal the literary range and to raise the status of many female authors hitherto more or less scanted by scholars and critics (such as Anne

Finch, George Sand, Elizabeth Barrett Browning, Elizabeth Gaskell, Christina Rossetti, Harriet Beecher Stowe, and Sidonie-Gabrielle Colette) and to bring into purview other authors who have been largely overlooked as subjects for serious criticism (among them Margaret Cavendish, Aphra Behn, Lady Mary Wortley Montagu, Kate Chopin, Charlotte Perkins Gilman, and a number of Black authors such as Zora Neale Hurston). For a study of the novels by women among *Black writers* in America, see Hazel V. Carby, *Reconstructing Womanhood: The Emergence of the Afro-American Woman Novelist* (1987).

American and English critics have for the most part engaged in empirical and thematic studies of writings by and about women. The most prominent feminist critics in France, however, have been occupied with the "theory" of the role of gender in writing, conceptualized within various *poststructural* frames of reference, such as Lacan's linguistic reworkings of Freudian *psychoanalysis*, the *semiotics* of Roland Barthes, and the *deconstruction* of Jacques Derrida. The common focus of these French feminists is a critique of the language which categorizes and structures our selves and the world. English-speaking feminists, for example, have drawn attention to observable evidence that a male bias is encoded in our linguistic conventions; instances include the use of "man" or "mankind" for human beings in general, of "chairman" and "spokesman" for people of either sex, and of the pronouns "he" and "his" to refer back to ostensibly gender-neutral nouns such as "God," "human being," "child," "inventor," "author," "poet" (see Sally McConnell-Ginet, Ruth Borker, and Nelly Furman, eds., *Women and Language in Literature and Society*, 1980). The sweepingly radical claim of French theorists, on the other hand, whatever their differences, is that all Western languages, in all their features, are utterly and irredeemably male-engendered, male-constituted, and male-dominated. Discourse, it is asserted, using a term coined by Derrida, is "phallogocentric"; that is, it is centered and organized throughout by implicit recourse to the phallus both as its supposed "logos," or ground, and as its prime signifier and power source; and not only in its vocabulary and syntax, but also in its rigorous rules of logic, its proclivity for fixed classifications and oppositions, and its criteria for what we take to be valid evidence and objective knowledge. The basic problem for such theorists is to establish the very possibility of a woman's language that will not, when she writes, automatically be appropriated into phallogocentric language, for such appropriation forces her into complicity with the features that impose on females a condition of marginality and subservience, or even linguistic nonentity.

Hélène Cixous, to evade this dilemma, posits the existence of an incipient "feminine writing" (écriture féminine) which has its source in the mother, in that stage of the mother-child relation before the child acquires a conventional language; thereafter, in her view, this prelinguistic potentiality manifests itself in texts, whether written by men or women, which work to undermine and subvert the significations, the logic, and the "closure" to the free play of meanings in our ordinary use of language. Alternatively, Luce Irigaray posits a "woman's language" which evades the male monopoly by establishing as its generative principle, in place of the monolithic phallus, the multiplicity and diversity of the female sexual organs and sexual experiences. Julia Kristeva proposes a "chora," or prelinguistic, pre-Oedipal, and unordered signifying process, centered on the mother, that she labels "semiotic"; this is repressed as we acquire the father-controlled language that she calls "symbolic," but can break out in a revolutionary way—her prime example is avant-garde poetry, whether by women or men—as a "heterogeneous destructive causality" that disrupts and disperses the authoritarian "subject," as well as the oppressive patriarchal order and logic, of our standard discourse, which inescapably consigns woman to a negative and marginal status.

Feminist critical and theoretical writings, although recent, expand yearly in volume and range. There exist already a number of specialized feminist journals and publishing houses, a growing quantity of colleges and universities have programs in women's studies and courses in women's literature and feminist criticism, and increasing place is given to writings by and about women in literary anthologies, periodicals, and conferences. Of the many critical and theoretical innovations of the last quarter-century, the concern with sexual difference in the writing, analysis, and assessment of literature seems destined to have the most prominent and enduring effects on literary history, criticism, and academic instruction, as conducted by men as well as women.

In addition to the books mentioned above, the following works are useful. Sandra M. Gilbert and Susan Gubar, eds., *The Norton Anthology of Literature by Women* (1985)—the editorial materials provide a concise history, as well as biographies and bibliographies, of female authors since the Middle Ages. Histories and critiques of feminist criticism: K. K. Ruthven, *Feminist Literary Studies: An Introduction* (1984); and Toril Moi, *Sexual/Textual Politics: Feminist Literary Theory* (1985)—more than half of this book is devoted to feminist theorists in France. Collections of essays in feminist criticism: Arlyn Diamond and Lee R. Edwards, eds., *The Authority of Experience* (1977); Cheryl L. Brown and Karen Olson, eds., *Feminist Criticism: Essays on Theory, Poetry and Prose* (1978); Mary Jacobus, ed., *Women Writing and Writing about Women* (1979); Elaine Marks and Isabelle de Courtivron, eds., *New French Feminisms* (1980); Gayle Green and Coppelia Kahn, eds., *Making a Difference: Feminist Literary Criticism* (1985); Elaine Showalter, ed., *The New Feminist Criticism* (1985). Among the books by French feminist theorists available in English are Hélène Cixous and Catherine Clement, *The Newly Born Woman* (1986); Luce Irigaray, *Speculum of the Other Woman* (1985), and *This Sex Which Is Not One* (1985); Julia Kristeva, *Desire in Language: A Semiotic Approach to Literature and Art* (1980). For examples in America of the adaptation of Marxist, Freudian, and deconstructive theory to feminist criticism see Gayatri Chakravorty Spivak, "Displacement and the Discourse of Women," in *Displacement: Derrida and After*, ed. Mark Krupnick (1983); and Mary Jacobus, *Reading Woman: Essays in Feminist Criticism* (1986); see also the list of suggested readings under *psychoanalytic criticism.*

Influence and the Anxiety of Influence. Critics and historians of literature have for many centuries dealt with the **influence** of one author upon a later author who is said to adopt, and at the same time to alter, the subject matter, form, or style of the earlier writer. Among traditional topics for discussion, for example, have been the influence of Homer on Virgil, of Spenser on Milton, of Milton on Wordsworth, or of Wordsworth on Wallace Stevens. The **anxiety of influence** is a phrase used by the influential contemporary critic Harold Bloom to identify his radical revision of this standard theory that influence consists in a direct "borrowing," or assimilation, of the materials and features found in earlier writers. Bloom's own view is that influence inescapably involves a drastic distortion of the work of a predecessor, and he uses this concept of influence to deal with the reading as well as the writing of poetry.

In Bloom's theory a poet (especially since the time of Milton) is motivated to write when his imagination is seized upon by a poem or poems of a "precursor," or father-poet. The "belated" poet's attitudes to his precursor, like those in Freud's analysis of the Oedipal relation of son to father, are ambivalent; that is, they are compounded not only of love and admiration but also (since a strong poet feels a compelling need to be autonomous and absolutely original) of hate, envy, and fear of the father-poet's preemption of the son's imaginative space. The belated poet unconsciously safeguards his own sense of autonomy and priority by reading a parent-poem "defensively," in such a way as to distort it beyond his own conscious recognition. Nonetheless, he cannot avoid embodying the malformed parent-poem into his own doomed attempt to write an unprecedentedly original poem; the most that even the best belated poet can achieve is to write a poem so "strong" that it effects an illusion of "priority"—that is, an illusion both that it precedes the father-poem in time and that it exceeds it in greatness.

Bloom identifies six distortive processes which operate in reading a precursor; he calls these processes "revisionary ratios" and defines them mainly on the model of Freud's defense mechanisms (see *psychoanalytic criticism*), although he equates the Freudian concepts with the interpretive devices of the Hebrew Kabbalists, as well as with various types of rhetorical *tropes*, or figurative language. Since in Bloom's view the revisionary ratios are the categories through which all of us necessarily read our precursors, his conclusion is that we can never know "the poem-in-itself"; all interpretation is "a necessary misprision," and all "reading is therefore misprision—or misreading." A "weak misreading" is an attempt (doomed to fail) to get at what a text really means, while a "strong misreading" is one in which an individual reader's defense mechanisms are unconsciously licensed to do violence to the text that the reader undertakes to interpret.

Since Bloom conceives that "every poem is a misinterpretation of a parent poem," he recommends that literary critics practice what he calls **antithetical criticism**—that is, that they learn "to read any poem as its poet's deliberate misinterpretation, *as a poet*, of a precursor poem or of poetry in general." The results of such strong readings will be antithetical both to what the poet himself thought he meant and to what standard weak misreadings have made out the poem to mean. In his own applied criticism, Bloom offers many examples of such antithetical criticism, applied to poets ranging from the eighteenth century to Yeats and Stevens. He is aware that, as a reader, he cannot escape adopting defensive tactics against his own anxiety concerning the influence exerted on him by precursor critics, hence that his own interpretations both of poets and critics are necessarily misreadings. His claim is that his antithetical interpretations are strong, and therefore "interesting," misreadings, and so will take their place in the ceaseless accumulation of misreadings which constitutes the total history both of poetry and of criticism, at least since the seventeenth century—although tragically, as time goes on, with an ever-narrowing sector of strong imaginative possibilities.

Harold Bloom's immediate precursor was Walter Jackson Bate's *The Burden of the Past and the English Poet* (1970), which told the history of the struggles by poets, since 1660, to overcome the inhibitive effect of fear that their predecessors might have exhausted all the possibilities of writing great original poems. Bloom presented his own theory of reading and writing poetry in *The Anxiety of Influence* (1973), then elaborated the theory, and demonstrated its application to diverse poetic texts, in three rapidly successive books, *A Map of Misreading* (1975), *Kabbalah and Criticism* (1975), and *Poetry and Repression* (1976), as well as in writings concerned with individual poets. For analyses and critiques of this theory of literature see M. H. Abrams, "How to Do Things with Texts," *Partisan Review*, 46 (1979); Frank Lentricchia, *After the New Criticism* (1980), Chap. 9; David Fite, *Harold Bloom: The Rhetoric of Romantic Vision* (1985). For a *feminist* application of Bloom's anxiety of influence, see Sandra M. Gilbert and Susan Gubar, *The Madwoman in the Attic* (1980).

Linguistics in Modern Criticism. **Linguistics** is the systematic study of the elements of language and the principles governing their combination and organization. Through the nineteenth century the study of language was known as "philology" and was mainly "comparative" (the analysis of similarities and differences within a family of related languages) and "historical" (the analysis of the evolution of a family of languages, or of changes within a particular language, over a long course of time). This latter study of the changes in language over a span of time has come to be called **diachronic;** the great advances in twentieth-century linguistics came with the shift to the **synchronic** study of the system of a single language at a particular time. A major contributor to modern synchronic linguistics was Ferdinand de Saussure, a French-speaking Swiss whose lectures on language as a self-sufficient system, delivered 1907–11, were published from students' notes in 1916, three years after Saussure's death; these lectures have been translated as *Course in General Linguistics* (1916). Important contributions were also made by American "descriptive" or "structural" linguists, notably Edward Sapir and Leonard Bloomfield, who set out to devise a linguistic theory and vocabulary adequate to analyze, as modes of verbal "behavior," the current state of various American Indian languages; a basic text in American linguistics is Bloomfield's *Language* (1933).

Both Continental and American linguistics have been applied to the analysis of the distinctive uses of language in literary texts (see *Russian formal-*

ism and *stylistics*), and Saussure's systematic procedures in analyzing a language have also been used as a model for analyzing the forms and organization of large-scale literary structures (see *structuralist criticism*). The following linguistic terms and concepts are often employed by current critics and theorists of literature.

Saussure introduced a crucial distinction between langue and parole. A **parole** is any particular utterance, spoken or written. The **langue** is the implicit system of elements, of distinctions and oppositions, and of principles of combination shared by members of a language community, which make it possible for a speaker to produce, and the auditor to understand, a parole. The linguist's primary concern, in Saussure's view, is to establish the nature of the underlying linguistic system, the langue. Noam Chomsky has substituted for Saussure's langue and parole the distinction between **competence** (the tacit knowledge on the part of native speakers who have mastered, or "internalized," the implicit rules of a language system which make possible the generation of well-formed and meaningful sentences) and **performance** (the actual utterance of particular sentences). Competent speakers know how to produce such sentences, without being able to specify the conventions and rules that enable them to do so; the function of the linguist is to identify and make explicit the system of linguistic conventions and rules that the speaker unconsciously puts into practice.

Modern linguists commonly distinguish three aspects which together constitute the **grammar** of a "natural language" (e.g., English, French, Japanese, and so on). (1) **Phonology** is the study of the elementary speech sounds; (2) **morphology** is the study of the organization of speech sounds into the smallest meaningful groups (morphemes and words); and (3) **syntax** is the study of the way that sequences of words are ordered into phrases, clauses, and sentences. Structural linguists usually represent these three aspects as successively higher and more complex levels of organization, in which each level manifests parallel principles of differentiation and ordering. A fourth aspect of language sometimes included within the area of linguistics is **semantics,** the study of the meaning of words and of word combinations in phrases and sentences. In this last area, Saussure introduced the terminology of the *sign* (a single word) as constituted by an inseparable union of **signifier** (the speech sounds or written marks composing the sign) and **signified** (the conceptual meaning of the sign).

(1) One branch of phonology is **phonetics:** the physical description of the elementary speech sounds in all known languages and the way they are produced by the vocal apparatus; the "phonetic alphabet" is a standardized set of symbols for transcribing such speech sounds in any language. Another branch is "phonemics," which deals with **phonemes:** the smallest units of speech sound which, within any one language, are functional—that is, which cannot vary without changing the word of which they form a part into a different word. Thus in the English word represented by the spelling "pin," if we change only the initial speech sound, we get three different words, pin-tin-din; if we change only the medial sound, we get pin-pen-pun; if we change only the final sound, we get

pin-pit-pill. From the matrix of such changes, we determine that each of the individual units represented by the spelling p,t,d; i,e,u; and n,t,l function as differentiating phonemes in the English language. Each language has its own phonemic system, which both overlaps with and diverges from the phonemic system of any other language; the imperfect success that a native speaker in one language, such as German, manifests in adapting his habitual pronunciations to the phonemic system of a different language, such as English, is a major feature of what we identify as a "foreign accent."

Even within a single language, however, a native speaker will vary the pronunciation of a single phonemic unit within different combinations of speech sounds, and will also vary the pronunciation from one utterance to another; still greater phonetic differences are apparent between two native speakers, especially if they speak the **dialects** of diverse regions, or diverse social groups. Saussure proposed the principle that what we identify as "the same phoneme" is not determined by the physical features of the speech sound itself, but by its **difference** from all other phonemes in a language—that is, by our ability to differentiate between a particular speech unit and all other functional speech units within a given linguistic system. Saussure's important claim is that the principle of difference, rather than any "positive" property, functions to establish identity not only for phonemes, but on all levels of linguistic organization, including morphemes, words, syntax, and semantic significations. All these types of items, then, are systemic facts, or identities, only within a single language, and they vary between one language and another. (This claim, that seeming linguistic identities are in fact constituted by networks of differences, has become a central feature in *structuralism*, *semiotics*, and *deconstruction*.)

(2) The next level of analysis, after phonology, is morphology—the combination of phonemes into morphemes and into words. A **morpheme** is the smallest meaningful unit of speech sounds within any one language; that is, a morphemic unit, composed of one or more phonemes, is one which is found to recur in a language with the same, or at least similar, meaning. Some morphemes, such as "man," "open," and "run" in English, constitute complete words; others, however, occur only as parts of words. For example, the noun "grace" is itself a morpheme. If we prefix to the root element, "grace," the morpheme "dis-," it becomes a different word with a sharply different meaning: "disgrace"; if we add to the root the morphemic suffix "-ful," the noun functions as an adjective, "graceful"; if we add to these two morphemes the further suffix, "-ly," the resulting word functions as an adverb, "gracefully"; if we prefix to this form either the morphemic "dis-" or "un-," we get the adverbial words, each composed of four morphemes, "disgracefully" and "ungracefully."

We find also an interesting set of phoneme combinations which do not constitute specific morphemes, yet are experienced by speakers and auditors of English as having a common, though very loose-boundaried, area of meaning. Examples are the initial sounds represented by "fl-" in the set of words "flash, flare, flame, flicker, flimmer," all of which signify a kind of moving light; while in the set "fly, flip, flap, flop, flit, flutter," the same initial sounds all signify a kind of movement in air. The terminal sounds represented by "-ash," as they occur in the set "bash, crash, clash, dash, flash, gash, mash, slash," have an overlapping significance of sudden or violent movement. Such combinations of phonemes are sometimes called "phonetic intensives," or else instances of **sound-symbolism;** they are important components in the type of words, exploited especially by poets, in which sounds seem peculiarly appropriate to their significance. See *onomatopoeia,* and refer to Leonard Bloomfield, *Language* (1933), pp. 244–46; I. A. Richards, *The Philosophy of Rhetoric* (1936), pp. 57–65.

Phonemes, morphemes, and words are all "segments" of the stream of the speech sounds which constitute an utterance. Linguists also distinguish a **suprasegmental** feature of language, consisting of stress, juncture, and intonation, all of which function morphemically, in that they alter the identity and significance of the segments. A shift in **stress**—that is, of relative forcefulness, or loudness, of a component element in an utterance—from the first to the second syllable converts the noun "ínvalid" into the adjective "inválid," and the noun "cónvict" into the verb "convíct." **Juncture** denotes the transition between adjacent speech sounds in an utterance, whether within a word, between words, or between groups of words. Linguists distinguish various functional classes of junctures in English utterances. **Intonation** is the variation of pitch, or voice-melody, in the course of an utterance. We utter the assertion "He is going home" with a different intonation from that of the question "Is he going home?"; and the use of the question-intonation even with the assertive sequence of words "He is going home" will make the sentence function to an auditor not as an assertion, but as a question. Uttering the following three words so as to alter the relative stress in the ways indicated, and at the same time using a variety of intonation-patterns and pauses, will reveal the extent to which suprasegmental features can affect the significance of a sentence constituted by the same words: "I like you." "I líke you." "I like yóu."

(3) The third level of analysis (after the level of phonemes and the level of the combination of phonemes into morphemes and words) is syntax: the combination of words into phrases, clauses, and sentences. Analysis of speech performances (paroles) in any language reveals regularities in such constructions, which are explained by postulating syntactic **rules** that are operative within the linguistic system, or langue, mastered by competent speakers and auditors. (These purely "descriptive" rules, or general regularities, of syntax are to be distinguished from the "prescriptive" rules of grammar which are presented in school handbooks designed to teach the "correct usage" of standard English.) A widely used distinction is that between **paradigmatic** relations (the "vertical" relations between any single word in a sentence and other words, phonologically, syntactically, or semantically similar, that might be substituted for it) and **syntagmatic** relations (the "horizontal" relations which determine the possibilities of putting words in a sequence so as to make a well-formed syntactic unit). The distinction is also made on the phonemic and morphemic levels between paradigmatic relations among single elements and syntagmatic relations of sequences of

elements. This distinction parallels that between metaphoric (vertical) and metonymic (horizontal) relations in analyzing *figurative language.*

Noam Chomsky in *Syntactic Structures* (1951) initiated what is known as "generative-transformational grammar." Chomsky's persistent emphasis is on the central feature he calls "creativity" in language—the fact that a competent native speaker can produce a meaningful sentence which has no precedent in the speaker's earlier linguistic experience, as well as the fact that competent auditors can understand the sentence immediately, though it is equally new to them. To explain this "rule-bound creativity" of a language, the linguist considers native speakers' and listeners' competence to consist in their mastery of a set of generative and transformational rules. This mode of linguistics is called **generative** in that it undertakes to establish a finite system of rules which will suffice to "generate"—in the sense that it will adequately account for—the totality of syntactically "well-formed" sentences that are possible in a given language. It is **transformational** in that it postulates, in the **deep structure** of a language system, a set of "kernel sentences" (such as "John is building a house") which, in accordance with diverse rules of transformation, serve to produce a great variety of sentences on the **surface structure** of a language system (e.g., the passive form "The house is being built by John" and the question form "Is John building a house?" as well as a large number of more complex derivatives from the simple kernel sentence).

For various applications of modern linguistics to literature, see *deconstruction, Russian formalism, semiotics, structuralism,* and *stylistics.* For Saussure's theories see Ferdinand de Saussure, *Course in General Linguistics,* transl. Wade Baskin (1966), and the concise analysis by Jonathan Culler *Ferdinand de Saussure* (rev., 1986). For American linguistics: Leonard Bloomfield, *Language* (1933); Zellig S. Harris, *Structural Linguistics* (2d ed., 1960); George L. Trager and Henry Lee Smith, Jr., *An Outline of English Structure* (1957). On "generative-transformational grammar": Noam Chomsky, *Selected Readings,* ed. J. P. B. Allen and Paul Van Buren (1971); *The Structure of Language,* ed. Jerry A. Fodor and Jerrold J. Katz (1964); John Lyons, *Noam Chomsky* (1970). Useful reviews of Continental and American linguistics and of their applications in literary criticism are included in Karl D. Uitti, *Linguistics and Literary Theory* (1969); William H. Youngren, *Semantics, Linguistics, and Criticism* (1972); Jonathan Culler, *Structuralist Poetics* (1975), and *The Pursuit of Signs* (1981). See Roman Jakobson's influential essay "Linguistics and Poetics," in *Style in Language,* ed. Thomas A. Sebeok (1960).

Marxist Criticism. A Marxist critic grounds his theory and practice on the economic and cultural theory of Karl Marx and his fellow-thinker Friedrich Engels, especially on the following claims: (1) "In the last analysis," the evolving history of humanity, its institutions, and its ways of thinking are determined by the changing mode of its "material production"—that is, of its basic economic organization. (2) Historical changes in the fundamental mode of production effect essential changes both in the constitution and the power relations of social classes, which carry on a conflict for economic, political, and social advantage. (3) Human consciousness in any era is constituted by an **ideology**—that is, a set of concepts, beliefs, values, and ways of thinking and feeling through which human beings perceive, and by which they explain, what they take to be reality. An ideology was often represented by Marx, in figurative terms, as a "superstructure" that, in a complex "dialectical" way, is generated by a "base," or "infrastructure," which is the socioeconomic system. The varied ideologies of social classes in particular eras are judged to be illusory or mistaken, in contrast to the true "scientific" (that is, Marxist) knowledge of the material determinants, the historical evolution, the present condition and class structure, and the classless future of social reality. In our current capitalist era the dominant cultural ideology is that which is held and successfully propagated by the "bourgeoisie"—the class of owners of the material means of production, as distinguished from the "proletariat," or wage-earning working class; this ideology has the primary, although concealed, function of legitimizing and sustaining the position and interests of the ruling social class. Bourgeois ideology permeates the religion, morality, philosophy, politics, and legal system of the present historical period; in a less direct and more subtle way, it also permeates our art and literature. All these cultural institutions not only manifest ideological components but are themselves to be regarded as diverse products of the reigning ideology.

In accordance with some version of these views, a Marxist critic typically undertakes to "explain" the literature in any era by revealing the economic, class, and ideological determinants of the way an author writes, and to examine the relation of the resulting literary product to the social reality of that time and place. What some Marxist critics themselves derogate as "vulgar Marxism" treats most literary works of our age as thoroughly dominated by bourgeois ideology, and demands instead a "social realism" which will represent the "true" reality and progressive forces of our era; in practice, this has often turned out to be the demand that literature conform to the official party line (see *socialist realism*). More flexible Marxists, on the other hand, building plausibly upon fragmentary comments about art and literature in Marx and Engels themselves, allow literature some degree of autonomy, and claim also that the greatest literary masters of the capitalist era have been able to transcend their bourgeois ideology sufficiently to represent (or in the frequent Marxist equivalent, to **reflect**) the truly "objective" reality of the class conflict, the social "contradictions," and the alienation of the individual under capitalism. (See *imitation*.) For example, the Hungarian thinker Georg Lukács, the most widely influential of Marxist critics, proposed that each great work of literature creates "its own world," which is unique and seemingly distinct from "everyday reality." But a master of realism in the novel such as Balzac or Tolstoy, by "bringing to life the greatest possible richness of the objective conditions of life," and by creating "typical" characters who manifest to an extreme the essential tendencies and determinants of the epoch, in fact—and "in opposition to [the author's] own conscious ideology"—produces a fictional world which is a "reflection of life in its total motion, as process and totality"; that is, a fictional world which accords with the Marxist conception of present and future history. (Georg Lukács, "Art and Objective Truth," in *Writer and Critic and Other Essays*, transl. 1970; the volume also includes Lukács' useful review of the foundational tenets of Marxist criticism, in "Marx and Engels on Aesthetics.")

Lukács, while lauding literary realism, attacked modernist experimental writers as "decadent" examples of the narrow concern with the subjectivity of the alienated individual in the fragmented world of our late stage of capitalism. The "Frankfurt School" of German Marxists such as Theodor Adorno and Herbert Marcuse, on the other hand, elevated the status of modernist writers such as Proust and Beckett, proposing that their formal experiments, by the very fact that they fragment and disrupt the life they "reflect," establish a distance and effect a detachment which serve as an implicit critique—or yield a "negative knowledge"—of the dehumanizing operations of society under capitalism.

Two other rather maverick German Marxists, Brecht and Benjamin, who also support modernist and nonrealistic art, have had considerable influence on non-Marxist as well as Marxist criticism. In his critical theory, and in his own dramatic writings (see *epic theater*), Bertolt Brecht rejected what he called the "Aristotelian" concept of a tragic play as an imitation of reality that has a unified plot and a universal theme and establishes an identification, or *empathy*, of the audience with the hero which produces a catharsis of the spectator's emotions. (See Aristotle, under *tragedy* and *plot*.) Brecht proposes instead that the illusion of reality should be deliberately shattered by the use of an episodic plot, by protagonists who do not attract the audience's sympathy, by emphasizing theatricality in staging and acting, and by other ways of producing *estrangement effects* that will jar audiences out of their complacent acceptance of modern capitalist society as a natural way of life into an attitude not only (as in Adorno) of critical understanding, but of active engagement with the forces of change. Another notable critic, Walter Benjamin, was both an admirer of Brecht and briefly an associate of the Frankfurt School. Particularly influential was Benjamin's emphasis, not on the relation of the content of a work of art to reality, but on the relation of the work to the changing conditions of the production of art itself, and particularly to the technological developments that have recently promoted "a revolutionary criticism of traditional concepts of art." In his essay "The Work of Art in the Age of Mechanical Reproduction," Benjamin proposes that modern technical innovations in artistic media—such as photography, the phonograph, the radio, and especially the cinema—have transformed the very concept and status of a work of art. Formerly an artist or author produced a work which was a single object, the special preserve of the bourgeois élite, around which developed a quasi-religious "aura" of uniqueness, autonomy, and aesthetic value independent of any social function—an aura which invites in the spectator a passive attitude of absorbed contemplation in the object itself. The new technical media not only make possible the infinite reproducibility of single objects of art, but effect the production of works which, like motion pictures, are designed for reproducibility. Such modes of art, Benjamin argues, not only destroy the traditional aura and ritual contemplation of the unique work, but open the way to "the formulation of revolutionary demands in the politics of art." (A useful collection of central essays by the Marxist critics Lukács, Brecht, Benjamin, and Adorno is R. Taylor, ed., *Aesthetics and Politics*, 1977.)

The Soviet critic Mikhail Bakhtin, although his writings go back to the '20s and '30s, remained largely unknown to the West until he attracted wide attention through recent translations. Bakhtin's emphasis was on language and discourse as themselves areas of societal conflict, and especially on the ways that the use of discourse in a literary work may disrupt the authority of a single voice. In *Problems of Dostoevsky's Poetics* (1929, expanded ed. 1963) he contrasts the "monologic" novels of writers such as Tolstoy, in which, according to Bakhtin, the voices of all the characters are subordinated to the authoritative voice and controlling purpose of the author, to the **dialogic** or "polyphonic" form created by Dostoevsky, which—in a way similar to various modes, which Bakhtin calls "carnivalistic," in classical, medieval, and Renaissance culture—liberates characters to speak "a plurality of independent and unmerged voices and consciousnesses, a genuine polyphony of fully valid voices." In the long essay "Discourse on the Novel" (1934–35), included in *The Dialogic Imagination*, transl., 1981, Bakhtin expands his earlier view, arguing that the "dialogic" form is characteristic of the novel in general, as distinguished from earlier literary genres.

In the last few decades there has been a resurgence of Marxist criticism, marked by an openness, on some level of literary analysis, to other current critical methods; a flexibility which acknowledges that Marxist critical theory is itself to some degree not a set of timeless truths but an evolving historical process; a subtilizing of the concept of ideology as applied to literary content and form; and a tendency to grant increased independence to internal, or artistic, determinants of literary structures. In the 1960s the influential French Marxist Louis Althusser assimilated the *structuralism* then current in France to his view that the social structure as a whole is constituted by diverse "nonsynchronous" structures, including literature; each of these, although interrelated in complex ways, possesses a "relative autonomy" and is determined by the material, or economic, basis only "in the last instance." A great work of literature is not a mere manifestation of ideology, for its fiction establishes a distance that serves to expose "the ideology from which it is born . . . from which it detaches itself as art, and to which it alludes." Pierre Macherey, in *A Theory of Literary Production* (1966), proposes that a literary text not only distances itself from its ideology by its fiction and form, but also reveals the "contradictions" inherent in that ideology by its "silences" or "gaps." Such textual "absences" are symptoms of repressions within the text of its own "unconscious." The aim of a Marxist critic, Macherey asserts, is to make these silences "speak" and so to make explicit, in opposition to the conscious intention of its author, the text's unconscious content—that is, its repressed awareness of the flaws and incoherence in the very ideology that it incorporates.

In England the many social and critical writings of Raymond Williams demonstrate an adaptation of Marxist concepts to his humanistic concern with the overall texture of an individual's "lived experience." The leading theorist of Marxist criticism in England is Terry Eagleton, who has expanded and elaborated the views of Althusser and Macherey about the way that a literary work assimilates and alters the ideology of its era at the same time that, by its artful distancing, it exposes the illusions, incoherencies, and limits of that ideology; in recent years, Eagleton has been increasingly hospitable to the tactical use, in dealing with ideology in literature, of concepts derived from *deconstruction*, Lacan's version of Freudian *psychoanalysis*, and current *feminist criticism*. The most prominent American theorist, Fredric Jameson, is also the most eclectic of current Marxist critics. In *The Political Unconscious: Narrative as a Socially Symbolic Act* (1981), Jameson expressly adapts to his critical enterprise such seemingly incompatible viewpoints as the medieval theory of fourfold levels of meaning in the *allegorical interpretation* of the Bible, the *archetypal criticism* of Northrop Frye, *structuralist criticism*, Lacan's reinterpretations of Freud, *semiotics*, and *deconstruction*. These methods are applicable at various stages of the critical interpretation of a literary work; but Marxism, he contends, "subsumes" all the other "interpretive modes," by retaining their positive findings in a "political interpretation of literary texts" which is the "final" or "absolute horizon of all reading and all interpretation." This "political interpretation" involves the revelation in a literary text of the hidden role of the "political unconscious," a concept which Jameson describes as his "collective," or "political," rendering of the Freudian concept that each individual's unconscious is a repository of repressed desires. In a literary work of our capitalist era the "rifts and discontinuities" in the text, as well as those elements of a text which are its "non-dit" (its not-said), are symptoms of the repression into the political unconscious of "History"; and this repressed History, he asserts, is that of the process through the ages of "the collective struggle to wrest a realm of Freedom from a realm of Necessity." In the final stage of a Marxist interpretation, according to Jameson, a critic "rewrites," in the mode of "allegory," "the literary text in such a way that the [text] may be seen as the . . . reconstruction of a prior historical or ideological *subtext*"—that is, of the text's unspoken, because repressed and unconscious, awareness of the ways it is determined both by current ideology and by the overall process of true "History."

See *sociology of literature*. Further references: Louis Althusser, *Lenin and Philosophy, and Other Essays* (1969, transl. 1971); Raymond Williams, *Culture and Society, 1780–1950* (1960), and *Marxism and Literature* (1977); Peter Demetz, *Marx, Engels and the Poets: Origins of Marxist Literary Criticism* (1967); Walter Benjamin, *Illuminations* (transl., 1968); Lee Baxandall and Stefan Morawski, eds., *Marx and Engels on Literature and Art* (1973); Terry Eagleton, *Criticism and Ideology* (1976), and *Marxism and Literary Criticism* (1976)—the latter is a useful introduction to Marxist criticism; Fredric Jameson, *Marxism and Form* (1971); J. J. McGann, *The Romantic Ideology* (1983); Chris Bullock and David Peck, eds., *Guide to Marxist Literary Criticism* (1980); J. G. Merquior, *Western Marxism* (1986). Various essays by Gayatri Chakravorty Spivak assimilate Marxist concepts both to *deconstruction* and to the viewpoint of *feminist criticism;* see her "Displacement and the Discourse of Women," in *Displacement: Derrida and After*, ed. Mark Krupnick (1983). For a sharp critique of recent theorists of Marxist criticism, see Frederick Crews, "Dialectical Immaterialism," in *Skeptical Engagements* (1986).

New Criticism. This term became current after the publication of John Crowe Ransom's book *The New Criticism* (1941). It came to be applied to a widespread tendency in American criticism, deriving in part from various elements in I. A. Richards' *Principles of Literary Criticism* (1924) and *Science and Poetry* (1926), and from the critical essays of T. S. Eliot, and directed against the prevailing concern of scholars and critics of that era with the lives and psychology of authors, with social background, and with literary history. Notable critics in this mode are the southerners Cleanth Brooks and Robert Penn Warren; their textbook *Understanding Poetry*, first published in 1938, did much to make the New Criticism the reigning point of view in American colleges, and even in high schools, for two or three decades. Other prominent writers of that time who, despite many individual differences, are often identified as New Critics are Allen Tate, R. P. Blackmur, and William K. Wimsatt. An important English critic, F. R. Leavis, in his emphasis on the detailed analysis of individual works and passages, shared some critical tenets and practices with these Americans.

The New Critics differ from one another in many ways, but the following points of view and procedures are common to many of them. (1) A poem, it is held, should be treated as such—in Eliot's words, "primarily as poetry and not another thing"—and should therefore be regarded as an independent and self-sufficient object. The first law of criticism, John Crowe Ransom said, "is that it shall be objective, shall cite the nature of the object" and shall recognize "the autonomy of the work itself as existing for its own sake." (See *objective criticism* and *formalism.*) New Critics warn the reader against critical practices which depart from a focus on the object itself (see *intentional fallacy* and *affective fallacy*), and in analyzing and evaluating a particular work, they eschew reference to the biography of the author, to the social conditions at the time of its production, or to its psychological and moral effects on the reader; they also tend to minimize recourse to the place of the work in the history of literary forms and subject matter. (2) The distinctive procedure of the New Critic is **explication,** or **close reading:** the detailed and subtle analysis of the complex interrelations and *ambiguities* (multiple meanings) of the components within a work. "Explication de texte" has long been a formal procedure for teaching literature in French schools, but the distinctive explicative procedure of the New Criticism derives from such books as I. A. Richards' *Practical Criticism* (1929) and William Empson's *Seven Types of Ambiguity* (1930). (3) The principles of the New Criticism are basically verbal. That is, literature is conceived to be a special kind of language whose attributes are defined by systematic opposition to the language of science and of practical and logical discourse; the key concepts of this criticism deal with the meanings and interactions of words, *figures of speech*, and *symbols*. There is emphasis on the "organic unity" of structure and meaning, and warnings against separating the two by what Cleanth Brooks has called "the heresy of paraphrase." (4) The distinction between literary *genres*, although casually recognized, is not essential in the New Criticism. The basic components of any work of literature, whether lyric, narrative, or dramatic, are conceived to be words, images, and symbols rather than character, thought, and plot. These linguistic elements are often said to be organized around a central and humanly significant *theme*, and to manifest "*tension*," "*irony*," and "*paradox*," within a structure which is a "reconciliation of diverse impulses" or an "equilibrium of opposed forces." The form of a work, whether or not it has characters and plot, is said to be primarily a "structure of meanings," and to develop into an integral and freestanding unity mainly through a play and counterplay of evolving "thematic imagery" and "symbolic action."

The basic orientation and modes of analysis in the New Criticism were adopted in the **contextual criticism** of Eliseo Vivas and Murray Krieger. Krieger defined contextualism as "the claim that the poem is a tight, compelling, finally closed context," which prevents "our escape to the world of reference and action beyond," and requires that we "judge the work's efficacy as an aesthetic object." (See Krieger, *The New Apologists for Poetry*, 1956, and *Theory of Criticism*, 1976.) The revolutionary thrust of the new mode, however, had lost much of its force by the late 1950s, when a number of New Critics began to reassay and broaden their critical premises and procedures, but it has left a permanent mark on the criticism and teaching of literature, in its primary emphasis on the individual work as such and in the variety and subtlety of the devices that it made available for the analysis of a literary text. This emphasis on close reading survives, for example, even in the radical mode of current literary criticism known as *deconstruction*.

Central instances of the theory and practice of the New Criticism are Cleanth Brooks, *The Well Wrought Urn* (1947), and W. K. Wimsatt, *The Verbal Icon* (1954). Robert W. Stallman's *Critiques and Essays in Criticism, 1920–1948* (1949) is a convenient collection of essays in this critical mode; the literary journal *The Explicator* (1942 ff.), devoted to close reading, is a characteristic product of its approach to literary texts, as are the items listed in *Poetry Explication: A Checklist of Interpretation Since 1924 of British and American Poems Past and Present*, ed. Joseph M. Kuntz (rev., 1962). See also Wimsatt, ed., *Explication as Criticism* (1963), and the review of the movement by René Wellek, *A History of Modern Criticism*, Vol. 6 (1986). Critiques of the theory and methods of the New Criticism: R. S. Crane, ed., *Critics and Criticism, Ancient and Modern* (1952), and *The Languages of Criticism and the Structure of Poetry* (1953); Gerald Graff, *Poetic Statement and Critical Dogma* (1970); and (on contextual criticism also) Grant Webster, *The Republic of Letters: A History of Postwar American Literary Opinion* (1979); Frank Lentricchia, *After the New Criticism* (1980), Chap. 6.

Phenomenology and Criticism. The modern philosophical perspective and method called **phenomenology** was established by the German thinker Edmund Husserl (1859–1938). Husserl set as his philosophical task to describe precisely human consciousness—that is, to describe the concrete "Lebenswelt" (lived world) as this is experienced independently of all prior suppositions, whether these suppositions come from philosophy or from common sense. He finds that consciousness is always **intentional.** By "intentional" he does not mean that it is deliberately willed, but that it is always directed to an "object"; in other words, to be conscious is always to be conscious of something. Husserl's claim is that in this unitary act of consciousness, the thinking subject and the object it "intends" or is aware of are interinvolved and inseparable. In order to be free of all prior conceptions, the phenomenological analysis of consciousness begins with an **epoché** (suspension) of all presuppositions about the nature of experience, and this suspension involves "bracketing" (holding in abeyance) any judgment as to whether or not the object of consciousness is real—that is, whether or not the object exists outside the consciousness which "intends" it.

Phenomenology has had widespread influence since it was put forward by Husserl in 1900 and later, and has been diversely developed by Martin Heidegger in Germany and Maurice Merleau-Ponty in France. It has greatly influenced Gadamer and other theorists concerned with analyzing the conscious activity of understanding language (see *interpretation and hermeneutics*), and has, directly or indirectly, affected the way in which many critics analyze specific works of literature.

In the 1930s the Polish theorist Roman Ingarden (1893–1970), who wrote his books both in Polish and German, adapted the phenomenological viewpoint and concepts to a theory of the way we experience a work of literature. In Ingarden's analysis, a literary work of art originates in the intentional acts of consciousness of its author—"intentional" in the phenomenological sense that they are directed toward an object. These intentional acts are recorded in a text, and so make it possible for a reader to reexperience the work in his or her own consciousness. The recorded literary work contains many elements which are potential rather than fully realized, as well as many "places of indeterminacy" in what it sets forth. An "active reading" responds to the sequence of the printed words by a temporal process of consciousness which "fills out" these potential and indeterminate aspects of the text, and in so doing, in Ingarden's term, **concretizes** the schematic work of literature. Such a reading is said to be "co-creative" with the conscious processes recorded by the author, and to result in the reader's consciousness of an actualized "aesthetic object," invested with values, which does not portray a reality that exists independently of the work, but a "quasi-reality"—that is to say, a fictional world. See Roman Ingarden, *The Literary Work of Art* (1931, transl. 1973), and *The Cognition of the Literary Work of Art* (1937, transl. 1973). For German critics strongly influenced by Ingarden, see Wolfgang Iser under *reader-response criticism,* and Hans Robert Jauss under *reception-theory.*

The term "phenomenological criticism" is often applied to the theory and practice of the **Geneva School** of critics, most of whose members taught at the University of Geneva, and all of whom are joined by friendship, interinfluence, and their general approach to literature. The older members of the Geneva School were Marcel Raymond and Albert Beguin; later members were Jean Rousset, Jean-Pierre Richard, and (currently the dominant figure) Georges Poulet. J. Hillis Miller, who for six years was a colleague of Poulet at Johns Hopkins University, was in his earlier career (before turning instead to *deconstructive criticism*) the leading American representative of the Geneva School of criticism, and applied this critical mode to the analysis of various American and English authors.

Geneva critics read a work of literature as the verbalized embodiment of the unique mode of consciousness of its author. In its approach to literature as primarily subjective, this criticism is opposed to the objective approach of *formalism,* both in its European variety and in American *New Criticism.* Its roots instead go back through the nineteenth century to that type of romantic *expressive criticism* which regarded a literary work as the revelation of the personality of its author and proposed that the awareness of this personality is the chief aim and value of reading literature. (As early as 1778, for example, the German critic Herder wrote: "This *living reading,* this divination into the soul of the author, is the sole mode of reading, and the most profound means of self-development.") In the course of time, however, Geneva critics absorbed a number of the concepts and methods of Husserl, Heidegger, and other phenomenologists. In the view of these critics the "cogito," or consciousness, of the author—related to, but not identical with, the author's "empirical," or biographical, self—pervades a work of literature, manifesting itself as the subjective correlate of the "contents" of the work; that is, of the objects, characters, imagery, and style in which the author's personal mode of awareness and feeling imaginatively projects itself. (For a related critical concept see *voice;* also, refer to *objective and subjective.*) By emptying their own minds of all personal prepossessions and particularities, the readers of a literary work make themselves purely receptive, and so achieve participation, or even identity, with the immanent consciousness of its author. The undertaking to read a work so as to experience the mode of consciousness of its author, and then to reproject this consciousness in the critic's own writing, underlies the frequent application to the Geneva School of the term **critics of consciousness** and the description of their critical aim as "consciousness of the consciousness of another." As Georges Poulet put it in "Phenomenology of Reading" (1969): "When I read as I ought . . . with the total commitment required of any reader," then "I am thinking the thoughts of another. . . . But I think it as my very own. . . . My consciousness behaves as though it were the consciousness of another." (It should be noted that whereas the philosopher Husserl's aim was to describe the essential features of consciousness which are common to all human beings, the Geneva critic's quite different aim is to identify—and also to identify oneself with—the unique consciousness of each individual author.)

Within this framework, Geneva critics differ in the extent to which they attend to specific elements in the contents, formal structure, and style of a text, on their way toward isolating the author's "interior" mode of consciousness. A conspicuous tendency in most of these critics is to put together widely separated passages within a single work, on the principle, as J. Hillis Miller says in his book *Charles Dickens,* that since these passages "reveal the persistence of certain obsessions, problems, and attitudes," the critic may, by analyzing them, "glimpse the original unity of a creative mind." Furthermore, the critics of consciousness often disregard the structure of a single work as an independent entity; instead, they treat the total body of an author's writings, as Miller in discussing Dickens said, in order "to identify what persists through all the swarming multiplicity of his novels as a view of the world which is unique and the same." Georges Poulet has also undertaken, in a number of books, to tell the history of the varying imaginative treatments of the topic of time throughout Western literature, as expressing diverse modes of lived experience. In these histories Poulet sets out to identify "for each epoch a consciousness common to all contemporary minds"; he claims, however, that within this shared period-consciousness, the consciousness of each author succeeds in showing its uniqueness.

Robert R. Magliola, *Phenomenology and Literature* (1977), deals with various types of phenomenological poetics and criticism in the context of an exposition of Husserl, Heidegger, and other phenomenological philosophers. Brief introductions to the Geneva School of criticism are Georges Poulet, "Phenomenology of Reading," *New Literary History*, 1 (1969–70); J. Hillis Miller, "The Geneva School . . . ," in *Modern French Criticism*, ed. J. K. Simon (1972). In "Geneva or Paris? The Recent Work of Georges Poulet," *University of Toronto Quarterly*, 39 (1970), Miller manifests his own transition from the criticism of consciousness to the very different critical mode called *deconstruction*. A detailed study of the Geneva School is Sarah Lawall's *Critics of Consciousness: The Existential Structures of Literature* (1968); see also Michael Murray, *Modern Critical Theory: A Phenomenological Introduction* (1976). Among the books of Geneva critics and other critics of consciousness available in English are Georges Poulet, *Studies in Human Time* (1949), *The Interior Distance* (1952), and *The Metamorphoses of the Circle* (1961); Jean Starobinski, *The Invention of Liberty, 1700–1789* (1964); J. Hillis Miller, *Charles Dickens: The World of His Novels* (1959), *The Disappearance of God* (1963), and *Poets of Reality* (1965). Other critical works influenced by phenomenology are Paul Brodtkorb, *Ishmael's White World: A Phenomenological Reading of Moby Dick* (1965); David Halliburton, *Edgar Allan Poe: A Phenomenological View* (1973); and Edward W. Said, *Joseph Conrad and the Fiction of Autobiography* (1975).

Psychological and Psychoanalytic Criticism. Psychological criticism deals with a work of literature primarily as an expression, in fictional form, of the personality, state of mind, feelings, and desires of its author. This approach emerged in the early decades of the nineteenth century, congruently with the romantic replacement of earlier mimetic and pragmatic views by an *expressive* view of the nature of literature; see *criticism*. By 1827 Thomas Carlyle could say that the usual question "with the best of our own critics at present" is one "mainly of a psychological sort, to be answered by discovering and delineating the peculiar nature of the poet from his poetry." During the Romantic Period, we find widely practiced all three variants of the critical procedures (still current today) that are based on the assumption that a work of literature is correlated with its author's mental traits: (1) reference to the author's personality in order to explain and interpret a literary work; (2) reference to literary works in order to establish, biographically, the personality of the author; and (3) the mode of reading a literary work itself as a way of experiencing the distinctive subjectivity, or consciousness, of its author (see *critics of consciousness*). We even find that John

Keble, in the series of Latin lectures *On the Healing Power of Poetry*—published in 1844, but delivered more than ten years earlier—proposed a thoroughgoing proto-Freudian literary theory. "Poetry," Keble claimed, "is the indirect expression . . . of some overpowering emotion, or ruling taste, or feeling, the direct indulgence whereof is somehow repressed"; this repression is imposed by the author's sentiments of "reticence" and "shame"; the conflict between the need for expression and the compulsion to repress such self-revelation is resolved by the poet's ability to give "healing relief to secret mental emotion, yet without detriment to modest reserve" by a literary "art which under certain veils and disguises . . . reveals the fervent emotions of the mind"; and this disguised mode of self-expression serves as "a safety valve, preserving men from madness." (The emergence and the varieties of romantic psychological criticism are described in M. H. Abrams, *The Mirror and the Lamp*, 1953, Chaps. 6 and 9.) In the present era many critics make at least passing references to the psychology of an author in discussing literary products, with the exception of those—see *formalists, New Critics, structuralists*—whose critical premises invalidate such reference. (For a debate concerning the relevance of the psychology of an author to literary criticism, see C. S. Lewis and E. M. W. Tillyard, *The Personal Heresy in Criticism*, 1934.)

Since the 1920s, a very widespread psychological approach to literature has come to be **psychoanalytic criticism,** whose premises and procedures were established by Sigmund Freud (1856–1939). Freud had developed the dynamic form of psychology that he called **psychoanalysis** as a means of therapy for neuroses, but soon expanded it to account for many developments in the history of civilization, including warfare, mythology, religion, and the arts. Freud's brief comment on the artist's imagination at the end of the twenty-third lecture of his *Introduction to Psychoanalysis* (1920), supplemented by relevant passages in the other lectures in that book, set forth what became the standard theoretical framework of psychoanalytic criticism: Literature and the other arts, as well as daydreams, nightdreams, and neurotic symptoms, consist primarily of the imagined, or fantasied, fulfillment of desires which are either denied by reality or are prohibited by the standards of morality and propriety that have been established by society. The forbidden, mainly sexual ("libidinal") desires come into conflict with, and are repressed by, the "censor" (the internalized representative of social standards) into the unconscious realm of the artist's mind, but are permitted by the censor to achieve fantasied satisfaction in distorted or disguised forms which serve to conceal their real nature and objects from the conscious ego. The chief mechanisms of such distortions are (1) "condensation" (the omission of parts of the unconscious material and the fusion of several unconscious elements into a single whole); (2) "displacement" (the substitution for an unconscious object of desire by one that is socially acceptable); and (3) "symbolism" (the representation of repressed, mainly sexual objects of desire by nonsexual objects which resemble them or are associated with them). The disguised fantasies that are evident to consciousness constitute the "manifest" content of a dream or work of literature; the unconscious wishes and their objects which are expressed in this distorted form are the "latent" content. The unconscious also harbors stages of psychosexual development, from earliest infancy onward, which have been outgrown by the mature person, but remain as "fixations" in the unconscious; when activated by some later event, these fixations may achieve disguised expression in fantasy, whether in the mode of dreams, neurotic symptoms, or literature. The chief enterprise of psychoanalytic criticism, consonant with the enterprise of the psychoanalyst in his therapeutic function, is to reveal the true content, and also to explain the effect on the reader, of a literary work by translating its manifest elements back into their latent, unconscious determinants.

Freud also asserts, however, that the artist possesses abilities in addition to the universal human ability to fantasize and dream, and that these abilities serve to differentiate the artist radically from the patently neurotic personality. The artistic person, for example, possesses to an especially high degree the power to "sublimate" (that is, to shift the instinctual drives from their original sexual goals to nonsexual "higher" goals, including the discipline of a particular art); the ability to elaborate fantasied wish-fulfillments in a way that conceals or deletes their personal or egoistic elements, and so makes them capable of satisfying the unconscious desires of people other than the individual artist; a greater than normal ability to disguise the despised unconscious content in the manifest features of a work of art; and a "puzzling" ability—which Freud elsewhere says that psychoanalysis cannot explain—to mold the artistic medium into "a faithful image of the creatures of his imagination," as well as into a satisfying artistic form. The result is a fantasied wish-fulfillment of a complex sort that not only allows the artist to overcome, at least partially and temporarily, personal conflicts and repressions, but also makes it possible for the artist's audience "to obtain solace and consolation from their own unconscious sources of gratification which had become inaccessible" to them. Literature and art, therefore, unlike dreams and neuroses, may serve the artist as a mode of fantasy that opens "the way back to reality." This outline of the psychoanalytic view of art was elaborated, but not radically altered, by Freud's later developments in his theory of mental structure, dynamics, and processes; he has himself summarized these developments, with his remarkable power for clear and dramatic exposition, in *New Introductory Lectures on Psychoanalysis* (1933) and *An Outline of Psychoanalysis* (1939).

Freud asserted that many of his insights had been anticipated by great authors in the Western literary tradition, and himself applied psychoanalysis to brief discussions of the latent content in characters or episodes of Shakespeare's *Hamlet, Macbeth, A Midsummer Night's Dream,* and *King Lear;* he also wrote a brilliant analysis of Dostoevsky's *The Brothers Karamazov* and a full-length study, *Delusion and Dream* (1917), of a novel, *Gradiva,* by the Danish writer Wilhelm Jensen. Especially since the 1930s there has been a flood of psychoanalytic criticism of literary authors and works. One of the best-known books in this mode is *Hamlet and Oedipus* (1949) by the psychoanalyst Ernest Jones. Building on earlier suggestions of Freud, Jones explains Hamlet's inability to make up his mind to kill his uncle as the result of the working of his **Oedipus complex**—that is, the repressed but continuing presence in the adult's unconscious of the infant's desire to possess his mother and to have his rival, the father, out of the way. (The term is derived from Sophocles' Greek tragedy *Oedipus the King*, whose protagonist has unknowingly killed his father and married his mother.) Jones then proposes that Hamlet's conflict is "an echo of a similar one in Shakespeare himself," and goes on to account for the audience's powerful response to the play, over the centuries, as a result of the repressed Oedipal conflict that is shared by all men. In more recent decades there has been increasing emphasis by psychoanalytic critics, in a mode suggested by Freud's later writings, on the role of "ego psychology" in elaborating the manifest content and artistic form of a work of literature; that is, on the way that the "ego" consciously manages to mediate and adjust the conflicting demands of the sexual instincts and unconscious compulsions (the "id"), the prohibitions of the "superego," and the limited possibilities for satisfying desires offered by reality. On such recent developments see Frederic C. Crews, "Literature and Psychology," in *Relations of Literary Study*, ed. James Thorpe (1967), and the issue on "Psychology and Literature: Some Contemporary Directions" in *New Literary History*, 12 (1980). Psychoanalytic criticism has been applied to the analysis of the personal dynamics both of the author of a literary work and to characters within that work. Norman Holland is the chief contemporary exponent of the application of psychoanalytic concepts to explain also the diverse responses of individual readers to a literary text; see *reader-response criticism.*

The term **psychobiography** has come to be applied to the procedure of writing the life of an author (see *biography*) which stresses the subject's psychological development, by reference both to external evidence and to evidence in the author's own writings; its procedure is to advert to unconscious and disguised motivations and dynamics in the formation of the author's character, often in accord with a version, or a revision, of the Freudian theory of psychosexual development. A major exemplar of the current mode was Erik H. Erikson's *Young Man Luther* (1958), in which Erikson stressed the importance of Luther's adolescent "identity crisis." Notable instances of literary psychobiography are Leon Edel, *Henry James* (5 vols.; 1953–72), and Justin Kaplan, *Mark Twain and His World* (1974).

Prominent examples of the varied applications of psychoanalytic criticism are in the collections listed below; it should be noted, however, that almost all modern literary critics, like almost all modern authors, owe some debt to Freud, while such important critics as Kenneth Burke, Edmund Wilson, and Lionel Trilling have assimilated central Freudian concepts into their overall critical procedures. In addition, recent literary "theorists" have made considerable, although diverse, use of Freud's views, including some *structuralist, poststructuralist,* and *Marxist critics,* but especially Harold Bloom, whose theory of the defensive "revisionary ratios," by which belated poets "misread" a precursor father-poet and disguise his presence in their own poems, is based in considerable part on Freud's concepts of the Oedipus complex and of the defense mechanisms operative in dreams and the literary imagination; see *influence and the anxiety of influence.* Jacques Lacan, "the French Freud," is a structuralist who developed a linguistic reinterpretation of Freud, restating Freud's basic concepts in terms derived from the analysis of language by Saussure and Jakobson; typical is his oft-quoted dictum "The unconscious is structured like a language." (See *structuralist criticism,* and the issue devoted to Lacan, "Literature and Psychoanalysis," *Yale French Studies,* No. 55/56, 1977.) Lacan's views have been especially influential for some leading French proponents of *feminist criticism.*

Carl G. Jung is sometimes called a psychoanalyst, but although he began as a disciple of Freud, his mature version of depth-psychology is very different from that of his predecessor. Jung posits the existence of a "racial memory" and of a "collective unconscious," which find expression both in myths and dreams and in major works of literature. He does not view literature as a form of wish-fulfillment which provides a way back from incipient neurosis to reality. Instead, he conceives a great author as possessing, and providing for readers, access to essential aspects of the human psyche which, although necessary to self-integration and human well-being, would otherwise remain buried as primordial images in the racial unconscious. Jung's theories have had an important formative effect on *archetypal criticism* and *myth criticism.* See Jung, *Contributions to Analytic Psychology* (1928), and *Modern Man in Search of a Soul* (1933); also Edward Glover, *Freud or Jung* (1950).

Some of Freud's psychoanalytic writings on literature and the arts have been collected by Benjamin Nelson, ed., *Sigmund Freud on Creativity and the Unconscious* (1958). Anthologies of psychoanalytic criticism by various authors are William Phillips, ed., *Art and Psychoanalysis* (1957), and Leonard and Eleanor Manheim, eds., *Hidden Patterns: Studies in Psychoanalytic Literary Criticism* (1966). Useful discussions of Freudian literary theory are Frederick J. Hoffman, *Freudianism and the Literary Mind* (rev., 1957), which also describes Freud's wide influence on writers and critics; and Norman N. Holland, *The Dynamics of Literary Response* (1968). Elizabeth Wright, *Psychoanalytic Criticism: Theory in Practice* (1984), reviews various recent developments in psychoanalytic theories and their applications to literary criticism. For two major critics who have adapted Freudian concepts to their enterprise, see Edmund Wilson, *The Wound and the Bow* (1941), and Lionel Trilling, "Freud and Literature," in *The Liberal Imagination* (1950). Frederic C. Crews, who in 1966 wrote an exemplary Freudian critical study, *The Sins of the Fathers: Hawthorne's Psychological Themes,* has more recently retracted his Freudian commitment; see his *Skeptical Engagements* (1986). Some *feminist* critiques and adaptations of Freudian theory are Juliet Mitchell, *Psychoanalysis and Feminism* (1975); Jane Gallop, *The Daughter's Seduction: Feminism and Psychoanalysis* (1982); Shirley N. Gardner, ed., *The (M)other Tongue: Essays in Feminist Psychoanalytic Interpretation* (1985); and Mary Jacobus, *Reading Woman: Essays in Feminist Criticism* (1986).

Reader-Response Criticism does not designate any one critical theory, but a primary focus on the activity of reading a work of literature that is shared by many of the critical theories, American and European, which have come into prominence since the 1960s. Reader-response critics turn from the traditional conception of a work as an achieved structure of meanings to the responses of readers as their eyes follow a text on the page before them. By this shift of perspective a literary work is converted into an activity that goes on in a reader's mind, and what in standard critical analysis had been features of the work itself—including narrator, plot, characters, style, and structure—are described as an evolving temporal process, consisting primarily of diverse kinds of expectations, and the violations, deferments, satisfactions, and restructuring of expectations, in the flow of a reader's experience. Reader-response critics of all theoretical persuasions agree that, at least to some degree, the meanings of a text are the "production" or "creation" of the individual reader, hence that there is no one "correct" meaning, either of the linguistic parts or of the artistic whole of a text. Where these critics differ is (1) in their view of the primary factors that shape a reader's responses; (2) in the place at which they draw the line between what is "objectively" given in a text and the "subjective" responses of an individual reader; and as a result of this difference, (3) in their conclusion about the extent, if any, to which a text "constrains" a reader's responses, so as to enable us to reject at least some readings as misreadings, even if, as almost all reader-response critics assert, we are unable to demonstrate that any one reading is the right one.

The following is a brief survey of some of the more prominent forms of reader-response theory:

The contemporary German critic Wolfgang Iser develops the phenomenological analysis of the reading process proposed by Roman Ingarden, but whereas Ingarden had limited himself to a description of the reading process in general, Iser applies his theory to the analysis of many individual works of literature, especially prose fiction. (For Ingarden, see *phenomenology and criticism.*) In Iser's view the literary text, as a product of the writer's intentional acts, in part controls the reader's responses, but always contains (to a degree that has greatly increased in modern literature) a number of "gaps" or "indeterminate elements." These the reader must fill in subjectively, by a creative participation with what is given in the text before him. The experience of reading is an evolving process of anticipation, frustration, retrospection, and reconstruction. This process of the reader's consciousness constitutes both the partial patterns (which we ordinarily attribute to objective features of the work itself) and the coherence, or unity, of the work as a whole. The fact, however, that the author's intentional acts establish limits, as well as incentives, to the reader's creative additions to a text allows us to reject some readings as misreadings. (For an historical application of reader-response theory in Germany, see *reception-theory.*)

French *structuralist criticism,* as Jonathan Culler said in *Structuralist Poetics* (1975), "is essentially a theory of reading," which aims to "specify how we go about making sense of texts" (pp. viii, 128). As practiced by critics such as Culler himself in this book, it stresses literary conventions, codes, and rules which, having been tacitly assimilated by competent readers, serve to structure their reading experience and so make possible, at the same time as they impose constraints on, the partially creative activity of interpretation. On the other hand, the poststructuralist movement known as *deconstruction* undermines the grounds of structuralist interpretation and invites us instead to read any writing "creatively," as a play of systemic "differences" which generate innumerable and contradictory but "undecidable" meanings.

American proponents of reader-response theory usually begin by explicitly rejecting the claim by the American *New Criticism* that a literary work is a self-sufficient object, invested with publicly available meanings, whose features and structure are to be analyzed without "external" reference to the responses of its readers (see *affective fallacy*). In opposition, these newer critics turn their attention exclusively to the reader's responses; they differ greatly, however, in the factors to which they appeal in order to explain how we in fact read.

Norman Holland accounts for the responses of a reader to a text in terms of psychoanalytic concepts (see *psychoanalytic criticism*). The contents of a work of literature are a projection of the fantasies, engendered by the interplay of unconscious needs and defenses, which constitute the particular "identity" of its author. The individual reader's "subjective" response is a "transactive" experience with the fantasies projected in the author's text—a response which is largely determined by the particular defenses, expectations, and wish-fulfilling fantasies that constitute the reader's own identity. In this transactive process the reader transforms the fantasy content, "which he has created from the materials of the story his defenses admitted," into a unity, or "meaningful totality," which is his particular interpretation of the text. There is no universally determinate meaning of a work; two readers will agree in their interpretation only insofar as their "identity themes" are sufficiently alike to enable each to assimilate to his or her own distinctive responses the other's re-creation of a text.

In his theory of the anxiety of influence in reading, Harold Bloom also employs psychoanalytic concepts—specifically, those of a reader's "defense mechanisms" against the "influence," or threat to the reader's imaginative autonomy, of the poet whose text is being read. He applies these concepts in a much more complex way than Holland. His general conclusion, however, is similar, that there can be no determinate or correct meanings of a text. All "reading is . . . misreading"; the only difference is that between a "strong" (because interesting) misreading and a "weak" misreading. See *anxiety of influence*.

Stanley Fish is the proponent of what he calls **affective stylistics.** He represents the activity of reading as one which converts the spatial sequence of printed words on a page into a temporal flow of experience in an "informed" reader. In following the printed text with his eye, "there is a point at which the reader has taken in only the first word, and then the second, and then the third, and so on." At each point at which the reader elects to stop, whether after a single word or a larger unit, he makes sense of what he has so far read by anticipating what is still to come. These anticipations may be fulfilled by what follows in the text; often, however, they will turn out to have been mistaken. But since, according to Fish, "the meaning of an utterance" is not some final, corrected result, but the reader's "experience—all of it," and the reader's mistakes are "part of the experience provided by the author's language," these mistakes are an integral part of the meaning of a text. ("Literature in the Reader: Affective Stylistics," published 1970 and reprinted with slight changes in *Self-Consuming Artifacts: The Experience of Seventeenth Century Literature*, 1974, and in *Is*

There a Text in This Class?, 1980.) Fish's analyses of large-scale literary works were designed to show a coherence in the kinds of mistakes, constitutive of specific types of meaning-experience, which are effected in the reader by the text of Milton's *Paradise Lost*, and by various essayists and poets of the seventeenth century.

In his earlier writings Fish claimed that he was simply describing what in fact happens in any encounter between a competent reader and a text; his analyses, he asserted, merely slow down the normal process so as to make us aware of aspects of the reading experience that we otherwise overlook. Recently, however, Fish has instead represented his method as merely one "strategy" among various other available reading strategies. Each separate strategy "creates," after its own fashion, all the seemingly objective features of the text itself, as well as the "intentions, speakers, and authors" that we infer from the text. There is, in consequence, no "right reading"; agreement in interpretation occurs only among readers in that one among a number of "interpretive communities" that happens to share a single strategy of reading (*Is There a Text in This Class?*, 1980).

A survey of reader-response theories is included in Steven Mailloux's own contribution to this mode in *Interpretive Conventions* (1982). Anthologies of diverse reader-response essays are Susan Sulleiman and Inge Crosman, eds., *The Reader in the Text* (1980), and Jane P. Tompkins, ed., *Reader-Response Criticism* (1980). Some prominent examples of the mode, in addition to the works mentioned above: Stephen Booth, *An Essay on Shakespeare's Sonnets* (1969); Walter J. Slatoff, *With Respect to Readers* (1970); Michael Riffaterre, *Semiotics of Poetry* (1978); David Bleich, *Subjective Criticism* (1978); Louise Rosenblatt, *The Reader, the Text, the Poem* (1978); Umberto Ecco, *The Role of the Reader* (transl., 1979).

By Wolfgang Iser: *The Implied Reader* (in prose fiction), 1974, and *The Act of Reading: A Theory of Aesthetic Response* (1978). By Norman Holland: *The Dynamics of Literary Response* (1968), and *Poems in Persons* (1973). By Stanley Fish: *Surprised by Sin: The Reader in "Paradise Lost"* (1967), and *The Living Temple: George Herbert and Catechizing* (1978). For discussions and critical views of Fish's "affective stylistics": Ralph W. Rader, "Fact, Theory, and Literary Explanation," *Critical Inquiry*, 1 (1974); M. H. Abrams, "How to Do Things with Texts," *Partisan Review*, 46 (1979); Jonathan Culler, *The Pursuit of Signs* (1981). A survey of, and response to, the diverse claims that all texts are indeterminate is Charles Altieri, "The Hermeneutics of Literary Indeterminacy: A Dissent from the New Orthodoxy," *New Literary History*, 10 (1978).

Reception-Theory is an historical application of a form of *reader-response* theory which has been much debated, especially in Germany, since it was proposed by Hans Robert Jauss in "Literary History as a Challenge to Literary Theory" (in *New Literary History*, Vol. 2, 1970–71). It focuses, like other reader-response criticism, on the reception of a text; its prime interest, however, is not on the response of a single reader at a given time, but on the changing responses, interpretive and evaluative, of the general reading public over a span of time. Jauss proposes that a text has no "objective meaning," yet does contain various objectively describable features. The response of a reader, which constitutes for that reader the meaning and aesthetic qualities of a text, is the joint product of the reader's own "horizon" of linguistic and aesthetic expectations and the confirmations, disappointments, refutations, and reformulations of these expectations when they are "challenged" by the features of the text itself. Since the horizons of readers change in the course of time, and since later readers and critics have access not only to the text but also to the published responses of earlier readers, there develops an evolving historical "tradition" of critical interpretations and evaluations of a given literary work. Following Hans-Georg Gadamer (see under *interpretation and hermeneutics*), Jauss conceives this tradition as a "dialectic," or "dialogue," between a text and the horizons of successive readers.

The study of literary reception as such a dialogue, or "fusion" of horizons, has a double aspect. As a **reception-aesthetic,** it serves to "define" the meaning and aesthetic character of any individual work of literature as a set of semantic and aesthetic "potentialities," which make themselves manifest only as they are realized by the cumulative responses of readers over a course of time. In its other aspect as a **reception-history,** this mode of study also transforms the history of literature—traditionally conceived as an account of the successive production of a variety of works with fixed meanings and values—by making it instead the history of the changing but cumulative way that selected texts are interpreted and assessed, as the horizons of its successive readers alter with the passage of time.

Among the diverse theorists discussed under *reader-response criticism,* above, the one most closely related to Jauss's work is Wolfgang Iser, a fellow faculty member at the University of Constance, Germany. See Hans Robert Jauss, *Towards an Aesthetic of Reception* (1982), and *The Aesthetic Experience and Literary Hermeneutics* (1982); and for a history and discussion of this viewpoint, Robert C. Holub, *Reception Theory: A Critical Introduction* (1984).

Russian Formalism. A type of literary theory and analysis which originated in Moscow and Petrograd in the second decade of this century, in connection with *avant-garde* experiments in literature and in reaction against the prevailing emphasis in Russian criticism on the content and social significance of literature. At first its opponents applied the term **formalism** derogatorily, because of its stress on the formal patterns of sounds, words, and literary devices instead of the subject matter and social values of literature; it has now become simply a designation for a mode of literary criticism. Among the Russian representatives of this movement were Boris Eichenbaum, Victor Shklovsky, and Roman Jakobson. When this critical procedure was suppressed by the Soviets in the early 1930s, the center of the formalist study of literature moved to Czechoslovakia, where it was continued especially by members of the **Prague Linguistic Circle,** which included Roman Jakobson (who had emigrated from Russia), Jan Mukarovsky, and René Wellek. Since the 1940s both Jakobson and Wellek have continued their very influential work as professors at American universities.

Formalism views literature as a special use of language, and rests on the assumption that there is a fundamental opposition between literary (or poetical) language and ordinary language. (Alternative formalist terms for the nonpoetic mode are "practical," "referential," "prosaic," or "scientific" language.) It conceives the primary function of ordinary language to be the communication to auditors of a message, or information, by references to the world existing outside of language. In contrast, it views literary language as self-focused: its function is not to make extrinsic references, but to draw attention to its own "formal" features—that is, to interrelationships among the linguistic signs themselves. Literature is held to be subject to critical analysis by the science of linguistics, but by a type of linguistics different from that adapted to ordinary discourse, because its laws produce the distinctive features of **literariness.** As Roman Jakobson wrote in 1921: "The object of study in literary science is not literature but 'literariness,' that is, what makes a given work a literary work." (See *linguistics in modern criticism.*)

The literariness of a work, as Jan Mukarovsky described it, consists "in the maximum of **foregrounding** of the utterance," that is, of "the act of expression, the act of speech itself." (To "foreground" is to bring something into the highest prominence, to make it dominant in perception.) By "backgrounding" the referential aspect and the logical connections in language, poetry makes the words themselves "palpable" as phonic signs. The primary aim of literature in thus foregrounding its medium, as Victor Shklovsky said, is to **estrange** or **defamiliarize;** that is, by disrupting the ordinary modes of linguistic discourse, literature "makes strange" the world of everyday perception and renews the reader's lost capacity for fresh sensation. (In the *Biographia Literaria,* 1817, Coleridge had described the "prime merit" of a literary genius as the representation of "familiar objects" so as to evoke "freshness of sensation"; but whereas the stress of the romantic critic had been on the world that is freshly perceived, that of the formalist is on the literary means for effecting such defamiliarization.) The foregrounded properties, or "artistic devices," which estrange poetic language are often described as "deviations" from the processes of ordinary language. Such deviations, which are analyzed most fully in the writings of Roman Jakobson, consist primarily of patterns in the sound and syntax of poetic language—that is, of repetitions, balance, and contrast in speech sounds, rhythm, rhyme, stanza forms—and also of patterned recurrences of key words or images.

Some of the most fruitful work of Jakobson and others, valid outside the formalist perspective, has been in the analysis of *meter* and of the repetitions of sounds in *alliteration* and *rhyme;* these features of poetry they regard not as supplementary adornments of the meaning, but as effecting a total reorganization of language on the semantic as well as the phonic and syntactic levels. Formalists have also made important contributions to the theory of prose fiction. With respect to this genre, a central distinction is that between the "story"—the simple enumeration of a chronological sequence of events—and a plot. An author is said to transform the raw material of a story into a literary plot by the use of various devices to violate sequence and deform and defamiliarize the story elements; the effect is to foreground the narrative medium and devices themselves, and so to make patent the fictionality of its subject matter. See Vladimir Propp, *Morphology of the Folktale* (1928), and refer to *fiction and narrative.*

American *New Criticism,* although it developed independently, is sometimes called "formalist" because, like European formalism, it stresses the analysis of the literary work as a self-sufficient object, independent of references to the "external" world. Like formalism, it also regards poetry as a special mode of language whose distinctive features are defined in terms of their opposition to ordinary or scientific language. Unlike the European formalists, however, the representative New Critic did not apply linguistic theory to poetry, and the new-critical emphasis was not on versification and other patterns in the linguistic medium itself, but on the complex interplay within a work of ironic, paradoxical, and metaphoric aspects of the meanings of its language, and on the organization of such aspects around a humanly important "theme." The direct influence of Russian and Czech formalism in recent decades has been on American *stylistics* and *narratology.* Roman Jakobson and Tzvetan Todorov have also been influential in introducing formalist concepts and methods into French *structuralism.* Strong opposition to formalism, both in its European and American varieties, has been voiced by some *Marxist critics* (who view it as the product of a reactionary ideology), and more recently by proponents of *reader-response criticism* and of *speech act theory;* both these critical modes reject the view that there is a sharp division between ordinary language and literary language. See, e.g., Mary Louise Pratt, *Toward a Speech Act Theory of Literary Discourse* (1977), Chap. 1, "The 'Poetic Language' Fallacy."

The standard treatment is by Victor Erlich, *Russian Formalism: History, Doctrine* (rev., 1981); a short survey is included in Terence Hawkes, *Structuralism and Semiotics* (1977), and Raman Selden, *A Reader's Guide to Contemporary Literary Theory* (1985); and René Wellek has described *The Literary Theory and Aesthetics of the Prague School* (1969). Representative formalist writings are collected in Lee T. Lemon and Marion Reese, eds., *Russian Formalist Criticism: Four Essays* (1965); Ladislav Matejka and Krystyna Pomorska, eds., *Readings in Russian Poetics: Formalist and Structuralist Views* (1971); and Paul L. Garvin, ed., *A Prague School Reader in Aesthetics, Literary Structure, and Style* (1964). A comprehensive and influential essay by Roman Jakobson, "Linguistics and Poetics," is included in Thomas A. Sebeok, ed., *Style in Language* (1960). Samuel Levin's *Linguistic Structures in Poetry* (1962) represents an American application of formalist principles, and E. M. Thompson discusses *Russian Formalism and Anglo-American New Criticism* (1971).

Semiotics. At the end of the nineteenth century Charles Sanders Peirce, the American philosopher, founded a study that he called "semiotic," and in his *Course in General Linguistics* (1915) the Swiss linguist Ferdinand de Saussure independently proposed a science which he called "semiology." Since then **semiotics** and **semiology** have become alternative names for a general science of signs, as these function in all areas of human experience. According to this science, the use of **signs** is not limited to explicit systems of communication such as language, the Morse code, and traffic signs and signals; a great diversity of other human activities and productions—our bodily postures and gestures, the social rituals we perform, the clothes we wear, the meals we serve, the buildings we inhabit—convey shared "meanings" to members of a particular culture, and so can be analyzed as signs which function in diverse kinds of signifying systems. Although the study of language (the use of specifically verbal signs) is regarded as itself only one branch of semiotics, *linguistics*, the highly developed science of language, supplies the basic methods and terms that a semiotician applies to the study of all other social sign-systems.

C. S. Peirce distinguished three classes of signs, defined in terms of the kind of relation between the signifying item and that which it signifies: (1) An **icon** functions as a sign by means of inherent similarities, or shared features, with what it signifies; examples are the similarity of a portrait to the person it depicts, or the similarity of a map to the geographical area it stands for. (2) An **index** is a sign which bears a causal relation to what it signifies; thus, smoke is a sign indicating fire, and a pointing weathervane indicates the direction of the wind. (3) In the **symbol** (or in a less ambiguous term, the "**sign proper**"), the relation between the signifying item and what it signifies is not a natural one, but entirely a matter of social convention. The gesture of shaking hands, for example, in many cultures is a conventional sign of greeting or parting, and a red traffic light conventionally signifies "Stop!" The major and most complex examples of this third type of sign, however, are the words that constitute a language.

Saussure introduced many of the terms and concepts exploited by current semioticians; see under *linguistics in modern criticism*. Most important are the following. (1) A sign consists of two inseparable components or aspects, the *signifier* (in language, a set of speech sounds, or of marks on a page) and the *signified* (the concept, or idea, which is the meaning of the sign). (2) A verbal sign, in Saussure's term, is "arbitrary." That is, with the minor exception of *onomatopoeia* (words which we perceive as similar to the sounds they signify), there is no inherent, or natural, connection between a verbal signifier and what it signifies. (3) The identity of all elements of a language, including its words, their component speech sounds, and the concepts the words signify, are not determined by "positive qualities," or objective features in these elements themselves, but by *differences*, or a network of relationships, consisting of distinctions and oppositions from other speech sounds, other words, and other signifieds that obtain only within a particular linguistic system. (4) The aim of linguistics, or of any other semiotic enterprise, is to regard the *parole* (a single verbal utterance, or a particular use of a sign or set of signs) as only a manifestation of the *langue* (that is, the general system of implicit differentiations and rules of combination which underlie and make possible a particular use of signs). The focus of semiotic interest is less on a particular parole than on the underlying system of the langue.

Modern semiotics has developed in France under the aegis of Saussure, so that many semioticians are also structuralists. They deal with any set of social phenomena or productions as "texts"; that is, as constituted by self-sufficient, self- ordering, hierarchical structures of differentially determined signs, functional *codes,* and rules of combination and transformation which make them "meaningful" to members of a society. (See *structuralist criticism.*) Claude Lévi-Strauss, in the 1960s and later, inaugurated both the application of semiotics to cultural anthropology and the foundations of French structuralism by using Saussure's linguistics as a model for analyzing a great variety of phenomena and practices in primitive societies, which he treated as quasi-languages, or independent signifying structures. These include kinship systems, totemic systems, ways of preparing food, myths, and prelogical modes of interpreting the world. Jacques Lacan has applied semiotics to Freudian *psychoanalysis,* interpreting the unconscious as, like language, a structure of signs; and Michel Foucault has deployed a similar analytic approach to discuss, in various historical eras, medical interpretations of symptoms of disease, the changing identification, classification, and treatment of insanity, and the conceptions of human sexuality. Roland Barthes, explicitly applying Saussurean principles and methods, has written semiotic analyses of the constituents and codes of the sign-system in advertisements which describe and promote women's fashions, as well as in many "bourgeois myths" about the world which, he claims, are exemplified in such social sign-systems as professional wrestling matches, children's toys, ornamental cookery, and the striptease. (See his *Mythologies,* transl., 1972.) Barthes was also in his earlier writings a major exponent of *structuralist criticism,* which deals with a literary text as "a second-order semiotic system"; that is, a literary text is viewed as employing the first-order system of language to form a higher-level structure, in accordance with a specifically literary system of differential elements, conventions, and codes.

Introductions to the elements of semiotic theory are included in Terence Hawkes, *Structuralism and Semiotics* (1977); in Jonathan Culler, *The Pursuit of Signs* (1981); and in Robert Scholes, *Semiotics and Interpretation* (1982). See also Pierre Guiraud, *Semiology* (transl., 1975); *The Tell-Tale Sign: A Survey of Semiotics,* ed. Thomas A. Sebeok (1975); Umberto Ecco, *A Theory of Semiotics* (1976); Roland Barthes, *Elements of Semiology* (transl., 1967); Edmund Leach, *Claude Lévi-Strauss* (1974). Among the semiotic treatments of diverse social phenomena available in English are Claude Lévi-Strauss, *Structural Anthropology* (1968), *Totemism* (1969), and *The Raw and the Cooked* (1966); Roland Barthes, *Mythologies* (1972); Jacques Lacan, *The Language of the Self: The Function of Language in Psychoanalysis* (1968); and Michel Foucault, *The Archaeology of Knowledge* (1972), *Madness and Civilization: A History of Insanity in the Age of Reason* (1965), and *The Birth of the Clinic: An Archaeology of Medical Perception* (1973). On semiotics and literary analysis: Maria Corti, *An Introduction to Literary Semiotics* (1978); Michael Riffaterre, *Semiotics of Poetry* (1978); Barbara Hernstein Smith, *On the Margins of Discourse: The Relation of Literature to Language* (1978). For a critical view, see J. G. Merquior, *From Prague to Paris* (1986).

Speech Act Theory was introduced by the philosopher John Austin, most fully in his posthumous book *How to Do Things with Words* (1962), and was developed in various ways by other "ordinary-language philosophers," including

John Searle, H. P. Grice, P. F. Strawson, and Max Black. The theory is directed against traditional tendencies of philosophers (1) to analyze the meaning of isolated sentences, abstracted from the context of discourse and the attendant circumstances in which a sentence is uttered, and (2) mistakenly to assume, in what Austin calls a logical obsession, that the standard sentence—of which other types are merely variants—is a statement which describes a situation or asserts a fact, and is to be judged as either true or false. John Searle's expansion of Austin's speech act theory opposes to this philosophical assumption the claim that when we attend to the overall linguistic and situational context—including the institutional conditions governing the uses of a language—we find that in speaking and writing we perform simultaneously three, and sometimes four, distinguishable kinds of "speech acts": (1) We utter a sentence. (2) We refer to an object, and predicate something about that object. (3) We perform an illocutionary act. (4) Often, we also perform a perlocutionary act.

An **illocutionary act** may indeed be the one exclusively stressed by traditional philosophy, to assert that something is true, but it may instead be one of many other possible speech acts, such as questioning, commanding, promising, warning, praising, thanking, and so on. A sentence consisting of the same words, such as "I will leave you tomorrow," may in its particular verbal and situational context turn out to have the "illocutionary force" either of an assertion, a promise, or a threat. In an illocutionary act that is not an assertion, the criterion by which it is to be judged is not its truth or falsity, but whether or not the act has been performed effectively, or in Austin's term, "felicitously." A felicitous performance of a particular illocutionary act depends on its meeting "appropriateness conditions" which obtain for that type of act; these conditions are tacit linguistic and social (or institutional) conventions, or rules, shared by competent speakers and interpreters of a language. For example, the successful performance of an illocutionary act of promising, such as "I will come to see you tomorrow," depends on its meeting its special variety of appropriateness conditions: the speaker must be capable of fulfilling his promise, must intend to do so, and must believe that the listener wants him to do so. Failing this last condition, for example, the same verbal utterance might have the illocutionary force of a threat. John Austin has drawn special attention to one kind of illocutionary act, the explicit **performative,** which is a sentence whose utterance itself, when executed under appropriate institutional and other conditions, accomplishes the state of affairs that it signifies. Examples are "I now pronounce you man and wife"; "I apologize"; "I call this meeting to order"; "Let spades be trumps"; "I bet you a dollar Ohio State will beat Michigan tomorrow."

If an illocutionary act has an effect on the actions or state of mind of the hearer which goes beyond merely understanding what has been said, it is also a **perlocutionary act.** Thus, the utterance "I am going to leave you," with the illocutionary force of a warning, may not only be understood as such, but have the additional perlocutionary effect of frightening the hearer. Similarly, by the illocutionary act of promising to do something, one may please (or else anger) the hearer; and by asserting something, one may enlighten, or inspire, or intimidate the hearer. Some perlocutionary effects may be intended by the speaker; others occur without the speaker's intention, and even against that intention.

Since 1970 speech act theory has influenced conspicuously both the theory and practice of literary criticism. When applied to the analysis of direct discourse by a character in a literary work, it provides a systematic but also rather cumbersome framework for identifying the unspoken presuppositions and implications of speech acts which competent readers and critics have always taken into account, subtly though unsystematically. Speech act theory has also been used, however, as a model on which to recast the theory of literature in general, and especially the theory of prose narratives (see *fiction and narrative*). What the author of a fictional work—or else what the author's invented narrator—narrates is held to constitute a "pretended" set of assertions, which are intended by the author, and understood by the reader, to be free from a speaker's ordinary commitment to the truth of what he asserts. Within the frame of the fictional world that the narrator thus sets up, however, the utterances of the fictional characters are held to be responsible to ordinary illocutionary commitments. Alternatively, some speech act theorists propose a new version of mimetic theory (see *imitation*). Traditional mimetic theorists had claimed that literature imitates reality by representing in a verbal medium the setting, actions, utterances, and interactions of human beings. Some speech act theorists, on the other hand, claim that all literature is simply "mimetic discourse." A lyric, for example, is an imitation of that form of ordinary discourse in which we express our feelings about something, and a novel is an imitation of a particular form of written discourse, such as biography (Fielding's *The History of Tom Jones*, 1749), or autobiography (Dickens' *David Copperfield*, 1849–50), or even a scholar's annotated edition of a poetic text (Nabokov's *Pale Fire*, 1962).

For the basic philosophical treatments of speech acts see John Austin's *How to Do Things with Words* (1962) and John R. Searle's *Speech Acts: An Essay in the Philosophy of Language* (1970). Among the numerous attempts to model the general theory of literature, or at least of prose fiction, on speech acts are Richard Ohmann, "Speech Acts and the Definition of Literature," *Philosophy and Rhetoric*, 4 (1971); Charles Altieri, "The Poem as Act," *Iowa Review*, 6 (1975); John R. Searle, "The Logical Status of Fictional Discourse," in *Expression and Meaning* (1979), Chap. 3. A detailed application to literary theory is Mary Louise Pratt's *Toward a Speech Act Theory of Literary Discourse* (1977), which also reviews speech act philosophy and expands upon H. P. Grice's analysis of the "implicature" (that is, the tacit assumptions) of utterances in the flow of everyday conversation. For views of the limitations of this theory when applied in literary criticism, see Stanley Fish, "How to Do Things with Austin and Searle: Speech Act Theory and Literary Criticism," in *Is There a Text in This Class?* (1980), and Joseph Margolis, "Literature and Speech Acts," *Philosophy and Literature*, 3 (1979). For Jacques Derrida's deconstructive analysis of Austin's views, and John Searle's reply, see under *deconstruction;* for Searle's speech act theory of metaphor, see *figurative language*.

Structuralist Criticism. Almost all literary theorists since Aristotle have emphasized the importance of *structure*, conceived in diverse ways, in analyzing a work of literature. "Structuralist criticism," however, now designates the practice of critics who analyze literature on the explicit model of modern linguistic theory. This class includes some *Russian formalists*, especially Roman Jakobson, but consists most prominently of a group of writers, with headquarters in Paris, who apply to literature primarily the methods and analytic terms developed by Ferdinand de Saussure in his *Course in General Linguistics* (1915). This mode of criticism is part of a larger movement, French **structuralism,** inaugurated in the 1950s by the cultural anthropologist Claude Lévi-Strauss, who analyzed, on the model of Saussure's structural linguistics, such cultural phenomena as mythology, kinship relations, and modes of preparing food. See *linguistics in modern criticism* and *semiotics*.

Structuralism conceives any cultural phenomenon, activity, or product (including literature) to be a social institution, or "signifying system," consisting of a self-sufficient and self-determining structure of interrelationships. The elementary units of the system (equivalent to *phonemes*, or elementary speech sounds of a language, in Saussure's linguistics) are not objective facts which are identifiable by their positive properties, but purely "relational" elements; that is, their identity is given to them by their relationships of differences from and binary oppositions to other elements inside the system itself. The system as a whole is conceived as a hierarchy of levels; at each successive level, the operation of the same principles serves to organize the lower-level units into ever more complex combinations and functions. The total system, or infrastructure of relationships and rules of combination (analogous to Saussure's concept of *langue*, the implicit system of a language), has been mastered by each adept within a given culture, even though he or she remains largely unaware of its nature and operations. The primary task is to make explicit the implicit structure, features, and rules of the underlying signifying system, as this system manifests itself in a particular cultural phenomenon (analogous to Saussure's concept of *parole*, a particular utterance in a language).

Structuralist criticism views literature as a second-order system which uses language, the first-order system, as its medium, and is itself to be analyzed primarily on the model of linguistic theory. Most structuralist critics concern themselves with single works of literature, or else with a limited group of related works, which they analyze by applying diverse linguistic concepts such as the distinction between *phonemic* and *morphemic* levels of organization, or the distinction between *paradigmatic* and *syntagmatic* relationships. Some critics analyze the structure of a literary work on the model of the *syntax* of a sentence, that is, as composed of elements whose functions in a literary work correspond to the role in a sentence of nouns, verbs, and adjectives. Other structuralists, applying more fully the model of linguistics, attend to individual works of literature mainly insofar as they provide evidence from which to construct the underlying system of literary conventions and rules of combination which has been unconsciously mastered by a competent author and reader of any given literary type, such as prose fiction. The ultimate goal of this latter structuralist enterprise is to make explicit, in a quasi-scientific way, the tacit *grammar* (the systematic and invariant rules and codes) of literature as a signifying social institution; as Jonathan Culler puts it, the aim is to "construct a poetics which stands to literature as linguistics stands to language" (*Structuralist Poetics*, p. 257).

Structuralism is in explicit opposition to *mimetic criticism* (the view that literature is primarily an imitation of reality), to *expressive criticism* (the view that literature primarily expresses the feelings or temperament or creative imagination of its author), and to any form of the view that literature is a mode of communication between author and reader; it also runs counter to the attempt by the *New Criticism* to analyze isolated works as independent verbal constructions endowed with fixed, inherent meanings.

The following are among the salient features of much structuralist criticism:

(1) In the structuralist view, a literary work is a mode of writing ("écriture"), constituted by a play of various component elements according to purely literary conventions and codes; these factors within the literary institution generate literary "effects" which, although they may provide an illusion of reality, have no truth-value, nor even any reference to a reality existing outside the system itself. See *text and writing (écriture)*.

(2) The individual author, or "subject," is assigned no initiative, expressive intentions, or design as the originator of a work of literature. Instead, the conscious "self" is declared to be a construct that is itself the product of linguistic conventions about the use of the pronoun "I," and the mind of an author is described as no more than an imputed "space" within which the impersonal, already existing system of literary language, conventions, codes, and rules of combination gets precipitated into a particular written text. As Roland Barthes expressed, dramatically, this subversion of the traditional humanistic view of literature: "As institution, the author is dead."

(3) In a similar fashion the reader, as a conscious, purposeful, and feeling individual, is dissolved into the impersonal activity of "reading," and what is read is not a text imbued with meanings, but écriture, writing. The focus of structuralist criticism is on the impersonal activity of reading which, by bringing into play the requisite expectations, conventions, and codes, makes literary sense of a text—that is, reading endows with form and significance the sequence of words, phrases, and sentences that constitute a piece of literary writing. Structuralist critics earlier held that such reading, although it produces a plurality of meaningful effects rather than a single correct meaning, is nonetheless to a considerable degree "constrained" by the implicit codes of the inherited system. Recently, however, a group of more radical critics have proposed that literary écriture provides only "marks" which set off (or should set off) in the reader a relatively free play of multiplex significations. (See *deconstruction*, and *reader-response criticism.*)

(4) Structuralist criticism has adopted many of the analytic terms developed over the centuries by traditional critics and rhetoricians, but it employs these terms within a drastically altered perspective. Thus, such familiar critical concepts as the unity of a work, its genre, plot, narrator, characters, and figures of speech, once regarded as objective features of a literary work, are translated into sets of prepared responses and expectations, generated in a reader by the knowledge of conventions acquired from earlier reading, which

may in the course of a text be either fulfilled, frustrated, or altered. A special value of literature, according to some structuralists, is that, by violating our standard expectations derived from the ordinary uses of language, it brings into high visibility the tacit conventions and codes which not only govern our language, but determine all our interpretations of the world. A number of structuralist critics, and notably Roland Barthes, therefore appraise most highly those "modern" writings, such as Joyce's *Finnegans Wake* or the French *nouveau roman,* which evade, parody, undermine, or frustrate—and so make us aware of—the codes of "classical" writings on which our literary expectations have been formed; as a consequence, such writings help to destroy our illusion that literature reflects, or imitates, or even has reference to, an external reality.

French structuralists have devoted relatively little attention to poetry, but a great deal to prose fiction. The pioneer in the structural analysis of the novel and of types of fictional plots was the Russian formalist Vladimir Propp, in his *Morphology of the Folktale* (first ed., 1928). Since the 1960s, such a treatment of prose fiction has been refined and expanded by the French structuralists A. J. Greimas, Tzvetan Todorov, and Gérard Genette (see the references below). The most thorough structural analysis of a single work of prose fiction is Roland Barthes's *S/Z* (1970), which breaks down the text of Balzac's novelette *Sarrasine* into its smallest functional units, called **lexies**—consisting of anywhere from one word to a sequence of sentences—and then distinguishes within these lexies the play of five types of *codes* which guide an interpretive reading. These codes consist in some part of stereotypes in the prevailing culture, but mainly of artifices, arousing conventional expectations, which function entirely within the system of literary writing itself, but serve to give Balzac's story the illusion of being a realistic representation of human life and society.

A clear and comprehensive introduction to the program and accomplishments of structuralist criticism, in poetry as well as narrative prose, is Jonathan Culler, *Structuralist Poetics* (1975); see also Robert Scholes, *Structuralism in Literature: An Introduction* (1974). For an introduction to the general movement of structuralism see Philip Pettit, *The Concept of Structuralism: A Critical Analysis* (1975); and Terence Hawkes, *Structuralism and Semiotics* (1977). For critical views of structuralism see Frederic Jameson, *The Prison-House of Language* (1972); Gerald Graff, *Literature Against Itself* (1979); Frank Lentricchia, *After the New Criticism* (1980), Chaps. 4–5; J. G. Merquior, *From Prague to Paris: A Critique of Structuralist and Post-Structuralist Thought* (1986). Some anthologies of structuralist writings: Richard T. De George and M. Fernande, eds., *The Structuralists: From Marx to Lévi-Strauss* (1972); David Robey, ed., *Structuralism: An Introduction* (1973); Richard Macksey and Eugenio Donato, eds., *The Structuralist Controversy: The Languages of Criticism and the Sciences of Man* (1970); and Josué V. Harari, *Textual Strategies: Perspectives in Post-Structuralist Criticism* (1979). Among the books of structuralist literary criticism available in English translations are Roland Barthes, *Critical Essays* (1964), *S/Z* (1970), and in Barthes's later poststructuralist phase, *The Pleasure of the Text* (1973); Stephen Heath, *The Nouveau Roman: A Study in the*

Practice of Writing (1972); Vladimir Propp, *Morphology of the Folktale* (2d ed., 1968); Tzvetan Todorov, *The Fantastic: A Structural Approach to a Literary Genre* (1975), and *Introduction to Poetics* (1981); Gérard Genette, *Narrative Discourse* (1979), and *Figures of Literary Discourse* (1982). Structuralist treatments of cinema are Christian Metz, *Language of Film* (1973), and Peter Wollen, *Signs and Meaning in the Cinema* (1969). For later developments that subvert the pretensions of structuralism to be a "science" or "grammar" of literature, see *poststructuralism* and *deconstruction*.

Stylistics. Especially since the 1950s, this term has been applied to a method of analyzing works of literature which proposes to replace the "subjectivity" and "impressionism" of standard criticism with an "objective" or "scientific" analysis of the *style* of literary texts. Style is identified, in the traditional way, by the distinction between what is said and how it is said, or between the content and the form of a text. The content is usually denoted, however, by terms such as "information," "message," or "propositional meaning," while the style is defined as variations in the way of presenting this information which alter its "aesthetic quality" or the reader's emotional response. The concepts of modern linguistics (see *linguistics in literary criticism*) are used to identify the stylistic features, or "formal properties," which are held to be distinctive of a single work, or of an author, or of a literary tradition, or of an era. These stylistic features may be (1) phonological (patterns of speech sounds, meter, or rhyme), or (2) syntactic (types of sentence structure), or (3) lexical (*abstract* vs. *concrete* words, the relative frequency of nouns, verbs, adjectives), or (4) rhetorical (the characteristic use of *figurative language*, *imagery*, and so on). A basic problem, acknowledged by a number of stylisticians, is to distinguish between the innumerable features and patterns of a text which can be isolated by linguistic analysis, and those features which are genuinely "stylistic"—that is, features which make an actual difference in aesthetic and other effects on a reader of the text. See, for example, Michael Riffaterre's objection to the elaborate stylistic analysis of Baudelaire's sonnet "Les Chats" (The Cats) by Roman Jakobson and Claude Lévi-Strauss, in *Structuralism*, ed. Jacques Ehrmann (1966).

Stylisticians who aim at scientific precision employ quantitative methods to calculate the relative frequencies of stylistic features, and often use electronic computers to establish frequency tables of the features which are held to identify a distinctive style. Others instead make use of linguistic concepts such as the distinction between *paradigmatic* and *syntagmatic* relations in language; or else of *transformational grammar*, with its distinction between surface structure and deep structure; or else of *speech act theory*, with its distinction between the propositional content and the *illocutionary force* of an utterance.

Sometimes the stylistic enterprise stops with the more or less quantitative determination, or "fingerprinting," of a distinctive style. Usually, however, the analyst tries also to relate distinctive stylistic features to traits in an author's psyche; or to an author's characteristic ways of perceiving the world and organizing experience (see Leo Spitzer, *Linguistics and Literary History*, 1948); or to the typical conceptual frame and attitude to reality of an era (Erich Auerbach,

Mimesis, 1953); or else to particular aesthetic and emotional functions and effects (Michael Riffaterre and others). A noticeable tendency is what René Wellek has called "the imperialism of modern stylistics," that is, the attempt to extend the analysis of style to include everything that is held to be valid in literary criticism. This tendency is particularly evident in the stylistic analysis of short lyric poems; see, for example, the exhaustive inventory of the linguistic patterns in a twelve-line poem by Yeats in Roman Jakobson and Stephen Rudy, *Yeats's "Sorrow of Love" Through the Years* (1977).

Stanley Fish, in "What Is Stylistics and Why Are They Saying Such Terrible Things About It?" (in *Is There a Text in This Class?*, 1980), offers a pungent critique of the scientific pretensions of many stylisticians. Fish proposes his own "affective stylistics" (see under *reader-response criticism*): the meaning of a text consists of a reader's total response to the sequence of words on the page; and within this response, Fish asserts, there is no valid way to distinguish between style and content. For a longer analysis, both of traditional analyses of style and of modern stylistics, based on the thesis that style is not a separable feature of language, see Bennison Gray, *Style: The Problem and Its Solution* (1969), and "Stylistics: The End of a Tradition," *Journal of Aesthetics and Art Criticism*, 31 (1973). On the other side, the validity of distinguishing between style and propositional meaning, although only on an appropriate level of analysis, is cogently defended by E. D. Hirsch, "Stylistics and Synonymity," in *The Aims of Interpretation* (1976).

In addition to the books and essays mentioned above, there are a number of recent anthologies which include discussions of stylistics, together with examples of stylistic analyses by exponents of *Russian formalism* and of French *structuralist criticism*, as well as by English and American stylisticians. Prominent in these anthologies are essays by Roman Jakobson, Leo Spitzer, Michael Riffaterre, Stephen Ullman, and Richard M. Ohmann. See Thomas A. Sebeok, ed., *Style in Language* (1960); Roger Fowler, ed., *Essays on Style and Language* (1966); Glen A. Love and Michael Payne, eds., *Contemporary Essays on Style* (1969); Donald C. Freeman, ed., *Linguistics and Literary Style* (1970); Seymour Chatman, ed., *Literary Style: A Symposium* (1971); Howard S. Babb, ed., *Essays in Stylistic Analysis* (1972); Braji B. Kachru, ed., *Current Trends in Stylistics* (1972).

Text and Writing (Écriture). The American *New Criticism* focused attention on the literary text, which it conceived as an autonomous verbal object endowed with "public" meanings that are accessible to competent and sensitive readers. French *structuralist* critics, on the other hand, conceive a literary text as one species of the social institution called **écriture** (writing); what makes it literary is the fact that the writing embodies a set of specifically literary conventions and codes. The author is conceived as an impersonal agency, or "space," in which the activity of "writing" precipitates aspects of the inherited linguistic and literary system into a particular literary text, manifested as marks on a page. The interpretation of this writing is effected by an impersonal "lecture" (French: activity of reading) which, by bringing to bear expectations formed by the experience of earlier texts, invests the marks on the page with what merely seem to be their objective meanings and structure. Structuralists differ on the degree to which the activity of reading is constrained by a participation in the literary conventions and codes that went into the writing; some *poststructuralists* propose that reading should ideally be "creative," by leaving itself open to the free play of textual significations. See *structuralist criticism* and *deconstruction.*

The system of linguistic and literary conventions that constitute a written text are said to be "naturalized" in the activity of reading, in that the artifices of a nonreferential "textuality" are made to seem **vraisemblable** (credible)—that is, is, made to give the illusion of reality—by being brought into accord with other modes of discourse and cultural stereotypes that are so familiar and habitual as to seem natural. **Naturalization** (an alternative term is **recuperation**) takes place through such procedures in reading as assigning the text to a specific *genre,* or assuming a fictional text to be the speech of a credibly human narrator, or interpreting its artifices as representing characters, actions, and values that are in accord with the real world. To a thoroughgoing structuralist critic, however, not only is the text's representation of, or accord with, the world an illusion, but the "real world" is itself held to be in its turn a text; that is, simply a structure of signs, whose significance is constituted by the conventions, codes, and ideology that happen to be shared by members of a cultural community. The term **intertextuality,** popularized by Julia Kristeva, is used to signify the multiple ways in which any one literary text echoes, or is inseparably linked to, other texts, whether by open or covert citations and *allusions,* or by the assimilation of the formal and substantive features of an earlier text, or simply by participation in a common stock of literary and linguistic procedures and conventions. In Kristeva's radical formulation, any text is regarded as an "intertext," constituted by an intersection of other texts, past and future.

Roland Barthes in *S/Z* (1970) proposed a distinction between a text which is "lisible" (readable) and one which, although "scriptible" (writable) is "illisible" (unreadable). A "readable" text is a traditional, or "classical," one which mainly conforms to the prevailing codes and conventions, literary and social, and so is readily and comfortably interpretable and naturalizable in the activity of reading. An "unreadable" text (such as Joyce's *Finnegans Wake,* or the French *new novel,* or a poem by a highly experimental poet) is one which largely evades, parodies, or innovates upon prevailing conventions, and thus persistently shocks, baffles, and frustrates standard expectations in the process of reading. By drawing attention in this way to the conventionality and artifice of literature, according to Barthes, an unreadable text laudably destroys the standard illusion that a literary text represents social reality. (See *fiction* and *imitation.*) In *The Pleasure of the Text* (published 1973), Barthes assigns to the readable text the response in reading of mere "plaisir" (quasi-erotic pleasure), but to the unreadable text the response of "jouissance" (orgasmic ecstasy); as Jonathan Culler has put Barthes's view, jouissance is "a rapture of dislocation produced by ruptures or violations of intelligibility" (*Structuralist Poetics,* p. 192).

For related matters, and relevant bibliographic references, see *semiotics, structuralist criticism, deconstruction, reader-response criticism.*

Index

The first number, in **boldface,** identifies the page of the text that contains the principal discussion of a term; in the text itself, that term is also printed in boldface. Succeeding numbers, in *italics*, identify other pages of the text in which the term occurs, in a context that illustrates its application or amplifies its meaning; on such pages, the term is also italicized. The term in the text may be a modified form of the term listed in the Index; the forms "parodies" and "parodied," for example, are listed in the Index under "parody," and "structuralist" and "structuralists" are listed under "structuralism."

Some entries in the Index are followed by one or more references to related terms that supplement the exposition; thus: "courtly love. *See:* Platonic love." A number of comprehensive terms, such as drama, figurative language, or novel, are followed by a list of the entries that deal with the species of a generic term, or with the component features of a literary form.

Terms likely to be mispronounced by a student—many of these are borrowings from a foreign language—are followed (in parentheses) by a simplified guide to pronunciation. This guide marks the stress—in some instances, both the primary and secondary stresses—and also indicates the pronunciation of those parts of the word about which the student is apt to be in doubt. The following vowel marks are used:

ā (fate)
ă (pat)
ä (father)
ē (meet)
ĕ (get)
ī (pine)
ĭ (pin)
ō (rope)
ŏ (pot)
oo (food)
ŭ (cut)